AUSTRALIA FOR WOMEN

Susan Hawthorne and Renate Klein have travelled widely throughout Australia while researching this book. Born in Australia and Switzerland, respectively, they share a love for deserts, rainforests, cockatoos and out-of-the-way places. Between travels they work as poet, writer and publisher at Spinifex Press (Susan Hawthorne) and writer, researcher and Senior Lecturer in Women's Studies at Deakin University (Renate Klein). They have worked together on many projects, including the anthology *Angels of Power* and amongst their publications are *The Falling Woman*, *The Language in My Tongue* and *The Spinifex Quiz Book* (Susan Hawthorne), *Test-Tube Women*, *Infertility*, *Radical Voices* and *RU 486: Misconceptions, Myths and Morals* (Renate Klein).

T0166861

OTHER BOOKS

Renate Klein
Theories of Women's Studies (with Gloria Bowles)
Test-Tube Women: What Future for Motherhood (with Rita Arditti
and Shelley Minden)
Man Made Women (with Gena Corea and others)
The Exploitation of a Desire: Women's Experiences with IVF
*Infertility: Women Speak Out About Their Experiences of Reproductive
Medicine*
Radical Voices: A Decade of Feminist Resistance (with Deborah Steinberg)
RU486: Misconceptions Myth and Morals (with Janice G. Raymond
and Lynette J. Dumble)

Susan Hawthorne
Difference: Writings by Women
Moments of Desire: Sex and Sensuality by Australian Women Writers
(with Jenny Pausacker)
*The Exploding Frangipani: Lesbian Writing from Australia and New
Zealand* (with Cathie Dunsford)
The Spinifex Quiz Book: A Book of Women's Answers
The Falling Woman
The Language in My Tongue

Joint publication
Angels of Power and Other Reproductive Creations

AUSTRALIA FOR WOMEN

TRAVEL AND CULTURE

Edited by
Susan Hawthorne and Renate Klein

SPINIFEX

Spinifex Press Pty Ltd
504 Queensberry Street
North Melbourne Vic 3051
Australia

First published by Spinifex Press 1994

Typeset in 10.5 pt Garamond by Claire Warren and Michelle Proctor
Cover design by Lin Tobias, Melbourne
Printed in Singapore on acid-free paper by Singapore National Printers

National Library of Australia
Cataloguing-in-Publication entry:
CIP
  Australia for women

  ISBN 1 875559 27 2

  1. Women – Travel – Australia – Guidebooks. 2. Women – Australia. 3. Australia
  – Guidebooks. I. Hawthorne, Susan, 1951– . II. Klein, Renate.

919.40463

This publication is assisted by the Australia Council, the
Australian Government's arts funding and advisory body.

CONTENTS

3
RESOURCES

FOREWORD

When travelling outside of Australia one is frequently confronted with stereotypes which, like stereotypes everywhere, bear little or no resemblance to one's own experience. For the dominant cultures of this world Australia is an exotic and faraway place and, accordingly, the myths are also exotic and far from real. Two recent ones arising from our film industry: Australian women resemble the girls in *Picnic at Hanging Rock*; Australian men resemble *Crocodile Dundee*. Nothing could be further from the truth. Australian women, to resort to a few generalisations, are energetic, forthright and often display both physical and emotional strength; Australian men are no worse or better than men anywhere, some are tough and outdoorish, others are cultured and scholarly. The whole range of characteristics is displayed in Australia, just as a huge range of linguistic and cultural backgrounds make up Australian culture.

Australia for Women is a guide to travellers of an Australia that is rarely depicted in the mainstream media, although, as is obvious from the huge range of cultural activity that women are engaged in, there is no shortage of material that the media could draw on (see chapters on the arts).

Australia for Women is a guide to both travel and culture. For further information on hotels and up-to-date information on tours you will need to consult a general travel guide.[1] This book contains information not available in standard travel books, and will provide you with an introduction to Australian culture in the words of many of those involved in developing and maintaining women's culture in Australia today.

The book is divided into three main sections. In Part 1 you will find essays, stories and poems that introduce you to Australian history, culture and everyday life. From Aboriginal origins, to convicts and slavery, we then move on to a history of some famous, and not so famous women, sheroes and the nurses of World War II. An introduction to the Australian political and legal systems is followed by some descriptions of particular cultural groups in Australia.

A cross-section of essays on Australian women's culture including the achievements of women in all areas of the arts follows. Here you'll find chapters dealing with literature, theatre, music, visual arts and film. This section ends with essays about Australian plants and animals.

Part 2 is divided into regions beginning in the North and East, across to the West and North, east again to the Centre and South and finishing with the densely populated South and East. Because state boundaries, or holidays, take little account of geographical regions, it is easier to divide the country into four main regions into which the states fall in the following way: West and North (all of Western Australia and north of Alice Springs in the Northern Territory); East and North (all of Queensland and New South Wales north of Coffs Harbour); South and Central (all of South Australia and NT south of Alice Springs); South and East (all of Victoria, Tasmania, and the Australian Capital Territory and NSW south of Coffs Harbour). For maps, see Lonely Planet's *Australia* guide.

Part 3 contains a list of useful resources including lists of women's books, films, music etc. which may interest the traveller. It also contains addresses of women's centres, lesbian centres, rape crisis centres, women's health centres, women's bookshops, cafes, galleries and organisations where information and new addresses can be found if the organisations shift. Also included are the addresses of women's tour companies, travel agents and women-run accommodation. Travellers should ring these organisations and accommodations for further information on availability of the resources listed here.

Australia is too large to get around in a few weeks, but if you plan your journey well you can incorporate both the culture of the urban centres as well as the immensity and beauty of rural and inland Australia.

Travellers these days can fly direct, or almost direct in to all Australian capital cities. Sydney, Melbourne, Perth, Cairns and Darwin are the usual first ports of entry, and recently Broome has opened an international airport. Brisbane, Adelaide, Hobart and Canberra are only an hour's flight away from one of these.

Each Australian city has its own character. Short descriptions of capital cities and other places of interest begin each section in Part 2. For further descriptive writing on Australian cities, a good resource is *Inner Cities: Australian Women's Memory of Place.*[2]

Australia for Women contains information on activities for women around the country, but inevitably things change. The attractions, sites and events included in this book are not the only ones available, but they give an indication of what you might expect to find in different centres around the country. There are numerous women working in art and craft, whose work you can find on display in local museums and galleries, or on the off-chance when taking the sign to a local pottery or craft studio.

The chapters in the book give a sense of the richness and diversity of women's lives, whether they be in remote areas or in the bustle of our cities. Similarly you will find Australian women from just about every culture, each adapting in her own way to new circumstances. It is not widely known that Australia has some of the largest migrant populations anywhere: Melbourne is the third largest Greek city in the world, while Bondi, a suburb of Sydney, has the largest urban Maori population in the world. These population centres are reflected in the culture of certain suburbs and towns. In Melbourne you can visit Lygon Street, Carlton for Italian culture; Victoria Street, Richmond for Vietnamese culture; Acland

Street, St Kilda for central European and Jewish culture; in Sydney the Haymarket area centred on Dixon Street is a long-established Chinese area (see Yen) – and these are just some of the possibilities. Australia has a long tradition of migration from the Macassans who travelled to Northern Australia prior to European contact. There were significant migrations of Chinese people in the nineteenth century as well as the various waves of migration throughout our history from Ireland, Italy, Greece, the Baltic States, Central Europe, the Middle East, Vietnam, Chile and again China. These lives will be reflected in the books, plays, music, visual arts and crafts, as well as the many cuisines, that you will find throughout the country. Keep your eyes open for exhibitions, concerts, festivals. Throughout the year festivals are held in areas where there are concentrations of particular cultures, some you may find include Greek, Spanish, Japanese, Chinese, Indian, Italian, Pacific and Aboriginal. If you discover something that you think should be included in a future edition, please write to us with details of addresses and contact numbers.

A word about words
Two hundred years ago there were over 250 languages and approximately 600 dialects being used in Australia. They were all Aboriginal languages. Australia is a large continent and one of the myths entertained by many people (including Australians) is that all Aboriginal cultures are the same. They are only the same in the way that Norway and Italy, Ireland and Turkey, Egypt and Zimbabwe are the same. Climate, landscape, cultural isolation and cultural borrowing have played the same part here as they have in other regions of the world, such as Europe, Asia, Africa and the Americas. As a result the names used by Aboriginal communities vary across the continent. In the Southeast most Aborigines refer to themselves as Koori (within that term are contained many distinct language and cultural groups); in Queensland Murri is frequently heard; in South Australia Nungga, in the South West Nyunga. In other parts of the country people will use specific terms such as Pitjantjatjara, Arunda, Yolngu, Pintupi and many others. When referring to all members of all the groups Aborigine, or Aboriginal person (with a capital A) is used, alternatively some prefer the word Koorie to be used as a general term.[3] White people are referred to as Gubba or Gub (from gov'ner) in the Southeast, and frequently as Balanda in the north, west and central areas.

Australian English has borrowed heavily from Aboriginal languages including words for plants and animals. For example, the word 'kangaroo' was recorded in 1770, on the northeast cost of Queensland. This use of 'kangaroo' was then extended to include all animals resembling what turns out now to be called a black wallaroo.[4] The words boomerang and woomera refer to artefacts, while the idea of 'dreaming' or jukurrpa, as it is referred to among the Walpiri is a conceptual borrowing. In recent years words such as tiddas, which means 'sisters' have come into use through the women's movement (although its best known use is probably through the Melbourne feminist band, Tiddas). You will also find many Aboriginal words as you pass through towns and suburbs in Melbourne, Mordialloc, in Sydney, Wooloomooloo and outside in the country there is Tallarook, Coolamon, Wagga Wagga, Maralinga, Muckinuppin, Tallangatta and many others. You can find out their meanings in Reed's *Aboriginal Place Names in Australia.*[5] Australian English also has its idiosyncracies as English. Words such as chook (chicken, hen), Vegemite (a breakfast spread used on toast), lamington (a small sponge cake covered in chocolate icing and desiccated coconut) are peculiar to Australia and New Zealand. But Australian English is sometimes incomprehensible to other English speakers due to the Australian habit of shortening words. Here is a list that may help you to decipher the rules when you're confronted with an Australian speaker.

mozzie	mosquito
sunnies	sunglasses
barbie	barbecue
piccies	pictures, movies, films
stubbie	small bottle of beer
trannie	transistor radio, transparency, transsexual
postie	post delivery wo/man
footy	football (Australian Rules)
cockie	cockatoo, a small farmer
relies or relos	relatives, relations
lesie or leso	lesbian (lesie has positive connotations, while leso is more usually used as an insult)
cosi or togs	swimming costume, bathers
arvo	afternoon
garbo	garbage collector
ute or tilly	utility truck, pick up truck

Notes
1. Such as *Australia* in the Lonely Planet Series.
2. See Resource List.
3. Eve Mumewa D. Fesl, 1994. *Conned.* St Lucia: UQP.
4. ibid.
5. A useful resource so long as you are aware that there is not a single language called 'Aboriginal'.

1
POLITICS AND DAILY LIFE

HISTORY AND POLITICS

Susan Hawthorne and Renate Klein
A BRIEF HISTORY

Australia is the only country in the world with a continuous cultural history of 60,000, possibly more, years. And Aboriginal women have been central to that cultural development and maintenance. Through a rich spiritual and religious life women have maintained and created important cultural artefacts including stories and songs that hold the earth together, visual arts and crafts, and dramatic ritual and dance. In addition they have made use of native medicinal and foodstuffs, sometimes developing elaborate means of collection (including leaching of poisons out of roots) to make them useable. Aboriginal women, in Australia as elsewhere, have played an important role in maintaining the cultural forms and memories throughout the period since European invasion, and they are central to the claims now being made to native land title – their continuous presence aids in the successful outcome of these claims.

A great deal of violence was brought to these shores with the invasion of the British. Violence against the original inhabitants with settlement at Sydney Cove, and later with the push to settle inland. Convicts were the mainstay of the workforce at Botany Bay and women, although greatly outnumbered by men, were central to that workforce (see Portia Robinson). 'Oh Trugganner' refers to Tasmania's most famous woman (also known as Truganini) who watched her relatives die around her (see Oodgeroo, 'Oh Trugganner'). This poem in honour of her opens the book while Terry Whitebeach, writing about the descendants of Trugganner and her people, closes the book. In Tasmania, the establishment of the convict colony of Port Arthur and the widespread violence against Aborigines went hand in hand with one another (see Oodgeroo, Whitebeach and Kelly). Throughout Australia the rush for agricultural land meant dispossession of those who had lived here for thousands of years. As the population moved north and sugar cane farming began, violence was also meted out to those on nearby islands. Vanuatu was a major source of 'blackbirded' labour – islanders were captured and forcibly removed to Queensland as slaves (see Faith Bandler). Mining and the rush for gold in many states brought a new influx of peoples – including Chinese (see Yen), Europeans and Americans. But with the advent of the twentieth century wars in which Australia would participate loomed on the horizon. The Great War of 1914–1918 may seem a long way from Australia, but one in ten Australian families

lost either a son or a daughter in this war. World War II came as far as the Australian mainland, and again women and men lost their lives (see Jeffs on the role of Australian nurses). Post-war migrations have also left an indelible mark on Australian culture (see Safransky, Gunew, Gleditsch).

Women in Australia have a long history of claiming their rights – as critical to the spiritual and material functioning of life in Aboriginal cultures, as resisters to slavery, as fighting for political and cultural power. Australian women were among the first in the world to win the right to vote (1894 in the State of South Australia, and 1902 federally) (see Janine Haines) and have continued to increase their share of political power. Faith Bandler and Oodgeroo Noonuccal were important in the struggle for the conferment of citizenship for Aboriginal people at the scandalously late date of 1967. And since the 1970s women have effected significant changes both in the culture and politics of Australia with the rise of the Women's Movement in the late 1960s and early 1970s (see Hawthorne, Starski and Deacon). Women from all walks of life and all backgrounds have contributed to this burgeoning of creativity (see Gleditsch, Gunew, Starski and Fraser). In spite of this, there remain serious problems in some areas, such as law reform, attitudinal shifts among both women and men, and in some areas racism and sexism tenaciously persist (see Scutt, Loewald, and Deacon).

Oodgeroo Noonuccal
OH TRUGGANNER!

Oh Trugganner,
I weep for you,
For Lanney and all your race,
As I read Ryan's damning thesis
After one hundred years.
Your desperate guerilla warfare
Failed to oust the white foe,
And spilt blood and tears
Freely flowed
Over your much loved land.
Your race
Was the trophy sought
By the 'Christian, civilised' man
Who carried his depravities
Even beyond the grave.
Oh Trugganner,
I feel deep pain and sorrow
For the life he made for you.
What did you feel
When the foreign Doctor of Science
Stole like a thief in the night to the morgue
To cut from his body
Lanney's not yet cold head and his hands
In the name of 'Christian' science?
Oh Trugganner,
What did your dreamtime spirit feel
As it watched them take you after death
As a rare museum piece,
To stay forever
Under the rude stares
Of vulgar public gaze?
Oh Trugganner,
Destined to be
Not just the last of your race,
But a prized specimen for science too.
Oh Trugganner,
Let your restless spirit
Bring comfort to us all.

Give us wisdom and strength,
For we have not yet found ourselves
In this now alien land.
This land we thought was ours for ever,
Now peopled with racists,
Murderers, manipulators,
Who know too well the art
Of conquer, enslave, kill and destroy.
Oh Trugganner,
Let your spirit rise from the foreign museum
And walk with us in our grief.
In our once loved Native land,
The love that sustains us,
Is what our race was
Before the invaders came.
Oh Trugganner,
As you cried in the past,
So too now do your people cry
And have cried for the last two hundred years.
Oh Trugganner,
Will the dreamtime spirits of our race
One day rise with us
As they did with you,
To the whispering sounds of stalking feet
With our guns in our hands
And an ambush plan
The nullas, the spears and stones?
Or will we in servitude,
Die like you?
And will 'modern' scientists rave and drool
Over our bones
As they 'religiously' did
With Lanney and you?
Oh Trugganner!

Oodgeroo of the tribe Noonuccal
(formerly Kath Walker)

Faith Bandler
SLAVERY AND RESISTANCE IN AUSTRALIA

Officially slavery was abolished throughout the British Empire in 1883, but an official enslavement of convicts continued till 1886, when the last boat of convicts arrived from England at the West Australian coast.

The intake of convicts had ended earlier in Eastern Australia because the colonials in the east became resentful of being used as a dump for British and Irish felons.

Opposition to the importation of convicts in the Eastern States came mainly from the workers who had come to Australia as free settlers and from the sons and daughters of the convicts who were now viewing Australia as their country, in which they could build a future. There was a strong element of nationalism among the free settlers and they didn't want the country now considered theirs to be an enormous prison for the villains of Britain and Ireland. Another aspect of their protest was their objection to cheap labour. The established new settlers who were now the employers supported the importation of the convicts because it was an endless supply of free labour. They lost the battle with the employed. When the gold rush began in Eastern Australia, it was hard to get labour – cheap or expensive.

Australia was young and new opportunities began to arise – for example, that cotton could be successfully grown in Queensland. The supply of cotton had been cut off to world markets from America by the American civil war. Australian growers saw the opportunity to develop the industry. Queensland beckoned. But cotton needed many people to work it. Profit was the major consideration so only cheap or unpaid labour would be considered.

The theory had been established that white-skinned people could not work in the tropics because they were constitutionally unfit for hard outdoor work in the tropical sun. Growers were therefore provided with a challenge, one that was soon solved by the businessman, Robert Towns.

The rise in the price of cotton which followed the blockade of North America (to subdue the Southern States) encouraged Towns to act with haste in search for a cheap workforce.

Towns, a member of the Legislative Council, plantation owner, and shipowner, had settled in Sydney in 1842. It was said he piloted his ship, *The Brothers* to take the first cargo of Australian wool to England. Later in his business pursuits he took up squatting in Queensland, where he planted two thousand acres of cotton on the Logan River, which is forty miles from Brisbane. He no doubt remembered another businessman who came before him: Benjaman Boyd, who took up land to graze sheep. He also owned ships and had sent a couple into the Pacific Islands to carry out raids for (men to be his) shepherds. Towns soon had his vessels sailing the Pacific to cajole or kidnap men or women to work on his cotton. The industry was short lived. At the end of the American civil war, the cotton exports were revived and the short boom in Australia came to an abrupt end. As a plantation industry, sugar took its place. The climate was right and the industry's growth flourished, making the demand for men and women from the Pacific Islands even greater. The Melanesian Islands were raided heavily mainly because their people were seen by the planters as reliable and servile labourers who were not only cheap but also loyal to their masters.

Although the number of women brought to the cane fields of Queensland from the Islands of the Pacific was much fewer than that of men, their contribution to the development of the sugar industry of Australia was significant.

My aunt Kate worked as a domestic in a planter's house in Mackay. This once small township is now one of the most prosperous cities in the North. It supports a broad band of enterprises. The sugar plantations border the city on three sides and beyond, dairy farms flourish on the Eungella Range.

Aunt Kate is portrayed as Emcon in my novel, *Wacvie.*

Extract from *Wacvie*

Some of the women, mainly those brought to Queensland at a tender age, were used as servants in the houses of the plantation owners or the white people in the towns. Emcon was one. She was Weloa's wife.

Emcon served in the house of Theodore Young. She was an observant girl and curious about the customs and habits of Amy Young – the washing and ironing of the family clothes, the scrubbing of the floors, the use of house linen, changed so freely in the hot weather. Above all, Emcon was interested in the methods of cooking. Although there were times when she thought that making a fire in a stove was a troublesome task, and longed for the simplicity of her mother's cooking arrangements in Biap, she quickly learned the new culinary skills and was soon cooking bread and buns with ease.

Before the Young's evening meal she would put the flour to rest with the yeast. After washing the dishes and carefully setting them upright in the dresser, she would then bring the dough from the side of the stove where it had been rising, and tipping it onto the well-floured kitchen table, she would pull and knead. Then she would fill the bread tins and put them in the oven, always leaving the buns until last because she liked to try out different shapes for them. Often she would make the shape of a shell, or a hibiscus. Remembering their incomparable beauty, she would sprinkle the dough with red and yellow jelly crystals. Mrs Young's pantry had many kinds of food and Emcon was not shy in experimenting with them. And somehow she always managed to get a hot bun, loaded with home-made butter, to Weloa who would share it with Wacvie.

Some days, her hands idle in the suds of the washing-up dish, her thoughts would wander far away, to where all the people ate the same food and there was never any need to steal food from one to give to another. Why was it, she wondered, that because their skin was white it gave them the right to eat good, well-cooked food, and when one's skin was brown one had to eat only poor food like heavy damper, and drink black, bitter tea? Why was it all so unjust, so unfair? One day she would talk to the other women about it all.

She compared the clothes she had been given with those that Amy Young wore, noticing how much finer those of the white woman were. They were made of soft linen and piles of lace. Certainly a bit of a nuisance to launder and perhaps unnecessary in the hot climate, but nevertheless nice to have. She still couldn't see the point of having to clothe herself, except when it was cool in the late of the evenings, but as she was not allowed to go without some covering, she would have preferred the light stuff that Mrs Young had, to the heavy, dark blue 'mother-hubbards'. Well, one day she might own a white lace blouse and a black skirt. For now she would continue smuggling the big, hot buns to Weloa.

Emcon was hanging the washing on the long clothes line when Amy Young noticed the girl's belly; it was beginning to swell. After Emcon finished the hanging, Mrs Young called her into the kitchen. Her cool, blue eyes were cold and hard as she cursed Emcon and ordered her to work in the field with the older women. Although she had been ill-treated and abused by Mrs Young, Emcon felt misgivings about working in the cane. She thought of the baby inside her and could only hope all would be well for it, if she had to lift the heavy cane in the hot sun.

Without any possessions, Emcon walked down the back steps of the house, through the house garden and the gate in the fence surrounding it, and down the hill to the cane field. Now she would have to obey those horrible field masters. She walked towards the other women, asking herself why they should work to kill themselves for such evil people. She determined she would speak to the women about it, but what she would say was not yet clear in her mind.

As the days and weeks passed she began to feel the baby within her. When the white demons were not in sight, she would lie on her back in the furrow, shaded by the cane, and rest. Unlike most of the women on Young's plantation, Emcon had become used to regular hours of work. She was still very young and memories of timelessness had almost faded.

The clocks in the big house had been more masters to obey; whenever they had chimed they had been ordering her to perform different duties for the comfort of the Young family.

Now she knew the time it would take the overseer to return to the furrow in which she lay. Sometimes a minute or two before his appearance she would rise and move back into the group of women. No one thought her lazy, all knew she needed rest. Bending to gather the long heavy stalks of cane, she would think of life beyond the fields.

She could now speak the master's language, called English, and could read and write a little. She had listened carefully to the conversations in the house and knew that there was a place where all food came from. It was the same place where the buggy horses were taken to be shod, and where the master and mistress went each Sunday morning, going to their 'church'. Some time, she thought, they might all go to the church. Already they could sing the hymns the white people sang, for some were those they had rejected in Biap when the long-nosed man tried to teach them about the man Jesus.

Emcon shared her knowledge of the white man's world with the others. The older women told her how the overseer would spread coins on the ground and tell the men that the bigger the coin, the greater its value. He lies, Emcon told them, explaining how the gold coins were of more value than the brown ones.

By the southern side of the barracks some of the men had turned the soil and planted the pumpkin seeds and cuttings of sweet potato vines that Emcon had brought from the house garden. One morning, while the men were working in the field, an overseer trampled on them. Wacvie had reminded them of how they had worked for their food on their island, and had advised them to do it now. 'We must use our hands for ourselves', he had told them. Now the plants had been destroyed, viciously, by one of the mean-minded white men.

'That was a most selfish thing to do!' Weloa said. Showing strong signs of anger, Wacvie answered: 'We should kill the one who did it'.

Although now heavy with her child, Emcon did not let the matter pass without voicing her protest and a scheme that, she said, 'will frighten hell out of the one I believe is the offender'. They listened to her idea; it was a daring one but they agreed to it.

For some days she patiently waited for a snake to appear. At last one did. While the snake lay curled in the dead cane leaves she quickly slipped her small basket over it, then pushed it into a hessian sugar bag. That night she found her way to the culprit's quarters and, with his heavy snores drowning any strange sounds, she slipped silently inside. Then, lifting the edge of the white sheet at the foot of his bed, she quickly and skillfully undid the string of the bag and placed it beneath the covering.

A few days later the Mackay weekly newspaper warned people of an invasion of dangerous black snakes in the district A man who had apparently been bitten while asleep in his bed, had died. 'One bad man gone will be replaced by another bad man', Wacvie told them, as they all sat eating their monotonous damper and beef. 'We must find a way to freedom.' 'Freedom!' they all repeated. The word now had heightened significance.

Portia Robinson
WOMEN CONVICTS

Australian colonial female society was unique in its origins. It was created artificially by the exile of British women and girls guilty of major statutory offences. As punishment, they were sentenced to transportation with penal servitude to England's convict colony of Botany Bay. During the first forty years of white settlement, most of the women in the colony of New South Wales had arrived as convicts. As convicted felons, respectable contemporaries had no doubt that colonial women were not only criminal but immoral, vicious and depraved, for criminality and immorality were seen as close bedfellows.

These convicted women arrived in Australia as adults, their average age being mid-twenties. Almost all were guilty of larceny, theft from the shop, the dwelling, the person. They arrived as technically single women in so far as that, as criminals, they were transported without their husbands or partners, their families and, in most cases, their children. Almost without exception, they were from the lower orders of British society – the poor, the illiterate, the unskilled, the labouring girls and women. These socio-economic origins placed them very firmly within that class regarded as 'the criminal class', defined by respectable contemporaries as 'that class which normally commit crimes, the poor and the indigent'.

For almost 200 years, these women were described by contemporaries, commentators and later generations of historians as whores and prostitutes, unable – or unwilling – to earn their livelihood by honest labour. The only economic avenue open to them in the convict colony of Botany Bay was a sexual one. Many twentieth century historians accepted contemporary opinion but excused the reputed immorality of the women by linking it with the low sex-ratio. Throughout the transportation period, the sex-ratio was never higher than one woman to four men and, in the outlying districts, could be as high as 1:15. This, it was argued, forced women to become sexual victims in a male dominated society.

Both the contemporary belief in the depravity of 'convict' women and the modern 'victim' interpretation are complete distortions of the social and economic roles of women in the foundation years of Australian society. Furthermore, both views obscure and misinterpret the nature and characteristics of the unique 'Australian' female society which had its origins in these early years of white settlement.

Admittedly, the first female workers in New South Wales were convicts under sentence of the law. Their labour was intended as punitive. There were, however, few occupations where female labour was needed in the establishment and development of the new colony. There were no mills, mines or factories requiring the cheap labour of women and children. Its economy was agriculture-based, the emphasis on small scale farming. There were no official orders to the governors regarding the specific nature of the labour required by the convict women. It was assumed that they would only be capable of following the traditional domestic work of women from their socio-economic class level. That is, cooking, sewing, nursing the sick, attending domestic animals, perhaps weaving, knitting, making butter and cheese. As technically single women, there was little expectation that these convict women would work as family women for the benefit, support and advancement of that family as, for example, in the pioneering colonies of settlement in North America.

On arrival, the convict women were usually assigned as servants to private masters or mistresses. Given the assumption as to the immorality of convict women – and the debauchery expected in a *convict* colony – it is understandable that respectable contemporaries stressed the 'enforced whoredom' aspects of the assignment of convict women to 'single' men. In 1809, Governor-designate Governor Lachlan Macquarie was told that New South Wales was 'a vast brothel' in which convict women were given indiscriminately as 'avowed objects of sexual intercourse . . .'

The convict women retained by Government were mainly those who could work at spinning or weaving at the Parramatta Female Factory. Eighty-seven of the 149 Government women at Parramatta in 1807 were employed in the linen and woollen manufactory. Others had special skills, useful to the Government, such as Bridget Kelsh (per *Lady Rowena*) a dairymaid convicted in Dublin, who was assigned to the Government Dairy at Parramatta; or Rebecca Hodges (per *Lord Wellington*) tried in Warwick, who, despite being a convicted felon, was considered a suitable assistant at the Female Orphan School; or Harriet Marsh (per *Lord Wellington*) who was assigned at Emu Plains, but discharged almost immediately as she married the government gardener.

The newly-arrived convict women who were to be assigned to private settlers outside the Sydney District, were usually taken up the river to the Female Factory at Parramatta and assigned from there as quickly as possible. It was not only colonial men who applied for the services of assigned female convicts. Came free and ex-convict women also applied for and received female assigned servants. Those assigned as domestic servants were in a far better situation than were most of the free and unconvicted female servants in Britain, being guaranteed accommodation, food and clothing. They were in far more acceptable situations than were those criminal women who remained in the gaols of England and Ireland.

It was after the convict women had served their sentences in New South Wales, or had been pardoned, that, as free women, they had a wider choice of occupation than domestic work. Choice was available to both

family women and single women and was not limited by age. The most attractive opportunity for married women was that of farmer or land-holder, either as the recipients of land grants in their own right, or as the wives of convict men who, because of their convict status, were ineligible to own land. In both cases the free or freed woman was the legal owner of the property, the 'master' of any assigned male or female servants, and responsible to Government for the clearing and cultivation of the land granted. The roles of these women in the development of colonial farming and grazing have been overlooked both by contemporaries and by historians.

For the women who settled the bush as farmers or agriculturalists or stock-owners, there was in all probability no prior awareness of the possible hardships of the Australian environment, of the 'differences' from Britain, of the problems of drought, of bush-fire, of floods, of the heartache of children wandering away, of drownings, of the dangers of snake and spider bite – of sickness and death – and of loneliness, all intensified by the great burden of isolation. Survival itself, for themselves and their families, depended on self-reliance. That so many women did endure such great difficulties and succeed, even if at the lowest levels of economic independence, was an achievement beyond any that could have been prophesied on the basis of their former lifestyles in their home countries. The rewards – and we are concerned with women from the lowest levels of British society – could be simple independence for themselves and their families, or far greater economic achievements.

One of the many convict wives who could and did improve their economic status in the colony was Rosetta Madden who came as a free woman with her husband, Edward Madden, on the *Hillsborough* in 1799. They were both from Lancaster. Madden died on the voyage to New South Wales and his widow married another convict, Henry Marsh. Widowed a second time, and left 'with three fatherless children and unprotected', she petitioned Governor Macquarie for additional pasture land:

. . . she has maintained and educated [her fatherless children] by the most perservering industry . . . and is now possessed of a considerable number of horse & cattle breeding Mares and other stock . . .

She purchased a farm for the accommodation of her stock which she found inadequate to the pasture ground required for the increasing stock and having in view nothing but the eventual benefit of her children she represented her case to Colonel Paterson who, in consideration of her Industry . . . granted to her one hundred and fifty acres of Pasture Land with a view still further to encourage . . . her Industry.

Rosetta Marsh told the Governor 'of her unremitting attention to her family . . . her perservering industry'. Was it these admirable characteristics which encouraged wealthy emancipist Samuel Terry to marry her early in 1810?[1]

Mary Sarjant had arrived as a convict on the *Glatton*, sentenced at Stafford in 1801 to transportation for life. Governor King granted her a conditional pardon in 1803 and an absolute pardon in 1804. In September 1813 she petitioned Governor Macquarie for an official Deed of Grant for the land she had been granted and which she had cultivated and improved 'on the Hawkesbury Road':

Memorialist is now in occupation of the Land [and] has erected buildings and had a large quantity of timber felled and burned off and is fully intended to proceed in Cultivating the Farm.

Your Excellency will of course believe that Memorialist has been at a Vast Expense as small Buildings cost a deal of Money. Memorialist feels herself in some measure injured by not holding in her possession any Kind of security for the Land – she has made two or three applications.[2]

Macquarie referred her request to his Surveyor-General Meehan and this ex-convict woman received her title deeds which no doubt eased her 'injured feelings'.

Not all Petitioners were as literate as Mary Sarjant and not all could afford the services of a professional letter writer. Some Memorials to the governor were obviously written with great difficulty, but lack of writing ability did not discourage women from petitioning. Jane Trotter had been sentenced to seven years transportation at Northumberland in 1793 and transported on the *Indispensable*. In 1810 she petitioned the newly-arrived Governor Macquarie:

The Humble pitition of Jane Trotter most Respectfully Sheweth . . . to yor Excellency is pitioner came to this Colony in the Ship Indisspenceable with Capt. Wilkinson going fourteen years and during this time Bihaved Meself upright and Honnost and mentade a Lifehod by my Industry.

is Honour Colonal Paterson has been plased to grant me thirty acers of Land for to support me in me old days. In hopes that your Execellency will be pleased to regrant the same and I will be Ever in Duty Bound Oged your Honnors Well fare.

Jane Trotter free woman got no indulgence from Government . . . arrived in the country I have been this 14 years. [sic].[3]

Jane Trotter kept her land for her support in her 'old years', but she doubly insured this support by living with James Ryan, a butcher who had arrived on the *Sugar Cane*.

Among the vast number of applications Governor Macquarie received for the necessary legal confirmation of land grants given after the deposition of Governor Bligh in 1808, there were many from women who feared loss of livelihood, or loss of farms or dwellings if they did not receive the necessary papers to ensure their right to legal title. It is significant that most of these female petitioners were ex-convict women and that their memorials not only stress their honest conduct and industry and include character testimonials, but that they indicate the ways in which they had obtained their 'honest livelihoods' since their arrival in New South Wales.

Ex-convict women, married to men who were prisoners for life were usually successful in their applications for grants of land. The essential prerequisites were that their 'good characters' could be proven beyond question. There was no hesitation by the wives of convicts to apply for the maximum indulgences once their husbands were assigned to them. Women who had arrived as convicts were as strident in their demands for Government assistance as were women who had arrived free. Isabella Roe who had arrived as convict Isabella Manson *alias* Smith on the *Lady Juliana*, sentenced at Middlesex in 1788 to transportation for seven years, wrote to Macquarie for confirmation of her husband's land grant and requested additional assigned servants to assist with their farm 'during her husband's indisposition.' They had suffered 'heavy losses at the Hawkesbury . . . my wheat being all destroyed at the last inundation' and her husband 'whose industry was well known . . . was confined to bed.' She found herself in such a distressing situation that she required the services of a Government man (Mick Higgins who had formerly been assigned to her by Colonel Foveaux), and she requested that her children be victualled from the Stores as she was 'totally destitute of dried provisions'. She concluded with this prayer, that His Excellency's approval of her petition would be:

An Act of Charity and for so benevolent a deed that the Almighty may shower down his choicest blessings on your Excellency and Families Heads and for which Memorialist and her unfortunate Family as in duty will every pray . . . [4]

How could Macquarie refuse such a supplicant? Isabella Roe, former convicted London thief, received her sixty acres, her specified Government man, the rations for her children, and, it would seem, her blessings rained on the governor and his family.

Many of the women who requested land, indulgences, or confirmation or extension of land grants had scarcely owned the very clothes they had worn at their trials in England or Ireland. Most of them had endured the overcrowded and filthy gaol conditions, had suffered the privations of lack of food and even water, being dependent on the meagre gaol rations which had to be shared with any children they had with them, supplemented only by 'the charity of the public'. It was these women who, in the convict colony of New South Wales, applied for assistance in times of floods or droughts, or personal misfortunes. In almost all cases, their petitions were successful. This was in direct contrast to the lives and opportunities of criminal women in Britain, before or after imprisonment. It was also completely outside the experiences of any of the women – or men – from the lower orders that, in times of poverty, distress or misadventure, they could apply to the Government for assistance and receive such assistance.

Mary Gotham had been destitute when she was tried and convicted in Stafford in 1801. In 1810 she wrote to Governor Macquarie for confirmation of title to her lease and dwelling. She explained that:

she has been seven years in this Colony and has always conducted herself in an honest industrious and becoming manner since her first arrival . . . [and] having by her industry built herself a house in Upper Pitt Row which William Paterson then Lieutenant Governor was pleased to grant a lease for fourteen years.[5]

That the former convict, Mary Gotham, could build and own a house was in itself an indication both of the opportunities for economic advancement which were available for either single or family women despite civil conditions. Elizabeth Giles purchased a House situated on the Rocks of Nathaniel Miller for the sum of One Hundred Pounds . . . and other improvements and additions has put her to a further expense of two Hundred and Thirty Pounds making the whole amount of purchase 350 pounds.[6]

Where she had obtained such a considerable sum is unknown. There is no evidence to suggest that it was earned in 'an immoral or improper way'. Was it her ownership of this house and her obvious ability to acquire capital which led to her marriage to ex-convict carpenter George Woodford? After their marriage he described her occupation as 'upholsterer' – a far more respectable craft than that of a humble carpenter.

Women were traditionally involved in brewing and had been so since medieval times. In New South Wales there were women from all civil conditions who were both brewer and victualler, involved in the distilling and sale of spirits – both retail and wholesale. Brewing and or distilling was frequently linked with the ownership of inns, taverns, public houses, Flash Houses licensed to retail spirits and beer. A licence from Government was necessary and the individual applicant had to be approved by the Governor as a person of good repute and character. Obligatory character testimonials were from magistrates or from the colonial chaplains. Few women were refused licences and, in these cases, the applicant appealed to the Governor to overrule the decision. Hanna Morley, (arrived convict per *Speke*) applied for the renewal of her liquor licence. The Superintendent of Police, D'Arcy Wentworth, refused her application on the grounds that her husband (Joseph Morley, convict per *Surprize*) was a known drunkard. Mrs Morley complained to the Governor:

she was in debt, as she had just erected a house suitable for a public house and if her licence was not granted she would become poverty-stricken and she could not repay the debt and she had six small children.[7]

Macquarie – a humane man – granted the licence on condition that the husband was barred from her licensed premises. Hannah Morley continued to run her public house, in Pitt Street Sydney at least until 1828. She appeared to be a good influence on her drunken husband, for, in the Census of that year, Joseph Morley, free by servitude, was recorded as the licensee, not his wife.

Most of the women who applied for and received liquor licences, licences to brew, distill and or sell beer and spirits, or who became 'officially' involved in the liquor trade in New South Wales had no previous known experience of these occupations in their native lands. Most began their new life in the English penal colony as women of bad character, as convict women, assumed to be debased, immoral, depraved, drunken and dissolute. These women needed not only to secure government approval and to obtain a liquor licence, but to have the finance to set up house, inn or tavern, to lease, rent or purchase the premises, to equip and maintain their businesses, to control their staff of government and freed servants.

In addition to these 'normal' business demands, the woman licence holder who had a convict husband had to petition for that husband to be assigned to her as her 'Government Man'. The normal family position was reversed, as with all women who had their convict husbands assigned to them. It was the wife who was the head of the household, the husband who was the servant.

Those family 'business' women with children had the normal duties and responsibilities associated with the raising of a family. And that family lived in an entirely different environment from any the women had previously experienced. Their children, for example, were not exploited labour, were not sent to mills, mines, factories or 'apprenticed out as poor parish children'. In most cases, the children remained within the household, working with and for the family until of an age to be apprenticed to a trade. The parent(s) paid the required indentures or obtained a Government apprenticeship.[8]

It had not been considered by either British or colonial officials that convicted women could, or would at any time, become part of the economic growth of the colony, that they would be as enterprising as the men in the diversity and success of their chosen occupations. There was no expectation – and almost no comment by contemporaries or later generations – that these 'infamous and depraved women', having served their penal sentences, might choose to set themselves up (despite lack of previous skills) as dealers, shopkeepers, hatmakers, dressmakers, shirt-makers, seamstresses, pastrycooks and bakers, confectioners, laundresses and washerwomen. That some would apply for and gain government licences as women of good character to brew and distill, to sell liquor, to run public houses, taverns and inns, to set up as butchers or blacksmiths. It was certainly not anticipated that some of these women would apply in their own right for grants of land, for convict servants to work that land – even applying for their own husbands, if convict, to be assigned to them as their servants. They became – in their own right – landowners, farmers, agriculturalists, stock keepers and dairywomen. Most of these achievements, whether at a level which gave bare self-subsistence, or higher, were in complete contrast to the opportunities, expectations and experiences of contemporaries from their socio-economic level in England and Ireland.

Women such as Mary Dillon who had arrived as a convict on the *Aeolus*, set up shop as a milliner while she was a ticket of leave woman. Her business expanded during her first two years of trading and she moved to larger premises in George Street. Unfortunately, she overreached herself, being declared insolvent the following year. Free and freed women were extensively involved in the sale of a variety of goods. Mrs Dockrell of 68 George Street, 'opposite the market', advertised clothing, books, tea, tobacco, gunpowder and pepper. Mrs Jones 'dealt in ladies wear and furniture from her house'. Mrs Nightingale, a 'Native Girl' and a widow, described herself as 'a dealer' at the age of nineteen. Madame Josephina Rens was more ambitious, advertising the opening of her 'shop of fashionable clothes from Paris' she traded from the house of Mrs Jones; Mrs Smith of 21 Castlereagh Street Sydney was a stationer; Mrs Stuart of Brickfield Hill, sold 'ladies wear and groceries' while Mrs Weavers of 19 Pitt Street was 'in business with her mother', Mrs Reynolds.[9] Elizabeth Killett was one of the most successful of the ex-convict businesswomen. Transported from Suffolk in 1800 (per *Nile*) at the age of nineteen, she married John Gray two years later. In 1818 Gray, the assistant clerk of the Market in Sydney, was accidentally drowned '. . . much respected as an old inhabitant of the Colony . . . [he] left a wife and seven children to lament his premature destiny'. The following year, his widow was appointed 'Lessee of Tolls of the Sydney Market'. She also held in her own right a spirit licence and ran *The Market House*, licensed for the accommodation of settlers and others, and the *Macquarie Arms* in George Street. She was both Clerk of the Markets and Poundkeeper for Sydney Town.[10]

It was not only the town women who became involved in trade and commerce. Women from the outer settlements – 'up country' – advertised in the *Sydney Gazette* and later in the *Australian*, sold or tendered their produce. Jane Codd was a successful 'convict' dairywoman. She was sentenced to transportation at West Pembroke in June 1788 and arrived at Sydney Cove in 1791. By 1796 she had a land grant in her own right at Balnarring, had planted four acres with maize, owned ten pigs and eight goats and was supporting herself without government rations. In 1806 she was living with Edward Edwards (arrived convict per *Royal Admiral*). By 1814 she was described as his wife. She continued to build up her dairy herd and after her death in November 1826 the following Notice appeared in the *Australian*:

FOR SALE
Mrs Jane Codd (deceased), Dairywoman of George Street Sydney. A Herd of 21 Milch Cows of the First Description, part of the well-known milking herd of the late Mrs Jane Codd . . . and now vested in her legal representatives.
    Sgd. D'Arcy Wentworth
    Trustee.[11]

From convicted thief to well-known and respected colonial dairywoman had been an unexpected change in the life of Jane Codd, an enterprising and hardworking woman of Botany Bay.

The diversity of women's occupations in the colony appeared unlimited, and, in many cases, exceeded those occupations traditionally described as male. There were, of course, those who followed the traditional women's occupations – such as the schoolmistresses. These were usually women who had arrived free. Others – also usually came free – ran 'seminaries for female education' – such as Mrs Geoffrey Eager who advertised that Instruction would be given in 'English Grammar, Ancient and Modern History, Geography (with the use of the Globes) and needle work.' Mrs Eager also advertised stores, sheds and cellars to let under her Seminary, these being unnecessary to her business. There were also women who opened boarding schools for young ladies, some of which were 'limited to ten genteel pupils' as Mrs James of 76 George Street advertised.

There seemed to be no limit to the type of businesses in which colonial women were engaged. Mary Ann Whitfield, who had arrived in the colony as a three-year-old with her convict mother on the *Britannia*, placed the following advertisement in the *Australian*, October 1824:

having removed to the house in George-Street, lately occupied by T. Harper, and known by the sign of the Cumberland Arms, where she intends carrying on a ready money-trade; and begs to inform the public that she will sell good rum at 13 shillings and sixpence per gallon, best tea at six shillings per pound, sugar at sixpence per pound, tobacco at five shillings and sixpence.[12]

Mary Whitfield, who lodged in Sydney with that enterprising shopkeeper and dealer, Elizabeth Jones, continued in the liquor trade, and became known as a business woman who 'gave no tick', all transactions being in ready cash only.

All women, of course, were not successful, but most managed to support themselves – and their families – at a far higher economic level than would have been possible had they remained in Great Britain. There were those who followed occupations which were customary for women in their socio-economic level. Mrs Leadbeater, for example, was a barrow-woman who had her stand at Clarence Street corner and who 'sells fruit about the town'. In 1826 she narrowly escaped injury after being knocked over by a recklessly driven horse and cart. There were charwomen, like Elizabeth Lambert and nursemaids 'who could support an unimpeachable character', or 'respectable middle-aged women', or housemaids 'who can work well at the needle and with good character', laundresses, servants of all types. In all advertisements for situations, the emphasis was on proven 'good character'.[13]

This was the essential prerequisite for employment, as in England and Ireland. The difference was that almost the entire female labour market in the colony had arrived as convicted felons. Despite this, there was little difficulty in finding servants with testimonials to good character and industry.

Why the economic achievements of these women have been ignored is linked with a lack of appreciation of the nature of colonial society, of the role of civil condition, and, above all, of the influence of that single word 'convict' and its infamous connotations. Most of the women arrived as convicts, but did not remain so indefinitely. By pardon or by completion of sentence, they became 'free' women, ex-convict. Still suffering the ignominy of having been a convict, they were, nevertheless, technically free, ex-convicts, able to choose where and how they would live. Colonial society could not be described with any accuracy as convict society. It was, of course divided vertically, on one side, those who had arrived as convicts and on the other, the 'free objects', those who had arrived unconvicted. There were, in effect, two societies, those who had come as convicts and those who had come free, for among the 'respectable', any person who had been convicted was forever tainted, and socially unacceptable.

With both societies, however, there developed an hierarchical class system, based not on birth or position but on economic achievement in the colony itself. Among the ex-convicts, women were to be found at every economic level, either in their own right or as wives/partners. Among the women who came free, few were 'working women' for most arrived as the wives/daughters of officials or military, the few free settlers. The 'working' free women were either the servants or governesses brought by free women, or those enterprising women who had come to the colony for the express purpose of employment as school teachers, instructors at Ladies' Seminaries or similar occupations. Additionally, there were the native-born girls, the daughters to women of every civil condition. So that female society (and male society) could be divided into four civil condition groups – the came free, the came convict, the ex-convict and the native-born. The largest group, at any time after about 1800, was the ex-convict women, and the analysis of their occupations and lifestyles when compared with an analysis of those women under sentence shows clearly that the distinctions between 'convict' and ex 'convict' are not merely semantic.[14]

It is therefore, a complete distortion to describe Australia's first women – her 'founding mothers' – as *convicts*. It is an even greater distortion to consider that their role in the colony was simply a sexual one – that of prostitutes. The diversity of their occupations and their economic contribution is distorted if only the labour of convict women is considered. It is as erroneous to equate *colonial* women's labour exclusively with that of *convict* women under sentence of law as it is to equate male achievements and failures solely with those of convict men. Those convict girls and women who laboured for the Government or for private masters/mistresses while under sentence of the law in no way reflected the opportunities, achievements and failures of colonial women. Nor did their labour influence the formation of a distinctive type of female society which was to become Australian. It was as ex-convict working women that their influence and contribution is reflected in the whole fabric of the economic life of New South Wales.

Notes

1. AONSW. CF Hillsborough with convict husband Charles Madden who died on the voyage, then married Henry Marsh who also died; 1806, self-employed; held a wine and spirit licence, 26 Feb 1808; subscribed to the fund for enclosing the Sydney burial ground.
2. Mary Sarjant. Memorials re land. 6 Sep 1813. Col Sec 4/1822A, reel 1066. no 44. AONSW.
3. Jane Trotter. Memorials re land 1810. 4/1822, reel 1066, no 316. AONSW.
4. Isabella Roe, incomplete source, 'no 286'. 'John Roe's Grant and his wife's Petition Rec'd 10th Jany 1810 . . . Granted lease . . . 60 Governor McQuarry'. AONSW. Isabella Manson alias Smith (Lady Juliana).
5. Mary Gotham, petitions re land 1810, reel 1066, no 119; received CP, 4 June 1804. Cert of Emancipation. 7 April 1814 (12/120 S).
6. Elizabeth Giles (Lady Juliana) married George Woodford (Duke of Portland), 15 Nov 1811, at St John's; on 26 June 1808 she advertised her house for sale; on 4 June subscribed to a fund for enclosing the Sydney burial ground, *Sydney Gazette.*
7. Petition of Hanna Morley, publican, CSIL. 4/1759 9/1444.
8. See Portia Robinson. 1985. *The Hatch and Brood of Time*: a study of the first generation of native-born white Australians. Melbourne: Oxford University Press.
9. Mrs Bodenham, Mary Dillon, Mrs Dockrell, Mrs Jones, Mrs Nightingale, Madame Josephina Rens, Mrs Smith, Mrs Stuart, Mrs Weavers: all representative of advertisements in the *Australian* 1824–28. Similar advertisements appeared in the Sydney Gazette.

10. Elizabeth Killett. D'Arcy Wentworth Papers. A765. p. 27. ML.
11. Jane Codd. 14 Oct 1828. *Australian*. Note that on 5 June 1808 Mrs Codd was assaulted and robbed; 12 June 1808 she gave evidence against her attacker, *Sydney Gazette*, 12 June 1808.
12. Mary Ann Whitfield. 28 Oct 1824. *Australian*.
13. Mrs Leadbeater; note list of Carts Licensed in Sydney 1819 included the names of 3 women: Sarah Watkins (Canada), son to 'James' Ellison bapt 5 Feb 1813, St Phillip's; 1828: Sarah Ellison FS, 10 children, with John Ellison (Albemarle) publican, Parramatta; Jane Stubbs, Phillip St, Sydney; Mary Greenwood (Northampton) Kent St, Sydney, BT Box 12, ML; note women employed as washerwomen included Judith Kelly (Sydney Cove), a washerwoman from Dublin, HO/2 PRO60. p. 85. 'female convicts 1810–19' AONSW.
14. For details of civil condition groups, see Portia Robinson. 1993. *The Women of Botany Bay*. Ringwood: Penguin.

Diane Bell

SHEROES OF MINE

Desert landscapes of Central Australia are the only ones I know with affection and confidence. My guides for these countries are wise in the ways of their land. Theirs is an ancient, dynamic civilisation superbly fashioned to the needs of the original peoples of this land. 'In the *jukurrpa*', my adoptive aunt is telling me, 'the *kurinpi* made this place, the old people told me. That's your place too Diane, you can follow-up for them; do the business; call out to the old people; they can hear.'

Known variously as the Law, the Dreamtime, and Dreamings, the *jukurrpa* heritage is made known through ritual re-enactment and subtly shaped to meet the needs of current generations. An all encompassing, enduring, sustaining, total world view, the *jukurrpa* is sensitive to gender, age, knowledge, human frailty, and has the capacity to accommodate change. In this oral culture, it is the responsibility of the living to follow-up the narratives of the ancestors, and to find relevance in them for the living. There are no books: features in the landscape stand as testimony to the ancestral travels, and it is for the living to interpret the symbols. Old people living, and old people deceased, are brought into communication in ceremonial celebration when the ancestral past moves concurrent with the present, when the edges of identity are blurred, merged and finally forged into one.

The narratives of the exploits of the *kurinpi* women vivify a tract of land extending from the Devil's Marbles to the Stirling Swamp in Central Australia. In the *jukurrpa* these women pioneered the land. At significant places in their travels they paused to perform particular rituals, to create and name features of the forming world. In significant encounters, especially with *ngapa* (rain), the *kurinpi* tracks criss-cross with those of other ancestors. Sacred sites, where ancestral spiritual power entered the land, are part of the heritage the living must maintain. They must follow-up the tracks, ensure the stories live, give form to the spiritual power in ceremony, and keep sacred places secure.

Within ritual recounting of the *kurinpi* narratives, a dilemma facing women is addressed, and possible outcomes explored. Here women may weigh their relationships with men as poised on a balance: tipping the scales for engaging with men is the desire for children and the company of a spouse, counter-balancing is the fear of the unpredictability of men, and men's challenge to the women's independence and autonomy. Stabilising the unsettling forces of this dilemma, is the constancy of the lives of the *kurinpi* women as ones of ritual observance and celebration of the bounty of their country.

In one account, two elderly, knowledgeable and respected *kurinpi* women, whose special power is manifest in their ability to turn red as they rub themselves with fat, travel from their swamp home in search of company. Once out of their homeland, they cease to name the country and travel more warily. They poke the ground with their spear-like sticks. As they pass from one swamp-land through another closer to Devil's Marbles, they enter a patch of tall spears. Fearing that perhaps someone might see them, they clutch their ritual packages, containing sacred objects, to themselves and continue. Several younger boys appear and dance flanking them. (This is the way of those who have responsibility through their mother's line for ceremonial performance and, in their travels, the *kurinpi* have already witnessed this ritual relationship.) The boys are carrying spears similar to the women's. The women teach the boys to throw spears in an overarm action.

The women wonder why the boys, who are also carrying ritual packages, such as are the right of older people, continue to travel with them. At the meeting, and while travelling with the boys, the women feel a mixture of shame and curiosity. Finally they reveal to each other the contents of their packages. The *kurinpi* attempt to leave, but the boys beg them to stay so they can show them everything. 'No,' say the women, 'You are too young and we are leaving.' Suddenly the boys disappear and reappear initiated as men. The women look on with amazement: these men are wearing their ritual headbands and armbands. Again the women hasten to leave and again the men beg them to stay. The women fear that these men might spear them for they now have long, strong spears such as men carry. The men follow the departing women who soon leave them far behind. 'Never mind,' say the men. 'We shall sharpen our spears, harden them in the fire, and spear the women when we catch them.'

The women say to each other, 'Come. Let them go their way. We have everything we need.' As the men travel they say, 'Let them go. We have all we need and can easily catch them later when we learn how to throw these spears.' As the *kurinpi* dance on, they see and join another group of women who are performing *yawulyu* (women's rituals for land, love and health). The men with the spears are unsuccessful in catching the women because they are not prepared to violate the restrictions of the women's ritual area. Each sex has residential and ritual spaces which are taboo to the other, and here the women are not only at a ceremonial site, they are also engaged in religious rituals.

This meeting with the boys has various connotations. Before encountering the boys, the women had never felt shame. They had confidently and authoritatively known their country and their relationship to it. The ambiguous status of the boys is compounded by their transformation, without ritual, into men. Each is prepared to respect the ritual packages of the other, but the men rather fancy the women and decide to pursue them. The women continue to display their power by rubbing fat into their bodies and by producing colour changes. The men decide to use force and a new technology to win the women, but are thwarted when they discover the women have sought sanctuary in the company of other women.

In another account of the *kurinpi* with men, the women do not escape, but are overpowered. In this *kurinpi* narrative, the women were returning to the camp after a day of hunting when some men began throwing stones at them. 'What is that?' asked the women. 'We want to get food, not to run away.' The women were unaware of the presence of the men. They continued home and on their way dug for grubs. One man ran after one of the women, stood on her digging stick, and asked the woman for food. She felt shamed because she had never met a man like that before. He told the woman to get up and they would dig together. 'Don't be shy,' he said, 'We shall go together.' He gently took the woman by the arm and they continued together. But as they travelled and the woman left her country behind, she held back and tried to go the other way. The man crippled the woman with a spear, and as she lay naked, complaining of his cruelty, he began to beautify himself so that she would love him. He brought her animal skins to warm her body and sat with her. She tried to straighten herself but it hurt too much. She looked back to her country but knew she must leave with her husband.

As a sustaining women's narrative, this is a cautionary tale: men are so insecure that violence is the only way they can express emotion. As a vindicating male narrative, the wild are being made quiet: man tames nature. But when the text remains in its context, a key value is that women's power base is shown to be land and she acknowledges that, through marriage, men can disrupt her ties to land. The once kind suitor who took her by the arm, now spears her. Her tie to her country is also damaged. In being crippled by the spear-wound the woman is also deprived of her land. In the loss of land she loses her autonomy and power base, but he gains a wife to whom he can now afford to show affection, and from whom he now seeks love by beautifying himself. In her crippled state, she feels pain, loss of movement, and loss of land. As they continue together she sees his country, like a mirage, come up before her, and he begins instructing her in the wonders of his country. Through men, women may thus gain knowledge of another country but the price is high. The reverse is also possible. Frequently men take up residence in their wife's country. On marriage men do not invariably succeed in carrying off young wives to another country: instead they may become part of the narratives of her land.

While travelling the *kurinpi* women take on the redness of the country. The rainbow-men they meet burst dangerously with all colours and use red of the ant-hill and green from the water to dull their brilliance. Women's and men's colours are not fixed in a colour spectrum, but are as fluid and as dramatic as the country itself, as ever changing and as unpredictable as the outcome of male-female encounters. Contact means that the stable, symbolically-ordered positions on the sexual axis are freed and negotiable. Like the shifts in colour, like the unpredictability of the country from which women draw their power, men constantly shift also.

For the most part, in the narratives, the *kurinpi* are depicted as old, but they also appear as younger women. The desirability of women is not a function of age. They do not have a self image of 'old hag'. What draws comment is the manifestations of knowledge of the *kurinpi*, not their age. The various encounters are not considered in temporal sequence, but are seen as co-existing in constant flux, an ever shifting, dynamic power on which women may draw. Different accounts are not considered as conflicting versions of the same story, but rather are taken as an illustration of the vagaries and complexities of male-female relations. At one moment in her life a women may need reassurance that a relationship with a man will not bring violence, at another she may need the assurance that she has options; at one that his affections are true, at another that his infidelity is not to be internalised. It is not necessarily her fault if a relationship fails, but rather is one of the many possible outcomes of leaving the security of known territory, and, by way of a safety net, returning to her own country or joining a women's camp remains accessible throughout her life. As long as one remains in contact (directly or through ritual activity) with one's land, one may draw on all one's forebears for assistance, explanation, sustenance, guidance, and life itself.

Men have narratives, women have narratives: like the ancestral travellers, these accounts criss-cross, are negotiable, and co-exist in tension-ridden, knotty webs of contradictions. Women and men have their own ceremonies in which each celebrates their own connectedness to the past and gives form to their responsibilities. There are times when women and men share their narratives, each fleshing out their segment of the ancestral exploits in a joint ceremony; there are times when men are the guests of women; and others when women are the guests of men.

In what narratives might the female newcomers to this land ground a sense of self, find a sense of place, maintain female solidarity? Western religions do not provide the comprehensive, interfunctional world view of the *jukurrpa*. The hierarchy is plain. Women have no female power to bestow names on the land, to generate explanatory texts, to celebrate sex-specific spaces sacred to women: to participate, women must seek concessions from patriarchal power; to ensure a proper marriage, promise to honour and obey. There is no public account of male violence as emotional insecurity: instead the narratives stress manly strength as heroic, sheroes are not canonised for making explicit their emotional needs. Frozen in non-negotiable texts of law and religion, the self-actuating woman is deemed deviant, a threat, insane, unnatural.

The *kurinpi* provide the charter to create and recreate images of women at every generation level. The living trace connections back to the *kurinpi* by reference to actual forebears and one direct link is through naming. Each person has many names, some are taboo at particular times in a person's life, some may only be used by certain kin, some are ego-centric, others socio-centric. A personal name is bestowed as acknowledgement of one's heritage, and with it comes the power of those who bore that name in earlier times. When visiting a new land, one calls out to the ancestors by name and brings their past into the lives of those present. My grandmother shares a name with me and her grandmother before her. In following-up through these grandmothers, I reach into the *jukurrpa*, imprint on the land, assert my right to access the *kurinpi* strength, and to read back into the present.

So now, encouraged that there are other ways to know my world, I'm in search of narratives of sheroes to sustain my generation of women in contemporary Australian society. I'm evoking a personal name 'Elizabeth' and all her other representations, Lizzie, Eliza, Bess, Beth, Bessie, Liza, Isabella, Belle, Bethal, Liz, Libby, Elizabeta. Through her I'll trace the possibilities, the ambiguities, the contradictions and the contextualisations: she offers multiple readings of her Elizabethness, but I know in one of her selves, she stood where I now stand, and can speak to the dilemmas I now confront. When I, in my turn, draw on this heritage, I mould herstory into my history. She must not be lost to the next generation, for if she is, woman is also. She is woven in the tapestries of this land and the threads are testimony of her traces. I chose the name arbitrarily I thought, but then, as I began to write, I realised that Lizzie was my mother's mother's mother's name. She lived in England and it was her daughter, my grandmother, who knew this land. Maybe that trace has drawn me to the name, or maybe it is a long held belief that Elizabeth, as in Macarthur, has been poorly served by the histories of pioneering development of this land as a place for sheep and men, and I want to accord her shero status.

From Elizabeth Macarthur, 1766–1850, we hear an educated woman speak of her role in 'inventing' the social norms of colonial married life. This Elizabeth arrived in her new land in 1790 on the second fleet. Her husband spent many years in England and during his absence she managed their property, Elizabeth Farm. Her sons went to school in England, and after a separation of nine years, reappeared as men. Their transformation, like that witnessed by the *kurinpi*, announced a new relationship: these men would henceforth direct the business. 'Macarthur', an identity imprinted on towns, rivers, schools and bank notes, evokes masculine deeds: Elizabeth's has remained localised, imprinted on the farm.

In letters home, Elizabeth offers a social history of the new land, documents her preoccupations, explores how she relates to the new land and its black inhabitants, and projects a strong sense of self. The narrative is not one of unrelenting domesticity, but of naming her new world. Her first letters to her mother concern her child's health, make mention of that of her husband, and document tasks of household management. The mother-daughter tie, rendered invisible by family histories which trace descent through men, is strongly evidenced. As part of maintenance of women's lore, this Elizabeth writes to women friends: on marriage she offers the advice, 'choose an equal'. Communication with relatives in England was only possibly by sea mail, or in other words, the ritual exchanges of women were constrained by circumstance.

Elizabeth Macarthur's sacred site, the place where her narratives now rest, the Mitchell Library, Sydney, will yield much of the shero activity of the colonial period. For all those Australian women who worked beside their menfolk in establishing farms; for all those women who worked alone; for those women who provided logistic support for their farmer brothers, fathers, sons and partners; could they not have 'shero Elizabeth', Mother of the Merino sheep industry? A contemporary shero, Eliza Forlonge, 1785–1859, who arrived in Australia in 1831, had already studied the sheep industry; had arranged for her sons to be suitably trained; and had hand-picked her flock. Pioneering a landscape further south, in what is now Victoria, she is remembered in a sundial at Kenilworth and a monument at Euroa, but not yet as part of a tradition of pastoral sheroes.

Convict women wrote new scripts in the land to which they had been transported, but the traces are faint, and rarely do we hear their voices. These women appear in routinely generated records, as statistics, rarely as full people. We know little of the everyday humdrum of making out in a foreign land. Their pioneering deeds in raising children, coping with the vicissitudes of male-female relations, mapping survival strategies, are subjects of speculation not an indelible imprint. And, their journeys in the new country were easily curtailed.

Reclamation of convict sheroes is thwarted as names change and are mis-spelt, as these women move in and out of temporary liaisons and de facto relationships. Negotiating relationships with men of some standing was one route to security. Eliza Batman, 1802–1852, also Callaghan, Thomson, Batman, Willoughby, and near the end of her life, Sarah, comes to our attention through her marriage to John Batman. For a short time the marriage brought stability to her life. John, a native-born son of a convict, is remembered for his 'treaty' with the Aborigines in his attempt to purchase land at Port Phillip: Eliza's changing life fortunes tell us of the convict mothers of the nation. Eliza was transported for fourteen years to Van Dieman's Land in 1821, a long sentence for a woman. As an assigned servant she found ways of dealing with sexual abuse from her colonial masters. When she married John in 1828, they already had three children. He died of syphilis in 1839: Eliza, now mother of eight, fell on hard times. Her next marriage failed. Her only son drowned tragically. She cut a lock of hair and sent it to her daughter. The accompanying letter is the only self-authored trace we have of Eliza: the gentle Christian sentiments of that text contrast with the violent murder of Eliza in a drunken fight in 1852.

Arriving in Sydney on the *Superb*, in February 1838 from Ireland, my next tradition-generating shero, Eliza Dunlop, 1796–1863, took the opportunity to study local languages and songs of Aborigines in her new land, and to write poetry. Fragments of her Aboriginal vocabularies survive in the Mitchell Library, obviously a sacred site where many tracks intersect. Other traces of her travels are in court records of the Myall Creek massacre trials. This was the first occasion on which whites were successfully tried for murder of Aborigines. Outraged by the testimony of one defendant who said, 'Only one female and her child got away from us', Eliza wrote 'The Aboriginal Mother' which concludes with this challenge:

To tell of hands – the cruel bands – that piled the fatal pyre;
To show our blood on Myab's ridge, our bones on the stockman's fire.

Relationships between immigrant and Aboriginal women in the colonial period were fraught with misunderstandings but also evidence flashes of sisterhood. The shero of Elizabeth Farm was moved by Aboriginal women's gentle handling of their babies, but thought their status akin to that of slaves. Unlike the colonial model of upper class female gentility, the Aboriginal women worked at making tools and Elizabeth observed them dexterously paddling about in boats.

Bessy Cameron, 1851–1895, encouraged to emulate the model of the refined lady, found the colonial narratives hostile. Born in Western Australia, given a good Christian education, an accomplished pianist, chosen by Moravian missionaries to teach other Aboriginal women, Bessy had come to expect more of life than the paternalists had in mind for her. Her desire to marry a similarly educated man was thwarted and, in keeping with the missionary perception of her proper place, she was married off to a peer. While 'marry an equal' was sage advice from shero Elizabeth, shero Bessy did not share her privileges: she was black and poor. Marriage limited her options for she was now seen as the Aboriginal wife of an Aboriginal man, not an educated woman pursuing a career.

Torn from the narratives of her place, and with no way of engaging with those of her new situation, her life became one of despair. She fought to stop her children being taken to be brought up as 'white', as she had been. Traces of her travels are in the narratives of countless Aboriginal mothers, lamenting the stolen generations, the children taken from Aboriginal mothers under policies of protectionism, segregation and assimilation. If Bessy's narrative had been a cautionary account, could Aboriginal women have been empowered to keep their children? If the right to work had been seen as a measure of independence, not a demeaning of one's femininity, might there have been greater solidarity between Aboriginal and white women?

Bessie Guthrie, 1905–1977, daughter of Jane Elizabeth, reared and privately educated by her Scottish spinster schoolteacher aunts, was advised, 'Never iron men's shirts'. Bessie's narratives have much in common with nineteenth-century sheroes and generated new contexts for contemporary sheroes. As designer, publisher, feminist theorist and activist, she pioneered new territory. War time paper shortages ended the work of her Viking Press, established in 1939, which published anti-war material and poetry including that of Elizabeth Riddell and Elizabeth Lambert. She was not deterred: in the 1970s she worked with the *MeJane* collective, Australia's first Women's Liberation paper. During the war she was head draughtswoman at Hawker de Havilland's experimental aircraft (gliders) factory. After the war she worked with the Young Women's Christian Association, not because of any commitment to Christianity but because of her commitment to the education of young women. She also worked to raise public consciousness of the plight of young women in trouble, provided them with refuge, and had one wall in her inner suburban Sydney home as a message exchange for girls in trouble. Like the *kurinpi* she understood the strength of shared experience; of female insights; and she worked hard to secure places. One of her sacred sites must surely be the Elsie Women's Refuge she helped to found. When Bessie died in 1977, women gathered outside her place to recall her work, women carried her coffin, and women sang over her. These mourning rituals for Bessie puzzled police who stopped the procession: Is this a funeral? Could women celebrate their own sheroes in ceremonies they created and managed? Was there no need for male approval?

The imprint of women's narratives on public spaces, decision-making, and resource allocation has been nourished, redrawn, reinvigorated, and recast by femtheorists, femactivists, and femocrats. These sheroes have rejoiced in the recovery of herstory and recoiled at the vehemence of the resistance to their vision. Just as it appeared women had a space, shifting fortunes destabilised their endeavours. Elizabeth Reid, a pioneering first, appointed as women's advisor to Prime Minister Gough Whitlam in

1973, transformed policies, was constantly harassed by media, starved of resources, and in 1975, when transfer of office was proposed, resigned. The continuing narrative of the journeys of that office, illustrate well the need for a secure site. But the traces of this generation of sheroes will not be lost. The narratives will be interwoven. Future political sheroes turning to the annals of the Women's Electoral Lobby (1972–), will learn that the founding sheroes were unaware of previous Australian feminist surveys of candidates for political office.

Tracing the travels of my Elizabeth sheroes, we have coloured in the maps of women. Their narratives like those of the *kurinpi* deal with conflicts, tragedy, triumph, loss, victory, relations with men, the need for a place to abide. The outline of the map is known to heroes also, the critical factors and actors appear in any history: the sequential litany is known – Aborigine, convict, colonialist, sheep, gold, boom, bust, self-government, suffrage, federation, war, depression, war, boom, immigration, social movements and global issues. But women with knowledge of shero deeds may elaborate this design in a way which is appropriate for her needs, may bend and blend chronology. Shero narratives issue in many forms, today radical and socialist, liberal and marxist feminists pioneer the land. The needs of current generations are many, they shift, they defy categorisation, but somewhere, there is a shero whose story could sustain. Evoke a name, tease out the traces, celebrate the narrative, Shero . . .

Notes
The narratives are based on my research of Elizabeths in Australian History, but rather than reference the material in the text, I list below the sources on which I drew.

Bibliography
Diane Bell. 1983. *Daughters of the Dreaming.* Sydney: Allen & Unwin.
Flora Eldershaw (ed). 1988. *The Peaceful Army.* Ringwood: Penguin. (Elizabeth Macarthur, pp. 3–25).
Norma Grieve and Ailsa Burns (eds). 1986. *Australian Women: New Feminist Perspectives.* Melbourne: Oxford University Press. (Elizabeth Reid, p. 61, p. 63).
Marilyn Lake and Farley Kelly (eds). 1985. *Double Time: Women in Victoria – 150 Years.* Ringwood: Penguin. (Eliza Batman, pp. 3–12).
Heather Radi (ed). 1988a. *200 Australian Women: A Redress Anthology.* Sydney: Women's Redress Press. (Eliza Forlonge, pp. 4–5/Eliza Dunlop, pp. 7–8/Bessy Cameron, pp. 58–9/Bessie Guthrie, pp. 220–22).
Marian Sawer and Marian Simms. 1984. *A Woman's Place: Women and Politics in Australia.* Sydney: Allen & Unwin. (Elizabeth Reid, pp. 175–76).
Dale Spender (ed). 1988. *The Penguin Anthology of Australian Women's Writing.* Ringwood: Penguin. (Elizabeth Macarthur, pp. 11–33).

Acknowledgements
I gratefully acknowledge permission of publishers Allen & Unwin to draw on material from *Daughters of the Dreaming* (1983).

Mavis Yen
MEMORIES OF SYDNEY'S CHINATOWN

Evelyn Yin Lo's story is as much a re-creation of Sydney's old Chinatown as it is about three generations of women, her mother, herself and her five daughters. It is a bridge between the old White Australia and today's multicultural society. Evelyn's Dad, G. Lai Park, was a chef who came from Tung Koon county to Sydney in 1898. Her mother was Annie Mary Chong from Jaang Sheng county. They ran small Chinese restaurants before Chinese food was popular with Australians as it is today. They never could afford a trip back to China.

Evelyn and her siblings became acculturated in the New South Wales public school system. There was always one big bully when she went to the Crown Street Primary School, she says. She lived in fear of being bashed up. Her brothers had to fight their way through school. However, helping in the restaurant after school gave Evelyn a window on society. It also enabled her to take over as chef when her father's health failed. She got to know everybody in the Chinese community. Their most distinguished guest was General Tsai Ting-kai who visited Sydney in 1935. He was acclaimed by the Sydney Chinese for defending Shanghai against the Japanese in 1932 and gave Evelyn his autograph.

The parents were always busy so the children sent themselves to Sunday school for something to do and Evelyn became a church activist. One of her brothers later went to Japan as a missionary. She tells of the festivals the family celebrated, particularly when the Chinese met each year to pay their respects to the spirits of dead clansmen at Rookwood cemetery.

After her marriage to Don Yin Lo, a former Chinese seaman who served four years in New Guinea with the US Airforce, they decided to stay in Australia instead of going to America. But because Don was Chinese his name was placed on a list of deportees under the Wartime Refugees Removal Act. Only timely intervention by the US authorities enabled him to stay. In order to raise a family of five daughters, like many other Chinese, Don worked in a factory by day, then came on duty to whatever business Evelyn ran during the day, a fish and chip shop or club dining room.

'The Chinese coming from overseas to Australia now spoil their children,' says Evelyn. 'The young ones complain they're having a hard time. I think the youngest generation are getting it the easiest of the lot. We battled through, but we could take a lot more because we went through a lot more.'

Evelyn's youngest daughter, Cheryle Yin Lo, contributes an appraisal of her parents. A Sydney artist, she travelled to China, Peru and Bangladesh in search of her cultural identity. She says she never suffered the vicious racism her parents had to put up with. She thinks her family was neither traditional, nor completely Australian. But with all the changes and opportunities now open to young Australian born Chinese women, she feels more conscious of her heritage and how much of an asset it is.

Evelyn Yin Lo 1890s to 1930s
My Dad was the first to make spring rolls in Sydney. We used to sell them for sixpence without mushrooms and eightpence with. He made the best prawn balls in Australia. I always remember him banging the fish balls. I only wish I could have learned more from him. Dad was going on to nineteen when he arrived in Sydney in 1898. He came with three other clan cousins, Lai War Hing, Lai Poy and another whose name I can't recall. They were all qualified cooks. They came from the same village in Tung Koon county, north of Hong Kong. Australia was the Golden Mountain and they came to build a new life for themselves.

When you're a kid, you don't know much. You just listen. Dad's friends said he had a pigtail when he first came. I don't know what he did at first, but eventually he went up to Tamworth where he had a little food shop. Lots of Chinese were growing tobacco there then.

Dad's name in Chinese was Lai Park, his surname being Lai, but in Australia he became known as G. Lai Park, and it was assumed his surname was Park. Mum was Annie Mary Chong. She came out when she was only thirteen from Jaang Sheng county, next to Tung Koon. While she was working as a housemaid for a Chinese family, friends in the furniture business thought it would be nice if she and Dad married. Dad was twenty years older than Mum.

Their first child, Basil, was born in Tamworth in 1920. They moved to Sydney when Basil was two years old, to Castlereagh Street. The area is now occupied by the Department of Main Roads. I believe Dad had a little shop there but only for a short period. I was the second child, born in the Paddington Women's Hospital in 1922.

Cecil was born in 1923 while we were still living in Castlereagh Street. Then we moved to a two-storeyed terrace house at 92 Campbell Street on the other side of the railway in Surry Hills. We thought it was a very nice house. It had two bedrooms, one of them upstairs, and a proper staircase. There was a toilet at the back and a little courtyard. The house had guttering which led the rainwater away. There was a laundry with a copper and a washtub. Some of those terrace houses, including the one we lived in, are still there. They look exactly the same today from the outside. They all had back entrances facing each other, though we had a factory behind us. At one time it caught fire and we were frightened the building would fall on the houses.

Dad often took Basil and myself to a recreation club called the Lai Gee Wooey, organized by the Lais. It used to be in the upstairs of one of the shops, next to the Nanking Restaurant in the downtown part of Campbell Street. We used to go up in a lift to it and Basil and I would play around there. Most of all I remember the launch picnics the Lai Gee Wooey held. The club had a very good connection with the Chinese then. Dad probably didn't have a restaurant then because he had the time to take Basil and myself to the club. Also, I think times must have been better than in the depression years later.

The Nanking Restaurant was started by Lai War Hing, who came out to Australia with my father. It was housed in a three-storeyed building midway between George and Pitt Streets with private rooms upstairs for special parties. The building is pulled down now. The Nanking was well-known in Sydney during the war years.

While we were living in Castlereagh Street, Dad had the earliest food shop that I can remember, in Harbour Street in Haymarket. This was the market area and the customers were Chinese. Not many Australians ate Chinese food then, like they do now. Dad was noted for offering a meal of rice and three dishes, including roast duck, steamed egg with minced pork and shallots, and barbequed pork or one other dish, all for one shilling! Dad did the cooking and Mum helped him. The same little shop is still there, facing the Entertainment Centre, but it's a Chinese butchery now.

Les was born in 92 Campbell Street in 1926. I remember the midwife coming. They used to have midwives in those days. Lindsay was born in 1928 and Henry in 1929.

On ordinary days Mum cooked for us. We always had rice, but not too much *haam yu*, salted fish. Dad always like *haam yu*, but we younger ones didn't. On Sunday Basil would push the billy cart down to Harbour Street to get Sunday night's tea. He would go right down to the bottom of Campbell Street and cross over George Street. There was always soup, chicken, pork, fish, prawns or whatever, the four main dishes that make up a Chinese meal. The menu varied with the chef. Dad was always giving us special food. That's why we go for food. We're used to eating the best.

Our Campbell Street house was almost directly opposite the Sydney City Mission, on the corner of Campbell and Mary Streets. Today, the same building houses the Australian Chinese Community Association. We used to go over and join the crowds inside. We had nowhere else to go. That's how we became influenced by church activities. There was a Scottish evangelist who went round with a concertina, playing all the old hymns. He had his headquarters in the mission, and he took his two daughters with him.

Mum and Dad were always busy at the restaurant. Basil was always with his friends. Besides, girls didn't get the same opportunities, so I had to entertain myself. I started going to Sunday school. I used to spend the whole day there. The boys went too, but I think they went for the company.

In 1931 I celebrated my ninth birthday in the lane at the back of our Campbell Street house. Dad and Mum fixed up trestle tables and all the neighbourhood kids came to the party, because we grew up together. Dad's friends would come up to the Campbell Street house for the Chinese new year. Dad always kept that up. He invited a lot of people to the house. They're all gone now. I was the only girl at the time and Dad's friends, having a bit of money, used to buy me beautiful dolls. They also gave us lucky money, *lishee* in red packets.

A half-Chinese lady with no children in Commonwealth Street always welcomed me to drop in to her place. She used to serve beautiful home-cooked meals in her front room. She and her husband lived upstairs and had a restaurant in the front room downstairs. I don't remember whether she used the kitchen, but she must have cooked with a fuel stove. She had a lovely set of lace tablecloths. Her dining room was very stylish, a bit classy for those days. It was the way she used to dish up the food that impressed me. She served it so nicely. She smoked too. The other kids used to be frightened of her, but I wasn't.

I used to go down the lane that ran past the back entrances to the houses in Commonwealth Street. It's blocked up now. We used to go down there to stickybeak the Pak-Ah-Pu lottery in one of the basements. We were only kids. They had two drawings a day, one at ten in the morning. The man who sold the tickets arranged all the numbers and that. He used to go round all the shops to sell the tickets. 'You know you're not supposed to tell the police,' he would say to us. I never saw the whole thing. You could win up to forty pounds, or something. It was two shillings a ticket, I think. That was a lot of money in those days. It could have been sixpence. People knew him and they would come down to the basement too. Now and again Dad bought a ticket. Dad wasn't a gambler. He only gambled because he thought he might make some money when there wasn't much business. Then he'd take a chance. I used to follow him and say: 'Dad, don't, you'll never win.' A lot of people used to play mahjong in those days, but this had nothing to do with the lottery.

Nobody ever closed their shop till late. There used to be an Australian who ran a mixed business at the corner of Commonwealth and Albion Streets. He used to boil up all the milk in the evening to make sure it didn't go bad. He didn't give it to you any cheaper though. We would take a billycan down. People going home late would also buy it. There were a few shops selling fruit and vegetables, as well as mixed businesses. But Mr. Lum Jack Hing had the monopoly of all the Chinese business. His little shop was on the corner of Reservoir and Batman Streets, in the heart of the terrace dwellings. They're all knocked down now. He used to give credit. That's why the Australians went to him. He had a very dry sense of humour, though. If you didn't pay your bill, then you didn't get any more credit. It was a very tiny shop with a counter and his wares on the side. The family lived upstairs. Mrs. Hing came from China and couldn't speak English. Their daughter, Eileen, and I grew up together. We went to the same Sunday school. We still exchange Christmas cards. She had all boys and I had all girls.

A friend of mine lived in Mary Street. I was fascinated by the houses there. You entered the house by a flight of steps leading to what I used to call a dungeon, actually a basement floor. The lounge room was down there. Then there was a floor at street level and a floor above that, three in all. The Chinese Masonic Society, the Gee Gong Tong, is still in Mary Street. Dad used to be a member. Like the Australian Masons, the Chinese

Masons are supposed to be brothers, to help each other. All the Chinese went to the Gee Gong Tong dances, but they don't have them now.

I still go to a little noodle shop on the corner of Reservoir and Commonwealth Streets to buy 'wun tun' wrappers and fresh noodles. I used to work in this shop when it was a mixed business run by Chang Way Shew. A clan cousin of mine, Lai Kuen, runs it now. Lai Kuen is the grandson of Lai War Hing, who came to Australia with my father in 1898. Lai Kuen still makes the noodles the old way, by hand and by machine too. Today the Chinese from Hong Kong are buying up property in Surry Hills. They like the area because it's close to Chinatown and to the city.

1940s

Sydney's Chinatown today is centred in Dixon Street in Haymarket. This used to be the market area where all the fruit and vegetable agents had their shops. During the war years however, the best restaurants were in Campbell Street. As you walked up Campbell Street from George Street towards Elizabeth Street, the Capital Theatre was on the right. Further up, the Tivoli Theatre was on the corner of Campbell and Castlereagh Streets. The Shanghai Restaurant, long since gone, was also on the right between Elizabeth and Mary Streets. The Tientsin Restaurant was upstairs, across the street on the left hand side of Campbell Street. If instead you turned right after reaching Elizabeth Street, the House of Five Sons, or Ng Gee Gooey, faced you across the road. The Nanking Restaurant was on the left hand side of Campbell Street, between Pitt and George Streets.

After Cecil and I returned from Hong Kong, Dad took up two shop fronts on the right hand side of Campbell Street, opposite the side exit of the Tivoli Theatre. Here he started the Canton restaurant, the Kwang Chow Lou. Now all the Tivoli stars started going to the Canton. Dad would make up their favourite dishes for them. He also served regular meals just like any other restaurant. He was the only one doing the cooking. Mum continued to run Ng Gee Gooey in Elizabeth Street, so we had two places going at the same time. We got to know the doorman of the Tivoli well. Some of the entertainers came from overseas, including America and China. Among them were the Kwan brothers and George Wallace. They used to give us tickets to their shows, but we had no time to go.

The man who was supposed to be arranging for another cook to come from China kept taking my father's money, but the cook never arrived. We got some help from some seamen who looked after the upstairs, the private wing, while Cecil and I took care of the downstairs. Dad's health was failing, but he was still able to cook and I became his off-sider. All the Hong Kong evacuees were coming in then. Some of the Chinese girls married to British servicemen asked us for jobs. It was a good time for the business.

I never did spend much time with my father before, but I did have to when his health failed. I had to more or less run the Canton on my own. Cecil was about sixteen after we came back from Hong Kong. Of course, we didn't run the Canton entirely by ourselves. Dad used to come over when he was able to. I helped to do the cooking. Dad had the stockpot ready. He told me exactly what to do. Everybody thinks I'm a good cook. Actually I just used the stockpot. You see, the flavour's already there. I had about four years' experience under Dad. So I did the cooking and Basil made the noodles. That's how we managed to keep the Canton going for a couple of years. I'm even more aware today of how important it is to do the best you can for your parents when they are not well. You don't blame your parents. It's a matter of survival.

In December 1941 the Japanese came into the war. We were still living in Foster Street near the central railway station when a midget Japanese submarine entered and shelled Sydney harbour. The expected cook never arrived. So Dad had to sell out. That's how he lost the Canton restaurant in the end. I always thought we shouldn't have sold it. Four or five seamen bought it cheap.

We only had the Ng Gee Gooey going after that. But Dad had to let someone else run it and everything was lacksadaisy. Dad was sick and tired. Two years later he sold the business very cheaply. I had already taken on a job in a fruit shop in Parramatta and Basil had gone off with the Allied Works Council, doing war construction work in Darwin. I was furious when I heard about it. I said to Dad:

'You didn't need to sell that business. I could have run it.'

But Dad was always worried the central railway station would be a target and he moved the family to Burwood, a suburb west of the city. At first we rented the house. Then Dad put down the deposit and Cecil and I put our money in and eventually the family bought it.

After we moved to Burwood, Dad and Mum just retired. By this time the older boys had jobs and were helping keep the family. Cecil was already working with Australian Wireless Amalgamated. But I was earning more than the boys. I was always lucky. Dad's health was failing fast now and he became a bit bored. He got in with a crowd of people who came from See Yup in China. They'd moved down from Darwin some years earlier.

Mum also made friends with a lady who lived around the corner from us. She was working in a woollen mill in Alexandria. Her name was Lee Tim-tay and her husband was Chin Loong Tong. We called her Yee Paw. They came from Toishan county. Mum wanted to go out to work too, but she wouldn't while Dad wasn't well. She just pottered around the house, took care of Dad, took up gardening and visited sick friends.

The only way Dad could tell which train to take to Burwood was by the two 'o's at the end of the word. The newsagent on the Burwood platform had a little stand with books and papers. Dad used to have a look and buy comics or story books for my young brother. The newsagent became quite friendly with Dad and would offer him his seat. When Dad's train came in, he would say:

'Here you are, Mr Park, your train.'

1980s

I'm very proud of my daughters. As far as education was concerned, it was up to the girls themselves, and they did look after themselves. I didn't know anything about education. I only knew we had to go and learn things at school. The only one who didn't like school was Beverly. Now she's making up for it by doing a mature-age university course. When I went to Japan to visit my sister-in-law, Kasue, I found that Japanese women are supposed to do what their husbands tell them. I didn't like that.

I didn't like school when I was a kid. But then, I think my mother and father needed me at home to help. They had waitresses working for them, but they were very unreliable in those days. Some days they wouldn't turn up and I had to help Dad and Mum. I used to do everything, cook and take the food out to the customers and collect the money at the same time. Everybody laughs at the way I used to do things. The main thing is, we got results. It doesn't matter how you go about it as long as you get results. That's what I think.

I think the Chinese coming from overseas to Australia now spoil their children. The young ones complain they're having a hard time. They never think how their grandparents survived and didn't do the things they wanted to do. It's only through hard work that we got to the position we're in today. We battled through, but we could take a lot more because we went through a lot more. I think the younger generation are getting it the easiest of the lot!

Postscript: Cheryle Yin Lo

As far back as I can remember, Dad and Mum were forever slaving over hot stoves, at home and at work. They shared a solid commitment and were a real support to each other. Even in times of difficulty, they always made sure we children had proper meals and enough to eat. The bond between them, their concern and love to provide and build a secure environment for our family is something my generation would have little understanding of.

Being the youngest of five girls, I was very spoilt and favoured. I was always surrounded by my family. I was the 'little baby sister' and spoilt with attention and gifts by my sisters. Because of the language barrier, I never knew my father as well as I would have liked to. I still wonder what his real thoughts and feelings were. I feel frustrated and disappointed that I missed the chance to retain all that valuable information about the Chinese way of life. Nevertheless, we shared a deep understanding. I think Dad missed not having a son and I was the substitute. He would get me to help him fix fences and cars and do other boy's jobs. He didn't ever cast me off for 'being a girl'.

I have memories of having to go with Mum and Wendy, during school holidays, to the fish shop at Pyrmont. Mum always preferred for me to go with her. I saw her as a very capable woman, assertive while not aggressive and always able to cope without having a man around. She also had a soft feminine touch about her. In her younger days, she was very fashion-conscious, wearing the best tailored suits and hats. She was not the 'traditional mould' of a Chinese woman. She was a balance between femininity and capability.

Australian born, Mum spoke both Cantonese and English fluently. She was 'the backbone' of the family and the 'mouthpiece' between the family and Dad. He had 'rules of the house' which were communicated to us by Mum. Of course, there was a difference in our ways of thinking. How could Dad possibly expect to understand us girls when he was brought up in a completely different tradition!

I have often wondered whether being Chinese was something that could be measured. Chinese girls of my age with both parents from overseas didn't have the same opportunity to mix with people outside the family circle. They led a more sheltered life-style. The amount of freedom they had was determined by family businesses. To me, my family didn't seem so 'strictly Chinese' as theirs.

As a family, we have always been very close. The family meal at night was mandatory. On weekends, we used to go on picnics or spend time together. When I was small, Sunday night was a 'must' at my Paw Paw's big house in Burwood, thirty or forty of us squeezing around the dinner table for *sihk faahn*.[1] We ate Chinese style. We went to the cemetery twice a year to pay our respects. My three elder sisters married people with Chinese backgrounds, obviously in respect of my parent's attitudes, especially of my father. But still we were not your 'traditional' family. Nor were we completely Australian. I don't think marriage was pushed on my sisters. It was peer pressure. It was the 'in' thing and expected of girls of that generation. If my sisters had wanted to pursue any career or further education, I am sure my parents would never have had any objections. Instead, they went to work to help support the family. It was their own choice out of their respect and obligation to my parents.

Mum and Dad never pushed us in any specific role that was Chinese. What was expected was more the usual 'female' role. They wanted us to always act like ladies, dress neatly and properly and hold ourselves well.

Mum encouraged being able to cook and at least able to sew on a button.

But things have changed over the years. Australia is changing. Opportunities of career, life-style, marriage and children have become more an individual choice rather than a trend or a necessity as before. Although the structure of Chinese families hasn't changed much, the Chinese community and its concerns have expanded enormously. Young Australian born Chinese women can now push their careers. Mixed marriages are being accepted. I realise how fortunate I am to have had the opportunity to study art and not be pressured into the marriage stream. With a culture of thousands of years behind them, it's just more difficult for Chinese women to maintain a balance between the traditional role and Australian values.

Unlike my mother's generation, I have never been subjected to any vicious racism, apart from the usual name-calling at school, 'Ching Chong', 'Chink' and more recently 'Slopehead'. Sometimes I have even forgotten that I look Chinese. But now that I am getting older, I feel the need to go back to my roots. I am more conscious of my heritage and how much of an asset it is. Perhaps we were more Chinese than we realized!

Note
1. Eat rice, to have a meal.

Sandy Jeffs
HOSPITAL TO HELL

Australian women served their country admirably during the Second World War. They took over the jobs the men left behind and helped Australia's war effort when it was most needed. Some women, the nurses in particular, saw active duty overseas and their contribution has been one of the 'quiet achievers'. They were paid less while serving their country, and did not receive the same benefits made available to their male colleagues on their return from the war. One particular group of Australian nurses suffered extreme deprivation. When they became Prisoners of War after the Fall of Singapore in 1942, they showed discipline and heroism equal to any. Their contribution to the development of the Australian way of life is no less important than the celebrated male tradition of the Anzacs. Their story should be told.

On the outbreak of the Second World War in 1939, when there was a call for volunteers, 4000 Australian nurses applied to serve overseas. They were motivated by patriotism and a wish to use their skills where most needed. There was also a great sense of adventure. In January 1940 the first contingent of the Australian Army Nursing Service (AANS) sailed with the 6th Division for the Middle East. In 1941 the second contingent sailed with the men of the 8th Division on the Queen Mary to Singapore. When they discovered their destination was Singapore, there was a feeling of having been cheated. They had been sent to a backwater of the Empire when they had hoped to follow the first contingent, which had been sent to where the action was.

In the 1930s nursing was a very acceptable vocation for young women of the middle and lower middle class in peace-time Australia. It was considered a profession of some standing with strict rules and hard training and the women who enrolled in the AANS had the benefit of this experience. The training was full of ethics of conduct and procedures that created an exceptionally disciplined and dedicated woman who saw herself in a chosen vocation. Indeed, the organisation and discipline of the hospital resembled that of the Navy or Army. At this time the nursing profession was considered to be on a higher plane than that of an ordinary occupation, and consequently required fitness, special and long training, and determined application. The successful nurse had to have the qualities of teachableness, enthusiasm, obedience, truthfulness and cleanliness. And amongst other attributes she must obey her senior officers and authorities without questioning the hierarchy. Doctors should be accorded respect and absolute loyalty. The nurse of that period had to be dignified, unselfish, courteous, observant, prompt, sympathetic, self-controlled and perceptive. This was the training the nurses of pre-war Australia received and it served as a perfect introduction to life as an Army nurse. It seems that the women who emerged from the general hospitals were an extraordinary creation, whose fortitude and training was an invaluable asset which would see them perform deeds above and beyond their call of duty as captives of the Japanese.

Right up until the surrender, there had been an air of unreality about the threat to Singapore, as though there was a certain immunity from the war. Even though there was news of the fighting on the mainland, the Japanese were still too distant to worry about. Cinemas and dance halls stayed open, and it was easy to eat lavishly – life went on as usual in a nonchalant, care-free manner that had typified the British colonial ethos.

When it became apparent that Singapore was to fall, hasty plans for the evacuation of the nurses were made. On the 11th of February fifty-three nurses boarded a cargo ship, the Empire Star, which after a difficult time at sea actually reached Australia. The remaining sixty-five nurses continued to work until they were ordered to leave their stations and meet at St Andrews Cathedral. The nurses felt terrible leaving the wounded men because this is what they had come to do; their job was to tend the helpless men and leaving was contrary to all their ethics and training.

Under orders, they met at the cathedral, then walked the final distance to the wharf amidst chaos and shelling, whereupon they were loaded on to a run down little boat called the Vyner Brooke. There were over 300, mainly women and children, on board. Two days out to sea, the over-crowded Vyner Brooke was attacked and sunk, just off Banka Island. Of the sixty-five nurses, twelve drowned and twenty-one were shot on Radji beach, in the infamous incident which was widely publicised after the war.

The Banka Island massacre has gone into Australian war history folklore, with the hero being Vivian Bullwinkel. A group of twenty-two nurses, some civilians and twenty British soldiers had come ashore to Radji beach. The island was in Japanese hands, and after considering their plight, it was decided to send the civilians and an officer from the Vyner Brooke in a deputation to Muntok, a town north of the island. The officer returned with a small party of Japanese troops. They immediately marched the men off to a cove and bayoneted them to death and returned wiping their bayonets. They then ordered the nurses to walk into the sea and machine gunned them from behind. Vivian Bullwinkel somehow survived the massacre and lay in the water until the Japanese had gone. Miraculously a bullet had shot through her side without injuring any vital organs. She finally came ashore and hid in the jungle where she discovered a survivor of the men who was badly wounded. With the help of women from a nearby village (the men would have nothing to do with them), they lasted ten days before deciding they had no choice but to surrender themselves, and thinking the Japanese were taking no prisoners, hoped they would make a clean job of their execution. The fickle Japanese were taking prisoners and Vivian Bullwinkel was reunited with the remainder of her colleagues. When she had told them what had happened, it was decided that not a word of the atrocity would be said, lest the Japanese find out and punish them or even kill them. As dribs and drabs of nurses came into captivity they finally numbered thirty-two.

Entering into captivity, the nurses had few possessions but they had the advantage of coming from a disciplined profession. They were strong and had group skills, they were good organisers and had a strong bond with each other which made them a formidable group. The AANS were a constant source of strength and encouragement to the other people in the camp with their ability to survive at all costs. They formed squads to do everything required in the camp and this became a source of income for them to use on the black market. They cleaned the latrines, chopped wood, nursed the sick, carted water; everything and anything.

The threat of rape was most intense in the first weeks of captivity when they were interned in a Dutch residential suburb, Irenelaan. They were to stay here for eighteen months, living in small houses originally intended for up to four people and not thirty people as they were to be. It was not long after their move here that the Japanese moved people out of two of the houses and commenced to clean them and install beds. The nurses, in jest, called the street 'Lavender Street' after the brothel area of Singapore. Their humour soon became a nightmare, when they realised the Japanese had intended the houses for that precise use, and the nurses were going to be the entertainment for the officers. The officers club demanded six nurses for the night. Fearing the worst, the nurses decided on a strategy of safety in numbers and sent all available personnel to the club looking as haggish as possible. They dressed themselves in rags with no make-up, and their hair was dragged down. After an hour they were told to go and the fiasco was over. The Japanese, however, still leered at the nurses, gave them no privacy and they felt they had to be on guard all the time.

Menstruation did not prove to be a problem. Some of the nurses said it stopped from the moment they jumped into the sea. Indeed, after the initial shock of the circumstances of captivity and the physical deprivation they endured, it was not long before menstruation simply stopped. They used to say 'ain't nature grand'. Ironically, after three years of captivity, the women were issued with cotton wool and voile-like material, as things the Japanese claimed women needed. It was a hollow gesture given the circumstances. Yet all this went hand in hand with the squalor and filth the nurses endured. Given the diet of rice, they all virtually lived on the toilets and often a woman would faint while using them. She would have to be washed and cleaned if water could be found. There was simply no privacy, no respite from the filth and degradation and no compassion on the part of the Japanese.

Amidst these inhuman conditions, the nurses tried to bring a little humanity and meaning into their lives, by celebrating birthdays and holidays. They boosted their morale by making and receiving little handmade gifts and cards. They excelled in creativity and produced marvellous dishes from their rice rations, with each being nonsensically named such things as Parachute Drop Scones, Ack Ack Puffs, Pre Freedom Sandwiches and so on. They made dolls, toys, games and clothes from whatever materials they could find. Some, like Betty Jeffrey, kept diaries, written on scraps of paper and hidden from the ever vigilant guards, lest they be discovered and punished severely.

Concerts were staged with the aid of a piano they had found in one of the houses. The ultimate artistic creation of the women's camp was the orchestra of voices. Nurses and civilian women joined forces to create a magic moment of music, which had been written and staged by three talented women. Margaret Dryburgh, one of the civilians, also wrote the anthem of the camp called 'The Captives Hymn', and when she died in April 1945, she left a huge gap in the lives of the rest of the camp. The most well known piece performed by the orchestra of voices, was the Largo from the 'New World Symphony', which even made the guards stop in their tracks and listen. For a while, captives and Japanese felt as one, such was the power of the music.

In 1944 the camp was shifted back to Banka Island, which was less than adequate because water was scarce and fever rife. Sores would not heal, and the chronic malnutrition was starting to weaken even the strongest of the nurses. Four nurses died on Banka Island, and after another draining move back to Sumatra in 1945 to Lubuk Linggau, an isolated rubber plantation, four more nurses died. It was when their own started to die that the nurses began to lose morale. These soul-destroying deaths were anguishing and deeply resented, but they still buried their dead with military dignity, proudly wearing their shabby uniforms as a mark of respect for their fallen comrades.

At the same time as the nurses in Sumatra were having a difficult captivity, the six nurses who had been captured on Rabaul were also experiencing extreme hardship. They also had to ward off Japanese soldiers who would attempt to chase and fondle them, but eventually were given a respite from the harassment by the arrival of a boatload of Geisha girls. In 1942 they were shipped to Yokohama in Japan where they spent the rest of their captivity.

The war ended on the 15th August 1945, but the prison camp was not informed of this. The Japanese had not been helpful to the Allies in finding the nurses camp, and it was only after the efforts of the war correspondent, Haydon Lennard, that they were found – three weeks after the Japanese had surrendered. In her diary, Betty Jeffrey describes the feeling of no more tenko and standing in the sun bowing to these 'little horrors', and no more face slapping. There was, however, genuine disbelief with the sensation of numbness. They were not even sure at first who had won the war! The war was over though and suddenly the Japanese released Red Cross parcels that they had withheld for the time of the nurses internment. Food, medicine, clothes and life saving quinine were now abundant. Three years and seven months of captivity had left the nurses emaciated; some weighing only five stone and all with yellow skin and reeking of camp stench.

After searching Sumatra, paratroopers arrived at Lubuk Linggua to an enthusiastic welcome and were immediately besieged by nurses asking questions such as who had won the football Grand Final, which horses had won the Melbourne Cup, the latest fashion in hair styles and so on; questions about a world they had not seen for three and a half years and about which they had slight reservations of seeing again fearing they would not belong.

Waiting in a nearby airstrip, in the full splendour of their patched up grey uniforms (they had declared when taken prisoners that they would save their uniforms for their day of liberation) a plane finally came. On the opening of the hatch of the plane, two women in trousers and safari jackets emerged – such attire was unheard of before the war! The nurses asked them who they were and Matron Sage said 'I am the mother of you all, but where are the rest of you?' hoping to find all sixty-five of them. The nurses numbered twenty-four and were half starved and almost beyond recognition. There was a silence.

After their rescue, the nurses spent time in Singapore preparing for the journey home, and having been nursed and fed, they looked almost presentable for the scrutiny of relatives and friends. Most did put on weight but some were still quite ill, and although they were determined to put on a good front, the marks of their internment were quite evident. They had all had, at some stage (and some still did) malaria, beri beri, dysentery, tape worm, and tuberculosis. All were suffering from malnutrition. They were given frocks, slippers, nightwear, writing paper, lots of flowers and the luxuries and trappings of civilised life they had been deprived of for so long.

On arriving in Australia, they were given a rapturous welcome home, quite unlike their British counterparts who received a muted reception. There was no sophisticated debriefing, as one would expect today, rather they were repatriated quickly, some settling into a nursing career they had begun before the war.

Sixteen of the nurses married, eight having children. Betty Jeffrey, whose war diary 'White Coolies' was published in 1954, and Vivian Bullwinkel, travelled around Victoria raising funds for a Nurses Memorial Centre. Vivian Bullwinkel had a distinguished nursing career receiving many honours including the Florence Nightingale Medal, the highest award of the International Red Cross.

Postscript
It is difficult to imagine the actual pain, deprivation and maltreatment the nurses endured, but the twenty-four who came home had survived a holocaust of their own, yet managed to retain much of the sense of propriety and humanity they possessed. For nearly four years they had relied upon each other for their basic survival, and had functioned with an egalitarian spirit, which was quite to the contrary of the male POWs who still adhered to discipline and hierarchy. They were each other's counsellors and entwined themselves in a strong bond that continues today. Although they are all in different locations, they still go out of their way to maintain contact with each other. Nothing interferes with the primacy of their relationships. The nurses claim that even the Returned Services League (RSL) thinks that they are too 'cliquey' – a testament to the nurses single-mindedness where their 'mates' are concerned. Such dedication can only arise out of experiences of the extraordinary of the human condition.

Some interesting sources

Kenneth Attwill. 1959. *The Singapore Story*. London: Frederick Muller.

J. Bassett. 1992. *Guns and Brooches: Australian Army Nursing from the Boer War to the Gulf War*. Australia: Oxford University Press.

Rupert Goodman. 1988. *Our War Nurses*. Brisbane: Boolarong Publications.

Betty Jeffrey. 1955. *White Coolies*. London: Angus and Robertson.

Catherine Kenny. 1986. *Captives: Australian Army Nurses in Japanese Prison Camps*. University of Queensland Press.

Hank Nelson. 1985. *P.O.W. Prisoners of War*. Australian Broadcasting Corporation.

Jessie Simons. 1954. *While History Passed: The Story of the Australian Nurses who were prisoners of the Japanese for three and a half years*. Melbourne: William Heinemann. Reprinted 1985 as *In Japanese Hands: Australian Nurses as POWs*. Melbourne: William Heinemann.

Laranina Warner and John Sandilands. 1982. *Women Beyond the Wire: A Story of Prisoners of the Japanese 1942–45*. London: Michael Joseph.

As well as the books mentioned, there have been other media presentations of the nurses' story. Warner and Sandilands were involved in the making of a television series called 'Tenko' in 1981. Hank Nelson produced a radio series for the ABC about the POWs which included an episode about the nurses called 'An Ordinary Bunch of Women' in 1985. There was a special programme on television retelling the saga of Vivian Bullwinkel's survival of the Banka Island atrocity. At various times there have been interviews with surviving nurses on radio. The Australian War Memorial holds in its archives various diaries, uniforms and artefacts, but they seem to be under-represented. There are also memorials scattered around Australia, including the monument at the Nurses Memorial Centre in Melbourne at which women, who were in the nursing service, gather for a memorial service on each Sunday before Anzac Day.

Janine Haines
WOMEN AND POLITICS

The day I walked into the Senate chamber in the old Parliament House for the first time in February 1978 I was struck by the maleness of the place. Of the 64 senators only seven were women. When the 124 all-male members of the House of Representatives joined us for the official opening of Parliament, the place was awash with testosterone. The Governor-General was male, so was the Prime Minister, the Deputy Prime Minister, the Leader of the Opposition, the President of the Senate and the Speaker of the House; all 124 members of the House of Representatives, all but seven of the senators, most of the clerks and all the attendants. Only one minister was female.

Nearly twelve years later, in December 1989, when I left the new Parliament House for the last time not much had changed. Women had been elected to both houses in greater numbers than in 1978, but not much greater. A woman had been elected Speaker of the House but not as President of the Senate, and two women held ministerial portfolios. There were more female clerks and a few female attendants. A different man was Governor-General.

Suffrage
Nations such as Australia and New Zealand led the way in electoral and social reforms because of, rather than in spite of, their infancy. As sites of white settlement, these two nations were very young indeed. That the efforts of women were needed and were acknowledged as important for the economic and social development and stability of these countries was a key factor in the relative ease with which the suffrage campaigns produced results. Thus change came more easily in the embryonic nations of Australia and New Zealand than in the more established ones, and while the suffrage campaigns were hard fought in the two southern hemisphere nations they were less violent than in Britain, and less drawn out than in the United States and Canada.

Within predominantly Protestant Australia the first states to grant female suffrage were the younger, less tradition-dominated South Australia and Western Australia, both of which were established in the middle of the nineteenth century – as was New Zealand – and both of which were settled – as New Zealand was – by free men and women rather than by convicts. This is not to say that the franchise was granted to women in those places without a fight. The proposal met with often hysterical and obdurate opposition from all sides of politics and from both men and women. Many more men and women supported the move, however, with the result that petitions and counter-petitions on both sides of the Tasman were presented to the respective parliaments in attempts by both sides to sway the members.

Furthermore, the well-organised and committed Woman's Christian Temperance Union (WCTU) was as much a leading force in the suffrage campaigns in New Zealand and South Australia as it was in the concurrent campaigns in Britain and the United States. In the end, and despite the efforts of the individuals and organisations involved in the pro-suffrage movement elsewhere, New Zealand, South Australia and Western Australia were the only places in the world to give women equal voting rights with men by the turn of the century. The other Australian states were much more reluctant to enfranchise women, and did so only after the federal government, faced with the electoral dilemma of having some women entitled to vote in federal elections but not others, amended the Electoral Act in 1902 to give all white Australian women the right to vote in those elections whether they had that right at state elections or not.

In Australia the push for female suffrage followed campaigns for other reforms to the education system, women's health care and adoption laws. In many cases the central figures and organisations behind these pressures for reform were also at the forefront of the suffrage campaigns. Catherine Helen Spence, Annie Martin and others who were active in the campaigns for better schools and modern teaching methods in South Australia in the 1860s and 1870s were also central figures in the campaigns for electoral reform in the 1880s and 1890s.

The Social Purity League, the Young Women's Christian Association, the Woman's Christian Temperance Union and, later, the Working Women's Trade Union were all established by the 1880s and early 1890s with social, economic and political reforms adopted at varying times as part of their agenda. To most of those women and the organisations to which they belonged, female suffrage and other social reforms were inextricably linked.

Catherine Helen Spence

This was certainly the case with Catherine Helen Spence, the doyen of the suffrage and reform movements in South Australia in the last decades of the twentieth century. Of Scottish descent, Spence arrived in Adelaide with her parents in 1839. She was fourteen years old and could hardly have had any idea of the mark she was to make on the young colony, and its female residents in particular, during the next 71 years. Her zeal for social reform was to affect elements of South Australia's population from the factory floor to the houses of parliament. She resented and opposed the idea that there were 'separate spheres' for men and women and was scathing in her attacks on conditions under which many women and children lived and worked. She railed against the lack of freedom women, and especially married women, faced, but was often forced to submit to those same restraints in order to achieve her ends.

Spence was a noted novelist and wrote pamphlets and articles dealing with social ills and deficiencies in legal protection for women and children. She addressed issues as diverse as the need for children's courts and for a more balanced taxation system. She campaigned for better education for girls, higher wages for their mothers and a fair and effective electoral system. Spence recognised the value of organisations established to lobby for issues which would improve the lot of women and children in Australia and maintained an association with groups in South Australia such as the Social Purity League and the Woman's Christian Temperance Union, among others, as well as being instrumental in forming the Effective Voting League.

Compared with the British, Canadian and American campaigns, the campaigns for female suffrage in Australia and New Zealand were relatively short: taking decades rather than generations to accomplish.

Suffrage movements were underway in all these countries by the 1870s and the leaders and individual suffragists maintained contact through letters and visits. They shared each others' successes, failures and frustrations; learned from each other and encouraged and supported each other. When women in New Zealand were given the vote in 1893 and the South Australian Parliament passed legislation in December 1894 giving women in that state both the right to vote and to sit in parliament, the suffrage movements elsewhere celebrated and used these successes to promote and justify their own campaigns.

For Catherine Spence prejudice against women was particularly galling. Unable to argue her case for electoral or social reforms in public because, she said, 'women as platform speakers were unheard of' in the late nineteenth century, she 'waited for some man to come forward and do the platform work for me'. None did and so 'I started to do the work myself'.[1] That work included campaigning for what she called 'effective voting' – i.e. proportional representation – believing it to be the fairest of all voting systems. Spence was concerned that without such a method adversarial politics and vested interest pressure groups would become entrenched.

It was Spence's determination to see the fairest voting system possible become part of the emerging nation's new Constitution – and her belief that she could not leave it to the men – that led her to seek election to the Constitutional Conventions due to meet in Adelaide and Melbourne in 1897–98. She was vastly amused, following her nomination being made public, to discover that 'in the list of the "10 best men" selected by a Liberal organisation my name appeared'. In her autobiography she wrote, with understandable pride, that 'I was the first woman in Australia to seek election in a political contest', and went on to report the fact that one newspaper had noted that 'Several unexpected candidates were announced, but the only nomination which evoked any expression of approval was that of Miss Spence'.[2]

Her nomination as a candidate for election to this Convention made her not only the first woman in Australia to run for elected office at a federal level but the first to do so anywhere in the British Empire. While many greeted it with approval, its very uniqueness proved a stumbling block. Notwithstanding the fact that the South Australian franchise legislation had been amended to remove the prohibition against women sitting in the parliament, there was considerable doubt, and therefore considerable debate, about whether or not women could in fact do so if the Constitution Act did not specifically allow them to. British legal precedent suggested they could not, because under British Common Law which applied to the colonies in Australia and elsewhere, women were not classified as 'persons' within the legal meaning of the term. 'Persons' meant 'men' unless otherwise specifically stated and the rulings enshrining this were legion.

Of the hundreds of candidates who nominated for the Senate and the House of Representatives in 1903, only four were women. Twenty-two year old Selina Sarah Elizabeth Anderson (later Siggins), stood for the House of Representatives' seat of Dalley in New South Wales, Mary Ann Moore-Bentley and Nellie Martel ran for the Senate in New South Wales, and Vida Goldstein nominated for the Senate in Victoria. They were the first women in the world to seek election to a national parliament, although women had stood for the presidency of the United States in the nineteenth century. While Vida Goldstein is undoubtedly the best known of those first Australian women candidates in terms of late twentieth-century history, the other three women were also exceptionally talented and committed to the role of women in politics.

Media attitudes and the status of women

Dr Carmen Lawrence made Australian history in February 1990 by becoming the first woman premier in the country. The media seemed non-plussed. How were they to write about a woman in such a senior position? In the end, the *Australian* solved the problem in the time-honoured way of, first, noting the approval of a male 'superior' and secondly linking her to several other women who had been elected to leadership positions internationally. The male approval validated her achievement, and the association with other women set her apart from the male norm. By any standards, the treatment Dr Lawrence received at the hands of the *Australian* that day was extraordinary.

The headline on the first page[3] proclaimed in letters two centimetres high that 'Hawke gives the nod to first woman premier'. It went on to note that the Australian Prime Minister was 'very favourably impressed' by Dr Lawrence and quoted him as saying that she 'strikes me as being a no-nonsense person, knows what she's about, says what she thinks, and I have a very high opinion of her'. No doubt Dr Lawrence was duly impressed by this encomium from her federal leader although she may well have wondered why such praise was necessary.

She must, however, have been less impressed by another article on the same page and the image conveyed by the photograph chosen to accompany it. There she was, arms folded at the waist, standing in a kitchen surrounded by pots and pans. The caption underneath the photo read: 'Dr Lawrence can stand the heat . . . inspecting the kitchen of an Aboriginal centre'. That particular piece of gratuitous stereotyping paled into insignificance compared with the opening paragraphs of the story beneath the photo. 'Dr Carmen Lawrence', wrote the male journalist, 'is no Margaret Thatcher. She hasn't the beauty of Pakistan's Benazir Bhutto. And while she might have the intellect, she hasn't the years of Israel's Golda Meir.' And he might well have added, apropos the last example, that

Dr Lawrence wasn't dead either. It is difficult to imagine any journalist, or anyone else, choosing to compare an Australian male politician with, say, Winston Churchill, John Kennedy and François Mitterand. Yet it was apparently regarded as perfectly acceptable to comment in this fashion about a prominent and capable woman. Not until the end of the second column did the journalist mention the fact that Dr Lawrence was 'a distinguished academic and speaker' and that she was 'one of the most heralded politicians in West [*sic*] Australian parliamentary history'.

The media have always had difficulty coping with women in politics both as individual MPs and with regard to the role they are expected to play. Journalists both male and female seem unable to deal with women in leadership positions in the same way they would deal with men – that is by analysing their policy priorities, their ability to hold the ministerial team together and their rapport or otherwise with the electorate. Instead they are far more likely to comment on the physical appearance of female MPs in a way they rarely do to men – their references to then Treasurer Paul Keating's suits was one of the few exceptions and that ceased when he became Prime Minister.

From the day she became Premier of Victoria, however, Joan Kirner was subjected to an almost continuous and offensive barrage of comments about her physical appearance. One newspaper picked up a comment made by a male member of the Liberal opposition and printed a hoarding which screamed 'Miss Piggy for Premier' after Kirner took over from John Cain as Premier in 1991. While the media seem to have no difficulty accepting often grossly overweight male politicians, they see nothing wrong with directing offensive epithets at women who do not conform to the desirable female figure type no matter how effective, articulate and intelligent they may also be. Thus the massively overweight Russ Hinze, Minister for Main Roads in the Bjelke-Petersen Government in Queensland was affectionately known as 'the Colossus of Roads' while few comments were directed publicly to the federal Labor Minister for Defence, Senator Robert Ray, whose excessive size was almost legendary.

When the appearance of women politicians is not the primary focus of articles and other media comment, their fecundity is, and this is true of all women who make news. Newspaper headlines are proof enough of that. References to 'Granny Bashings' or 'Woolies seeks "mums" in float' a reference to Woolworths wanting to attract ordinary people to buy shares) found in the Australian media are replicated in other countries. Few stories about any successful woman end without some reference to her marital status and the number of children she has. It is almost as if the journalists need to reassure themselves and the readers that the women are 'normal' – that they haven't rocked the boat completely because at some stage in their lives they have rocked the cradle. Physicist or farmer, engineer or entertainer, politician or plumber, the female of the species will find that her private life and appearance take precedence over her professional career in the minds of the media although those of her male colleagues do not.

While this attitude may have been understandable, if not appropriate, in the days when women were first beginning to make their mark in business, the professions and politics decades ago, it is no longer either understandable or acceptable. That these comments are still made in the 1990s indicates that women are tolerated, at best, when they move out of traditional jobs into those wielding power and paying well. That this patronising attitude to women is still widespread makes it even more of a problem for women, whether they are the specific targets of it or not.

Whatever disadvantages women face, in the main they are perceived as more honest, more trustworthy, less ruthless and less self-interested than their male colleagues. Many female MPs also see themselves as having a particular responsibility to be different from men, to clean up the image of politicians and to change the political agenda so that 'clear goals for improved legislation to make women's lives easier and more flexible . . . can be achieved'.[4]

Just as Dame Enid Lyons had entered parliament determined to raise issues of importance to the women of the 1940s, so Senator Susan Ryan in Australia, Dr Marilyn Waring in New Zealand, Clare Short and Teresa Gorman in Britain, I and many other women went into parliament decades later with two broad objectives. As Susan Ryan put it:

one was to bring into consideration matters of vital importance to women which had been neglected; the other was to establish, through my work and by supporting the work of other women, that women were capable parliamentarians.[5]

Most of us were determined not to be portrayed as single issue politicians, nor as just another politician. We made our gender a plus willingly, if sometimes uncomfortably, becoming role models and capitalising on the fact that the uniqueness of our position made us natural focal points for the media. Like many other women in parliaments around the world, Ryan was aware of 'the diminishing credibility' of the institution and its inmates. She was also aware, however, that 'women parliamentarians . . . have been able to establish more credibility with the electorate than their male colleagues.'[6]

Margaret Guilfoyle also did aspiring female politicians a service. She was virtually unshakable during question time, during tough parliamentary debates, or under fire from the media, and earned considerable respect albeit grudging from all sides. As the Fraser Liberal Government's Minister for Finance she dispelled any idea that women couldn't cope with economic policies. She had sufficient support within the Victorian division of the Liberal Party to be placed on the top of the Senate ticket until her retirement in 1987. In the valedictory that year a left-wing Labor senator trying to describe Guilfoyle adequately as a person as well as a senator and minister finished up saying 'When one is looking at something so fine, it is often very difficult to find words to describe effectively that fineness'.[7] Senator John Button said of her that

> She brought great skills and . . . intellectual stringency to her role as a Minister. She was a very fine Minister for Finance. Throughout her career she brought both dignity and good humour to this chamber.[8]

The legislative imperatives of economic rationalism reinforce the double standards applied to women both in and out of the workforce. In their demands for cuts to welfare benefits; in their refusal to acknowledge the value of unpaid work in the home; in their persistent underpayment of work done predominantly by women in the workforce, employer groups along with unions, politicians, the media and the community generally have made it as difficult as possible for women to attain economic and personal independence and for them to break free of restrictive gender stereotyping. It has also reinforced traditional theories about the proper division of physical and emotional resources within the family in which mothers nurture husbands and children, while fathers primarily earn money.

I worked both as a teacher and as a member of parliament because that was what I wanted to do, and I refused to be made to feel guilty despite the best efforts of a lot of other people. Even after I left the parliament there were people who suspected that the psychological skeletons of my children littered my closet.

Their assumption that my family must have suffered during my years in parliament and their often imperfectly disguised astonishment that this had not happened, stems from the fact that even in the 1990s there seems to be a desperate and ongoing need for the media and some sections of the community to tell themselves and others how unusual, if not downright odd and improper, it is for women to be anything other than somebody else's wife and mother.

Somehow the media – both reflecting and entrenching social attitudes – seem unable to accept that women have the drive, the talent, the need and the right to make it to the top. Those who do succeed are not, indeed must not be allowed to be, portrayed as representing the norm for women. So they are trivialised; their achievements are minimised or ignored; they are accused of being tokens; their abilities are called into question; and they receive publicity only when they speak about 'women's issues'. This in turn perpetuates the myth that women have a narrower range of interests than men and that those interests are, by definition, less important.

Within the wider political sphere the belief, conscious or otherwise, that women are of secondary importance in the scheme of things is seen again and again in debates dealing with issues most frequently affecting women such as child-care, pension levels, family assistance programs and so on. The relative importance, influence and emphasis given to issues of interest to men in parliament is greater than that given to those issues which are seen as more the concern of women. Non-legislative debates on, and time given to, matters concerning finance, tax, property and defence are more extensive than those on health, welfare, education and housing.

In the Australian Senate two hours is set aside each day immediately after question time for a debate on a Matter of Public Importance (MPI). The most frequently raised topics are tax levels and industrial relations. Invariably time runs out before the list of speakers does. Occasionally issues specific to women and children are raised. On these occasions it is sometimes difficult even to fill the two hours. An MPI debate on the question of violence against women and children lapsed after 67 minutes.[9] Three of the four speakers were women and neither the Minister for Community Services nor any other minister in the Senate took part. In fact, so little interest was shown by Labor and Liberal senators that, for the first time ever in an MPI debate two Democrat senators got the President's call. A debate on the imposition of a ten per cent wholesale tax on wine, however, ran for the full two hours allocated to an MPI, and attracted seven speakers including the Minister for Resources and Energy.[10]

The so-called 'welfare' issues have become women's issues partly because more women than men are in receipt of age pensions and other welfare benefits, and partly because they are seen as an extension of that very under-rated occupation, mothering. They are underfunded on a per capita basis in comparison to issues seen as of interest to and therefore importance to men such as defence, industry assistance and so on, in the same way that work traditionally done by women is underpaid relative to work traditionally done by men and is similarly undervalued. The total Federal Budget allocation for 1984–85 on housing, social security, child-care, aged care and education came to fifteen per cent more than that allocated to defence.

Furthermore, family allowances and other direct benefits to mothers bear no relation to the value of the work done in the home. Duncan Ironmonger and Evelyn Sonius from Melbourne University estimated that the productive output of the cooking and washing up done by women in

Australian homes during the 1976–77 financial year was valued at $15,425 million compared with the $15,667 million value of gross product of all manufacturing industry.[11] Out in the paid workforce where female full-time wages are still significantly lower than those of men another problem arises. Whereas the needs of men are routinely considered by governments, unions and private sector management, the needs of women, frequently stemming from the weight of responsibility society expects them to bear in the areas of child-rearing and housekeeping, are rarely considered. When they are raised by women in the parliament or the bureaucracy or the private sector, and when it is suggested that employers should consider these needs and allow for them in awards and other elements of employment, cries are raised about 'special treatment' being meted out to women to the disadvantage of men.

Letters to the editor regularly express rage and fear at women who do not conform to tradition and at the idea that lifestyles for so long geared to the needs of men should be made flexible enough to meet the needs of women. There is a frightening malice behind some of those letters which indicates that women still have a long way to go before they are allowed the same freedom men have to choose their direction in life. They reveal just how far women still have to go to establish their right to the same choices that men take for granted. Whether it is the man who notes snidely that women are a bargain for employers because while they are only 90 per cent as efficient as men, they are twenty per cent cheaper to employ,[12] or the woman who asks when the Liberal Party is going to 'stand up to the sisterhood' and consider the needs of 'real Australian women[13] they send a clear signal that, nearly a century after suffrage women are barely tolerated in politics and are still not accepted as fully functioning beings in society.

Notes
1. *Catherine Helen Spence, An autobiography*, ed. Jeanne Young, reprinted from the Register, 1910, p. 41.
2. ibid., p. 41.
3. *Australian*, 8 February 1990, p. 1.
4. Teresa Gorman, answer to author's questionnaire.
5. Susan Ryan, 'Women in parliament: fishes on bicycles' *Senate Occasional Lecture Series*, March 1992, p. 9.
6. ibid., p. 15.
7. *Commonwealth Parliamentary Debates*, Senate, 29 November 1983, p. 2963.
8. ibid., p. 3685.
9. *Commonwealth Parliamentary Debates*, Senate, 22 May 1985, p. 2348.
10. *Commonwealth Parliamentary Debates*, Senate, 23 August 1984, p. 262.
11. Duncan Ironmonger (ed.) 1989. *Household Work*, Allen & Unwin, Sydney.
12. Letters page, *Australian*, 13 March 1992.
13. *Australian*, 25 February 1992, p. 8.

Jocelynne Scutt

THE INCREDIBLE WOMAN

A young woman hit by a car and killed as she crawled across a road in Moonee Ponds at the weekend was screaming that she had been raped and wanted to die, police said yesterday . . .

Detective Sergeant Bruce Smith, of Moonee Ponds police, said that after Miss Kelly apparently scaled a 1.5m fence from Ormond Park on to the Brunswick Rd entrance of the Tullamarine Freeway, she cried hysterically to a motorist: 'I have been raped. I'm in trouble. Leave me alone. I want to die.'

An autopsy found that Lisa Jane Kelly, 18, was heavily intoxicated when she died early on Saturday morning.

But police said the results on whether she had been sexually assaulted were inconclusive and would not be confirmed until the end of the week.

– From a report headed 'Woman screamed of rape: police', *Age*, 24 May 1990

To be a woman, whether as victim of crime or accused, is to be incredible in the context of the law.

This is nowhere more clearly illustrated than in the case of Lisa Jane Kelly. Lisa Jane Kelly is a young woman (now dead) whom we, as women, know without any modicum of doubt was raped on May 19, 1990. We know that as a direct consequence of that rape, she died on Melbourne's Brunswick Rd entrance to Tullamarine Freeway. We know further that if the law were interpreted appropriately, those who raped Lisa Jane Kelly ought also to be held guilty of murder or at least criminal manslaughter.

They intentionally committed the act of grievous psychological harm constituting the rape (together with the physical damage associated with it), as a direct consequence of which Lisa Jane Kelly died on a Melbourne road.

Yet what does the legal system, through its enforcement arm – the police – say of this rape and unlawful killing?

. . . the results of tests on whether she had been sexually assaulted were inconclusive and could not be confirmed until the end of the week.

Thus are the dying words of a woman incredible in law. They are unable to be taken as the truth: that the woman was raped. If these dying words are unable to be believed and medical confirmation is necessary – that is, the credible words of a (no doubt) male professional, a police surgeon or doctor, what price the words of live women in the criminal justice system?

Nowhere is 'the incredible woman' more in evidence than in laws relating to rape. Chief Justice Hale's aphorism that rape is crime 'easily charged and hard to be disproved' though the accused be ever so innocent founds the basic body of rape law. It underlies special rules developed over time, through judicial decisions, that set rape law apart from the general run of criminal law.

If a women did not promptly complain of rape then there was an assumption, at law, that she was not raped at all. If she did complain promptly, however, this was no evidence that she had, in fact, been raped.

It was evidence solely of the reality that she had complained soon after the alleged act. Thus the woman who, for whatever reason, did not make a complaint to anyone as soon as the opportunity arose after the act of sexual intercourse was incredible in law: she was not to be believed. Complaining as soon as possible did not, however, render a woman credible.

The corroboration rule is also illustrative of the incredible woman syndrome. Prior to amendments to laws around Australia in the early 1980s, judges were required to warn juries in all sexual cases of the danger of of conflicting an accused unless the evidence of the chief witness for the prosecution – the woman stating she had been raped – was corroborated.

A jury was entitled to convict on the word of the woman alone but if a judge failed to warn them against the purported dangers of doing so, the conviction could be quashed on appeal.

The only other actors in the criminal justice system whose evidence had to be highlighted by judges as requiring additional scrutiny and considered 'safer' if supported by the words of others were children and accomplices.

This is instructive in itself. Women, children and so-called 'idiots' were a known category at law.

The equations of women victims of sexual offences with accomplices to crime is telling. A person who is in the accomplice category is one who has participated with another in a criminal act.

The woman who has been raped, or who complains of rape, is not an accomplice to a crime: she is a victim of it. There may be accomplices – in group rape, for example – but the woman cannot be an accomplice to a crime committed upon her. Or can she?

What the law appears to be saying here is that if she says she is raped, the woman falls into a suspect category, one akin to an accomplice in crime.

In the 1980s, jurisdictions around Australia modified the corroboration rule so that a judge was no longer mandatorily required to give the corroboration warning. But it remained the law that a judge had a discretion to apply the warning.

This could hardly be said to be an advance. Indeed, it left the way open for there to be no effective change at all: if judges continued to subscribe to long-held beliefs (and there is hardly any reason why they should change their views overnight), the lack of credibility of women giving evidence about their own rape remains, with a consequent application of the corroboration rule, unchanged.

Other aspects of the law impose a similar lack of credibility upon women who are raped.

Thus, in December 1990, the Victorian Court of Criminal Appeal set aside a jury's convictions of a man for indecent assault and two counts of rape, and entered verdicts of acquittal.

What the court said was that the jury acting reasonably [sic] should have had a reasonable doubt as to the guilt of the accused. However, where the accused's story contained conflict (and, indeed, a prior inconsistent statement), this was not considered to be any evidence of dissimulation but rather evidence of the veracity of the accused.

The woman who alleged rape was described as 'a single woman aged 30 years having been divorced from her husband'. What relevance this has to whether she was raped or not or whether she was truthful or not is not readily ascertainable.

The category of incredible woman as victim has taken a new turn with the reality that has been brought about by the decriminalisation of criminal assault at home through the passage of laws relating to non-molestation orders, injunctions, intervention orders and the like.

The problem for women has been that because we lacked credibility as legitimate victims of crime where our husbands, 'boyfriends', 'lovers' and sons beat us, rather than demanding that the criminal justice system take us seriously as legitimate citizens, the path was taken of passing 'new' laws.

Thousands of women around Australia have been diverted from the criminal justice system into the quasi-criminal system.

Simultaneously, men who are in truth guilty of crimes of violence against women with whom they are living, or with whom they have lived, escape criminal intervention. They are led yet again into a position of being figuratively patted on the head and asked (politely, now) not to 'do it' again.

Within this system, women still lack credibility. To present a man who has inflicted criminal acts upon another human being with an order that he 'not do it again' is hardly confirmation that women are equal citizens, with equal rights not to be bashed, brutalised and abused.

On August 14, 1991, women demonstrated outside the county Court in Melbourne then marched to the *Age* building in Spencer Street to protest their anger at a decision by a judge that rape was likely to cause women working as prostitutes less psychological harm than other women. The week in between had seen scads of letters to the editor published on a daily basis, the huge majority of which declared opposition to the judgement.

The case highlights a certain 'grading' of credibility of women as victims of crime, and a categorisation of women-harm-damage calculated with reference to a woman's sexual experience. The defence counsel in this case argued (among other matters) that the defendant should be sentenced, taking into account that he had raped a prostitute.

It was rather akin, counsel's argument ran, to raping a woman wearing a mini-skirt, make-up and 'wandering through a Housing Commission car park'.

This astonishing proposition was not accepted by the court. But the court did accept, and confirm as a legal proposition, the notion that sex-for-money (or consensual) sexual experience is relevant to psychological damage in rape.

This case shows an inability of the courts, yet again, to comprehend the nature of rape. Rape is a frightening, damaging and highly destructive form of attack on any woman, whatever her sexual experience.

The 'principle' that women with sexual experience warrant lesser penalties for their rapists on the basis that they are less harmed by the activity confirms simply that male-orientated and dominated courts are unable to establish a set of principles that recognise the reality of rape: that it is violence and power-centred in sexually dominant and dominating activity; that it is detrimental to the very essence of being a woman.

Women are placed in a special category in the criminal law, particularly where they are accused of crimes relating to violence at home.

Women are not credible in terms of provocation law and self-defence laws. A woman is more likely to be prosecuted for murder; where an argument as to provocation is made, the experience in Australian courts is that such an argument is not well considered. Self-defence is not only not considered, it is rarely, if ever, put forward.

Women are also rendered incredible through a definition of an accused woman as 'ill': the raging hormones theory.

Every aspect of the menstrual cycle has at one time or another been called upon to define women out from being competent participators in the world. The argument generally runs that women are suffering from 'diminished responsibility' during these times, and thus have no, or little, or lesser, control over their actions.

To recognise this definition of women into the category of 'sick' is not to refuse to acknowledge that some women suffer real premenstrual and menstrual pain. But it is important to ensure that 'research' which purports to attribute every antisocial or criminal act of women as arising out of our hormonal 'nature' or 'character' is recognised for what it is: unwise, or not recognised at all.

The criminal law shows some little evidence of a move towards a more credible future for women as participants in the justice system.

The jury's decision and judge's sentence in a Melbourne case where Garry John Norwood was found guilty of rape and four other charges and sentenced to five years and nine months' jail when he forced unprotected sexual intercourse on a woman who had consented to intercourse provided he used a condom, illustrates what is hopefully a shift in the way women are regarded.

The legal system is being pushed into a position where it will have to begin to accommodate women as credible figures in criminal law.

Women in other areas of the law – family law, paternity law, contract law, consumer law – have suffered from the failure of the legal system to take women seriously, to grant to women the same allowance that is extended to men: that of characters with full mental powers, with full human status.

At the same time, there are apparent moves towards extending credible status to women so that the incredible woman becomes a creature of a misogynist past.

Sadly, in the interim, while we fight to advance the new millennium, too many women are being disregarded or distorted by a criminal justice system that should take women, like men, seriously.

Renate Klein

Of Test-tube Heroes and Feminist Resistance

Although Australian 'technodocs' missed out on the birth of the first test-tube baby – Louise Brown was born in England in 1978 which would have caused a lot of long faces amongst the Aussie team – Australian in vitro fertilisation (IVF) doctors are often called 'world-leaders'. And indeed Australia has a few dubious 'world firsts' to claim. A Melbourne team headed by Carl Wood introduced the use of superovulatory drugs which not only create serious short- and long term health hazards for the women involved, but also greatly increase the odds for multiple births. Thus Australia announced the world's first test-tube twins in 1981, triplets in 1983 and 'test-tube quads' in 1984. The same year also saw the birth of Zoe: the first baby born from a frozen – and then thawed – embryo. TV and print media heavily promoted these messages, creating test-tube heroes and picturing 'our boys' as benevolent baby makers in white coats. Carl Wood, Zoe's 'lab-father', had especially good news. Kids from the glass, he was reported as saying, are brighter and better – and he and other techno-docs knew how to produce them.[1]

Australian IVF expertise was deemed so superior that in 1985 the Monash University team established IVF Australia, a company whose intention was to export its know-how to the USA where, according to the chairman of its board, a $19 billion market from the 'three million baby-starved couples in the United States' was waiting to be conquered. West Australian IVF teams were quick to follow suit and in 1985 PIVET established a clinic in Malaysia to be followed by similar establishments in Kuala Lumpur, Athens, Cairo, Singapore and even Britain.

Meanwhile in Australia, the local market was exploited too. A private test-tube baby clinic in Sydney and another at the Gold Coast – at Surfer's Paradise in Queensland – geared their services particularly to Japanese tourists. As the director of the Sydney clinic explained: 'It's a form of assisting the tourist industry. What could be more natural than to go for a month's holiday and when you come back, be pregnant.'

The boys seemed to be up and running and the 'Sun-Rise Industry' was all set to win. At least for a while, the general public was seduced by the glamour of a technology which promised to boost Australian trade and its image as a clever country. National pride was stirred by the promoted spirit of the IVF teams to do good – that is to alleviate the plight of infertile couples around the world. These themes struck a chord with the Australian public for two reasons. The first is the long-term association of Australia with a country that breeds: as a wheat growing nation the breeding of rust resistant wheat was an important national program, and the sheep industry is so important that a saying goes that Australia 'rode to prominence on the sheep's back'. So the breeding of 'better' plants and 'better' animals in order to survive is a well-known story in white Australia. Breeding 'better kids' – and exporting the technology – was seen as doing Australia proud. Furthermore, a lot of the technologies used in IVF had been previously used in sheep and cattle breeding. Professionals trained in animal reproduction such as veterinary surgeon Alan Trounson joined the Monash IVF team to expand technologies used in sheep and cattle to women in what its promoters benevolently call 'assisted reproduction' – critics call it experimentation on live real women. Moreover, Australia has a long pre-IVF history of 'Rambotechnology' – trial and error experimentation on healthy women. In the 1960s a follicle stimulating extract from pituitary glands collected from dead bodies was administered to infertile women. This experimentation with over 1500 women was hailed as 'unique in the world' and seen as highly promising for early IVF attempts. Unfortunately, it caused a frenzy of multiple births up to septuplets as well as many ectopic pregnancies and serious accidents with ovarian hyper-stimulation. And Australia now also holds the sad world record of four deaths of women who recently died from the cruel neurological Creutzfeldt-Jakob disease (CJD) which was transmitted with the pituitary extract and strikes only some 15–30 years later. Since the specifics of the CJD agent remain elusive, all hormone recipients are at risk (including the 600 children who were given growth hormones from the same source) and the threat of an epidemic cannot be ruled out. Nevertheless, some of the same doctors and endocrinologists who were leaders in the pituitary fiasco continue to be prominently involved in the current IVF programs![2]

The second reason for the initial general acceptance of test-tube technologies is the continuing pronatalist orientation of white Australians. This too can be explained as a colonial legacy: when the first white invaders arrived – convicts included – they were predominantly male. The chronic shortage of white women persisted until the post-war migration of the 1940s. Marriage and the production of children thus became the desired way of life. Despite the influence of the Women's Movement, which has greatly enhanced Australian women's life-options, even in the 1980s and 90s, the 'child-free' alternative is still seen as frivolous by many. The stereotype that only a mother is a proper woman continues alive and well. There are not many visible role models of famous women politicians, artists or writers who decide either to remain child-free or have found happy alternatives to their unmet desire for a child. The expectation for biological parenthood makes it especially hard for involuntarily childless women and men to resist the lure of IVF. I must emphasise here, however, that in the case of IVF we are talking about an exclusive clientele of white and some Asian women. Aboriginal women are conspicuously absent from IVF programs although infertility, for instance from chlamydia and other sexually transmitted diseases, no doubt exists. Pronatalism is for the dominant groups only. Besides, the cost of approximately $3000 for each IVF cycle is prohibitive for the majority of Aborigines whose ongoing problem is high morbidity and mortality among their children, especially babies.

However, the fairy-tale story of good doctors and beaming parents with the much longed-for baby in their arms is as false in Australia as it is in the rest of the world. Despite extraordinary statistical acrobatics (for instance counting pregnancies or even egg-transfers rather than actual births), 'success rates' remain so low that it makes more sense to call them failure rates: out of every 100 women who begin IVF a mere five to ten leave the program with a healthy child and this often only after several attempts. In 1993 IVF doctors suggest in all seriousness that a woman should pursue her luck up to twelve times. But being on IVF means having one's life totally medicalised, being prodded and poked. As a woman in a study I conducted among women who had gone through IVF put it: 'I felt like a baby machine, no one was interested in me as a person. I was just a chook with growing eggs inside . . .' It also means emotional turmoil: hopes up, then dashed, up again at the next attempt. Above all it means being sick from the drug treatment for superovulation and experiencing dizziness, vision problem, depression and irritability as well as cysts and ovarian hyper-stimulation which is life threatening and can lead to strokes and in fact death. Two women have also died from problems during a general anaesthetic for egg retrieval in Perth, West Australia. Recently, a group of Victorian women, who underwent IVF, claim that they got breast cancer from drugs used in IVF (their cases are being investigated). All of this is extremely destabilising: life on a roller coaster. It causes economic hardship and puts severe pressure on relationships (IVF is notorious for breaking up marriages). And sadly, even after years of trying there is often no baby at the end. For many women what remains is a deep sense of failure – not technology's failure but their internalised own.

Australian feminists have played a key role in alerting the general public to the many myths and misconceptions surrounding reproductive technologies. As part of the international network FINRRAGE (Feminist International Network of Resistance to Reproductive and Genetic Engineering), founded in 1984 in the Netherlands, Australia has staged a lively debate on whether these technologies will lead to 'liberation' or 'loss' for women – the theme of a 1986 national conference 'Women Act on the New Reproductive Technologies' in Canberra. That there was a feminist stance which saw these technologies as a violation of women's bodily integrity was put on Australia's map by social psychologist Robyn Rowland in 1984. In a courageous act she resigned as Chairperson of the

Queen Victoria Medical Centre's Ethic Committee when Carl Wood's team announced its intention of introducing the 'flushing' technique for obtaining embryos from women's bodies. By going public at the prestigious Australian and New Zealand Association for the Advancement of Science (ANZAAS) and denouncing IVF as degrading women to 'living laboratories', Robyn Rowland marked the beginning of an Australia-based women-centred resistance to reproductive technologies which to this day has kept strong links with similar feminist movements in European and Asian countries, notably Germany and Bangladesh. Her protest caused a media storm and sparked an inquiry by the National Health and Medical Research Council (NH&MRC) which led to a moratorium on flushing. Since then feminists have tirelessly written submissions, spoken as witnesses before various government committees, appeared on TV, radio and in the written press and networked behind the scenes with other critics of these technologies. Australia, and in particular Victoria and Western Australia have enacted regulatory laws which, while far from being perfect, at least are restrictive enough to make life hard for IVF technodocs who threaten periodically to emigrate because their research, especially human embryo experimentation, is now subject to some control. A landmark decision in 1991 by the Health Ministers to make commercial as well as so-called altruistic surrogacy illegal is fiercely resented by IVF teams who are after lucrative business from IVF surrogacies in which the embryo produced from the 'commissioning' couple's egg cell and sperm is inserted into the womb of a sister or close friend. Through making public US 'surrogate' mothers' distressing tales after relinquishing their babies, Australian FINRRAGE members countered the ludicrous assertions by promoters of IVF surrogacy that the birth-mother would not bond with her baby because it was not her own egg. Funding from the Victorian Women's Trust from 1989 to 1992 enabled FINRRAGE to produce a newsletter and hold seminars on legal and technical developments as well as offer workshops for women with a fertility problem. Our expertise is also sought by women's health centres who offer feminist support and facilitate self-help and counselling groups. Consciousness-raising of individuals and distribution of information about the latest research developments through print and TV media are crucial to counter the technodocs' message that these technologies are in women's best interest. Robyn Rowland's and my own 1988 research into the adverse effects of fertility drugs was vindicated in January 1993 by the US Food and Drug Administration who now require the manufacturers of Clomid and Pergonal (two frequently used drugs in infertility treatment), to add a warning about the increased risk of ovarian cancer to their package insert. Despite attempts by IVF promoters to shut us up, we are confident that our message is getting through to more and more women. In 1992, a

Perth IVF program bemoaned the drop in clients, blaming this on the recession. As eternal optimists we would hope that this reflects women's increasing knowledge of the false promises of reproductive technologies and the decrease in numbers is the result of their informed decision against IVF. It is also encouraging to see that these days, in general, glossy women's magazines report 'IVF miracles' much less glowingly than ten years ago.

We cannot rest on our laurels, however, as the pro-reproductive technology group is a powerful lobby which must not be underestimated. At the time of this writing (September 1993) the current liberal government in Victoria, driven by heavy lobbying from IVF doctors and the prospect of making money to fill the empty state coffers, is considering changing the Infertility (Medical Procedures) Act 1984 to allow non-commercial surrogacy. Such a change of the Act would be a breach of the 1991 Health Ministers' decision. IVF research too continues. The latest 'breakthrough' is this year's announcement of one (!) pregnancy from maturing immature eggs. Aside from the fact that one pregnancy does not equal the birth of a healthy child, and, even more importantly, that to use a real live woman as a living incubator to test a new technique is an outrageous example of an extraordinarily unethical experiment, this 'progress' is great cause for alarm. The point was already made in 1989 that once the technique of egg maturation was perfected, even a foetus could become a mother since after the twelfth week in pregnancy, the ovary with its thousands of immature eggs is formed! Such bizarre developments belong to the same category as using neomorts as baby incubators, poor black women as 'surrogates' for white embryos and the development of in-vitro wombs. They cannot be dismissed as science fiction but need to be taken seriously. Some IVF scientists will do whatever is doable. Legislation is urgently needed to curtail the use of immature eggs cells. If this does not happen, then IVF scientists will finally have their egg heaven – as British IVF scientist Robert Edwards dreamt of in the 70s – from which they will be able to make as many embryos as they wish: not very far away from producing babies without women.

Feminist resistance is thus needed more than ever. Other attempts to medicalise and 'drug' healthy women under the guise of 'doing good' and offering 'choice' such as the French abortion pill RU 486, and hormone replacement therapy for menopausal woman, are also exposed in Australia and New Zealand. Needless to say that at times whistle blowing gets tiring and one needs a thick skin to laugh off attempts to undermine us which range from the silly – 'they are all rad.fem.les.seps.' – to the truly damaging: we've had nervous breakdowns and are locked up in asylums; or we are being sued by drug companies and are therefore not reliable sources. What helps is knowing that we are not alone, that there are international links, and that there are many women in other countries who fight equally hard for a future when involuntary childlessness is no longer a tragedy which is then used to justify the development of dangerous and damaging technologies who have the potential to change the nature of reproduction for all women. What also helps is keeping in mind that women have always resisted male-take overs with passion and irreverent wit, and the stubborn trust that even in the face of this latest technological frenzy we will survive.

Notes

1. This article is based on my own work in Australia. I also recommend the following literature for further insights into the Australian test-tube saga including feminist resistance. *Angels of Power* is a unique book as it deals with the topic through fiction, prose and poetry.

   Susan Hawthorne and Renate Klein. 1991. *Angels of Power and Other Reproductive Creations*. Melbourne: Spinifex Press.

   Lorraine Hepburn. 1992. *Ova-Dose? Australian Women and the New Reproductive Technologies*. Sydney: Allen & Unwin.

   Renate Klein. 1989a. *The Exploitation of a Desire: Women's Experiences with In Vitro Fertilisation*. Geelong: Women's Studies Summer Institute Deakin University; Melbourne: distributed by Spinifex Press.

   Renate Klein (ed). 1989b. *Infertility: Women Speak Out About Their Experiences of Reproductive Medicine*. London: Pandora Press; Sydney: Allen & Unwin; San Francisco: Harper Collins; Melbourne: distributed by Spinifex Press.

   Renate Klein and Robyn Rowland. 1988. Women as Test-Sites for Fertility Drugs: Clomiphene Citrate and Hormonal Cocktails. Reproductive and Genetic Engineering. *Journal of International Feminist Analysis* Vol. 1 No. 3. pp. 251–75.

   Susan Powell and Helen Stagoll. 1992. *When You Can't Have a Child*. Sydney: Allen & Unwin.

   Robyn Rowland. 1992. *Living Laboratories: Women and the New Reproductive Technologies*. Sydney: Macmillan; USA: Indiana University Press; UK: Limetree.

   Jocelynne Scutt (ed). 1988. *The Baby Machine: Commercialisation of Motherhood*. Melbourne: McCulloch Publishing; Melbourne: distributed by Artemis Press.

2. For further information on hormone-related Creutzfeldt-Jakob disease – including the many walls of silence that went up when we began to investigate the events that took place between 1964 and 1985 when the program was stopped after three young adults who had been given the growth hormone died in the UK and the USA – see the following articles:

   Lynette J. Dumble and Renate Klein. 1992. Creutzfeldt-Jakob legacy for Australian women treated with human pituitary gland hormone for infertility. *The Lancet* 340. pp. 847–848.

   Lynette J. Dumble and Renate Klein. 1993. Walls of Silence. *Medical Observer*. January 22. pp. 6 and 43.

   Renate Klein and Lynette J. Dumble. 1993. Transmission of Creutzfeldt-Jakob disease by blood transfusion. *The Lancet* 341. p. 768.

Uyen Loewald
FEMINISM AND COLONIALISM

You will be intrigued by the complexity of new immigrant settlements in Australia in general and of Vietnamese ones in particular whether you choose to visit Sydney, Melbourne, Adelaide, Perth, Darwin or Hobart. Many peoples have come to Australia to find their pasts. Some Australians still wear costumes which have become history in other parts of the world; others speak dialects popular some half a century ago. Australia can be seen as a cultural museum or a radical nation, depending on the interest of the tourist.

Vietnamese settlers in Australia must be among the most fascinating of the new arrivals. Since 1975, they have settled in large groups. Some immediately felt at home while others continued to long for the day they could return to their homeland. They are Christians, Buddhists, Confucians, Cao Dai, Hoa Hao, Bah'ai and Muslims.

Vietnamese are as 'sophisticated' as the French, the Americans, or the British who have conquered, dominated and betrayed them. As new settlers in any part of the Western world, they are easily adaptable to their new environments and become high achievers. They speak many languages including Khmer, Laotian, Chinese, Japanese, German, Spanish, Russian. There are the most intelligent Vietnamese who manage to enter medical schools all over the world a year or two after their arrival, but there are also illiterate Vietnamese who have been ignored, exploited, and forgotten by their own community leaders.

Vietnamese and many other Asians need to live in groups due to lack of space and wealth.To live in groups, it is necessary not to alienate oneself from the rest of the group (community), so Vietnamese culture has become necessarily indirect over thousands of years. Western culture, on the other hand, is direct as Western society can afford individualism which requires space and affluence.

While Vietnamese food is well received and well recognised in France, the US and Australia as one of the world's best, Vietnamese people are much less welcome. While political debate about Asian migration continues to change immigration policies, Vietnamese are facing increasing hostility and discrimination. When I was in Germany, people commented loudly as I walked with my husband in a park: 'He must have picked her up when he was last in Bangkok.' Racial violence in Australia is equally harsh.

In Canberra, I have experienced racial violence half a dozen times during the past six years while walking in the centre of the city. One afternoon a drunken man tried to attack me physically while shouting, 'fucking Chinese take jobs away from Australians.' A truck driver attempted to run me down at noon in another street. A woman working for the Department of Foreign Affairs and Trade drove into me on a pedestrian crossing and destroyed my bicycle. After recovering from shock with the help of by-standers, I called the woman in her office only to be abused over the phone. Two white males threw paper balls at me while shouting obscenities as I walked past them. A group of teenagers threw dozens of empty beer bottles after me as I rode my bicycle in the park. The bottles crashed just inches away from me. At Parramatta station near the centre of Sydney I barely escaped physical violence in daylight.

Migration undermines social status. Unemployment denies Vietnamese men respect because they can no longer function as heads of family. Following their peers, Vietnamese children often act like 'Australians' and ignore their father's command. While compulsory education liberates Vietnamese children, Vietnamese women have been imprisoned by social isolation. They have become men's last target for oppression. In 1988, my interviews with Vietnamese women in Australian refuges revealed that unfortunate women who were married to gangsters and crime bosses have suffered dangerous abuse and even death.

The vast majority of Vietnamese in Australia are innocent people living in fear. Until recently they were denied the very freedom for which they risked their lives: freedom of movement.[1] To visit their loved ones left behind in Vietnam, they had to go through socialist East Germany, because going directly from capitalist Australia could mean death or financial ruin. Doing business with Vietnam could also mean physical danger or execution by anti-communist Vietnamese who collected protection money from businesses and professionals in the name of patriotism, only to spend it on personal improvement.In 1985, the murder rate in the Vietnamese community in Australia was just below that of a country at war.[2]

The interpretation of the Confucian doctrine which dictates that 'men and wives respect each other like invited guests' enabled Ba Huyen Thanh Quan in the 18th century to assume her husband's position of a local magistrate to allow Nguyen Thi Dao divorce and remarriage against the forces of 18th century tradition. In the same century, Ho Zuan Huong wrote poems condemning social injustice and unequal status between men and women. In addition, Ho Xuan Huong defied literary convention to create a unique poetic style recognised as unmatched by others until today. Men of her time discredited her by saying that Ho Xuan Huong was in fact a man and not a woman forced to be a secondary wife to a village idiot because her face was scarred by pox marks. Unfortunately, like Emily Dickinson's poetry, Ho Xuan Huong's is too culturally specific and therefore untranslatable.

Since 1986, the Marriage and Family Act in Vietnam has stated that housework is to be shared equally between husband and wife, that men are not allowed to get divorced from their wives until their child is at least one year old, and that no proceedings covering the Act can be legal without the presence of a representative of the Vietnam Women's Union which has the power to arrest men who are violent to women. Affirmative Action has been implemented to the middle level. In 1989, fifty per cent of visiting Vietnamese students in Canberra were women; in 1990, more than fifty per cent.

The first Vietnamese doctor in the Australian Army was a woman but the majority of Vietnamese women in the West are kept like birds in cages despite their superior language skills and acculturation. Like their Aboriginal sisters, Vietnamese women believe that oppression has been aggravated by Western colonialism which robbed them of financial independence. Before Western occupation initiated by French colonialism, Vietnamese women used to be breadwinners while their husbands pursued their fame to honour their families and clans. Vietnamese status in a rural democracy was independent of financial gain until the introduction of the economic middle class by western colonialism which removed power from Vietnamese women. They were reduced to housewives waiting to be kept while exploiting their servants, their even less fortunate sisters.

Confucian systems are also patriarchal, for example, Confucianism highly values the status of the mother and grandmother who produce sons. Since most mothers produce sons, there is some room for negotiation within this value system, but due to sons being favoured it is not infrequent for domestic violence in Vietnam and in the Vietnamese community to be by women against women. Mothers-in-law have beaten or ordered their sons to beat their daughters-in-law. Because people live in extended families, age is respected, and women live longer, Vietnamese women have become matriarchs. As matriarchs they perpetrate against their daughters-in-law what has been done to them but they do also use their power in positive ways. Domestic violence in the Vietnamese communities outside Vietnam has been further aggravated by the reduction and dysfunction of the extended family. An extended Vietnamese family in Australia often comprises a couple, their aged parents and young children competing for service.

As refugees, Vietnamese women have been denied access to power in their host country, and not infrequently by their mainstream sisters. One of my clients told me how her job had been terminated because her two 'feminist' supervisors accused her of being mentally ill. Having researched cross-cultural psychology for the past three years, with the assistance of mainstream clinical psychologists, I have found that the woman's mind was sound. I then helped her contact the Human Rights Commission and other authorities. All agreed that an injustice occurred, but none could do anything for her because the current law against racial discrimination is inadequate.

Whether Vietnamese women's perception that some of their mainstream feminist sisters are racist and that Western feminism is connected with colonialism is correct needs further research; the validity of their claim is important as we function according to our perception and construct of the world. Analysing my own involvement with the women's movement in Australia since 1973, I realise that, to stay within the movement, I had to alienate myself from my own cultural heritage and my own Vietnamese sisters. I felt resistance every time I proposed to discuss cultural differences.

Lack of understanding towards women who speak English as a second language is also obvious within the education field. Now I am in the work force attending conferences and encountering teachers. The female TAFE teachers I have worked with say they are feminists. I have been outvoted many times when proposing that people who do not speak English should not be classified illiterate unless they are illiterate in their primary languages. Another cultural insensitivity I have experienced is the lack of awareness towards the indirect way Vietnamese women deal with situations. A feminist theory is valuable only if it benefits the majority if not all women.

So, when you interact with Vietnamese or other non-western women, it is necessary to keep in mind the question, 'What can I learn from this opportunity?' instead of seeing these women as objects of aid or a source of problems. They may not need your assistance as much as you may need theirs. Their inability to speak the mainstream language may have nothing to do with their intelligence or wisdom. Their unconscious communication may be stronger than their articulate words. When I say different I do not imply superior or inferior; I merely employ the word as defined in dictionaries. Disallowing differences has caused genocide of Aboriginal peoples and assimilation of migrants.

Australia has the potential to be a radical nation, not just a cultural museum. After New Zealand (1893), Australia (1902) gave women the right to vote long before Europe and North America. However it wasn't until 1967 that Aboriginal men and women won the right to vote. Thankfully Australian Western feminism has not been as slow to accept difference. In the last five years, Western feminists have begun the process of working with differences instead of against them, a process which I believe needs more rigorous attention.

Notes
1. 'Free World', one of my stories about Vietnam published in *Short Story International*, 6 Sheffield Road, Great Neck, New York.
2. *Youth Crime in the Vietnamese Community*. 1989. Canberra: Australian Institute of Criminology.

Sabine Gleditsch

MULTICULTURALISM

The history of white Australia began with the denial of the existence of the continent's original inhabitants, Australia's Aborigines. Australia was considered terra nullius – uninhabited land. It took the Australian government more than 200 years to recognise that that was a tragic mistake which had claimed hundreds of thousands of lives among Aboriginal people. In 1993 the Australian High Court acknowledged that at the time of white settlement in 1788, Australia was inhabited. The court ruling has now opened up the path to reconciliation and led to numerous claims of land by Aborigines, mainly in the remote areas where such land claims clash with the interests of Australia's mining industry. However, what Australia's whites view as a step towards reconciliation, is perceived with scepticism by Aboriginal people and land rights activists.

When England, in the early eighteenth century, opened its overcrowded prisons and began dumping mostly male convicts – murderers, petty thieves and political prisoners – on Australia's shores, those who settled here brought with them the belief system of their colonial masters which included beliefs of superiority of one race over another, of men over women and children, of white over black. Australia's colonial history provides a good example of the links between racism and sexism, how male power came to be at its roots, and how racism and sexism are used to sustain male supremacy.

The history of immigration to Australia is the history of colonisation of a continent – a process in which women followed men to suit male sexual, cultural and economic needs. In the early stages, female settlers from Britain worked either as prostitutes if they were convicts, or if they were free settlers were imported as potential brides in a bid to 'civilise' and enculture the working men. In later stages, they were imported as factory fodder, willingly doing monotonous, repetitive work under appalling conditions, often at under-award wages and ready to be sacked at any time. Those women, it seems, were as much a male colony as was the country itself. And for the process of colonisation it doesn't matter where those women came or come from. The concept of woman as a male colony has been adopted by radical feminists who point out that sexism and racism share the same origin: male aggression aimed at control over other human beings and material objects, combined with an economy based on competition. Australia's colonial history justifies that position.

Women – despite their physical presence – are curiously absent from the history of immigration, and only recently have the contributions of migrant women to Australian society begun to receive some recognition.

The following is an attempt to make those women more visible.

In the 1830s, Australia's colonial wealth in primary products and Britain's increasing demand for them led to a severe labour shortage in Australia which allowed for the development of a strong labour movement and high wages. Immigration appeared to be the solution to the labour shortage. Due to a lack of childbearers, the new colony's fertility rate was too low to supply the necessary numbers of labourers needed to exploit Australia's raw materials and ship them to Britain to support its growing manufacturing industry. The British government encouraged migration to Australia by offering financial assistance for the voyage of potential settlers. But men outnumbered women by at least three to one, and those women who chose Australia as their new home, were mostly convicts and financially desperate enough to turn to prostitution as a means of survival. A Presbyterian minister of that time reported that they 'rendered the whole colony and especially the town of Sydney, a sink of prostitution'.[1] Within three years, three thousand women – unmarried of course – were shipped from England to Australia.

The mid-nineteenth century saw a shift in occupations of British migrants. Those who followed the first generation of settlers were the ones who migrated to provide services to their predecessors. Many of the migrants of the second wave were skilled, middle-class white-collar workers who faced an oversupply in their professions in England. Among them were considerable numbers of women, trained as governesses and domestic labourers – and desperate to get married for which chances in England were low because of an oversupply of women.[2] So, many of them chose Australia as their 'lucky country', some of them using the services of a private women-only employment agency. Once in Australia, those women could earn more money than in England, but often only by undertaking more menial work, if they found work at all.[3] If they didn't, Caroline Chisholm picked up the pieces – that is, the would-be governesses – from the streets and founded the first Female Immigrants' Home in Sydney in 1841. Within a year, several employment agencies were established throughout New South Wales.[4] In 1862, 33-year-old Marie Rye founded the Female Middle Class Emigration Society designed to assist unmarried women of respectable background to find work in Australia despite an oversupply of governesses.

Around the same time, the mid-nineteenth century, discoveries of gold attracted Chinese, Pacific Islanders, and Indians to Australia who worked under conditions that no white worker was willing to accept. The established white, Anglo-dominated labour movement feared competition and reduction of wages. In 1859, Chinese migrants made up eight per cent of Victoria's population, but the colony's attempts to control the influx of migrants remained unsuccessful. Migrants simply chose other colonies on the Australian mainland as port of entry and then rushed to the goldfields of Victoria and later, to New South Wales. Being of different colour and speaking a different language, they suffered violent attacks by British migrants who accused the Chinese on the goldfields of depriving them of their livelihood.[5] These were the first incidents of overt racism directed against a group other than the indigenous people.

A debate of who should be allowed to migrate to Australia flared up, and the federation of the colonies in 1901 allowed for the introduction of uniform entry regulations. The newly created Commonwealth of Australia was still uncertain as to what would make Australia a nation, but it was already very certain about whom to exclude. The Immigration Restriction Act of 1901 declared official policy what earlier colonial legislation unsuccessfully tried to achieve: the restriction of entry on non-whites to a temporary basis under a permit. The policy became infamously known as the White Australia Policy, and reinforced the dominance of British culture. Until 1947, almost 90 per cent of Australia's population was of British origin. Until then, in line with the White Australia Policy, Aboriginal people were decimated by acts of murder and through disease to ten per cent of their pre-colonial numbers of about one million who spoke an estimated 260 languages and between 500 and 600 dialects.[6] At the 1986 census, 230,000 people identified as Aboriginal or Torres Strait Islander, sharing ninety languages between them. Seventy languages face a severe threat of extinction and are no longer transmitted. Only twenty Aboriginal languages are used by children and are taught. Eve Fesl writes that Aboriginal languages are dying at a rate of one a year, a figure that the National Languages Institute of Australia confirmed.

The economic depression of the 1890s brought a shift in destinations of British immigrants who appeared to prefer the United States. When the world economy began to recover, Australia was again facing a shortage of labour which consequently increased assisted migration from Britain. With the British economy plagued by high inflation and widening gaps between the classes, lower middle-class, white-collar employees were ready targets for British emigration propaganda, and in particular single women who were conned into satisfying the demand for 'brides' in a country where men still heavily outnumbered women

Until the Second World War, Australia remained primarily monocultural, and its main trading partner was Britain. Its population rose from 3.7 million in 1911 to 5.7 million in 1933, mainly through migration from Britain, steadily supplying around 85 per cent of the country's immigrants in those years.[7] Only after the Second World War, Australia's monocultural British identity started to change. In 1945 Australia embarked on its biggest immigration programme ever. The then Labor government's Immigration Minister, Arthur Calwell formed the slogan 'populate or perish' to describe the need for a policy that was aimed at increasing the labour force to modernise the manufacturing sector and create a larger domestic market. The reason was largely due to politicians realising that Australia could no longer rely on Britain as its major trading partner. But Calwell's expectation that 70,000 migrants per year and a quota of only 7,000 non-British migrants could be attracted failed to materialise. Migrants of Eastern European countries were favoured because of their anti-communist and largely apolitical convictions. Gradually, the concept of who was racially acceptable was extended to include central, northern and southern Europeans. In the 1960s, migrant intake averaged 90,000 a year, with migrants from Britain still making up over half the total.

Ironically, Australia's assimilationist policy produced exactly those ethnic ghettos assimilationism was meant to prevent. Lack of English, lack of culturally appropriate services and lack of access to existing services resulted in the creation of ethno-specific community support networks. Often, small businesses such as milkbars and restaurants which could be run from home without women neglecting their childcare commitments, served as meeting places for friends and families who provided comfort and practical support. The Melbourne suburb, Carlton, was dominated by Italians, the Vietnamese seemed to prefer Footscray and Richmond. In Sydney, local residents have jokingly renamed the suburb Parramatta 'Vietnamatta'. Generally the less time an ethnic group has been present in Australia, the lower their living standards and social status. In the early years of mass migration, ghettoisation was perceived to be anti-assimilationist. Only a few Australians valued those ghettos as a source of a meal not based on mutton or for a European-style cup of coffee. The ghettos sustained the notion of 'them' and 'us' and reinforced the belief that more effort had to be made to assimilate foreigners in order to rescue Anglo-Australia from the abyss of foreign cultures. Complaints against the pressures of quickly turning into what was then called 'a new Australian', were countered with the ultimate insult, 'why don't you go back to where you came from?'

Despite overt racism and sexism inside Australia, hardly anything was known about it overseas. Instead, the continent represented itself as the lucky country, tolerant to newcomers, with a pleasant climate, and job vacancies as abundant as space. In fact, these were the promises with which the 'Australian Dream' was sold to potential migrants overseas. But the late sixties saw the Australian dream falling to pieces. A world economy in crisis led Australia into recession. In its search for new markets, Australia began to look to Asia, and increasing trade with countries in the Pacific region made the White Australia Policy a major embarrassment. In 1972, the Labor Government under Prime Minister Gough Whitlam took office and finally abolished the White Australia Policy, and broader immigration criteria were introduced that no longer discriminated on grounds of race,

ethnic origin or religion. 1972 also saw the demise of assimilationism because its self-defeating effect became glaringly obvious.

During its three-year stint, the Labor government also began to speak of multiculturalism aimed at adapting welfare and education for a multi-ethnic society, thereby introducing the concept of structural multicultur-alism. Representatives of ethnic communities were consulted in planning and delivering services. The consultations led to increasing political involvement of male-dominated ethnic community organisations which strengthened their position by linking up to form Ethnic Community Councils in all states. These Councils in each state in turn linked up to form the powerful and influential Federation of Ethnic Community Councils of Australia (FECCA).

After the sacking of Prime Minister Whitlam in 1975, the Liberal-Country Party Coalition was re-elected. By that time, the first and second generation migrant population had grown politically mature enough to make its presence felt during elections, and the Liberals could not return to assimilationist policies. Building on the notion of multiculturalism, they introduced a policy of cultural pluralism distinct from the Labor proposal of structural pluralism. Contemporary multicultural policy maintained by today's Labor government is based on the definition of multiculturalism as cultural pluralism which means that ethnic groups should be allowed and encouraged to retain their languages, traditions and cultural practices to the benefit of Australian society as a whole, but should have a loyalty to the overriding (predominantly Anglo) values of Australian society.

A major shortcoming of multiculturalism is its inbuilt sexism, as it allows sexist behaviour to be attributed to ethnicity which – under multicultural policies – is considered worth preserving. Thus, leering, catcalls, abuse and misogynist jokes can be excused and even encouraged by a policy that protects what is called 'that nice mediterranean temper', rather than be dismissed as the woman-hating behaviours they really are. In its 1989 National Agenda for a Multicultural Australia, the federal government has outlined its multicultural policies for the near future and defined multiculturalism as a policy for 'managing the consequences of cultural diversity in the interests of the individual and society as a whole.'[8] The aim of the policy is 'to protect the rights of all members of society to enjoy their culture and language and practise their religion . . . Fundamentally, multiculturalism is about the rights of the individual . . . to be accepted as an Australian without having to assimilate to some stereotyped model of behaviour.'[9] However, at least in writing, there are limits to the freedom of expression granted under that definition: '. . . multicultural policies require all Australians to accept the basic structures and principles of Australian society – the Constitution and the rule of law, tolerance and equality, Parliamentary democracy, freedom of speech and religion, English as the national language and equality of the sexes . . .'[10] According to this definition, there seems to be no room for sexist behaviour. But what if sexism is part of the cultural baggage a migrant imports?

The Australian Law Reform Commission has recently begun to invite submissions and comments on a discussion paper on multiculturalism and criminal law. One of the submissions proposed that there should be an exemption from the prohibition of possessing and carrying knives without lawful excuse to allow male Sikhs to carry ceremonial kirpans, an important religious symbol.[11] The issue of female genital mutilation has not been raised in this paper. There are no official records on such practice in Australia – although anecdotally it is obvious that it is going on – but there is no law either that explicitly bans clitoridectomy. It would be a tricky legal question to decide whether infibulation is sufficiently covered by legislation in relation to assault and bodily harm, or whether special legislation banning genital mutilation should be introduced. On the other hand, doctors practising infibulation with the parents' consent, could even argue that in a multicultural society s/he felt entitled to support the cultural beliefs expressed by their patient's parents by responding to their request that their daughter be infibulated.

Over the past five years, federal and state governments in most states have embarked on programs aimed at improving the status of women in general, and the status of migrant women in particular. An entire network of professional feminist bureaucrats has been set up to advise government authorities on policies aimed at improving the status of women. At their top is the Minister Assisting the Prime Minister for the Status of Women, usually a female bureaucrat. She presides over the Office of the Status of Women (OSW) within the Department of the Prime Minister and the Cabinet. OSW is responsible for developing and implementing government policies in relation to women. Part of its activities include consultations with organisations representing women from non-English speaking backgrounds to assess their special needs and to communicate them to the government. A number of programs have been developed aimed at meeting the special needs of migrant women in relation to health, community services, employment and training, and the government has outlined its policy on women in general in its 1988 National Agenda For Women.[12]

In 1989, OSW established a Council on Non-English Speaking Background (NESB) Women's Issues to co-ordinate and develop policies and advise state, federal and territory governments on the particular needs of women of non-English speaking backgrounds in Australia. Its nineteen members include government and community representatives and four members of the Association of Non-English Speaking Background Women of Australia (ANESBWA).

ANESBWA was established in 1986, after ethnic women decided they would no longer put up with male domination in ethnic lobby groups. They applied through FECCA for a grant from OSW to employ a part-time worker to explore the feasibility of an independent ethnic women's organisation, ANESBWA. After funds from OSW had run out, the Office of Multicultural Affairs, responsible for the development of multicultural policies, commissioned ANESBWA to prepare a 'policy options paper' on issues for migrant women. ANESBWA approached all federal government departments for information on programmes targeted at migrant women. Only five departments were able to provide such information, and only two of them – the Office of the Prime Minister and Cabinet, and Immigration and Ethnic Affairs – provided more details. One of the agencies without specific policies for migrant women was the Human Rights and Equal Opportunity Commission, which in 1988–89 began a pilot program in major community languages to increase migrant women's awareness of existing anti-discrimination legislation.[13] Australia's radical feminists argue that this form of institutionalised feminism is a tokenistic exercise concealing the structural inequalities in society, and some would say that the feminist bureaucrats – or femocrats as they are called – are out of touch with their grassroots sisters.

However, migrant women appear to be more visible in the femocrats' activities than in the non-institutionalised feminist movement which is being criticised for projecting women as universally Anglo and of marginalising those who are different. Only recently have migrant women begun to demand autonomy, and for the first time in Australian feminism, racism within the movement was openly discussed at the 1984 Women and Labour Conference in Brisbane. The absence of migrant women from the movement in the past had a very practical reason. Most migrant women worked (and many still work) two full shifts a day, eight hours in the work-place to supplement the family income, and another eight hours a day at home because for many men – depending on their cultural traditions – it is still out of the question to share housework equally with other family members. Only an educated minority of migrant women in well-paid jobs or without families have been able to make time available to make their voices heard in the women's movement. In the past, women endowed with such privileges hardly felt the necessity to organise themselves. However, the daughters of first generation migrant women of the 1960s seem to be keener to become part of the feminist agenda.

Several groups, catering specifically to the needs of migrant women, have existed for quite some time. One of them is Sydney Asian Lesbians, and the other is the Gay and Lesbian Immigration Task Force (GLITF) with representatives in most state capitals (see Resource List). GLITF aims at achieving equality in the Migration Act for gay/lesbian couples with one overseas partner, so that the overseas partner can legally join his or her partner living in Australia. In 1991, for the first time in Australian history, lesbian and gay relationships were officially recognised in regulations of the Immigration Act. Since April 1991, regulations have been in force to allow for so-called relationships of interdependency, be they gay or straight, with an Australian citizen or permanent resident. In other words, gay and lesbian relationships have been given equal recognition in the Migration Act with heterosexual de facto couples. Before April 1991, it was up to the discretion of the Minister for Immigration to personally grant residency to the overseas partner under a compassionate category in immigration law. But now with the official recognition, the overseas partner of a lesbian or gay couple enjoys the same rights as the overseas partner in a straight relationship does. That includes appeals rights in the case of the rejection of an application. The criticism this decision received, ranged from calls for compulsory AIDS testing for migrants to renewed calls for the reduction in migrant intake, fuelled by controversies over an ecologically and economically sustainable population in times of an economic recession.

A further group is the Migrant Women Writers Group in Melbourne which published four collections of short stories, poems and essays depicting the lives of migrant women in Australia.

However, despite all these flourishing activities, the malestream does not appear to have taken much notice of the efforts of femocrats and feminists to raise the status of migrant women. In television commercials, migrants are still viewed as if they lived on trees, and migrant women are always presented in inferior roles, such as the cleaner of artist Pro Hart's carpet. Occasionally they are recognised as consumers promoting a certain spaghetti brand or advising another customer on the benefits of a supermarket home brand. But roles such as the company executive or the professional – on the rare occasion that they are allocated to women at all – are reserved for white women of Anglo background. Not only on the television screen.

Notes
1. Geoffrey Sherington. 1982. *Australia's Immigrants.* George Allen & Unwin: Sydney. p. 37.
2. For an example in literature, see the novel by Catherine Helen Spence. 1988. *Mr Hogarth's Will.* Ringwood: Penguin. Distributed by Spinifex Press.
3. Sherington. 1982. p. 63 ff.
4. Ann Summers. 1994. *Damned Whores and God's Police: The Colonisation of Womanhood in Australia.* Ringwood: Penguin.
5. Sherington. 1982. p. 65 ff.
6. Eve Fesl. 1988. Koories and the English Language. In Yvonne Smith Ed. *Taking Time: A Woman's Historical Data Kit.* Melbourne: Union of Australian Women.
7. John Dique. 1985. *Immigration: The Quiet Invasion.* Bullsbrook, WA: Veritas Publishing Co.
8. Department of Prime Minister and the Cabinet, Office of Multicultural Affairs. 1989. *National Agenda for a Multicultural Australia.* Canberra: Australian Government Publishing Services.
9. *National Agenda.* p. 15.
10. *National Agenda.* p. viii.
11. Australian Law Reform Commission. May 1991. *Discussion Paper 48. Multiculturalism: Criminal Law.* Canberra: Australian Government Publishing Services. p. 12.
12. Department of Prime Minister and the Cabinet, Office of the Status of Women. 1988. *A say, a choice, a fair go: The Government's National Agenda for Women.* Canberra: Australian Government Publishing Services.
13. Marian Sawer. 1990. *Sisters in Suits: Women and Public Policy in Australia.* Sydney: Allen & Unwin.

Susan Hawthorne

A HISTORY OF THE CONTEMPORARY WOMEN'S MOVEMENT

Introduction

In the 1990s it is very easy to forget that, in 1971, the women's movement was a fledgling movement with a lot of dreams that had no material parallel. In 1971, there were no women's health centres; there were no women's bookshops, and certainly no publishing companies, galleries or theatre groups owned and controlled by women; abortion was difficult to obtain without entering the criminal arena; there were no refuges for women and no sexual assault centres; no one believed that women would soon be holding conferences to discuss women's liberation; there was no paid maternity leave; there was no such discipline as 'Women's Studies', and few tertiary education courses included any information about women at all; there were no lesbian festivals and few places for lesbians to meet. None of this could have happened without a political movement committed to changing the shape of the culture.

My involvement in the women's movement (or the Women's Liberation Movement, as it was called when I joined in 1973) has been wide ranging in the activities I have undertaken. But it has been fairly consistent in its political agenda, namely, an insistence on a radical shift in the cultural and political paradigm that takes women and other oppressed groups as central. This is, therefore, partly memoir, partly analysis that takes a radical feminist stance and follows the progress of that political agenda through a twenty-year period. There are peaks and troughs in the narrative, just as there are peaks and troughs in life. Sometimes, my involvement was intense – establishing links, discussion and creating theory, participating in political actions. At other times I have retreated in order to consolidate, to gather energy, to take time out.[1]

There are several false views of the women's movement that tend to be presented by the media. One is that the entire movement is made up of lesbians; another is that it is made up of middle-class, highly educated white women; yet another view is that it is made up of women who have had bad experiences with men. All of these women are in the women's movement. Indeed, without the lesbian presence we would not have progressed as far as we have. Lesbians have been at the forefront of every political challenge, including the establishment of refuges and halfway houses, rape crisis centres, centres against sexual assault, bookshops, galleries, publishing houses, and in the public sector as 'femocrats' (to name just a few examples). But what we don't hear very often is that Aboriginal women have been involved in the women's movement in Australia since it began; that women from non-English speaking backgrounds have always been active in the women's movement; that women from every imaginable class background have worked side-by-side in the development of feminist theory over the last twenty years; that women of all ages have contributed in different ways to the women's movement; and that women all around the world – Bangladesh, Japan, Brazil, Nigeria, East Germany – have expanded the horizons of feminist thought well beyond any imagined borders that any one women might have drawn twenty years ago. Women have not always agreed on every aspect of feminist theory and action, but a diversity of voices is what has made the women's movement in Australia, and internationally, a vigorous and everchanging pool of thought.[2]

Beginnings

In 1970, five women participated in a direct action on Melbourne's trams. They refused to pay more than 60 per cent of the adult fare, in protest against the fact that women's wages were only 60 per cent of men's wages. To gain further publicity, they also chained themselves to the railings of a Commonwealth government building. The same women were responsible for establishing Melbourne's first consciousness raising group. The women were: Zelda D'Aprano,[3] Thelma Solomon, Alma Morton, Alva Giekie and Bon Hull. They came from a mix of ethnic and language backgrounds, all but one identified as working class, and most were in their forties and fifties – hardly the stereotypical young, middle-class, anglo women projected by the media.

In 1972, the first Women's Liberation Conference in Australia was held at Mt Beauty in Victoria. Six months later, the first national lesbian conference, organised by the Radicalesbians, was held at Sorrento, also in Victoria. In between these two events, the first Women's Centre in Melbourne was established, followed by the first issues of *Melbourne Women's Liberation Newsletter* and *Vashti's Voice*, the latter a newspaper that continued for a decade. The dates of comparable events in other cities reflect those of Melbourne, although there were variations of order, and some differences in time.

The issues that made women become involved in the women's movement between 1971 and 1975 included: equal pay, abortion law repeal, violence against women, rape, health, sexism in education, advertising, mainstream political agendas, and the arts. These issues were addressed by establishing refuges, rape crisis centres, women's health centres, women's studies courses, The Women's Electoral Lobby (WEL) and various groups active across all the arts.

All these things had happened by 1975, a mere three years later. Critical to this success was the election of the Whitlam federal government, with its mandate of social reform and its grants of money to fund that reform. Many of the centres, services and groups were set up without on-going funding, while some received financial or bureaucratic support from government agencies.

Issues and Actions

In 1973, a pirate edition of Robin Morgan's collection of poems, *Monster*,[4] was published by Radicalesbians in Melbourne. The US publishers of *Monster*, Random House, had agreed to publish the book only on condition that publication was limited to the US. The reason for this restriction was the poem 'Arraignment', in which Robin finds Sylvia Plath's husband, Ted Hughes, guilty of her death. Random House's legal advice was that Hughes would not sue if Robin re-wrote the poem, making her accusations hypothetical rather than direct and overt, and publication was confined to the US. The pirate publication of *Monster* was regarded at the time as an action that undermined the censorship imposed by patriarchal institutions. Radicalesbians was committed to speaking out about violence, including emotional violence, against women.

Similarly, in the following year, the campaign against the advertising of Bradfield cigarettes as 'not mild' (i.e. as 'manly') protested against the positive portrayal of a macho image. Feminists sprayed the billboards depicting the ads with the words 'but sexist', changing the message to read: 'not mild, but sexist'. It wasn't long before the cigarette was withdrawn from the market.

The fight for safe abortion has been an on-going issue for the women's movement. The early years of this fight are well documented in the magazine, *Right to Choose*, which provided legal, medical and social analyses of abortion issues. Large demonstrations were the norm, and the issue of abortion was one that drew together women from a wide range of political positions. It was, in fact, one of the issues that feminists agreed on – constituting a powerful example of the feminist challenge to male control over women.

In April 1974, the Melbourne Women's Liberation Halfway House opened in a quiet street in Kew. Its address was kept a secret, even from government funding bodies, because of the danger from violent men. Women who needed the house and its services would ring the phone number of the Women's Information and Referral Service, and someone would come and pick them up.[5] Also in 1974, Melbourne's first Women's Health Centre opened. There are now over thirty women's health centres in operation throughout Australia, and more are being opened each year. The first Rape Crisis Centre in Melbourne also opened in 1974. It was run by the Women Against Rape collective, and shared premises with the Health Centre. Meanwhile, Aboriginal and feminist activist, Molly Dyer, was involved in setting up the Aboriginal Child Care Service in Fitzroy.

Alongside the establishment of these politically-based services, other areas were also being explored. The Melbourne Women's Theatre Group put on its first show, 'The Love Show', and others followed over the next four years, finishing with 'Edges' in 1977. Songs, poetry and women's bands played a big part in the development of a feminist culture. 'Women's Electric Band' (known as WEB) played in Melbourne; in Sydney, 'Clitoris' (pronounced with the emphasis on the second syllable) was popular; and 'Shameless Hussies' came out of Adelaide. These bands, as well as many artistic and political movements, were predominantly composed of lesbians. In the world of literature, *All That False Instruction* by 'Elizabeth Riley' (a pseudonym – the author had been one of the Radicalesbians) was the first novel published in Australia to deal with the lives of lesbians in a positive way;[6] while Helen Garner's *Monkey Grip* portrayed an alternative and heterosexual view of feminist life in the inner city.[7] Both books have become classics in their own right. Some ten years later, Finola Moorhead's *Remember the Tarantella* looked back on this period of the women's movement.[8]

The mid-1970s saw the establishment of women's studies courses in universities. The impetus for this came in part from the huge increase in written materials arising out of conferences. The Socialist Feminist Conference of 1974, for instance, produced a wide range of political agendas, as did other conferences that followed close on its heels. The first Women's Studies Conference was held at Adelaide University in 1976. There were other conferences, combining teachers from primary, secondary, adult and tertiary education, held in Victoria in the early 1980s. In 1978, the first Women and Labour Conference was held at Macquarie University in Sydney; others followed at two year intervals in Melbourne, Adelaide and Brisbane. These were effectively a combination of women's studies practitioners and Women's Liberation activists. Other conferences on specific areas of theory and action had been held in different cities.

Crisis and Change
Melbourne Women's Liberation Movement went through a crisis in 1976. At a general meeting at the Women's Building, a group of women passed a motion dissolving the women's movement. Women at the meeting had been frustrated by the lack of commitment and attendance at the meetings, as well as a lack of structural support for policy and decision-making. As a consequence of this motion, three special general meetings were held. These meetings were attended by hundreds of women in reaction to the dissolution. Papers were presented, ideas aired, and a number of breakaway groups formed to discuss strategies for decision-making, political agendas for the women's movement, and a way forward, theoretically and practically. The motion clarified the difficulties of Women's Liberation policy-making. At the time, there were few 'femocrats', very few structural

positions held by feminists, and almost no funding for feminist purposes. The movement, though wide-ranging in its effect on the social fabric, was still relatively small. Activists in different areas tended to know one another informally, and most policy and political decision-making occurred on an ad hoc basis.

The women's movement's priorities have, on the whole, reflected shifts in community attitudes, generally preceding these changes and often being in part responsible for them. Discussions of racism and prejudice were always an integral part of women's movement philosophy. Early Women's Liberationists had, after all, been actively involved in the anti-Vietnam war movement, and in the demonstrations against apartheid and the Springbok tours. Widespread publicity and involvement by white/anglo women in campaigns and projects run by Aboriginal and non-English speaking women was sporadic. White and anglo involvement in such campaigns was also sometimes misdirected. Migrant and Aboriginal women, though at the forefront of Women's Liberation action, had even fewer avenues and resources to draw on. Similarly, action on disability issues moved slowly. In these and other political movements, e.g. environmental politics, feminists were often at the forefront of shifting attitudes through political action. Involvement in the women's movement – in political action groups; in group dynamics through participation in collectives; in strategies such as lobbying, meeting procedures, writing minutes and press releases; in widespread networking; and in a political analysis that allowed us to move across a range of issues in a politically challenging fashion – gave a good grounding for establishing services and developing political strategies in a range of arenas.

The first Aboriginal Women's Arts Festival took place in Adelaide in 1985, with a range of events including dance, film, literature, story telling, visual arts and theatre. Adelaide was also the location for the First International Indigenous Women's Conference four years later. In 1991, the Victorian Indigenous Women's Writers Festival took place as part of the Australian Feminist Book Fortnight. These, along with a range of other political actions, such as the Pine Gap protest and the establishment of Aboriginal and Torres Strait Islander health centres, have helped to forge links between women of different backgrounds and with different political agendas.

Conclusion
There have been considerable shifts in priorities, strategies and outcomes over the last twenty years. The 1970s saw a huge explosion of services and centres for women, but some of these collapsed in the early 80s due to lack of funding or other support.[9] The 1980s has seen a widening of the feminist agenda. At the same time, the threat of depoliticisation – through

co-option or simple retreat from radical stances – has also occurred. As the movement's base has broadened, and some feminists have moved into positions of power in the workplace, there has been an inevitable shift in the way in which change comes about. What is required in the 90s is a strengthening of networks and links between those providing services, outlets and opportunities for women, and those who have the power to provide structural support, such as funding or backup through government, institutional or corporate agencies.

The Australian women's movement has had a sometimes torrid history, which cannot be adequately conveyed in a short summary. Original newsletter debates, conference papers and other documentation are the best source of this material. It has also had periods when the media has cried out: 'Is feminism dead?' To date, there has always been a resounding 'No!' to this question. Understanding the roots of the contemporary movement provides a foundation for further developments in theory and practice. The 1990s mark a new phase in the history of feminism. With economies tight all around the world, services established by and for women will be increasingly under attack. Likewise, funding for women's arts events is likely to decrease, in spite of the fact that higher education courses that focus on women are extremely popular and tend to fill their quotas long before many mainstream courses. If the movement is to survive these ravages, we can only gain by appreciating the energy and vision that has created what now exists.

Notes
1. This essay concentrates on the contemporary women's movement in Australia from 1973–1994. Although the essay takes in a national perspective, it focuses particularly on events during the 1970s and in Victoria, as that is where I have lived over the last twenty years.
2. For parallel developments in the US see Robin Morgan, 'Goodbye to all That', reprinted in *The Word of a Woman*. 1993. London: Virago; New York: W. W. Norton.
3. Zelda D'Aprano. 1977. *The Becoming of a Woman*. North Carlton, Victoria: Self-published.
4. Robin Morgan. 1974. *Monster*. Melbourne: Radicalesbians.
5. The first women's refuge in Australia was 'Elsie', set up in March 1974, a month earlier than Melbourne's Halfway House. It consisted of two small houses in the Glebe Estate in Sydney, owned at the time by the Anglican Church. 'Elsie' was squatted by feminists concerned about the plight of women trapped in their homes by violent husbands, and impatient with bureaucratic delays on the part of governmental funding and housing authorities.
6. Elizabeth Riley. 1975. *All That False Instruction*. Sydney: Angus and Robertson.
7. Helen Garner. 1977. *Monkey Grip*. Melbourne: McPhee Gribble.
8. Finola Moorhead. 1994. *Remember the Tarantella*. London: The Women's Press.
9. Dorothy Broom. 1991. *Damned If We Do: Contradictions in Women's Health Care*. Sydney: Allen & Unwin.

Destiny Deacon
KOORI WOMEN: RACISM AND POLITICS

Twenty years hey. It's a spit in the ocean for Aboriginal people, as you all know.

I was there. I was there at the Tent Embassy. I was there. I was a high school student and handing out 'It's Time' badges for the Whitlam government to be elected. I was there at the Women's conference in Canberra in 1975. The Women and Politics Conference which was very important. I was there at the Commonwealth Games in '82 where we tried to boycott it as Aboriginal people. I was there at the Bicentennial demonstrations in 1988 and I was there – now I'm here, so what do I do? Talk to you guys. Where do I start?

I know I'm preaching to the converted. That seems to have been happening for the past twenty years. White women, white feminists, maybe even white men, believe that the struggle of Aboriginal and Islander Australians is important. I mean you live in our country, you should make some concessions and your ideas about learning what we're all about and that's kind of happening. And the audience we've got here – there's no use in me saying to you, 'You white bastards, you took our land, this, that and the other.'

But what I want to say is, let's think about racism in terms of feminism. That's probably where we're not communicating properly.

Everyone thinks male Kooris are dirty, lazy, bludging alcoholics. There's also myths about Aboriginal women. We're like the new wave version of the Drover's Wife – since the 70s – battlers, strong, survivors, looking after the family, living without husbands – what a luxury! – the Earth Mother, backbone of the family and so on.

But there's a lot of burnout happening, not just since the 70s – since way back when, before you even came here. And lots of things have happened since the 70s. There were Aboriginal women's groups way back when, with men invited too, and white people. There was no sort of division. Just people believing in a common cause. That was for Aboriginal people to have justice in this country.

Like 1967[1] – the vote – remember that? They used to say the criminals, the insane and the Aborigines couldn't vote? It doesn't make any difference though does it? Oh that was a joke! But no one laughed!

It's important to realise that Aboriginal women have been mythicised. We're supposed to be strong. We're supposed to be tough. Everyone has this ideal view of us. When there are conferences, everyone expects us to get up and give them a piece of our mind and say 'You oppressors, you bastards,' etc.

It's been like that since the 1970s. But what has been done? What are you doing about it? These are the sort of things we've got to start questioning if we are feminists and believe in the female principle, or whatever they call it. What do we actually believe in? What are we going to do about racism? This is a black person's country. What's happening?

These are the things – we know the white men are bad – we all agree on that, don't we? For what it's worth. And all these sort of things, Capitalism's bad and this is bad, and we don't like these oppressive ideas, but what are we doing? I think as people who believe in a feminist perspective on life, let's look at racism and let's look at where we're living at this point of time.

We have the strength and power to have principles and believe – you know you're in Australia – an Aboriginal country – what are you doing?

A lot of people say, 'I've never met an Aborigine.' I've given talks at conferences before and I might be talking about something I've said a hundred times before. After I finish, people say, 'Do you eat witchetty grubs?'

'Can you speak some Aboriginal for me?'

I say 'Ugga Booga!' That was in the 70s but it still happens today. But in the 80s I noticed they said things like, 'Does incest exist in Aboriginal society?' This is the transition that's happening.

'Are there any Aboriginal lesbians?' So it's really complicated. Yes, I have eaten witchetty grubs, but I can't get 'em in Brunswick!

'Can you speak some Aboriginal for us?'

My mum wanted to teach us the language, but I wanted to watch Mickey Mouse and Zig and Zag.

'Does incest exist in Aboriginal society?'

Yes it does, it's like everywhere else in the world and I'm one of the lucky few who can say it didn't happen to me.

'Are there any Aboriginal lesbians?'

Oh well, there's stacks.

Anyway let's go back to the history since the 70s. When I was growing up in the 70s – a young teenager may I add – the questions asked were – this is the flavour of a decade which is very hard to encapsulate – What can we do for you? This is the white people talking.

In the 1980s – What do you want now?

The 90s – question mark.

I want to go back to voyeurism and Aboriginal women being mythicised. We know we're tough; we know that we're the battlers and the new-wave Drover's Wife.

100

OK we started up all these things, you can read it in any book – the health services, the legal services, welfare organisations and childcare. Battles for education and employment – but there were some men involved and some white people also. I suppose you realise that some men and some white people got the good jobs, and the Aboriginal women were stuck at home with the kids.

The early fighters are the grandmothers of today. They're still fighting and keeping up the struggle which is very important; always being the backbone of the family, being forceful, putting up the class, race and sex battle.

When we look back in the 70s, who was the Aboriginal woman hero? I thought to myself – Evonne Goolagong.

The 80s, who was the Aboriginal woman hero – Sally Morgan.

The 90s, who was the Aboriginal woman hero – whoever wants to be!

Note
1. In 1967 a national referendum belatedly gave citizenship and the vote to Aboriginal people.

Diana Starski
LESBIANS IN AUSTRALIA

Access to lesbian culture is much easier now in the 90s than it was in 1971 when I became a lesbian. I met my first lover when I was eighteen. She was nineteen. We hardly knew any other lesbians. There had been a private lesbian organisation running in Melbourne for some years, but it was difficult to find. When my girlfriend finally made contact, the secretary told her that members had to be twenty-one before they were eligible to join. We could hardly bear the idea of waiting for several years before meeting other lesbians! But things were soon to change in Australian cities.

The Women's Liberation Movement and Gay Liberation Front were both established in Australia in the early 1970s. I remember attending my first Gay Lib meeting and being overwhelmed by the mere fact of being in a room with so many other homosexual people. It was very exciting.

The first emergence of lesbian feminism in Australia took place in these years. The Women's Movement had maintained a largely heterosexual profile until then, and the Gay Movement, whilst adopting the ideology of sexual revolution, had homosexual law reform high on its agenda. (Male homosexual acts were illegal in Australia at this time.) Lesbians from both movements felt that they were invisible, and began meeting separately.

In 1973 the first national lesbian conference was held in Sorrento, a bayside town in Victoria. It was attended by over sixty women, a huge gathering for that time. Many papers were presented for discussion concerning the nature of lesbian feminist philosophy, identity and culture.

The conference connected women from different states in Australia, both politically and amorously, and gave rise to a lot of political activism in the following years. It was in these years that the slogan 'Lesbians are Lovely' was graffitied all over city walls.

Lesbians were also actively involved in the running of Women's Buildings in different cities, as well as in feminist struggles. The first domestic refuge in Australia was established by a lesbian group.

Alongside this political activism ran the CR groups (consciousness raising groups, where women shared their histories and thoughts with each other). Lesbian rock bands were formed and the first women's dances were held. Women's restaurants, run by lesbians and catering mostly for women, were opened in different cities. Women's theatre groups, many of them lesbian, became involved in experimental theatre. For a brief time, the Women's Cultural Palace in Melbourne was a haven of lesbian culture. Women met there to eat in the restaurant, to plan political action, to run courses for other women and to party. With the advent of community radio in Melbourne, lesbian voices had broadcasting space for the first time in Australian history.

One of the directions taken by lesbians at this time was the purchase of land in the country. One collective of women bought a thousand acres of mountainous bush land in NSW for the purpose of establishing women-only space. This was a reflection of the 'separatist' philosophy adopted by many lesbians at this time.

The new wave of lesbian feminism of the 70s was accompanied by a growth in non-feminist lesbian culture. Commercial entrepreneurs, catering for the gay male entertainment dollar, opened their hotels for one or two nights a week to gay-only clientele, and the gay disco bars were born. 'Ruby's', a Sydney lesbian bar, was very well known and attended for many years. In Melbourne, several hotels ran women-only nights for lesbians. 'Penny's' in St Kilda was the longest running of these disco bars.

In the Australian summer of 1987–88 I met two travelling lesbians from Germany (there have been many over the years) who came to Melbourne on their journey across this continent. They had arrived in time for the Women's Ball, an annual or sometimes biannual event.

The Women's Balls usually attract over a thousand lesbian women. On this occasion, we went to an Italian bistro after the ball for snacks and coffee. Making cross-cultural comparisons of lesbian dances, Margit and Gaby were struck by one essential difference. The clothes, they said. All the dresses, the ball gowns, the dinner suits, amid the casual jeans and runners. They said they were used to women in white shirts and leather pants.

Australian lesbian culture is extremely diverse, and exists in interconnecting webs across the continent. Some of it is highly visible, such as the summer Lesbian Festival in Melbourne, the Gay and Lesbian film festivals of Sydney and Melbourne, and the Sydney Gay Mardi Gras which has become a national event with a high public profile. Lesbians participate in large numbers in the Mardi Gras, which is held in February.

One of the important areas for lesbian contact in Australia is sport. Women's sporting clubs for cricket, hockey, netball and softball all have their fair share of lesbian team members. In the early eighties in Melbourne a lesbian softball team formed to play competition sport. They called themselves 'Radclyffe Runners' and fielded a fairly anarchic team and group of supporters.

As the political climate in Australia changed in the eighties, so did lesbian feminism. The Women's Liberation Movement broadened its scope and activities, in a sense becoming less centralised as more women espoused feminism and sought change in their work places, in unions, in schools and in government policy. Women's Studies was established in universities and in local learning centres, and several healing centres were opened for women in New South Wales.

A national forum held in Melbourne in 1981 entitled Women, Patriarchy and the Future Forum was organised by lesbian feminists and helped to give some impetus to lesbian culture. In the following years a monthly 'Salon' was run as a venue where the work of women artists could be exhibited and discussed. Not specifically lesbian in focus, it was feminist in philosophy and was run by lesbians.

Women's spirituality was also a new area of exploration for different lesbian groups throughout the eighties, and a gathering was held in South Australia to share information and celebrate women's rituals.

Generally, it can be said that the eighties saw the absorption of many lesbian feminists into the professional workforce, where feminist networking was established at local levels. Lesbianism did not emerge again with a national focus until January 1989, when a festival was held in Adelaide in South Australia. Limited by numbers, the organisers were overwhelmed by the response, and the following year another national lesbian festival was held in Melbourne. This was so successful that it has become an annual event in Melbourne and also in other states. The festivals have included art displays, music, plays, readings, workshops, dances and markets where women can sell their wares.

Over the past few years a smaller type of annual conference has been attended by many lesbians. This is the 10/40 conference, organised by and for women over forty who have been involved with feminism for at least ten years or more. It is held in a different state each year over the Easter holidays, and is attended mostly by lesbian feminists.

There are now many facets to lesbian culture in Australia. The large attendances at the festivals have brought together different types of lesbian communities – feminist, professional, artistic, sporting, unemployed. Within all these communities there are also issues which are being explored, lesbian motherhood and sexuality amongst them.

In July of 1991 a national lesbian conference was held in Sydney with the theme 'celebrating our differences'. It was well attended and for the first time gave prominence to lesbian women of different ethnic origins in Australia. A festival was also held to coincide with the conference. One of the most interesting features of the festival was the emergence of a-capella choirs, from all around Australia. The most memorable event of this festival was the Concert at the Sydney Opera House. Entitled 'Living our Passion' it brought together some excellent lesbian performers, including Robyn Archer, Judy Small, the Topp Twins Trio, comedian Sue Ann Post, the Bangarra Dance Company, and singers Deborah and Donna who sang for us the duet from Lakmé. The concert hall was filled with over two thousand wildly appreciative lesbians. It was an exciting night.

It was exciting also to realise that in the space of twenty years lesbian visibility in Australia has emerged as a strong presence, and in the creation of our communities and our culture we are also making our own history.

Virginia Fraser
RENAISSANCE OF THE SALON

Salon-A-Muse was established in Melbourne in March 1982. It ran for about three years. This article was written for the National Times *in 1983.*

When the Salon-A-Muse started in Melbourne, its aim was monthly gatherings that fused informal performances of a feminist and artistic bent with something like a private party of about 30 women where the arts, and particularly the art of conversation, were the focus.

Motivated by a desire for intellectual and aesthetic refreshment and broader social lives in what seemed a sluggish cultural environment, and with a degree of idealism about bridging yawning gulfs between women in and out of the women's movement, the six-member Salon-A-Muse collective launched its venture after three months preparation, and with rather formal language, as 'a venue along the lines of the centuries-old tradition of the salon.'

'We wish,' they said, 'to follow the model of Nathalie Barney (1876–1972) Parisian heiress, lesbian, writer who turned her house into a salon for 60 years (and) unlike other women *salonières*, did not derive power from the stature of her male visitors, but rather encouraged women to be artists in their own right and held frequent all-female evenings. We want a place where performers (poets/dramatists/speakers) . . . are of equal status to the audience – where we can learn ways of avoiding that familiar split between active and passive . . . each woman contributing her experience to the perceptions of the whole group. We want a place where publishers and poets can get together, as well as artists of all kinds, so that a creative interchange may take place with women talking about their work in an atmosphere of trust. We want the stress to be on artists contributing rather than defending their work.'

They hired a room in the National Book Council's Carlton office for the last Monday evening of March 1982, invited a guitarist, the poet Judith Rodriguez and collective member, comedy writer, dramatist and actor Sandra Shotlander to perform. They organised supper, set a modest entrance fee, advertised in a small way – and were swamped.

About 80 women squeezed into what was really only a terrace house living room while more were turned away at the door by a 'house full' sign.

Between word of mouth following that night and an unsolicited write-up in the *Age*, they were off and rolling at considerably more speed and in a rather different direction than the one they had planned.

'We felt if there was a need we should cater for it,' Sandra Shotlander

says. 'It's really hard to turn women away. It's a rotten job.'

They moved to a larger space at Tsakpina, a Greek-Australian coffee lounge in the city, where it was still shoulder-to-shoulder but could hold more shoulders, and expanded to two nights, the last Sunday and Monday of the month.

They then moved to their third venue, Rumpoles, a cinema-restaurant resembling a cross between a dining car of an opulent Victorian train and the foyer of a 1950s movie house, where they can accommodate about 300 over the two nights, which is as big as they want to get.

Jenny Cameron says: 'As we realised it was financially viable,' (which means it pays its costs, adds to a small fund for a rainy day or more ambitious projects later, but does not include a fee for the organisers) 'we had to look at whether we should keep doing it, making ourselves exhausted or should we share resources with other women? Should we cut back on prices? We decided to provide a service that complemented the whole idea of the salon and didn't totally destroy the experience for us – because that was what was happening, we were running off our feet and never got a chance to talk to anybody, which was the idea of the whole thing. So I think the first thing we did was to get other women to do the catering and after that we were also able to pay other women to do the cleaning up, and so there's a sort of permanent on-going job for four women, plus the women who get paid for performing.'

Robyn Arianrhod adds: 'We've had to assimilate the decision to go for the large number, so the emphasis on conversation has changed. The first couple of times we were trying to push it. I think we accept that the discussion that happens is limited by numbers and that's not what we intended. We're all opposed to large groups, but now it seems to me that the conversation happens in the breaks, that the performances become material for discussion.' Besides the change wrought by size, their approach has also altered. Jenny Cameron recalls: 'Originally we made approaches specifically to people who were in the arts, or in print or in publishing, and the advertising was for artists to get together and talk. And I remember that at the first salon, women had brought their stuff along and they thought that they would be talking with other artists only and they got a kind of shock to realise there were women there who were just interested to talk, to view, and weren't themselves artists. So there was a sort of drop-off of some people who wanted to go into cliques – a private group of little women artists.'

Not all the salon members are practising artists. Two original members, Merrilee Moss and Vivienne Ray moved on last year and the present group consists of Sandra Shotlander, Vera Ray, a teacher; Jenny Cameron, a CYSS worker who is also writing a part of a book on matriarchies; Katy Noad, a self-defence instructor and broadcaster on the community radio station, 3CR; Jenny Plant, at the moment unemployed but with an occupational interest in childcare and also involved with 3CR; and Robyn Arianrhod, a mathematician who is being pressed to put on some 'mathematical street theatre'.

Of the salon's success, Jenny Cameron says, with some understatement, 'it was the right place at the right time. There's nothing like it in any other city in Australia and I think it's got something to do with Melbourne . . . vaguely cultural, vaguely keeping warm and togetherness, sort of stately.'

Their policy is to be varied in their material and to keep a mix of lesbian and heterosexual perspectives. 'If we look and see that lesbians haven't been represented for a while, we try to juggle the program around and vice versa or mix it,' Jenny Cameron says. And likewise with kinds of performances.

Besides plays, poetry and music, their programs have included Liz Paterson's performance art, Barbara Creed's dissection of Mills and Boon books (everyone was asked to come dressed as a romantic fantasy), a launching, with readings, of *Frictions*, a well-reviewed anthology of women's writing, and ceramicist-turned-papier machéist, Pierrette Boustany talking about and showing slides of her work.

This largely featured the various incarnations of Beryl, a hugely proportioned female figure who appears, alone and en masse, sunning herself in bathers under umbrellas and palm trees, playing sports and lately as Super-Beryl in cape and leopard skin, and who, in all cases, enjoys herself and especially enjoys the company of other women.

Comedy, one of the more contentious areas, seems to come in for harder scrutiny, perhaps because in laughing you openly commit yourself to a position about which, later, it is possible to feel ambiguous.

The comedy, Sandra Shotlander says, has been 'interesting from a feminist perspective – what's good to laugh at – the satirical target. They've been pretty fiery discussions sometimes.'

Jenny Plant believes that one of the frequent problems is that 'you're still setting up the stereotypes for women to laugh at, which is a danger, isn't it?'

But, says Vera Ray: 'Women have many opinions and many views and sometimes we get locked into these views and we start feeling alone or we start feeling that, you know, we can only trust one or two others. And I do have an overview of feminism as a very strong, potentially revolutionary movement that actually can change things quite significantly – but not while we are not able to communicate. And to me, another old-fashioned word is sisterhood which I really quite believe in. I don't mean that I want to feel sisterly towards every woman who wants to be one but doesn't know how to do it, but I do feel that most feminists have enough in common to develop that kind of feeling. There has not been a venue for that sort of thing in Melbourne since the old days when the old Women's Liberation House actually functioned properly. That was a long time ago. And so the salon for me has this purpose of bringing in a variety of women from all over Melbourne, coming together and losing that sense of strangeness, this sense of "I can't talk to her because she's so and so and I'm not".'

In 1984 the Salon-A-Muse collective decided it was time for other women to take over the organization. A new group resumed the responsibility but the salon had lost its impetus and ceased to exist in 1985.

CULTURE

Susan Hawthorne and Renate Klein
CULTURAL LIFE

Aboriginal women are central in the burgeoning of recent cultural expression in all the arts. Among them are writers such as Oodgeroo Noonuccal and Ruby Langford; artists including Donna Burak, Sally Morgan, Destiny Deacon and a host of others; playwrights such as Eva Johnson, singers and musicians such as country and western singer, Betty Little, The Mills Sisters from Thursday Island, and Tiddas from Melbourne, but frequently the work of these women is underrepresented at national and international gatherings. This book will introduce you to the work of some of these women and others and there is a great deal else being produced. In this and other areas *Australia for Women* is only a starting point for further unguided journeys into culture and landscape.

Australian literature in the 1990s is a rich amalgam of oral and written work produced over millennia – in the case of oral literature – and over the past two centuries by Australian women writers. Elizabeth Macarthur and Rachel Henning wrote letters 'home' about their new environment; Caroline Leakey (writing as Oliné Keese) wrote the first convict novel, *The Broad Arrow* (some fifteen years ahead of the more famous novel by Marcus Clarke, *For the Term of His Natural Life*). Others such as Mary Fortune, Mary Gaunt and Ellen Clancy wrote journalism and fiction of the goldfields. The struggle for the vote and for women's emancipation in the early years of the twentieth century was documented marvellously by Catherine Helen Spence and works by writers such as Miles Franklin (*My Brilliant Career*), Barbara Baynton (*Bush Studies*), Henry Handel Richardson (*The Fortunes of Richard Mahoney*) and M. Barnard Eldershaw (Marjorie Barnard and Flora Eldershaw, *A House is Built*) described in great detail the lives of rural, urban and business women.

Australian literature of the 1940s was an exceptionally rich period for women writers. This period is marked by a concern for leftist political causes and themes. Many of the novels of the period centre on working class settings and characters, both urban and rural. Among those whose work continues to thrill Australian audiences are works by Dymphna Cusak (*Jungfrau*) and with Florence James (*Come in Spinner*), Christina Stead (*For Love Alone*), Kylie Tennant (*The Battlers*), Eve Langley (*The Pea Pickers*), Katharine Susannah Pritchard (*Coonardoo*).

From the 1950s to the 1970s writers whose works are considered central in any discussion of contemporary writing began to emerge. Thea Astley's tropical novels evoke the north eastern shores of Australia and the Pacific Islands, as does much of the work of Oodgeroo Noonuccal; Dorothy Hewett draws on her background in Western Australia and working class and bohemian life in Sydney; Jessica Anderson writes from a base firmly centred in Sydney, while Glen Tomasetti and Helen Garner are at home in the inner suburbs of Melbourne, and Barbara Hanrahan in Adelaide.

Since the 1970s there has been a huge literary output by Australian women writers and in this time we have seen the emergence of fiction and poetry by Aboriginal writers (see Oodgeroo, Johnson, Bellear, Langford), migrant writers from diverse backgrounds (see Gunew, Loewald, Gleditsch), and by lesbian writers (see Hawthorne, Johnson, Fraser, Starski). For further reading see the Resource list in Part 3.

It has also sparked the formation of independent women-run publishing houses. Sybylla Press was established in Melbourne in 1975, Women's Redress Press, in Sydney, has been publishing for around a decade; in Adelaide, Tantrum Press was established in the late 80s; and with the 90s has come Artemis Publishing and Spinifex Press in Melbourne. Australia was also one of the earliest to establish Women's Studies courses in universities and other continuing education centres.

The 1970s also saw a huge explosion of creativity in the other arts. Women's theatre groups came into existence in most states (see Fraser, Johnson, Moss, Richards, Edmonds); women musicians came together and formed bands, they composed and sang and frequently travelled interstate (see Edmonds, Ellis and Martyn-Ellis, McCarthur); and women in the visual arts also drew on their rich history (see Burke) and developed new ventures together (see Ricketson, Bellamy).

With women moving in large numbers into the arts, this created a need to know about what was going on. Women had been running newsletters and magazines within the women's movement since its inception, but radio was the next area that women entered in significant numbers. In 1975 the Australian Women's Broadcasting Collective established 'The Coming Out Show' and it has been running weekly at 5 o'clock on Saturdays since then. A large audience hungry for information about women's lives, women's culture, women's events and women's politics. Primarily national in focus the programmes have ranged hugely across an enormous variety of topics. Programmes have included celebrations of women's writing such as the work of Miles Franklin or Virginia Woolf; another memorable programme focused on Bea Miles, a Sydney eccentric of the 1950s and 60s who is also the basis of a novel by Kate Grenville, *Lilian's Story*. In recent years there has been more emphasis on programmes about Aboriginal women as inidividuals (e.g. programmes on Ruby Hammond and June Mills of the Mills Sisters) as well as on issues

raised by Aboriginal women. Multicultural issues, including programmes centring on Asian and Pacific cultures have also received more attention recently.

'The Coming Out Show' has its parallels in a number of similar shows on community and local public radio stations. Give Men-A-Pause in Melbourne, and Crystal Set in Sydney were two early FM programmes for women. Give Men-A-Pause had a three hour Sunday morning slot on 3RRR and ran a mix of music, arts reviews, interviews and announcements.

'Women on the Line' is a national programme that is contributed to by community radio stations around the country. These programmes are selected from a range of women-run programmes on the station, shared between stations and played nationally. In addition there are programmes such as 'Not Another Koorie Show', run jointly in Melbourne by Lisa Bellear and Destiny Deacon, that focus on Aboriginal issues with particular emphasis on Koori women's lives (see Resource list for specific information on stations and programmes).

While print and radio have been relatively easy to gain access to, TV and video have proven more difficult. Although newsreaders, dramatic and comedy roles have been filled by many women, production, direction, budgets and control over what gets shown when has generally remained outside the control of women. The professional organisation, Women in Film and Television (WIFT) is also very active with over 600 members working in a range of different fields (for information on film see Creed, also see Resource List).

An additional aspect of culture in Australia is sport which is perceived, from both within and without, as central to our national image. Australian sportswomen have had considerable achievements. Dawn Fraser in swimming is the only female Olympic competitor to win gold medals in the same event in three successive Olympic Games; while Betty Cuthbert and Heather McKay have made their mark in athletics and squash respectively. Likewise, Evonne Goolagong Cawley, in tennis will not be the last Aboriginal woman to make her mark in sport, especially with the recent performance of Cathy Freeman, who looks set to make her mark as a sprinter. Similarly in team sports Australian women have also secured world titles and gold medals in softball, netball and hockey, among others.

There are many amateur women's sports clubs – and some lesbian sports clubs – around the country. National sporting associations such as the Australian Ladies' Golf Union, the Australian Netball Association and Women's Cricket, Tennis, Athletics, Swimming etc. Associations can be contacted for information.

Any kind of travel is made enjoyable by good food, and in Australia you will find high quality, relatively inexpensive food. Australian food and beverages have become a central part of the culture over the past couple of decades. Australian wines and beers are sought after internationally; and the quality and range of fresh foods – vegetables, fruits, meat and fish – is very high. You might like to look out for the wines produced by women winemakers, such as Ursula Pridham's Marienberg label, from South Australia.

The markets in each city provide a huge array of foods – from European staple vegetables to tropical fruits, as well as vegetables and fruits that originated in China, Vietnam, Indonesia, Malaysia and the Pacific.

Seafood around the coast is generally good. You should try Sydney rock oysters and Tasmanian oysters, and in some places river oysters are available. Likewise fresh fish caught in local rivers, or yabbies – a freshwater crayfish – can be a delicacy. Crayfish or lobster is good when freshly caught, as are Moreton Bay bugs and mud crabs. Some indigenous foods are making their way to the gourmet table. Macadamia nuts are native to Australia (in spite of Hawai'ian advertisements to the contrary), and you may get a chance to sample wattle seeds or or a nutty-flavoured witchetty grub soup. For the carnivores there is crocodile steak (that resembles chicken in flavour and texture) or kangaroo. Honey made from the blossoms of various Australian trees is amongst the nicest anywhere in the world (Tasmanian leatherwood honey is particularly well known).

In the cities you can eat well and cheaply in cafés, small restaurants, bistros and delis (The Angel Café in Brunswick Street, Fitzroy is a women's café, while Tilley's in Canberra is well known for its women's nights – see Dowse). The larger metropolitan centres publish *Good Food Guides* to restaurants as well as *Cheap Eats* guides which will help you find your way around the plethora of possibilities.

Lisa Bellear
CHOPS 'N' THINGS

for Eva Johnson

I can't wait to curl around
a lemon scented gum tree
light a fire and
watch it burn down to
the embers as the sun
floats away, far away
our ancestors are
yarning and laughing
at this Koori woman
and through the
flames, the embers
and the burnt chops
and charcoaled
potatoes wrapped in foil
they're saying, tidda girl
you're okay,
keep on dreaming
keep on believing

Dale Spender

SOME EARLY AUSTRALIAN WOMEN WRITERS

Only when all the women writers of Australia are brought together is it possible to identify common patterns and themes, and to speak of a distinctive female literary tradition. Yet surprisingly, this simple exercise of gathering the women together and of constructing their tradition, has not been undertaken recently.

It cannot be because there are not enough of them, or because they have not produced sufficient work to form the substance of a literary heritage, that the women writers of Australia have been overlooked. Debra Adelaide lists the astonishing number of four hundred and fifty women in her compendium of Australian women authors[1] and their publications can be counted in thousands. If the women do not feature in mainstream literary records, it cannot be because they have not written or because what they have written does not warrant inclusion. Rather, there have been so many women writers whose work has been so good, so many like the nineteenth-century novelists Rosa Praed, 'Tasma' and Ada Cambridge who achieved international fame and acclaim, that their omission is more a reflection of their refusal to conform to the masculine image of the mainstream than it is an indication of the force and fascination of their work.

Too frequently the characteristics of Australian literature are held to be exclusively those of the 'outback'; of the contest and the conquest of land and life that was carried out by brave men; yet even as this particular image of people and place was being pieced together, there were women writers who were giving expression to very different concerns. They were writing about different issues and in different ways from the men; they were even writing about the men in a way that men rarely wrote about themselves. What women writers saw and made of the continent and its inhabitants was a long way from the world of 'mateship' and marks a decidedly different body of literature with distinctively different traditions.

The literary traditions of white women in Australia can be traced to an identifiable source; letter writing was the formative activity. Apart from the fact that it was a type of writing permitted – even encouraged – among women (who were invariably denied access to more professional literary pursuits) letter writing was in keeping with women's responsibility for maintaining family ties. So the first white women who settled in Australia soon turned to letter writing, even if they had not always cultivated the habit before. From convict woman Margaret Catchpole (1762–1819) to Elizabeth Macarthur (1769–1850), officer's wife, they wrote and they wrote, and they wrote – to friends and family back home, whenever the opportunity was available. The limits placed on their letter writing were those of literacy, paper, ships and time.

This need to write, however, was not prompted solely by the desire to discover what was going on 'back home': it was also to recount what was happening in the new world. It was a strange country the women had journeyed to; it often did strange things to them. So many women were changed by their Australian experience that they used their letters to describe and define their new identities, to make sense of their new selves and their new lives, which is why self-analysis and self-development feature so prominently in the literary traditions of Australian women.[2]

But this is not the end of the influence that the penchant for letter writing exerted. In the first few decades of settlement in Australia the post was – to say the least – erratic.

So they wrote 'monologues': many of their letters were written over long periods, a 'chapter' at a time in serial form. Day by day, week by week, even month by month, women added to their narratives, reported on themselves and their lives, although they did not know how family and friends fared far away, even whether loved ones were still alive. But they went on keeping the records as they waited for a ship to bring the news, and to take away their stories to the old world.

In many respects this was a migrant literature; letters sent from those who willingly or unwillingly had left their home and whose security was linked with people, places, pressures, in another land. The voice of 'the exile' continues to resonate through Australian women's writing.

The women who wrote these important letters were often acutely conscious of their audiences, and the manner in which their letters would be treated. They knew it was likely that the long letter from Australia would be read aloud to the assembled family, that it would provide drama, entertainment, fascination, before being passed on to scattered relatives and preserved as a record of exciting events in exotic places. The letter writers knew that they could be the heroines in these thrilling tales. So the letters of Rachel Henning (1826–1914) (which have recently been reprinted and are now widely available) were written with a strong sense of story-telling, with an awareness of the interest they would arouse in the listener, and an appreciation of the letter writer's role, centre-stage.

On reading the letters of Rachel Henning, the links between the letter and the novel become readily apparent. While Fanny Burney (1752–1840), that outstanding epistolary novelist of the eighteenth century, may have drawn more on 'fantasy' and Rachel Henning more on 'fact' for the substance of their accounts, few other distinctions can be made about the form of their work. The published letters of Rachel Henning tell such an exciting, and such a romantic tale.

Another reason these letters contained such wonderful stories was that the writers did not want to cause their relations undue concern. Although some or the events the women recounted were truly terrible, they were often transformed by the pen into amusing and entertaining yarns. After all, the letter-writer had obviously survived the danger, the drama, the disaster, the disappointment, and lived to tell the tale. So best to make light of the flood, the drought, the fire, the accident, the snake bite, the childbirth. This typical facility for transforming some of the trials and the tragedies of life into funny stories, has some of its foundations in women's desire to write reassuring and soothing letters to those 'back home'.

Such a consideration, however, is not to be found in much of the journal writing undertaken by women in Australia. Like the letter, the diary or the journal is part of the traditional literature of women and has for centuries served numerous personal needs, although not always the same ones as those that have found expression in letters. For whereas Elizabeth Macarthur and Rachel Henning wrote to their families to let them know all was well, Georgiana McCrae (1804–1890), for example, wrote in her journal to dispel some of her darkest doubts. White women in the early days of settlement and from all walks of life, who were cut off from familiar sources of replenishment, who were deprived of so many of their cultural forms and the comforts of home, often took up their pens as a form of therapy, to make sense of self and the world. Through writing they were able to break their silence, to create an audience, to keep their sanity.

Even in the traditional writing of women it is possible to see the two strands coming together in the cultural heritage. There are the good yarns and outgoing reassurances, as well as the bitter reflections, the personal fears, failures and recriminations. Both frames of reference have helped to shape the women's world of letters. And just as specific conditions and specific activities have contributed to the development of particular literary styles, so too has the specific experience of women led to the evolution of some identifiable common themes.

One of the most striking patterns to emerge when the women writers are placed together is the extent to which white women have expressed concern at the plight of the Aborigines. It is no exaggeration to state that most white women writers have made reference to black experiences and not always as something that is alien.

Again and again women's literature exposes the cruel exploitation of black women by white men; sometimes, when women writers raise the issue of exploitation of white women by white men, connections are made about the common experience of women. There are numerous stories within women's literary heritage which depict black women subjected to the same master, and experiencing an inextricably linked fate.

Stories too about childbirth; about black and white women in remote regions, each offering the other assistance and support. And while there are references to disasters and difficulties, while there may be accounts of anger, antagonism, antipathy, there is nothing in the literature of white women which symbolises black women as the 'enemy'. White women did not live in fear of black women, they did not see them as a physical threat, a force to be subdued. Not only does this make their literature about the dispossessed Aborigines crucially different from that of their male counterparts, but women's writing provides another, often subversive perspective, on the attitudes and values of the country and its development.

By contemporary standards some of the expressions of empathy and understanding of nineteenth and early twentieth century women writers are racist. While not wanting to exonerate them it is as well to remember that they were – as we are – products of the time. Sentiments which may now give offence could well have branded the writer as a radical in her own day, and brought censure. However, the racism of some of the women of the past certainly poses a problem which it would be irresponsible to ignore.

Australian literature reflects the views and values of women in Australia. Much of it is predominantly by white women about black women, and some of it is racist.

It is co-existence rather than conflict which often characterises the literature of women and it extends to many aspects of their environment. Search as one might through the reams that Australian women have written over the centuries, there is little to be found which would support a theme of conquest, little which shows women trying to subdue a people, or a place: there is much, however, which shows women being subdued.

Far from finding friendship and fulfilment in the bush, the drover's wife was more likely to go mad, or to become a victim of the harrowing conditions of outback life. Many women persevered in such unremittingly harsh circumstances yet female deeds of heroism generally remain unsung. But the horrendously hard work, the pressure of child bearing and child rearing, of illness, isolation and pain, took their toll. When women like Rosa Praed, Mary Gaunt, Barbara Baynton and Katherine Susannah Prichard wrote about female experience of the bush, they did not romanticise.

For women there were few compensations for the brutal nature of their existence. Not for them the contentment of the campfire, the opportunity to break bread, tell tales, make mates.

This is not to suggest that women were unaware of the freedoms that their rural and pioneering life could afford. Miles Franklin was not alone in extolling the virtues of a horse – and mobility – for Australian womanhood; directly and indirectly, there were women authors who portrayed the absence of 'polite' conventions and painful clothing in a positive light. When their labour was needed, they were more likely to be valued, although it must be said that there was sometimes a fine line between being necessary and being exploited.

But if work provided a purpose, it also posed something of a dilemma, particularly for those who aspired to being seen as 'young ladies'. While the number of English roses who were confined to couches could well have been exaggerated, the fact remains that the coveted image of womanhood was frequently one of a fragile soul – often consumptive – who languished away her idle days. Such a model did not fit easily with the realities of a young woman's existence in Australia.

Perhaps it was her sense of self which also inspired her spirited challenge to the subordinated status of her sex, for the Australian heroine has a long tradition of seeking independence, self realisation – and creative fulfilment. For more than twenty years before Miles Franklin's Sybylla made her spectacular entry in *My Brilliant Career* (1901) women writers of Australia had been presenting a parade of heroines who would not be satisfied with being the mere appendages of men. Germaine Greer had a heritage of resistance, rebellion and reason on which to draw when she wrote her outstanding analysis of women's position in Western society (*The Female Eunuch*, 1970).

High on the list for criticism of these erstwhile women writers was the institution of marriage which was seen to constrain the existence of women, and there were many writers like Catherine Helen Spence, for example, who suggested that in the interest of women's self-realisation, the institution of marriage should be modified, even abandoned. Her novel which put forward alternatives – *Handfasted* – was completed in 1879, but was considered too radical for publication and not until 1984 did it appear in print.

And she was by no means the only woman writer to examine the pros and cons of marriage, to contrast what a woman gained with what she lost when she became a wife. Like Miles Franklin, there were many women writers who reached the conclusion that the single woman led the better life. When today questions continue to be asked about women's relationship to marriage, and to men, these provocative, often profound and highly popular writers of the past retain their relevance; it is their range of experience and understanding which provides such a rich and rewarding heritage for the modern reader.

However, if the questions about the merits of matrimony, about women's bodies and women's rights, continue to arise, less common now are the concerns about the sins of the fathers being visited upon the sons. It is understandable of course that at a time when Charles Darwin introduced his controversial theories about evolution, the issue would find expression in literary form; there are numerous works of nineteenth-century fiction which explore the relative influence of environment versus heredity. But when to this international scientific debate was added the Australian apprehension about the origin of individuals – of whether once a criminal always a criminal, perhaps even producing criminal offspring – the focus on the importance of heredity in national literature is to be expected.

Rosa Praed, for example, was a writer who raised fascinating questions about the way the weakness of one generation might taint the life of the next (*An Australian Heroine*, 1880); she was genuine in her quest to determine whether a criminal could be rehabilitated, whether a convict could put his past behind him and become a trusted community member. *Policy and Passion* (1881 and 1988), and *Outlaw and Lawmaker* (1893 and 1988) are just two of her novels which explore some of these contradictions which were thrown up in colonial society.

It was partly because the antecedents of many prominent Australian figures could not bear close scrutiny that the practice arose of 'taking people on appearances'; if individuals were wealthy, it was not always wise to enquire too closely into the way their fortunes were acquired. Better to congratulate – and elevate the achievements of 'the self-made-man' than to be concerned with birth or breeding – or so some insisted.

But to women who have always been required to make crucial judgements about the worth and value of a man, the new practical morality of Australia presented a number of difficulties.

How could they take a measure of a man when the yardstick of the old world could no longer be used? This vital question demanded an answer, since the circumstances of women's lives could depend on the choice that was allowed them. Where they would live, how much money they would possess, what freedoms they would enjoy, how many children they would have – even if they were to be happy or ill-used – could all be determined by the character of one man. No wonder this issue was so important; no wonder it has been the theme of so many women's books.

Was it better to marry a rough, rich man, or a poor but noble lord? Was it better to have money in the bank or genteel manners and an impoverished but cultured life? Virtually all the women writers raised these issues as they tried to reconcile the manners of the old world with that of the new, and as they tried to assess the price that women paid for making mistakes. In one novel, *Sisters* (1904 and 1989), Ada Cambridge used the various matrimonial experiences of four sisters to suggest that all marriages (and most men) meant unhappiness for women.

No minor matters, these, in women's lives; they are issues of paramount importance. In the tradition that encompasses Jane Austen, Elizabeth Gaskell and Charlotte Brontë, women writers had asked – what happens to the woman who marries the wrong man? And the Australian novelists continued in this vein. Again and again, Ada Cambridge's wives lead lives of distress and misery; and when in Rosa Praed's best-selling novel, *The Bond of Wedlock* (1887 and 1987), Ariana Lomax's husband beats her, the author asks whether the wife has the right to leave.

Some of the problems and priorities of women's existence may remain constant over time, but their expression and the solutions have varied according to period and place. And as Australian women writers tried to reconcile some of the practices of the home country with the pressures of colonial reality, they frequently forged their own refreshing and revitalised forms. So, for example, Ada Cambridge, who was born in England and moved to Australia in 1870, attempted to retain a refining influence in the face of frightening freedom; so Rosa Praed, who was born in outback Queensland, and who moved to England in 1875, attempted to introduce a note of frankness and freshness to the somewhat stultifying London literary scene. Both were influenced by their expansive new world experience at home and abroad; they were but two of the novelists who helped to establish the distinctive and distinguished traditions of Australian women writers.

Finding and formulating this admirable tradition is such a full and fascinating task that it is tempting to go on tracing the common concerns, the creative forces, and the differences too, in interpretation and execution. There have been so many women who have written so many letters, diaries, autobiographies, as well as the genres of journalism, drama and fiction, that the possibilities for locating the links and discerning patterns are virtually never-ending. This is why it can be salutary to find that despite the diversity in women's literary contributions, there is often an identifiable common core. It cannot be simply coincidence that so many of these writers have expressed such a sustained concern for the status of their sex, and such a distrust for the dominance of men. Sometimes it is the subtext, sometimes it is the subject, but invariably women writers have found the power of men problematic.

In Australia, where women have enjoyed a peculiar degree of freedom, they have also been obliged on occasion to take particular precautions. A recurring plot in women's literature is one in which women masquerade as men. Not only does such disguise afford them a certain degree of protection, it also helps to emphasise the distance between the privileges the characters can enjoy when they are permitted to pass as men, and the privations they can be required to endure when they are perceived as women.

One of the reasons that women have – in such numbers – taken up their pen is because it has allowed them to create their own world. It has allowed them to set the conditions of existence – free from the direct interference of men. One of the reasons that women have – in such numbers – taken to reading women's writing is because it allows them a 'safe place' from which they can explore a wide range of experiences of the world, from which they can identify with a range of characters and a variety of existences. This is why women's writing has occupied, and still can occupy, such a significant and central place in women's lives. It is also why women's writing can share much the same disparaged status as women in a world dominated by men.

It is but a brief and broad outline of some of the salient features of women's literary traditions in Australia which has been presented here, and there is much more that could be stated about the nature of women's writing, and its contribution to the cultural heritage. For its influence is not on the wane; far from experiencing a decline, women writers past and present are now enjoying an increasing popularity and prestige.

The reason could lie in the shifts in power in the realms of print, since the information revolution has reduced the importance of the printed word;[3] men may have moved out to follow the new technologies and thereby allowed greater opportunities for women in print. But regardless of the cause, the reality is that women writers have achieved an impressive record of success. There is growing interest in reclaiming some of the lost contributions of the past, and in documenting the nature and influence of the great female tradition.

Some literary studies have a lot to offer in this increasingly technological and often alienating age; it is through the accumulated wisdom of the women writers that the values of the culture can be reflected, and revised, and reaffirmed. Through their eyes we can see a different world, with their assistance we can seek to realise the potential of human achievement. In any appraisal of the Australian continent, its people, its place, an appreciation of the writing of its women is essential.

Notes
1. Debra Adelaide. 1988. *Australian Women Writers: A Bibliographic Guide.* Sydney: Pandora.
2. For examples of writing by all those named in this article see: Dale Spender (ed). 1988. *The Penguin Anthology of Australian Women Writers.* Ringwood: Penguin.
3. Lynne Spender. 1983. *Intruders on the Rights of Men.* Sydney: Pandora.

Sneja Gunew
THE PEOPLE IN BETWEEN

The complexity of the migrant subject in recent fiction is exemplified by the work of four writers. Their differences from each other as well as their difference from Australian Anglo-Celtic writing is apparent. Antigone Kefala is a Rumanian Greek who emigrated to and spent her youth in New Zealand before moving to Sydney. Zeny Giles (Zenovia Doratis) was born in Sydney of Greek-Cypriot parents. Ania Walwicz was born in Poland and arrived in Australia in her adolescence. Anna Couani is a second-generation Australian of Greek-Polish extraction (a Polish grandfather arrived here in 1860). On the face of it Couani does not belong in the category of migrant women writer yet she chooses to speak from various migrant positions, as we shall see. All four writers are transgressive in ways that interweave the voices of women and of migrants: testing the limits of languages, the limits of gender.

One common challenge to the notion of a unified subject is in connection with names, those social labels which, when questioned, or changed, or mutilated, throw everything concerned with identity into question.

She could see that Manoli was right – they had to learn to live in two worlds. At school they would answer to Nina and Herb. They would speak English, trying to copy every characteristic of the accent around them. They would join in lessons and sport and play with their Australian friends, trying in every way to fit in. But as soon as they stopped at the back door of their house, they were different people. Herb would become Manoli, Nina would become Finnaki or Chrisaphina, as Father called her. (Giles, *Between Two Worlds*)[1]

How does one project the self onto a world when the prime signifier, the personal name, has either disappeared or become multiplied?

And I stayed alone in my room watching my face in the mirror. Caged in myself. Petrified in this frame out of which I could never hope to come except by a definite act. A positive act of will that would destroy me at the same time. And in the mean-time the other one stayed inside me unimpressed. For there were always two inside. The one that moved and laughed, cried and was angry, had attitudes and demanded things and was stubborn in wanting, that felt the vacuum and was afraid. And there was the second one. The one that undermined every effort towards an involvement. The one that dwelt somewhere at the roots of my being and knew with an absolute certainty that everything was futile. That I was making far too much noise about all these not very important matters. The second one that could see through everything. That was merciless. Absolutely indifferent. That watched the very movement of people with a sharp clinical eye, when I, the other one, was totally involved. So that the moment became split, between a doer and a watcher, and the watcher being the stronger, the doer tried to maintain such a level of concentration and involvement leaving no room, no crack, for the second one to insinuate itself.   (Kefala, *The First Journey*)

That second 'I' perceives the fragility of the constructs of the self as they impinge on the equally fragile surrounding world. In Giles' *Between Two Worlds* the mirror functions to confirm a past socio-cultural self that has been interrogated too soon.

Before he'd started school in Australia, he had always fitted in so comfortably that he never even thought of what he looked like. He didn't remember even bothering to look in a mirror in Castellorizo, except perhaps to pull a funny face. Now he would stare into the bathroom mirror and he was ashamed of his brown skin and his short black hair. He was determined never to allow Maria to cut his hair again. But most of all he hated the old-fashioned knitted suit Maria had bought in Port Said. It made him look so different from the others. He had been at school for well over a month and he still dreaded the time each day when one bully or another would poke fun at him. And the terrible part about it was that although he despised those bullies for making fun of him, he wanted to be like them. He wanted light hair and fair skin and, most of all, he wanted to wear not-good clothes.   (Giles, *Between Two Worlds*)

Implied in both these quotations is the arbitrary nature of these social images which in turn reflect, or cast doubts on, the nature of the larger social structures which prescribe certain convention of behaviour and speech. Compare this with Ania Walwicz's two prose poems: 'I' and 'Sitting Pretty'.[2] In the latter there is once again the splintering of the self into the social selves of certain kinds of female stereotypes: an amalgamation of doll and child. Again, as in the Kefala extract, there is the caged self but in this case, paradoxically, because the images are so definitive, it is possible to escape them. The enunciating 'I', from a third place (not doll, not child), discards them. 'And I was nice and quiet and no trouble to anyone. And clean and tidy. And I left me.' In the poem 'I' there is a movement where the 'I' finally engulfs everything, but also remains 'I'. 'My objects are pieces of me . . . They speak my words. I wrote them.' Although it embraces the universe, the 'I' is subject and object still. Compare this with the fifth section of Couani's prose poem, 'Untitled'.

The two white chiffon curtains are being blown into the room by the wind from the open window. They are twisting like cigarette smoke and obscure the view which is of a hazy grey block of a building. Through the open doorway to the next room can be seen a mirror which reflects the mattress on the floor and some pillows, sheets and clothes. There is a small tinkling sound and then a door closing softly. The curtains are blowing over the table just touching the top of a glass without moving it.[3]

126

Here the 'I' is displaced by the description of objects, akin to the putative objectivity of a camera eye. Gradually, in succeeding sections, across the fixed frame of the mirror, there drift further details, including limited human statements. In this case it is the reflected listener, the reader, who is left free to draw connections between these fragments. In a later poem sequence in that volume, 'The View', the various sections keep re-playing the same perceived sequence of events in order to tease out various meanings. In this case more of the process is completed for the reader but, nonetheless, there is never a total unification or closure. The ends are not tied up. It is never a question of a unified perspective mediating or enclosing an event. This refusal of closure, this interrogative approach, reinforces the notion of language itself as a network of territories where boundaries keep shifting in accordance with prevailing ideologies. These transgressions query constantly the concept of a 'natural' language in which one gains competence. 'You step outside convention and then you forget it. The convention seems arbitrary – for anyone who does it anywhere in the world.[4] Amongst other things the migrant voice can alert readers to the arbitrary nature of place, that the mother or father land amounts to an imaginary territory perilously shored up by conventions which may melt away on close scrutiny. In an interview about her writing, Ania Walwicz stated:

As both woman and migrant I have been given no sense of belonging in the world, no set place. I have to state my identity. I have to reconstruct the world . . . I join me to the world.[5]

This awareness, that the 'world' comes into being through the 'I' is echoed by the narrator in *The First Journey*:

The old fear in me again that they might all disappear some day because of a negligence of awareness on my part. A moment when I would fail to lend them my constant support as an onlooker, that gave substance to their limbs.[6]

At the same time since communication needs to involve the recognition of a shared base, that 'I' is the result of construction in and through language. In *Between Two Worlds*, Manoli is unable to articulate his sense of self in the alien language but breaks through when he recognises a familiar place in the universal language of numbers.[7] Later, the book includes an important section where Greek and English words are juxtaposed so that the shared base is extended by means of this either/and rather than either/or approach. In Kefala's story 'Alexia' the eponymous protagonist is introduced to the vagaries of the English language by a teacher who demands:

"Are you happy?"

Alexia went immediately into a panic. For she felt HAPPY to be an Enormous Word, a word full of flamboyant colours, which only people who had reached an ecstatic state had a right to use. She saw it as the apotheosis, so to speak, of a series of events which, as far as she could see, lay totally outside her life. But she could not explain this, for everyone on the Island kept asking, as if this Fantastic Word was the basic measure of their days –

. . .

And the more she thought about it, the more confused she became. Did Miss Prudence mean:

Was she happy eating her mashed potatoes?

Being in the house with the grandfather clock chiming?

Happy living on the Island?

or

Happy living in the world?

There she was, with the salt cellar in her hand, which she had been asked to pass on to Mary, not knowing what to say, getting more and more confused between Happiness and Salt.[8]

What can be more transgressive than such comedy? Almost comparable in the sardonic confusion of meaning and representation is Lucija Berzins' story 'The Berlitz Method'[9] in which an earnestly conducted English language class is anarchically sustained by the promise of a strip-tease.

Edward Said has explored in detail how the Orient becomes an object constructed by the Orientalist. So too the migrant becomes an object constructed by Australian culture, in particular, by its officialdom. Paternalistic institutions reduce the migrant to the status of child as is seen in Walwicz's poems 'So I Little'[10] and 'helpless'.[11]

before they were big i was small they could do things more than me they were something now they are nothing he was a doctor of animals now he was learning to speak properly he talked funny they made mistakes she was clumsy she works in a factory he cleans the floors of the serum laboratory now life can be everybody clean and nice and we ate all wrong here i was the translator i was the mother of my mother they were more helpless they were useless nervous didn't know what to do i was too serious for me it was too early to be like this we walked lost on the street we were looking for john street i was bigger than them my parents were again small old children they were heavy for me they couldn't do much you are helpless useless.

So that another trope in migrant writing becomes, not surprisingly, the government institution, be it a hospital (as in Kefala's 'The Waiting Room',[12] Walwicz's 'Hospital'[13]), or even the academy, as in the following extract from Kefala's novel, *The Island*, where the speaker feels reduced to the status of an object:

I spoke. One could see from his face that he had not the faintest idea what I was saying, the meaning stopped somewhere mid air between us, he incredulous that he will ever understand me, I incredulous that he will ever understand me. He was busy swallowing thin mouthfuls of vinegar, watching me with preoccupied eyes, rubbing his hands as if drying them of sand, trying to get rid of it. One could see in his whole attitude the immense surprise of being confronted, here in his own room, at the University, by something as foreign as myself. The implied extravagance of my voice, the rapid nervousness of my movements, my eyes that looked too directly at him.

As well, however, there is a reversal of this process of objectification when the migrant, in turn, transforms the Australian experience into an object. Compare, for example, Walwicz's poem 'Australia':[14] 'You big ugly. You too empty. You desert with your nothing nothing. . . You don't like me and you don't like women' and its counterpoint poem 'Wogs'.[15]

you can't speak to them why don't you learn to speak english properly they are not like you or me they're not the same as everybody they change us is your child educated by an australian? is it? do you know if? you don't know what they think you don't know what they can do here they change us they paint their houses blue green have you seen blue houses who ever heard of that they live too many together they're too noisy

In a sense the 'you' addressed in the former is the speaker of the latter. In the former the speaker is oppressed, migrant and female and attacks the assumptions of the 'you' which is loosely defined as Ocker and male but also, strangely, oppressed, 'You go to work in the morning. You shiver on a tram.' In the fourth chapter of Couani's *Were All Women Sex-mad?* there is a long section of Australia as object for scrutiny by, presumably, the 'citizen of the world' mentioned elsewhere:

It's unique I'll say that. Anyone can feel at home there because it has a strange character or atmosphere which is like an absence of character, a kind of neutrality. I think it's very tolerant or maybe just very anonymous. No really, I do like Australia. When I lived there I liked it. But I realize coming away again that there's some strange pressure there. It's subliminal, very subtle. I don't think I could describe it exactly because it's an abstract quality which pervades everything there, the work situation, the politics, the social life. It's a place that gets you down. The amount of drinking the people do is phenomenal. And it's as though everyone's bitten by the same bug . . . some kind of desperation or hysteria which is never expressed. They're stoics, the Aussies. The most cynical people in the world. Beyond morality. . . like the English but more sophisti-cated because they never say anything.

And later, even more damning:

But now it's changing a bit at last. They're starting to come in from the cold like the old stockman returning to the bright lights of the station after 2 weeks riding the fences in the cold and the dust. While he's away he has to remember the warmth and light of his home but when he comes back he can forget it.
–He says. And then I get home and wouldn't you know – the wife started her period today. Forget it.
–I think you're starting to understand.

Migrant women's writing speaks from positions which interrogate socio-cultural conventions, notions of linguistic competence, and gender certainties. Migrant, and women's, and migrant women's writing are the 'excess' of Anglo-Celtic writing, a luxury which is an index of what? Civilised scepticism? The mining rights to an unknown territory? New histories for new subjects?

He claimed that in order to understand history, one needed a type of vision that only people placed at the crossroads could provide. That is, people that lived between cultures, who were forced to live double lives, belonging to no group, and these he called 'the people in between'. This type of vision he maintained, was necessary to the alchemy of cultural understanding.   (Kefala, *The Island*)[15]

For those inclined to take territorial metaphors for certainties, migrant writing indicates that Australia is really off the planet.

Notes
1. Zeny Giles. 1981. *Between Two Worlds*. Cammeray NSW: Saturday Centre Books.
2. Ania Walwicz. 1982. *Writing*. Melbourne: Rigmarole. p. 27.
3. Anna Couani. 1977. *Italy*. Melbourne: Rigmarole. p. 11.
4. Anna Couani. 1982. *Were All Women Sex-mad?* Melbourne: Rigmarole. p. 20.
5. Ania Walwicz. 1981. *Mattoid*. Vol. 13. p. 14.
6. Antigone Kefala. 1975. *The First Journey*. Sydney: Wild & Woolley. p. 27.
7. Zeny Giles. 1981. *Between Two Worlds*. p. 50.
8. Antigone Kefala. 1981. *Mattoid*. Vol. 13. pp. 38–43.
9. M. Jurgensen (ed.). 1981. *Ethnic Australia*. Brisbane: Phoenix.
10. 1981. *Mattoid*. Vol. 13. p. 19.
11. Sneja Gunew (ed.). 1982. *Displacements: Migrant Storytellers*. Victoria: Deakin University. p. 2.
12. D. White and Anna Couani (eds.). 1981. *Island in the Sun 2*. Glebe: Sea Cruise Books. pp. 58–9.
13. Ania Walwicz. *Writing*. pp. 20–21.
14. Ania Walwicz. 1981. In *Island in the Sun 2*. pp. 90–91.
15. Ania Walwicz. 1981. *Mattoid*. Vol. 13. pp. 16–17.
16. Antigone Kefala. 1984. *The Island*. Sydney: Hale & Iremonger. p. 22.

Susan Hawthorne

RECENT INNOVATIVE AUSTRALIAN FEMINIST FICTION

In Australia there has been a rich experimental literary output. And most of it has been done by feminists and some of it also represents the innovations that small presses have brought to Australian literature: the vast majority of the writers and their books have been first published by small feminist and/or literary presses. Many of these books defy classification, blending fiction, prose, poetry, and performance together.

One of the things I like about innovative feminist writing is the attention to form and language. Marion Campbell's work provides a good example. Her first novel, *Lines of Flight*, unfolds, onion-like, in concentric circles – representing in part the unfolding of the artist self, Rita Finnerty, (and simultaneously the movement out from the centre of the canvas) to the world at large. But visual art isn't her only concern, the protagonist also has to work her way out through the duplicity of language – as it's spoken in France and in Australia. There are echos of this in her second novel, *Not Being Miriam*, when one of her characters, Bess, spends time working as an au pair with a Swiss family. *Not Being Miriam* has a very different form, perhaps more in keeping with its mesh of theatrical themes. This book's structure is more like a cross-hatched fabric in which threads are pulled and thereby showing a pattern by their absence. It's a strange kind of structure but completely in keeping with the intersecting lives of the women who come out of myth and suburbia.

Marion Campbell isn't alone in her interest in different art forms and their relationship to myth. Finola Moorhead's *Remember the Tarantella* is also a kind of weaving of dancers and artists of various kinds. Five central characters, Arachne, Etama, Iona, Oona and Ursula stitch the narrative pieces together. Iona, the central vowel of the alphabet, is also the central character, who one day, muses Helen, will be the centre of the dance. The dance that is referred to throughout the narrative takes place as an epilogue, and though timeless in a way, as the dancers 'possess past and future vision', nevertheless takes place in the distant past: in 4553 B.C. somewhere between the Tigris and the Euphrates. Moorhead's concern for putting the pieces together is reflected in her other books, *Quilt*, a collection prose and in her most recent novel, *Still Murder*, in which the viewpoints of the characters are presented to the reader as different sized pieces of cloth, flapping in the wind. Moorhead is also fascinated by mathematical and geometrical patterns, reminiscent of Marion Campbell's enigmatic chapters on Johannes Kepler's mother, Katerina, in *Not Being Miriam* and of Helen Hodgman's random events in her black comedy, *Broken Words*.

The fractured narrative of *Broken Words* takes us from London to

Vancouver to Goondiwindi as Hazel tries to work out what she wants. Is it Moss, her lover? or Walter whom she meets in the park when he's looking for his dog, Angst? The complicated pattern of wants and don't-wants are used to play with the reader's sense of belief and disbelief. The reader is later left wondering if she should have laughed.

Susan Hampton's irreverent *Surly Girls* takes the reader on an excursion, a wonderfully rich and candid excursion, through contemporary feminist and lesbian culture. There are short aphoristic pieces, long moving stories, poems, performance pieces and prose pieces that play with theory. Although the pieces are not connected specifically, there are links and some recurring characters and by the time you reach the end of the book you feel as though you know some of these people, as though you might sit down and continue a conversation begun in the narrative. Susan Hampton shares a move from poetry to prose along with Pamela Brown and Joanne Burns, both of whom have produced books of short crisp prose in the last couple of years. My favourite piece in *Keep it Quiet* by Pamela Brown is 'If Life Could Have A Soundtrack', a story about friendship between two young girls that has all the pathos of a much longer work without for-going complexity. *blowing bubbles in the 7th lane* contains five prose sequences, the first of which was produced as a radio play. No one is safe from Joanne Burns; her wit is sometimes scorching, her iconoclasm touches on the urban and the suburban, the universal concerns of the nuclear arms race and the peculiarly local environments of swimming pools and city to surf races.

There is a great deal of fragmentation in all the narratives mentioned so far, and Mary Fallon's *Working Hot* continues in the same vein. A wonder-ful array of odd but believable characters, among them Freda Peach, One Iota, Toto, ECR Saidthandone, Top Value and Kinky Trinkets sprawl, laugh and make love across the pages of this novel/play/poem/opera/radio script.

But not all the books produced in the last ten years are fragmentary. Drusilla Modjeska's *Poppy* and Sue Woolfe's *Painted Woman* bring us full circle to another kind of avant garde. This one is the shifting sand that appears solid, but which moves invisibly under one, so that when you stop to look you find that the perspective has somehow shifted without you noticing it. *Poppy* is an exploration of memory and of mother/daughter relationships. Modjeska's seemless web is an extraordinarily rewarding read for anyone intrigued by the way memory invents us, and we invent it. *Painted Woman*, on the other hand, explores the illusions created in a father/daughter relationship and the reassertion of self through artistic endeavour, this time through painting the interior and the domestic and thereby transforming them out of the ordinary into something like the dance invoked by Finola Moorhead some 6000 years ago. Fiona Place's *Cardboard*, a novel about anorexia falls somewhere between the fragmentation of *Working Hot* and the shifting perspectives of *Poppy*. While most of the narrative is from Lucy's perspective, the voice shifts into the third person, distancing Lucy from herself, perhaps as a way of finding her external self again.

Gillian Hanscombe, too, blurs the boundary of prose and poetry with her prose poem sequence, *Sybil: The Glide of Her Tongue*. The central image of the sequence is the prophet/poet Sybil, who, mythologically speaking, spoke her prophetic utterances on the ancient goddess site of Delphi. But the Sybil of this sequence is a multiplicity of voices, specifically lesbian voices. In a sense, Gillian Hanscombe's work is a coming together of many of the strands in Australian, mostly lesbian, certainly feminist, experimental writing. Dorothy Porter's verse novel. *Akhenaten*, takes form in another direction, through giving a mythical/historical narrative a verse form. Dorothy Porter plays with the challenges of perspective in taking on a male voice as her narrator. Drawing on the history of Egypt and some of its most enigmatic characters – amongst them Nefertiti and Akhenaten – Porter expands the possibilities of feminist poetry. Amongst other recent poetry published, comes the work of Sandy Jeffs and Deborah Staines in a joint collection, *Poems from the Madhouse/Now Millenium*. While Deborah Staines explores the mythic past and the technological future, Sandy Jeffs slides along the continuum between sanity and madness. Both write across the gap between prose and poetry, challenging our sense of reality, whether it be through the distorted perception of madness or through the artifice of video and virtual realities. Beth Yahp's novel, *Crocodile Fury*, set in Malaysia, also follows the refractions of reality through the uncertainties of three generations of women's memories. This novel is like a series of distorted mirrors, each reflecting the repeated imagery of the original story, each distorting it in her own way.

All these books have appeared since 1985. It's an extraordinary achievement. And these are not the only ones, but I have chosen these books because all the writers identify as feminist and further, each is breaking the rules in her own way. In some cases stretching the parameters of a particular form, such as *Poppy* achieves for biography; for others it's a matter of crossing genres or mixing them in new ways. Whatever the innovation, Australian feminist writing is amongst the most interesting anywhere.

Books mentioned

Marion Campbell. 1985. *Lines of Flight*. Fremantle: Fremantle Arts Centre Press.
— 1988. Not Being Miriam. Fremantle: Fremantle Arts Centre Press.
Finola Moorhead. 1985. *Quilt*. Melbourne: Sybylla Press.
— 1987. *Remember the Tarantella*. Sydney: Primavera Press; 1994. London: The Women's Press.

— 1991. *Still Murder*. Ringwood: Penguin Books.

Helen Hodgman. 1988. *Broken Words*. Ringwood: Penguin Books.

Susan Hampton. 1989. *Surly Girls*. Sydney: Collins Angus & Robertson.

Gillian Hanscombe. 1992. *Sybil: The Glide of Her Tongue*. Melbourne: Spinifex Press.

Sandy Jeffs / Deborah Staines. 1993. *Poems from the Madhouse/Now Millennium*. Melbourne: Spinifex Press.

Dorothy Porter. 1992. *Akhenaten*. St Lucia: University of Queensland Press.

Beth Yahp. 1993. *Crocodile Fury*. Sydney: Collins/Angus & Robertson.

Pamela Brown. 1987. *Keep It Quiet*. Sydney: Sea Cruise Press.

Joanne Burns. 1988. *blowing bubbles in the 7th lane*. Sydney: Fab Press.

Mary Fallon. 1989. *Working Hot*. Melbourne: Sybylla Press.

Drusilla Modjeska. 1990. *Poppy*. Melbourne: McPhee Gribble.

Sue Woolfe. 1990. *Painted Woman*. Sydney: Allen & Unwin.

Fiona Place. 1989. *Cardboard*. Sydney: Local Consumption Publications.

Eva Johnson
A PROFILE

My name is Eva Johnson and I was born of the Malak Malak people of Daly River in the Northern Territory, Australia. I am a playwright and have so far written five plays. I guess I became a writer by accident, or perhaps writing chose me. In 1984 the first National Aboriginal Women's Arts Festival was held in Adelaide South Australia, and I was approached to write a play for this event. Previous to this, I had seen myself as being a poet, and I still am, as poetry has been my interest.

The play written for the Arts Festival was called *Tjindarella* which is an analogy of Cinderella. The word Tjindarella is pronounced 'Gindarella' the word 'Gin' derives from the derogatory terms that was applied to Aboriginal Women. Cinderella is a nursery rhyme common to western culture, and is the fairytale story of a white girl's experience of poverty, persecution and the alternate success. *Tjindarella* is the story of a Black Woman, her experiences follow the same line as that of Cinderella, only the political implications, of racism, sexism, and outcome differ. My writing also involved my participation in the first National Black Playwrights' Conference in 1987, and out of that eventuated the founding of the Aboriginal National Theatre Trust.

So why do I write? I write to record the events in my life I have experienced. I write about the people in my life, those close to me, those who are important to me, the people who are also the victims of this society. And many of them are my relatives, my friends, and family. I write to expose the inhumane treatment of a people, of the imbalance and the injustice implied on my race. I try to motivate change, to inform people, to communicate and to make known the problems of my race, to confront issues from the society that oppresses me and other Aboriginal people. I write because I must keep this revolution awake, to keep the spirit of my revolt alive. Most importantly I attempt to rewrite the myths the untruths that others have written about me. I believe that what I have to say is useful, and to demonstrate that the reality of politics through writing is essential in the struggle for justice. Being black confirms that politics for me, which leads me to identity.

Where do I fit into everything? Firstly as an individual, and secondly as a member of the Aboriginal race? When I write for theatre, I write from the perspective of a black Woman, and on Aboriginal Woman and therefore look at the conditioning of Aboriginal people, our representation, and status in this society. I see the focus as one to promote theatre for purposes of change, for perceiving social issues, from the realistic point of view, and attempt to give a black perspective at seeing how these issues affect our lives and our community. I see theatre vital in promoting humanistic values which contribute to the moral growth of society.

I began to write in 1979. My first poem became the title of the first play ever produced by Black Theatre in Adelaide called *When I Die You'll All Stop Laughing*. In those days, there was no money, no theatre, and no-one with any skills. We busked on the streets, rehearsed in parklands, and every performance relied on donations. The Union Theatre in the University of Adelaide became our first theatre venue.

Our visibility lit many fuses, raised curiosity and most importantly stamped the beginning for Black performers and Writers. We moved on to our second production in 1981. The company has a name, and we called ourselves 'Wujuruki Theatre', which is the name given to the Willy Wagtail, the bird that carries messages for people as believed by the Aboriginal people of South Australia.

Then came *Tjindarella*. This was the changing point of my life as a Writer. I originally wrote *Tjindarella* with a cast member of ten. However the response to invitations for Aboriginal Women to audition for the play proved overwhelming. Twenty-five Women auditioned, and to me that meant twenty five Women coming from their own situations who were interested in committing themselves to this production. I immediately thought that everyone should be included in this play. That night I proceeded to re-write Tjindarella, and came up with a play that included eighteen players and a musical band of four members. We joined our circle and developed the first Women's Theatre in Adelaide.

Within the circle we committed ourselves to the play and to working together, we talked our business, anything of any context was free to be spoken within the trust of the circle. To many this symbolised our sacredness and place, within contemporary mode of Women's Business. My role was that of the Co-Director. The Director was a Woman who had worked in theatre for many years both on an International level and in Australia. My decision to co-direct the play was based on the fact that I wanted to learn more about theatre, not just from the writers perspective but also from a broader creative focus. The backstage and technical crew were all Women, some feminists, some lesbians, which were indeed a new phenomena for most Aboriginal Women.

The play *Tjindarella* proved a success, and continued to tour to Victoria. In 1985 the performance of *Tjindarella* was an important inclusion in the New Moods Women 150 Festival as part of Women Writers Week. So with the experience of *Tjindarella* I learned many things, not only about myself but about Aboriginal people and our diversities. I had experienced racism, and a sense of jealousy, resentment of my work and my first confrontation with homophobia, even from those I thought were my friends.

Of course, as a Writer I have a responsibility. Firstly to myself to be honest about who and what I am, and secondly to exposing the truths of how racism and sexism operate in the attempt to silence those who challenge the establishment and the rules of the norm.

There are very few black writers, in particular Aboriginal Women playwrights in Australia. There are many black male writers who in many cases hold the monopoly on funding and publishing. Many of them have preference in publishing because none of these writers are feminist, lesbians and black. Some of the issues that I deal with are confrontative to men, particularly to black men who see me as a threat and are afraid of me, those men who want me to change my life and to be 'normal' again. So I say to those men 'I cannot be what you want, and I cannot speak from your personal experience because I am not a black man. But I do understand that you have a responsibility to confront your own oppression and talk about black men's hostilities. I don't know how you feel as a black man. And I don't necessarily agree with the way many of you act and behave towards black women and other women. I would like to address that, and when you do then we can talk. And that does not mean that I hate you.'

For myself as a Black Woman, I need to find ways in creative self-conscious representation of ourselves by using a variety of artistic forms. And to find ways to break down the isolation and to create our own places where we can be the Women that we are, and gain respect for the amazing depth of perception that our identity brings us. I believe that it is important to focus also on humour in my plays as the irony within any oppressive situation can turn into a kind of humour that only we can laugh at, but it is to us, maintaining some form of survival inside us. As Women we need to recreate our identity because it is ours that is forgotten in a male dominated patriarchal society.

Extract from *What do they call you?*
. . . and when I finally find my real mother
I'm worried that she'll think I'm too white.

. . . Hello, are you Connie? Connie Brumbie?
You don't know me, my name is Ali . . . Alison Brumbie
I was told you worked here, it's taken me all this time
to pluck up enough courage to come and meet you.
Yes, it's been thirty-two years
I, I don't know what to say
just that I work in a shelter, and, I, I never got married.
and, and I'm glad that I've found you . . .

God Sara, I felt so stupid.
I thought that my mother would be so disappointed in me.
All I was thinking of was how I was presenting
I didn't worry how she felt, I didn't ask her how she felt
after all these years, I wasn't even worried about her pain.
My God, Sara, how can you tell a mother you've never known,
that you're a radical feminist, anarchist, amazon, lesbian warrior?
that you belong to a collective,
that you march for peace, for whales, for land.
that you march to reclaim the night,
and that you live with a woman?
Well, I finally told her,
I wonder what she really thinks.
As for my sister, Regina
I completely freaked her out
all she knows is husband, kids, house, tupperware,
avon, two cars, dogs, cats and microwaves.
It was a struggle for her to accept that she WAS Aboriginal
let alone the fact that her mother is an alcoholic, her
sister's a radical feminist lesbian, and her brother is
wanted for murder,
she was in total SHOCK!!
Yes, I'd say that she's had a pretty tough identity crisis
. . . well, it's taken her all this time to come to terms
with her Aboriginality . . .
And where? where could she go to find her identity?
Who has the magical formula to say what makes you Aboriginal?
Where can she go where she can be accepted as an Aboriginal
despite her white orientation? without being called a
coconut?
Brown on the outside, white on the inside.
On the one hand she's called a Boong
on the other she's called a coconut.
In a way we are both victims,
our credibility, our identity is at risk.
The irony, my mother, my sister, and I, after all these
years, coming together, as strangers, needing desperately
to reclaim our identity, our Aboriginality.
The very tool that was the source of our separation . . .

. . . But Sara, just look, just look how far we've come
just look how far Aboriginal women have come in the
struggle against oppression.

Take my mother, Connie Brumbie for example
she's the most courageous woman I've ever had the pleasure to know.
When I was born, the racist rules of the day
gave her every disadvantage.
She never demanded anything
whatever she wanted for herself –
just for her sanity's sake – was denied her.
She was continually bashed, her head permanently scarred,
her physical image criminally assaulted and mutilated,
she was raped and denied the right to cry out in pain.
She's been sworn at, spat at, rounded up and accused.
She's been called a lubra, gin, slut, whore, black velvet
her children confiscated from her, as if illegal merchandise
and jailed in a government compound.
She's confused, frustrated, hurt, resentful,
she's frightened and angry – and
who dares to brand her now?
what can they do to her now?
what can they do to Connie Brumbie now?

Merrilee Moss

Puppets to Playwrights: Girls on Stage

A new form of women's theatre originated in Melbourne in the early seventies with a burst of excitement which still sends a glow of nostalgia to the cheeks and a sparkle to the eyes of those who were involved, whether as audience or participant. A form of radical alternative theatre had evolved in the sixties, and it was appropriate and inevitable that when feminism hit town, women working in theatre would use their work to express their politics.

Frustrated with the stereotypical roles available to female actors, lack of scripts written by women (or even for women), lack of opportunity to become involved in direction or to develop skills in technical work, and with the hierarchical structures in general, women got up and did their own thing with spontaneity, enthusiasm and optimism.

In the beginning there was street theatre – initiated by women in Melbourne from the Australian Performing Group (APG), but open to all interested women, skilled or unskilled. A sketch involving a 'baby machine' was used at an abortion demonstration in 1971. Another sketch, called *The Perfect Woman Kit* included huge phallic noses. 'We really sent up that type of woman who has all the stuff you need to be a so-called "perfect woman". Things like tampons, mops, hair-rollers . . .' (Marg Jacobs)

In 1972 Kerry Dwyer directed *Betty Can Jump* at the Pram Factory (home to the Australian Performing Group). 'The audacity of women working alone and developing a play without a writer was staggering . . . the APG was primarily a theatre whose aim was to develop new Australian writers and as those writers were all men with particularly masculine and male perspectives, the attempt was seen as a dangerously divisive one.' (Kerry Dwyer)

Two years later, a separate group, the Women's Theatre Group (WTG) was formed and eighteen women were involved in a group-developed revue, satirising advertising and media images of women, using scripted scenes and songs and lots of comedy. The mix of experienced and inexperienced women worked well. Performances of *Women's Weekly Shows (Vol. I & Vol. II)* in the back theatre of the Pram Factory were packed out, with more than a hundred turned away each night.

Role-reversal – sending up men – was very common, with humour and song holding everything together. '. . . there was so much exuberance in the early days of the women's movement,' Marg Jacobs said. 'Theatre was perfect to express it. We were very evangelical. In a way, humour softened that tendency.'

But those *Women's Weekly* shows were very frustrating for the women involved. 'We could have done a lot more,' said Marg. 'Here you were being given this theatre for scraps of time, like Friday, Saturday and Sunday at eleven pm, and the place was packed out!' Eventually they took over the Front Theatre – for two weeks. A Feminist Festival called Out of the Frying Pan was held, including documentary theatre, *The Revised Love Show*, a Talent show, a Bake-Off and lots more.

Lesbian content fitted easily into the early shows, despite the fact that 'most of the women involved in performances were straight, or at least not "out".' But specific roles and references to lesbianism did not appear until 1975 (International Women's Year) when scripts were solicited – such as the sketch *But This Is Chris* by Barbara Creed. The story told of parents awaiting the arrival of a glorious new son-in-law, only to discover that their expected guest is a woman. *Shift* by Di Q was a naturalistic performance about a woman discovering her lesbian sexuality.

International Women's Year meant funds for the Women's Theatre Group. There was a festival in the Carlton Gardens, a travelling *Women and Work Show*, the *Women and Madness: Add a Grated Laugh or Two* (again in the Front Theatre) and a Summer Solstice Celebration.

'The WTG was hot property in 1975,' said Ursula Harrison. 'Organisational structures, or non-structures, had to be worked out. There was a rotating administrator and everything else was group directed and devised. But it was also in 1975 that the clashes started to happen. How much should experienced women be allowed to take the lead? There was a strong pressure to get shows together and that stopped a lot of the workshopping. There were new women coming in all the time who had to be taught skills and a whole lot of administrative work had suddenly appeared. It was harder to take risks with money involved.'

In 1976 the Women's Theatre Group moved to The Space in Faraday Street, Carlton, where it 'pioneered experiments in non-scripted group-devised performance; non-hierarchical group organisation; collective direction of production and the breaking down of amateur/professional dichotomies in theatre' (Suzanne Spunner). Spunner praises the Women's Theatre Group for having a profound and lasting impact on theatre in Melbourne,' despite the fact that the group itself divided into 'those women who wished to pursue a form of separatist women's theatre', and 'those who wished to pursue feminism in the theatre world at large.'[1]

In 1976, the performance at the Pram Factory of *Sisters*, written by Robin Thurston, and the group-devised performance of *Wonder Woman's Revenge* at the Salvation Army Hall, symbolised the return of some women to the APG and the differing concentration on process and product between the two groups. Bronwyn Handyside wrote a particularly scathing review of *Wonder Woman's Revenge* where she referred to an 'insistence on subjectivity' leading to 'a fatal lack of self-criticism which produces the kind of self-absorbed, self-congratulatory show that *Wonder Woman's Revenge* turned out to be.'[2]

A lot of women were very angry about her review at the time, but some now remember that there was a self-conscious insertion of lesbian content in the show. And it was a very extreme form of personal theatre. On the other hand, *Sisters*, written by a man, was a very sombre production which concentrated on suffering and imprisonment. Neither of these performances followed the model of the earlier exuberant WTG.

It was very difficult for women in both positions: some wanting to move on in an established theatre world which offered few appropriate scripts or opportunities; others wanting to develop their feminism through drama and provide opportunities for other women to join them.

In the same year that all this was happening in Melbourne, theatre for women in Adelaide was just getting off the ground. Jude Kuring received an International Women's Year grant for a cabaret performance and in late 1976 gathered interested women together to begin planning for what became *The Carolina Chisel Show*. It was basically a series of songs, from rock to musical comedy, strung together on a story line about three sisters – all called Grace, who inherited the possibility of putting on a show. A plot which allowed for anything, and anything was literally fitted in. 'Someone would say I want to sing "Bobby's Girl" and I'd have to find a place to put it' (Jenny Pausacker, playwright).

Adelaide productions were very large affairs. 'About every twelve months sixty to eighty people would gather together and in a rather miraculous process of disorganisation produce a show that people would like.' (Jenny)

International Women's Day, 1977, was celebrated by singing, dancing, performance and fire-eating, all inspired by the work of *The Carolina Chisel Show*. This event marked and signified the existence of feminist theatre in Adelaide.

Next was a musical comedy called *Chores*, remarkable because it was more or less a group-written script (six women sat around in backyards for a year while one person took down all the jokes) and because it was unashamedly a play by feminists about feminists and for feminists. The plot involved Radclyffe Hall visiting a suffragist's household and converting them to lesbianism, while they convert her to 'ideological soundness'. It was a great success.

The Redheads Revenge followed – a melodrama focusing on role reversal. Embedded in the mesh of plot was a lesbian relationship between the working and upper class heroines. The poorer woman spent her time encouraging the match-girls to strike, while the rich girl (a governess) had set up a school (Freda Stare's Academy).

The program notes echo the idealism and optimism of Melbourne shows:

In *The Redheads Revenge* (May 3–13, 1977) all the various jobs have been done by groups of women working co-operatively . . . It is not a simple matter to work collectively, and we have made a number of mistakes down the way. But we believe that we have established a pattern of working that can be improved on by future women's shows, and that we have gained greatly from the process of working it out.

Redheads was a huge hit, with enthusiastic reviews and hundreds of people turned away from the door. However there was conflict over the venue. A number of women felt that the use of Festival Theatre space was an attempt to 'make it' in 'mainstream' terms and formed a protest group called the Redherrings.

A post-production discussion whose agenda included such questions as: 'Auditions – good or bad? What audience do we want – general public or feminist? Does the collective structure work, especially with actors and director? What should we do with the profits?' resulted in the setting up of a Feminist Theatre Fund. A meeting in October 1978 decided to begin two major projects: a revival of *Chores* and the establishment of a women's performing space (an idea that had strongly been argued as an alternative to the Fund).

The women's space was established at the Bakery in St Peters, which was the setting for various learning groups and a number of dances and supper shows. As in Melbourne in 1976 this represented a division in the women's theatre community, and again the different directions were seen as conflict rather than diversity.

Common to both Melbourne and Adelaide feminists who look back on that time is a longing for the fresh, spontaneous enthusiasm which seemed to hold those first few shows together. The phenomenon of 'funding' was of remarkable significance. But the facts were – women had come a long way, fast. In 1980 Suzanne Spunner wrote, 'Experience of women became acceptable, even fashionable'.[3]

Women's theatre tended to be non-naturalistic and imagistic. Individual work such as Jenny Kemp's *Sheila Alone* (Back Theatre, Pram 1979), Margot Hilton's *Potiphar's Wife* (Nimrod, 1979), Elizabeth Patterson's short sketch *Old Woman at a Window* (1981), *The Case of Katherine Mansfield*, by Cathy Downes (Pram Factory 1980) and Patricia Cornelius' *Witch* (La Mama,1982) were all monologues based on imagery. Groups such as Canberra's Fools Gallery (*Standard Operating Procedure*, 1981), Home Cooking (*Not Still Lives*, 1982) and Footfall Theatre (*The Balek Scales*, 1982) all presented their ideas with movement-based image, using poetry, song, mime etc to imprint concepts on the minds of their audience. Jan Cornall's rock musical *Failing in Love Again* was a big hit, as were Robyn Archer's two shows *A Star is Torn* (Universal Theatre, 1980) and *The Pack of Women* (1983).

Comedy too has been an important element of most women's performances. Often with a sharp edge to it, like *The Women and Madness Show: Add A Grated Laugh or Two* (1975) and Sue Ingleton's biting one-woman performance as Bill Rawlins, the 'pregnant man' in *From Here to Maternity*. The Wimmin's Circus (1979–81) concentrated on a sort of bizarre humour (1979–81) when women performed as clowns instead of 'beauties' and showed their muscles along with their skills.

In the eighties women like Wendy Harmer, Maryanne Fahey, Liz Sadler, Jan Cornall and many others took up the challenge of stand-up comedy, breaking into a very risky and highly 'male' arena. By 1985, The New Moods Festival was able to present several evenings of all-women stand-up entertainment, including *It's A Joke, Joyce* and *In Stitches*. It also included a touring production of Eva Johnson's *Tjindarella*.

Individual playwrights researched the role of women in Australian history and produced scripts about Australian women such as Margaret Preston, Thea Proctor, Katherine Mansfield and Edna Walling as well as plays that focused on the lives of overseas writers such as Radclyffe Hall, Gertrude Stein, Georgia O'Keefe, Virginia Woolf and Vita Sackville-West.

However, the most difficult thing for all women theatre workers – writers, directors, technicians or performers, is breaking into the already established networks.

Jobs for older female performers are almost non-existent. 'As I got older my earning capacity has diminished as my ability has increased. It's as though we have to disappear,' Maggie Miller said.[4]

Scripts are still problematic, parts are hard to get, funding's a worry if you're political (and even if you're not) and there are still few female technicians, directors and writers. But there are more than there were.

'The problem for women will be learning how to write for a theatre they've been locked out of,' playwright John Romeril wrote in 1980.[5] Playwriting is still a very male dominated domain.

Skilled female directors are finding it hard to break through what they call 'the glass ceiling' (an invisible barrier to their progress). In 1993 the Australian Women Directors' Association (AWDA) was formed and it is calling for 50% equity. In the meantime, the group has uncovered some revealing statistics. Of nine new shows from May to October 1993 at the Melbourne Theatre Company, none are directed by a woman. Only one woman was listed as directing a show in the previous season. The current Royal Queensland Theatre Company season lists two women directors for eight plays. In Adelaide, no women will direct the seven major works to be staged at the prime Playhouse venue. Out of 14 Sydney Theatre Company productions this year, women have scored only three positions.

'. . . if you are decisive and pushy, you are seen as being difficult.' (Ariette Taylor)

146

'If you're not bossy, you're seen to be a weak, vacillating female; if you are bossy you're threatening, asexual or a lesbian.' (Kim Durban)

Some argue that we have to start at the top. We need female artistic directors to choose female directors, who will in turn choose scripts written by women.

Three women have recently (1992–3) won prestigious artistic positions: Chris Johnson as artistic director of the Royal Queensland Theatre Company, Chris Westwood as executive producer of the newly structured State Theatre Company of South Australia, and Robyn Archer as head of the Community Cultural Development Unit of the Australia Council, the Federal Government's Arts advisory and funding body. But a lot still has to be done before women directors can enjoy any measure of job security.

Generally, when women are given a job in mainstream theatre, it is as an assistant director or in the lower-risk exploration program for school students. They also find positions in community theatre, struggle for grants on the fringe scene or develop new writer's work at smaller venues such as La Mama (Melbourne).

It has been argued that directing is tough, male work. That women lack natural authority, they can't make decisions under pressure, they're too emotional, they keep changing their minds. . . They're better at making costumes and cutting hair. But others argue that women have better skills of negotiation, flexibility, nurturing and diplomacy.

Apart from the industrial battle, women working in theatre are faced with many exciting and challenging questions that are only just beginning to be discussed. 'Are there assumptions that being female equals a particular ideological base?' 'Is there a recognisable difference in the processes used by women?' 'How does the notion of "Feminist Theatre" blend with modern concepts such as post-modernism and deconstruction?' 'How does the label "women director" affect work/funding?' 'Do women have the potential to create a new vocabulary?' 'Does women's "voice" in theatre exist to undermine existing language?' 'How much has the work of the early women's theatre groups informed the shape of theatre today?'

There are still very few published scripts, and there is a tendency for women to re-invent the wheel with each new burst of energy. As yet, there is no body of theory to reference these questions and very little documentation. But we're working on it.

Notes
1. Suzanne Spunner. February 1980. Theatre and Feminism From Then Till Now. *Theatre Australia.*
2. Bronwyn Handyside. 1976. *Lip Magazine.*
3. Spunner. February 1980. *Theatre Australia.*
4. Maggie Miller. 18 May 1993. The lady vanishes. *Age.* p.14.
5. John Romeril. January 1980. *Perambulator.*

References

Michelene Wandor. 1981. *Understudies: Theatre and Sexual Politics*. London: Methuen.

Merrilee Moss. August 1984. Puppets to Playwrights, Girls on Stage. *OutRage*.

Lip Magazine, 1974, 1975, 1976, 1979, 1980.

Helen Keyssar. 1984. *Feminist Theatre*. Macmillan.

Iris O'Loughlin. Australian Women Playwrights Project. English Dept. Monash University. Frankston.

Points of Interest (1993)

- Iris O'Loughlin, Lecturer in English, Monash University has recently received funding to conduct a study of all Australian women playwrights with the aim of making them visible and known to the community.
- Some playwrights already listed:
  Dorothy Hewett, Teresa Radic, Betty Roland, Topsha Learner, Jenny Kemp, Alma De Groen, Mona Brand, Hanny Rayson, Sandra Shotlander, Joanna Murray-Smith, Rhondda Johnson, Dymphna Cusack, Merrilee Moss, Doreen Clarke, Peta Murray, Patricia Cornelius, Kate McNamara.
- The Third International Women's Playwrights Conference will be held in Adelaide in July 1994.
- Vitalstatistix, is the only fully-funded all-women's theatre group in Australia. It's home is – Waterside Nile Street, Port Adelaide.
  PO Box 459, Pt Adelaide 5015 (Ph: 08 476211)
- Peta Tait (University of NSW) has published a monograph, *Original Women's Theatre: The Melbourne Women's Theatre Group 1974–77*. Melbourne: Artmoves, 1993.
- The Pram Factory, Drummond Street, Carlton, Melbourne (home to the Women's Theatre Group) was demolished and replaced by a large modern shopping complex.
- The nineties has seen a revival of women's circus skills with the unique and highly successful Women's Circus formed by director Donna Jackson. This group – made up of more than eighty women – is housed at the Footscray Community Centre, Melbourne.

Some Supportive Theatres Across Australia

Adelaide
    Doppio Teatro
    Vitalstatistix
    Red Shed
    Junction Theatre Co.

Melbourne
    La Mama
    Carlton Courthouse
    Napier Street Theatre
    Melbourne Workers Theatre
    Theatreworks
    New Theatre

Brisbane
    La Boite

Canberra
    Women On A Shoestring
    Canberra Youth Theatre

Darwin
    Brown's Mart

Perth
    Hole in the Wall
    SWY Theatre
    Black Swan Theatre

Sydney
    Belvoir St
    Performance Space
    The Wharf Theatre
    The Stables

Alison Richards
WOMEN'S CIRCUS ... LEAPING OFF THE EDGE

The background – Australian circus old and new

Circus in Australia has a long and colourful history; circus performers were among convicts transported for petty theft in the early days of the colony. Until the mid 1970s, it was pretty much a traditional family affair. Members of prominent circus families, the Ashtons and the St Leons (who had changed their name from the much less exotic Jones), performed in equestrian shows in the 1840s. Others, such as the Perrys and the FitzGeralds, were also of English origin and had established themselves in Australia over several generations.

One of the earliest circus entrepreneurs was an Italian, Luigi delle Case. The originally Bavarian Wirth brothers and much later the originally Swiss Gassers progressed from being immigrant artists to circus proprietors and the founders of circus dynasties. Other families such as the Soles, the Colleanos (who claimed Spanish ancestry but who were actually of Aboriginal/Irish origin) and the American Herberts were well known.

The major circuses such as Ashtons, Wirth's, Bullens and Sole Brothers, modelled themselves on those of Europe. The small and sparsely settled population of Australia meant that outside Sydney and Melbourne it was not possible to establish the permanent circus arenas which were both the glory and the graveyard of circus abroad. Australia's circuses were always tenting operations, often struggling to cover costs as they travelled thousands of kilometres following city and country agricultural shows. Often in the company of, if not actually doubling as, sideshow and fight promoters, they nevertheless kept up the 'traditional' circus acts and circus skills – animal acts with horses, dogs, lions and elephants; acrobatic acts, knife acts, trapeze (sometimes even flying trapeze), Risley and other balance acts and magic acts; clowning and of course always glamorous girls in spangled tights and leotards.

By the 1970s Australian circuses were generally in decline. Then, along with a new and vital alternative theatre scene, came a generation of performers who wanted not so much to reform circus as to reinvent it. Some of them came from traditional circus or showbusiness backgrounds; more emerged from the student and other radical theatre groups who saw in the circus form a chance to explore a popular theatre tradition and to give it new life.

The new Australian circus was characterised by a wonderfully eclectic approach. It borrowed from Chinese as well as European acrobatic traditions; it incorporated clowning, puppetry, popular mechanics and political and social satire. At first, the newcomers were resented by the 'traditional'

151

circus people. However, their success, their survival by replicating the family support traditions of the circus in less traditional ways, and the efforts they have made to build bridges back to the existing artists including holding the first Circus Summit in Australia in 1990, has gradually led many 'old' circus artists to welcome the development as a renaissance.

The new circus in Australia produced a fresh and irreverent homegrown style that is still recognisable in the companies that have emerged from that time. From its beginning, another characteristic feature of this new circus movement has been the strong participation of feminists. These women have had an enormous influence on the development of non-sexist humour (sometimes not without a struggle) and on the way performing roles have been allocated within the circus troupes.

The amalgamation of the small New Circus, originally from Adelaide, with the enthusiastic but less skilled Soapbox Circus in 1976 led to the creation of the now famous Circus Oz. Members of the Australian Performing Group at the Pram Factory, which supported Circus Oz in its early years, joined with members of the Captain Matchbox Whoopee Band and the Melbourne Women's Theatre Group in laying the foundations of a circus style which emphasised political commitment as well as entertainment, refused animal acts (apart from a pack of outrageously sex-starved fur-fabric 'kangaroos') and combined circus skills from Asia and Europe with rock music and a non-sexist approach to acrobatics.

Seeing Sue Broadway, Robin Laurie, Pixie Robertson, Jane Mullett and Hellen Sky, and later on younger women such as Judy Pascoe, Teresa Blake and Annie Davey, acting in traditionally 'strong male' support roles as well as being encouraged to develop their own brand of character clowning, has been an inspiration and a joy to other women now for over fifteen years.

The new circus women refused to be confined to the traditional roles of women as performers. The list of women who have made major contributions to the new Australian circus as administrators, publicists and technical crew (in some cases performing as well) is too long to include here. However, women who contributed to the design, direction and technical shaping of the performances, challenging the 'macho' technical culture as well as contributing to costume, lighting and sound design include Laurel Frank, Ponch Hawkes, Eve Glenn, Georgine Sparks, Lisa Small, Clare Gallagher and Gail Davidson. The by no means desk bound managers and administrators, as well as Robin Laurie and Sue Broadway (now artistic director of Circus Oz) have included Jenny Saunders and Elizabeth Walsh. Tanya Lester, who as a child 'Fruit Fly' enchanted audiences with her web act, is now a leading member of Brisbane's Rock 'n Roll Circus.

Members of this group helped train the bunch of country kids from

Albury who, under the auspices of the Murray River Performing Group, became the Flying Fruit Fly Circus. They helped found Australia's first secondary school devoted to circus arts; they invited and worked with Chinese acrobatic specialists; and they briefly but memorably formed Australia's first circus group run by, for and with women – the Wimmins Circus which trained and toured in 1979–80.

It was the memory of this season which led Donna Jackson, the Theatre Co-ordinator at the Footscray Community Arts Centre in Melbourne's industrial western suburbs, to propose the formation of a new Women's Circus in 1991. This Circus is a good example of the way in which the new circus movement has grown in a community context, with many organisers and most participants working on an unpaid basis.

The Women's Circus at Footscray

Donna was inspired by reading about the 1980 Wimmins Circus in *Lip*, a feminist arts magazine. Building on the experience of a theatre project with survivors of incest, 'No Frills', in which circus skills had proved a particularly fruitful working method, she set about creating a small budget, big outcome process. With the support of the staff and board members of the Community Arts Centre she lobbied private foundations and women's health and sexual assault survivors' groups for help with finance and publicity. The circus process, she argued, would allow incest survivors and other women to discover their own strength, and demonstrate ways of making feminist principles work in practice.

In an era of political gloom and economic recession, the two Women's Circus seasons in 1991 and 1992 have hit a particular spot with Melbourne audiences. The prospect of seeing more than 50 women tumbling, juggling, playing music, cracking whips, hanging from high places and balancing on narrow ledges has proved so inspiring that hundreds of eager spectators have had to be turned away over the three week seasons. Women of all ages have flocked to the workshops – there is now a substantial waiting list, and as the Circus enters its third year of operations, trainers led by chief trainer Sally Forth are dealing with the problem of supporting the integration of 'raw recruits' into a group which now contains some highly skilled members.

Word of a revival of activity in women's performance has drawn feminists and theatre workers from interstate as well, including women who'd been involved in the original Women's Theatre Group and Wimmins Circus. The Centre at Footscray runs a wide range of other programs with an emphasis on multicultural activities; while its resources have been stretched to the limit as the Circus has grown, the strongly supportive staff including Director, Elizabeth Walsh have continued to make the Circus a high priority.

What of the pressure to turn professional? Some women who have received their training in the Women's Circus have become paid trainers with other community groups, and it is possible to hire small groups of Women's Circus artists for special performances. However, the emphasis is still on the community of women in relation to their local communities, and the development of an organic feminist theatre culture, rather than on professional aspirations.

What is it that has made the circus so special? What has made such a large number of women, many lacking in either previous performing experience or a high level of physical skill, give up their time and torture their bodies over months and even years to make it happen?

The sight of a crowd of fit and alert women, proud of their bodies and of their capability, is meaningful in itself in a culture that encourages passivity and a lack of physical confidence in post-adolescent women. But it was the potential of circus on a metaphoric level, rather than simply its promise of physical challenge or spectacular entertainment, that inspired Donna Jackson and the women who flocked to join the project.

As well as building and exchanging physical skills, they have worked hard to generate a supportive and non-competitive environment. A commitment to individual challenge and democratic process is emphasised, and a feeling of participation and ownership among those involved.

The photographs taken by Vivienne Mehes show some of the sweat, strain and concentration that goes on in the workshops. The process involves twice-weekly sessions on circus and theatre skills including sound and lighting. As well as these, a music group, a mural project, and a group newsletter have been options for members. Proposals for the future include courses in engine maintenance, and ideas for extending the 'labour exchange' scheme, which allows women to contribute work rather than cash as payment for training, into a fully fledged alternative barter system.

The first season – a personal record
As an 'old' community theatre practitioner and member of the board of the Community Centre, I was privileged to attend workshops and follow the development of the first season of the Women's Circus. The following observations are based on my own notes, and on interviews with participants.

From the beginning, skill development was balanced with personal discovery and the generation of a self consciously feminist group spirit. Support groups were set up to discuss body image, sexual abuse, and other issues that might be a focus of fear for performers. There was an emphasis on practice, research and the exchange of personal experiences. These exchanges not only helped individuals deal with issues brought up in the work, but also helped the group to build a coherent set of images, worth sharing with an audience in performance, from the diverse skills and possibilities being developed in the workshops.

To survivors of earlier women's performance projects – intense and exciting, but often searingly confrontational – it was the politics of interpersonal support that most clearly marked this circus project as having been influenced by both community arts and feminist politics. Difficulties certainly arose in dealing with differences of perspective and position, and there were problems in giving as much support to each woman as the original statement of principle had offered. Differences in ability and skill level, and issues of emotional security as well as physical safety, were highlighted during the rehearsal period. In the absence of Sally Forth, one woman ended up in hospital with a cracked sacrum as a result of rushed preparations for a pre-season publicity event.

There was, however, a consistent emphasis on process as a matter of both individual and group responsibility. Each woman was given a job description on entry to the project. The first item – to have fun! – was followed by guidelines on consistency, punctuality, conflict resolution and safety. Respect for your own and others' bodies – Sally mentioned the need to 'maintain a healthy fear of the various skills' – was balanced by the recognition that conflict, while 'natural and healthy' required resolution. Each woman was asked to keep a circus book, to contribute to the group circus journal and newsletter if she wished, and, if necessary, to negotiate a work exchange agreement in lieu of payment for training.

The foundation of energy, enjoyment and mutual appreciation, and the enormous growth in confidence and expressive capacity that took place over the workshop period, were very much in evidence. The workshops concentrated on traditional circus skills such as tumbling, tightwire, juggling and trapeze, together with abseiling, whip cracking, and manipulative routines borrowed from Chinese and Maori traditions. They also drew extensively on Donna's repertoire of developmental theatre techniques such as trust games, exchanging stories and drawing together a symbolic vocabulary and an expressionist metanarrative that would link individual experience into a political statement told in time, space and motion. The structure of the final performance was generated as an organic part of the workshop process.

The workshop plan forecast a series of 'thresholds' over the six months of preparation where the focus – and incidentally both the elation and the pressure of performance – would become more intense. After a series of exploratory workshops, women were expected to specialise in two areas and develop a level of expertise in both. A further period was spent in developmental rehearsals to integrate the storyline, music and circus skills. Then followed seven weeks of intensive rehearsal which included preview performances by various subgroups. Consultative process moved into decision-making here, and all decisions became final. A tech week was followed by three weeks of performances, and then it was all over.

These 'thresholds' are familiar to anyone who has been through a developmental performance process. Both physical and psychological barriers would present each woman with particular difficulties and challenges. A sample of their written and verbal reactions: 'I've made a breakthrough on forward rolls, just when I was ready to pack up and leave.' 'This is nearly impossible.' 'She's so much better than me.' 'I feel isolated.' 'I have to stop imagining my teeth hitting the concrete.' 'It was terrifying.' 'I really had to trust that I would survive.' 'I feel so amazingly strong.' 'The excruciating pins and needles of dammed-up emotion often seem unbearable.' 'I'm being ignored.' 'It's all going too fast now, I can't work out what's going on.'

As the work progressed, women were encouraged to form smaller work and support groups in order to facilitate communication and assistance, and to maintain energy and a sense of humour. Routines developed by the groups were polished and integrated with larger set pieces choreographed from scratch. This complexity of invention and the interrelationships it produced became a strong feature of the final production. From the moment the audience began to walk along the riverbank towards the stage area, the many levels of the picnic ground, turned amphitheatre, came alive with one small event after another. Rather than a traditional sequence with one trick or routine at a time occupying centre stage, this circus' story was told with images flowing into, supplementing and supplanting each other. The small group combinations effectively used and transformed the large performance space, creating an emotional and theatrical richness of texture difficult to achieve with more conventional external or hierarchical production methods.

The sweat of the workshops produced, in performance, a story about institutions. How women are confined by institutions. How all too often we betray one another. How, in slow and frequently painful ways, we can begin to recognise our mutual strength. How we can even transform rebellion against the institution from a frightening undertaking into a powerful and joyful activity.

The future?

The second season, in 1992, was based around the theme of women and work. Traditional images of women washing, sweeping and scrubbing merged into a strong political satire on economic rationalism, made especially pointed by the fact that the season coincided with the election of a conservative State government with a harsh industrial relations policy. New skills including juggling with fire, a posse of roller-blading 'police' and a finale featuring spectacular spinning ladders contributed to the conviction that the audience was witnessing the growth of a truly original, creative and exciting example of women's culture, as well as a real contribution to a new performance form in its own right. As I write, training is beginning for the third season!

The Women's Circus offers us a rare opportunity to see a different kind of human institution develop: a group of women working together, 'leaping off the edge'.

Sue Edmonds

ON THE BAND WAGON

> I know I can make it now,
> give me a song and I'll sing it in tune.
> I know I can take it now,
> there's not a goddam thing I have to prove . . .
> to be a woman
>
> Judy Small, 1976[1]

Music is a great mixer. It combines well with a dinner, it's essential for a dance and can make or break a march or rally. It charts the passions and preoccupations of a community and there's been plenty of that in the last 20 years in the Australian women's movement. As the Refuges, Women's Health and Rape Crisis Centres and other services emerged in the mid-1970s, women gathered at conferences and events, and of course they needed to be entertained.

Robyn Archer set a cracking pace when she released *Ladies' Choice* in 1977.[2] The Broadcasting Control Board assisted the album's promotion by banning 'Menstruation Blues' from the air waves. Things were hot in Australia in the 70s; women's issues were clearly on the public agenda and there was plenty to sing about. Singer/songwriters, bands and street theatre groups appeared everywhere, in backyards and community halls, shopping centres and lounge rooms, women performed to each other with fun and flair. They ate fire, juggled on stilts, sang songs, wrote plays and sketches developing an emerging culture and consciousness.

I was living in Hobart, Tasmania, isolated from the action by Bass Strait and airfares. Travellers would arrive on 'The Apple Isle' with stories of groups with names like 'Shameless Hussies', 'Lavender Blues', 'Clitoris' and 'Furious Chicken' and shows like *The Redheads Revenge.*

In Hobart we talked the politics of the day, housework, education, domestic violence and abortion, and tried to keep up with the action on the mainland. The national newspapers, Rouge and Mabel kept us in touch as we sat out the winter, autumn and spring by the fire.

> It was so cold I nearly got married, so cold I nearly got wed,
> seemed a lot better than freezing in my bed.
> Just when I thought I'd have to do it, I realised I'd rue it
> so I bought a hot water bottle instead.
>
> – Lian Tanner[3]

Women's music made its way into our lives when the Hobart Women's Centre came under direct attack from 'Right to Lifers'. They rallied against

158

our right to discuss abortion and 150 of their passionate supporters crushed into our little premises to stack a meeting. We had prior warning and had one night to stack the agenda. Women's music became item three and abortion was relegated to item eight. That night we managed to silence 150 antagonists with a ukulele, six voices and four bastardised folk songs.

'The Ovarian Sisters' were born and for the next five years we sang anywhere and everywhere. We took lessons in guitar, banjo and how to remember words and gave up going to so many collective meetings. After two years of playing to supportive audiences at political rallies and celebrations, the Ovarian Sisters had an original repertoire as Lian and I wrote songs like it was going out of business.

We expanded into the realm of concerts, doing magic tricks from books and home-made sketches to break up the torrent of songs. The various children of the 'Oves' sold tickets and pulled the curtains. Our chance of cracking the 'Mainland' stage came when a slush fund called 'Girlenes Giveaways' allocated the necessary thousands of dollars, with no questions asked. The Ovarian Sisters recorded 'Beat Your Breasts' in record time.

We parked the kids with hippy friends on Bruny Island, a spot more remote even than Hobart, and moved into the only commercial studio in town. An album was a rare event in the late 70s and we were particularly fortunate to come across 'funny money'. It meant a bit of air-play on the radio, mostly on the community FM stations, and a profile beyond Tasmania.

In current terms, the Ovarian Sisters were a big band. We had six members playing guitar, banjo, mandolin, bass and violin plus as many voices as available microphones. It required a massive organisational feat for us to tour. There were kids, chooks, cats and a few jobs to consider as well as airfares, accommodation and venues, all on a shoe-string budget. We had two major tours, each a week long, in Melbourne and Sydney, where we cross-pollinated with other performers and strutted our stuff on larger stages.

The concerts were becoming more ambitious. Fabulous posters, varied programmes, lights, sound, the works. During 1982, Women's Arts festivals were held in most major cities. In Tasmania, we decided to concentrate on an operetta by bastardising a Gilbert and Sullivan. A cast and crew of twenty set to and devised a collaborative piece with a confidence and style unheard of ten years previously. Women's culture was on the march.

Artists started to travel. Judy Small recorded her first of five albums in 1982, other groups recorded tapes and performed far afield and their profiles edged out of the lounge-rooms to a wider audience. Judy has gone on to become one of Australia's foremost singer/songwriters and has built a successful career with massive touring and recording. She recorded an Ovarian Sisters smash hit, 'The IPD' (Intra-Penile Device)[4] and Lian and I still get an occasional royalty cheque.

In 1983 I moved to Wollongong, an hour and a half south of Sydney, with my kids. We started our migration to NSW in the Gross Valley, 70 km west at the foot of the Blue Mountains. My plan was for Cris and Meg to do their schooling by correspondence while I sat on the verandah and learnt the guitar from a book. Possums stole our food in broad daylight, insects covered the mahjong board at night. It was 40 degrees in the shade and, with no power or water on at the old farm house, we survived by lying in the river or driving to the air-conditioned library. A friend offered to take Cris and Meg to the South Coast while I recuperated in Sydney for a weekend. The drive to Wollongong was enough to convince me that we should move. As well as being a steel city dominated by BHP,[5] Wollongong has beautiful beaches, a dramatic escarpment as a backdrop and is within a quick train ride of Sydney. And we could live in a house with fly-wire screens and a frig. Next day we moved.

The major arts funding body, The Australia Council, has a policy of assisting development of work-place artistic expression and it was with such a grant that I became the musician-in-residence of the South Coast Labour Council, the combined unions of the region, for a year in 1986. One of my briefs was to write topical songs and among many issues, I chose the case of the thirty-four women from eight ethnic backgrounds who took BHP to court on a charge of discrimination, and won, after eight years.

> There's tales about the heroes who faced the giant's wrath,
> stories 'bout the heroines forced to spin gold cloth.
> Jack and the beanstalk, Rumplestiltskin the dwarf,
> now the women from Wollongong have met that giant's force.
>> The giant's made of iron and steel,
>> didn't feel a thing.
>> The women worked together,
>> now the giant feels their sting.
>> Sue Edmonds, 1986
>> *When the Whistle Blows Songbook*

Another of my activities during that year was to build a large Sound Sculpture off a wall of a factory in the Steelworks. That project led to Carribean Steel Drums a few years later which, in turn, has led to the Hubaphone in 1992, an instrument made of tuned hub caps, played like a glockenspiel or xylophone with a sound somewhere between a gamelan and a steel drum.

The women's community of Lismore hosted the first national women's music festival in 1985 and the long weekend in October became an annual event for eight years, held once at Moruya on the far south coast, once in

Wollongong, ['It had to happen somewhere Festival'] and regularly in Lismore, the tropics for us southerners. Festie-goers would usually camp in caravan parks or in backyards and it was always perfect weather. Women's Music Festivals and good weather, as well as a good time, were synonymous.

'Mixed Bag',[6] a two-woman band of Lioba and myself, travelled to all the festivals and as many other events we could possibly organise. We could go to Canberra and Melbourne by car for a long weekend and be back home in time for other regular work. We lashed out and got sleepers on the train to Brisbane or Lismore. Or we could dash up to Newcastle overnight for a job. Along the way we would come across other women doing similar things. Betty Little, a Koori singer/songwriter was often on the same trail, and we developed firm friendships and networks of performers and promoters.

The National Women's Music Network started in 1990[7] and now it's possible to buy, mail order, tapes and CDs of innumerable women artists. These enterprising women have also started a quarterly magazine about current events in the women's music scene. Out Loud is available in the feminist bookshops in the major cities or through the post. The bookshops are usually a good way of finding out what's on in town at any one time. Amongst the regular big celebrations are International Women's Day, March 8; the Gay and Lesbian Festival happens in Sydney every February; the Lesbian Festival moves each 18 months; in 1993 it's across the Nullabor in Perth.

Women's music is an area of constant change. Groups come and go after a few years but you can be sure that there will be something on the boil. A capella has taken off in the last few years and there are some stunning groups. 'Arremmieda', originally from Tasmania; 'Tiddas' a Koori group, and 'Crying in Public Places' from Melbourne; 'Blindman's Holiday', and 'The Lesbian Choir' in Sydney; 'Hammer and Tongues' in Perth, are amongst the many.

The Lesbian Festival held in Sydney in 1991 showed clearly how far we have come in such a short time. The finale of the festival was held at the Opera House, where 2500 women celebrated as Robyn Archer, Judy Small, choirs and dance groups, opera singers and musicians combined forces for a spectacular night. I had the privilege of compering the show and as I walked out to the microphone the electricity in the air was tangible. I said 'Good evening' and the roof came off.

In my years of messing around with musical instruments and words I've become enchanted with its travel aspect, so this year I'm off . . . have hubaphone, will travel! Equipped with Vera Volvo 1977, (big boot full of camping equipment and musical instruments and a heart like an amazon) I'll drive and busk in Wagga, Mildura and Adelaide, then Vera and I will load on to a train and head for the desert and Alice Springs for a look around. I think the hubaphone will sound amazing in all that space. It's a far cry from a lounge room in Hobart.

> Boobtitty, boobtitty, boobtitty, boobtitty,
> Boobtitty, boobtitty, boobtitty, boobtitty,
> Boobtitty, boobtitty, boobtitty, boobtitty,
> Boobtitty, boobtitty, boobtitty, boob,
> Beat your breasts.

> Long tits, short tits, even wrinkly wart tits,
> Low tits, high tits, reach up to the sky tits,
> Sweet tits, sour tits, get 'em any flavour tits,
> to semaphore your neighbour with the minimum of labour
> Stick 'em out, thrust them forth,
> Beat your breasts
> > Sue Edmonds and Janet Planet, 1979[8]

Notes

1. Judy Small. 1976. 'To Be A Woman.' Recorded on *A Natural Selection*. 1982. Crafty Maid Records CMM001. © Copyright 1990. Larrikin Music Publishing. Reprinted with permission.
2. Robyn Archer. 1973. 'The Menstruation Blues.' Recorded on *Take Your Partners for . . . The Ladies' Choice*. Larrikin Records. 1978. LRF023.
3. Lian Tanner. 1979. 'It Was So Cold.' Recorded on *Women's Business*. Mixed Bag. 1990. © Copyright 1990. Reprinted with permission.
4. Lian Tanner and Sue Edmonds. 1979. 'IPD.' First recorded on *Beat Your Breasts*. Candle Recordings. 1980. © Copyright 1979. CFPS104.
5. BHP is one of Australia's largest companies, involved in mining and steel-making.
6. Mixed Bag comprised of Lioba Rist, guitar, trumpet, recorder, piano, vocals and Sue Edmonds, guitar, banjo, charango, ukulele, vocals. Recordings: Red and Rough, Wollongong lounge room. 1987. Women's Business. 1990.
7. National Women's Music Network. PO Box 535, Eltham, Victoria 3095. Mail order service. Publishers of *Out Loud*. First issue, June 1992.
8. Sue Edmonds and Janet Planet. 1980. 'Beat Your Breasts.' (Written when marooned on Bruny Island waiting for a ferry.) © Copyright 1980. Potential anthem.

Catherine Ellis and Judith Martyn-Ellis
The Sung World of Aboriginal and Islander Women

The vast regions of the centre of Australia are harsh and forbidding, and have rejected many white people who have attempted to settle there. Imposition of the consumer lifestyle and primarily European agricultural techniques generally have been unsuccessful and destructive of the fragile Australian ecosystems, and, as is slowly being understood, knowledge and maintenance of the balanced indigenous wildlife is vital to survival within Australia.

Aboriginal people have extensive knowledge, maintained over thousands of years, on healthy survival in these environmental conditions. It is directly associated with Aboriginal song traditions, and perhaps because of this has rarely been recognised by white people. Thus, travellers unacquainted with this country who become stranded in a remote area may die of thirst while waiting to be found by searchers; yet, if it were accessible to them, a local song could well contain all the necessary information for finding drinking water and food close by. In the absence of this knowledge, the land seems to have little to offer those who are alien to it.

The remaining traditional inhabitants in the north of South Australia are not as knowledgeable now as they were even thirty years ago when our family (Catherine and husband Max, both researchers, with two, and later three, children) first started visiting them to record their songs. Despite this loss, their knowledge is still extensive and important. It portrays a country that is loved by those who are its custodians, and who must regularly sing its health.

Although the desert areas form an enormous swathe of the Australian landscape, there are also coastal and island localities with traditional performers still preserving their customs. For the most part, however, these are the places of greatest white contact have experienced sweeping cultural changes.

Every tree, rocky outcrop, unusual ground surface, water reservoir, hill, creek or river is known to have been made by the Ancestors at the beginning of time, in the Creation Era. They left both diaries and maps of their creation journeys in the form of songs that they taught to their own offspring, and the latter to their children in perpetuity to the present time. These songs have often been claimed as the property of present generations of men, yet women have played an important part in conjunction with men, and as well they have an active musical tradition of their own.

Aboriginal music is primarily vocal, and (according to the performers) songs have been transmitted without change since their composition by the Ancestors at the beginning of time, the Dreamtime. The Ancestors are

163

the fountain of all life – human, animal and plant – as well as the creators of all landforms, and their songs, when performed in the present, tap the life forces of the Dreamtime. They have the power to maintain, heal and regenerate all life forms associated with the specific Ancestor. Aboriginal people are thus the custodians of the Australian landscape and of all its inhabitants, which are maintained through the correct presentation of their songs of power.

The term 'business' is often used by performers to describe the most important of their songs, indicating that singing is not an idle pastime, but an important action which can change the given world either economically, politically, physically, or spiritually. 'Business' refers to the Laws of the land, and these are all encapsulated within the song tradition.

Women's 'business' is usually performed away from the main living area, at a site out of ear-shot from it. It is often in an important food-gathering area and the women arrive at the ceremonial ground with food which they have collected along the way. Once on the ceremonial ground they divide into two contiguous groups sitting in a semi-circle around a fire lit in the middle of a cleared area. They commence singing and beating their thighs in a metronomic pulse, with the most senior woman, the song owner, leading the performance. After some preliminary singing and dancing, some of the women from the side of the song leader go away to an obscured area at some distance from the singers and paint their bodies. Both the singers and the dancers must sing during the painting of the body designs. When these are completed, the two dancers involved in the next item in the song series move towards the dancing area with their designs covered. As the song leader commences the appropriate song these dancers reveal their body designs simultaneously with commencing to dance towards the singing group. Whenever the singers pause for a break, the dancers turn their backs to again obscure the design, turning when the singing recommences; and when they finally reach the singers, who then stop singing, they obliterate the design from their bodies. Senior women come forward and touch the dancers to earth the great power that has been released through them during their performance.

A women's ceremony may last for up to five days, with the women returning home each evening and coming back to the ceremonial ground each morning. The songs depict the journey of a particular Ancestor through the singers' country, and each item, of about thirty seconds duration (which is repeated many times) describes one place or event along the route. Dancing songs last longer than descriptive songs (perhaps up to four minutes with pauses within this time). The whole ceremony moves through the song series gradually, with many repetitions and pauses for informal chatter and laughter. The song leader, any time she feels that the group is losing concentration, reiterates the present song. In

164

this way, a song needed for a particular body design, for instance, can be kept active over a period of one or two hours if necessary.

The only musical instrument throughout Australia which is reported to have been used by women is a bundle of skin used as a percussive accompaniment by being beaten on the ground. It is rarely used and only in scattered locations. The didjeridu, which is unique to the north of the country, is a male instrument.

Senior tribal men, who have traditionally held authority over the most powerful songs, have been displaced by the changes that Europeanisation has caused, and they often lack the motivation to solve the challenges that survival in the modern world entails. Women, on the other hand, have been strengthened by new contact. Traditionally they adapted to shifts to new country if that was necessary when they married, and an important part of their learning included encompassing new sacred sites into their old song-knowledge. They could incorporate new ideas without losing their own sense of identity.

In the 1990s women throughout Australia are taking on the role of custodians of the ancient song-maps, known as 'big songs' or 'history songs' of the Ancestors, as well as passing on the songs known by some as 'little histories', which have been personally composed by human beings within the much narrower time-scale of remembered human experience.

An example of the flexibility of modern women's thinking, showing this preparedness to embrace new ideas, is the recently formed Ernabella media association known as PY Media. The women at Ernabella have taken a new approach to the education of their children, videoing representations of their sacred ceremonies and the accompanying stories in their appropriate settings 'for our children's culture' (as stated in *Mount Connor Video*, PY Media). In this way the women are adapting to their changing situations, where there is marked reluctance among young people to learn the old songs, and they are protecting for posterity what remains of their traditions.

As a result of their culturally inherent adaptability, the roles of Aboriginal women have been maintained much better than those of their menfolk in the course of transition from the traditional, hunter-gatherer life, to contemporary urban Europeanised situations. Traditional roles such as food-gathering (seeds, fruits, edible plants, reptiles, small marsupials, fish etc.) and as carers of the children have been transplanted into the lifestyle of the city-dwelling Aboriginal family. Contemporary Aboriginal women remain the mainstay of food supply and familial support, particularly attempting to combat the destructive forces of alcoholism in their men, largely caused by the de-personalisation created by their low status in our society.

Music is integral to all traditional societal roles, and in many areas the most knowledgeable person, the senior leader, is selected for that status because he or she is the person knowing most songs. This is an aspect of urban living in which men are reasserting their individuality, especially within rock music.

Women's role as community healers has had a much less successful transmission into contemporary culture than have their other roles, as the practice has been so denigrated by European-based Australian culture, but it is still sometimes used in the urban setting. However, their constant task of dealing with the disempowerment of their men and prejudice against their children can be seen as an adaptation of the process of healing. Older women traditionally taught their grand-daughters through the use of song; this process is tending to degenerate as a result of the overwhelming influence of rock and other popular musics on young people, even in remote areas. Added to this is the white tendency to isolate the elderly from the young, through both the use of Old People's Homes, and the necessity in rural areas for many children to board in the city to undertake their compulsory white education.

Aboriginal women are starting to take an active role in the socio-political framework of Australia, and have thus begun to overcome the sexism inherent in European values to re-access their lost traditional political status. The Borroloola women from Northern Australia, quoted in Fay Gale's *We Are Bosses Ourselves*, say:

White men come here now and having all the business and we can't listen and [Aboriginal] men listen then and they won't tell us, and even they won't speak up right, speak up to the white man what he say . . . Maybe if woman may be sitting in the front of the people maybe we could speak too. We can ask questions too.[1]

Nganyintja, a Pitjantjatjara woman from Central Australia, in discussing Land-rights claims, quoted in the same paper, states:

We have always spoken up strongly at men's meetings that we want to have meetings with the men and together, speak out for our land rights. But they have always told us to go because the men's sacred stories would be discussed and it would frighten us.[2]

As well as these traditionally based women, there are many urban and city-dwelling Aboriginal women voicing their discontent through their active political work, and also through media such as the creative arts.

In the localities in which traditional music and the related ceremonies are still practised, there has been strong emphasis amongst researchers on documenting the last surviving fragments of a great tradition which spanned possibly more than 40,000 years and crumbled in the space of the two centuries after white invasion. Initially, researchers were almost all male, and their findings created a severe imbalance in the general perception of gender roles and status within the culture. An increase in the number of women researchers working in the field since the 1960s has uncovered a core of musical, spiritual and practical information which was unknown to the researchers from the previously male-dominated fields of ethno-musicology and anthropology.

All these early and more recent collections are housed in the Australian Institute of Aboriginal and Torres Strait Islander Studies (AIATSIS) in Canberra, where they can be studied by non-fieldworkers. There are special prohibitions placed on access to secret information, to protect the rights of the performers.

Due to the latent power in the ancient 'history songs' of the Aboriginal people, strict controls are enforced by the performers on admission to and knowledge of the powerful songs, and an intensive process of initiation ensures that only the oldest and most knowledgeable people may participate or be present at the performance of them. There are three broad access-levels to the song repertoire of Central Australia: open access, closed access to all but mature members of one sex, and closed access to all but a few knowledgeable senior song people. Open versions are available to the entire community, and are used to reinforce cultural values and teach the youngsters their ancestral history and tribal laws. Access to closed performances which are often erotic in nature is limited by gender and a certain level of initiation (for women, this is often to have borne two children); and access to closed esoteric performances, including the most powerful songs, is for only the most knowledgeable older people of one gender. Both men and women have secret ceremonies of great power, and the one ancestral songline/map may occur as an open ceremony, a closed women's ceremony and a closed men's ceremony, with certain omissions or additions depending on which of these contextual settings is being used in the performance.

Despite statements to the contrary, it is common for the wisest women to be knowledgeable about the men's secret ceremonies, although they must never admit publicly to this knowledge; and men likewise can have a detailed understanding of women's song. Interaction occurs between the sexes in some of the powerful repertoire, though rarely on an equal basis: women are permitted to participate to a limited extent in certain parts of some of the men's ceremonies, and men though generally excluded from any form of participation in women's ceremonies can take part in the introductory singing or the open versions of some women's songs. Social and political status can be gained by both men and women through ownership and extensive knowledge of ceremonies.

Traditional women's music functions on several levels, related to the specific function of the performance. Thus, songs for teaching children are particular 'open' ones; through them the children are taught correct behaviour and history, and a store of information on such things as the localities of specific foods, permanent water supplies, etc. Some of these are passed on to the younger females as part of their education. The 'closed/ erotic' ceremonies contain often explicit erotic information concerning the experiences on the original journeys of the Ancestor, and these can be used to teach adolescent girls how to behave correctly as sexually active members of their community. Another function of women's ceremonies at this level is 'love-magic', which can be used to ensnare a particular male, and men stand in considerable awe of this and other psychic capacities of the women. The 'closed/esoteric', 'big' or powerful ceremonies, function for the healing not only of the land and animals, but of specific ailments of individuals, such as a particular illness, injury or a difficult birth.

The women's closed ceremonies are less strictly formal than the men's closed ceremonies, as children may be present at all except the most powerful ones. Thus, uninitiates are permitted to attend, though generally not participate, but are excluded from the 'correct' explanation of the ceremonial story, being given instead a 'false front' explanation. The open community-based ceremonies are also considered 'false-fronts', because the real ancestral information is never disclosed, and cannot be discovered from the sung form of the Ancestor's history.

These 'false fronts' will, in time, be transcended by the maturing musician, to reveal new perspectives on the ambiguities embodied in both the story and song structures. These new levels will eventually also be 'turned over' to reveal deeper understanding and progressively increased secret information at each more advanced level. The 'false fronts' can be seen as paradoxical when eventually they can be compared with the real information embodied in secret song and ceremony. Thus continues the process of education through many different forms of initiation to the pinnacle of the social, political and intellectual hierarchy.

As the traditional function of both men's and women's music was to ensure the health and preservation of both the human and non-human world, including the land in which the necessary power was embedded, the issues of access to land and land-rights impact greatly on the capacity for Aboriginal people to re-negotiate their ritual roles in an urban or rural setting. Removal of land ownership has robbed Aboriginal people of their traditional and fundamental role as caretakers and protectors of the fragile Australian environment, and the extinction of many of the native fauna and flora (being totemic relations to the original inhabitants of that locality) has resulted in a sense of guilt and hopelessness which dramatically affects their capacity to survive in the world at large. Where people have had large tracts of land returned to them, the regeneration of both the land and its inhabitants is remarkable.

There are pockets of lifestyle as described above still occurring throughout the more remote areas of Central and Western Australia and in some parts of northern Australia. In these, certain elements of the culture and gender roles are maintained in traditional form. The impact of Western culture, however, has been extensive and often violent, leaving no domain of traditional life unaffected.

In response to this cultural devastation, Aboriginal women's contemporary popular music is a rapidly growing industry, embracing a whole range of styles and backgrounds from country, gospel and blues to funk, jazz and rap. Although differing in aspects of performance and musical elements, contemporary Aboriginal women's music maintains a bond with traditional culture in expressions of identity and the roles and functions of the music. These women are consciously attempting to raise their profile and fight for space in the soundscape of contemporary music.[3]

The role of Aboriginal women in contemporary music varies from case to case, with many implied as well as articulated functions in both single-sex and mixed performance situations. Rock music, as seen elsewhere throughout the world, is a largely male-dominated idiom, which women musicians are tending to avoid. Instances can be recounted, however, in which women have been used in the Aboriginal male rock bands, such as Yothu Yindi: a female singer requested by the white director of their video-clip for the award-winning song *Treaty*, wanted for her visual impact.[4] The reverse of this is also true, with Aboriginal rock bands like No Fixed Address using competent female and male musicians on an equal basis (see, for instance, their film *The Wrong Side of the Road*).

The Centre for Aboriginal Studies in Music (CASM), at the University of Adelaide, is an institution for the teaching and integration of both traditional Aboriginal music and contemporary idioms, for both Aboriginal and non-Aboriginal students. Staff and students work on an equal basis, regardless of gender, to create works such as *Indulkana Suite* and *Urban Corroboree*, which fuse the different musics, and use both contemporary and traditional performers. Equally, the Aboriginal and Islander Dance Theatre, in Sydney, uses contemporary and traditional dance techniques in newly created performances which express the Aboriginality of the male and female performers.

There is, however, a growing number of female contemporary musicians who are functioning independently, as solo artists or in all-women groups. Many of these groups have a political message, combating both sexism and racism, but these groups are also formed for the sheer pleasure of making music with other women, a process taken directly from traditional performance practice.

For some years now the Sing Loud, Play Strong festival of contemporary Aboriginal music, has been held annually, but it was only in 1992 that Aboriginal women's music was recognised as an important medium in its own right. The inaugural National Aboriginal and Torres Strait Islander Women's Music Festival, held in Sydney, provided the platform for Aboriginal women to combine forces on a national level and let their voices be heard. The festival was designed for indigenous women only and musicians travelled from all over Australia to attend. Performers included the Mills Sisters from Thursday Island, the Seven Sisters (taking their name from a traditional women's ceremony) from Adelaide, and Ruby Hunter from Melbourne, to name but a few.

In European-based cultures little attention is paid to the social functions of music, and this greatly hampers our understanding of the many differing perspectives on life found in the multicultural society which now constitutes the Australian community. Aboriginal women have, for many centuries, used the spiritual, emotional, physical and political properties of music to love, heal, fight, and communicate, and this process is continuing today, despite their vastly changed circumstances in the often cruel and prejudiced world they now inhabit.

Notes

1. Gale, Fay (ed.) 1983. *We are Bosses Ourselves: The Status and Role of Aboriginal Women Today.* Canberra: Australian Institute of Aboriginal Studies.
2. ibid.
3. Mackinlay, E. 1992. *Urban Aboriginal Women's Dreaming: an examination of the significance of the Dreaming for urban Aboriginal women and their music at the Centre for Aboriginal Studies in Music.* Unpublished B.Mus Honours Thesis, The University of Adelaide.
4. Hayward, Philip. 1993. Safe, Exotic and Somewhere Else. *Perfect Beat: The Journal of Research into Contemporary Music and Popular Culture, Sound Alliances.* Vol.1, No.2, January.

Sources for Further Information
Aboriginal performers, both male and female, will have entries in the forthcoming Encyclopaedia of Aboriginal Australia, being produced by AIATSIS. Information concerning contemporary Aboriginal musicians can also be found in *Our Place Our Music* edited by Marcus Breen. Discussion of both Central Australian and urban music can be found in *Aboriginal Music: Education for Living* by Catherine Ellis.

There are many indigenous media associations and performing-arts bodies throughout Australia, of which the following lists show just a few. For further information on any Aboriginal group contact the Aboriginal Cultural Centre or Land Council in the area of your specific interest.

Media Associations
- Central Australian Aboriginal Media Association (CAAMA, and 8-KIN Radio), Alice Springs, NT.
- Brisbane Indigenous Media Association, Qld.
- Townsville Aboriginal and Islander Media Association, Qld.
- Umeewarra Aboriginal Media Association, Port Augusta, SA.
- Western Australian Aboriginal Media Association (WAAMA), Perth, WA.
- Warlpiri Media, Yuendemu, NT.
- Broome Aboriginal Media Association, WA.
- PY Media (EVTV), Ernabella, SA.

Performing Arts Bodies
- Centre for Aboriginal Studies in Music (CASM), The University of Adelaide, Adelaide, SA.
- Ab. Music, Perth, WA.
- Aboriginal and Torres Strait Islander Dance Theatre, Sydney, NSW.
- Tjapukai Dance Theatre, Kuranda, Qld.

Additional Sources
Breen, Marcus (ed.) 1989. *Our Place Our Music; Aboriginal Music: Australian Popular Music in Perspective Volume 2.* Canberra: Aboriginal Studies Press.
Ellis, Catherine J. 1985. *Aboriginal Music: Education for Living.* St Lucia: University of Queensland Press; reprinted in paperback 1989 and 1993.
Mt Connor Video. 1990. Ernabella: PY Media.

Sally Macarthur
WOMEN COMPOSERS HAVE GOT AUSTRALIA COVERED

Within the last five of years or so, there has been a noticeable shift in attitude towards women composers in Australia. It is now much more widely acknowledged than ever before that women *do* write music. The current policy of the Performing Arts Board of the Australia Council positively discriminates in women's favour, ensuring that they receive an appropriate level of funding. But this has not always been the case.

In 1948, Margaret Sutherland (1897–1984), latterly lauded as the doyen of Australian composers, submitted her Concerto for string orchestra to the music publishing firm, Boosey and Hawkes, inscribing it, 'M. Sutherland'. It was rejected when it was found out that she was a woman. She responded '. . . the world at large thinks that a woman cannot be creative. A woman can contribute in a special way. I don't think that women want to write the same type of things as men, but their contribution is no less important.'[1]

Moya Henderson (b. 1941), on the other hand, is a regular voice on the radio, advocating equal opportunities with her male opposites. Like Sutherland, Henderson is aware that her music might be different. In 1991, she asked, '. . . does my being a woman, and consequently different in culture as much as gender, give idiosyncratic qualities to my work?' Answering her own question, she replied, 'We hardly know what we are talking about here. Western art music has been men's music for so long. It may take many years before women are able to exploit the richness of their difference; or, maybe that is already happening and only the recognition of it is lacking.'[2]

An indicator of a raising of consciousness *vis-à-vis* discrimination and a growing solidarity among women composers, was the formation in October 1990 of the Australian Women Composers Network with an ultimate aim of making itself redundant. A loose affiliation of people (not just composers and not just women) linking themselves by fax, phone and personal computer, the Network was set up to address the general under-representation of women composers. In the dispassionate language of statistics, the iniquities were (and are) pretty stark. The *Directory of Australian Composers* published in 1988 by the Australian Music Centre lists 23 women composers and while there has been a slight increase since then, the proportion seems to hover around the 15 per cent mark of the Australian composer total.

During the 1988 Australian bicentennial celebrations, not one woman received a Federal Bicentenary commission. This, despite the fact there were some 40 opportunities from the Bicentenary. In 1990, however, the real crunch came for the women of Australian music when the Australian Broadcasting Corporation (ABC) sponsored the Brisbane Musica Nova Festival for new music composition and performance and not one Australian woman was invited to participate as a commissioned composer. It was incongruous that Sophia Gubaidulinah from Russia had been invited as a special guest composer from overseas. What must she have thought when she heard not a note from her female colleagues from 'down-under'?

In a concentrated networking effort, the Australian Women Composers Network (AWCN) targeted the ABC's Concert Music Department as first port of call, writing letters to important people from within the organisation, holding interviews on national radio programs, participating in public forums and publishing articles in the press and other music journals. Although an Equal Opportunity Employer, the ABC's response to the question of why Australian women were not offered orchestral commissions was: 'Australian women are not commissioned by Musica Nova because none of them are writing orchestral music. The ABC's criteria when awarding commissions are primarily to do with talent. We would be doing a disservice to ourselves and to the cause of contemporary music if we operated under some crude equality rule.'[3]

As the composer, Mary Mageau, concluded from this statement: 'Australian women composers must be a sorry and untalented lot who carry some inherited gender-specific inability to structure works of large scope for major forces.'[4]

Now, the facts should speak for themselves. There is an immensely rich tradition of musical composition in all the represented genres and styles associated exclusively with the names of women in Australia. Contrary to the myth which is still being perpetuated by the ABC – which controls all six symphony orchestras based in each of the capital cities (excluding Canberra and Darwin) – women composers have accepted overseas residencies, are recognised as performers, teachers and lecturers, and are continuing to be performed, published and recorded outside Australia. As Mary Mageau points out in her landmark article about the AWCN, women composers in Australia also do well when it comes to receiving funding (grants and fellowships) from the Performing Arts Board of the Australia Council. She also notes that music written by Australian women has generally received its portion of broadcast time allotted to 'Australian content' on the ABC and listener-supported public radio stations.

In the early history of 'art-music' composition in Australia (not begun until the late 1800s), there was an attitude of amazement from the Australian community towards anyone who had the temerity to call themselves a 'composer'. Melbourne-based musicologist, Thérèse Radic writes, 'Australian composers were very rare birds indeed. On the few occasions when one was spotted, its colonial status embarrassed listeners. Worse, since British music was considered vastly inferior to the German or even the Italian models, the unfortunate Australian composer was left in a crippling double cringe. In that environment a woman composer was as puzzling and as miraculous as a heat mirage in the desert.'[5]

Radic and others have, over the last decade, begun to discover and describe the music of some of these early women composers. When the English composer, Marshall Hall, was appointed the first professor of music at The University of Melbourne, he apparently saw no reason why his many female students should not be trained in musical composition. Indeed, Margaret Sutherland was one of his students. But there were two other women worthy of mention: Mona McBurney (1862–1932) and Florence Ewart (1864–1949). Radic says that their achievements were quite remarkable. McBurney's opera, *The Dalmations*, first produced in 1910, won second place in a Ricordi competition for an English opera. Ewart, while composing some five operas, managed to get a concert performance for one of these, the *Courtship of Miles Standish*, in 1931. Both women, says Radic, found many performance outlets for their numerous smaller works and the only stigma from which they suffered, like their male colleagues, was from that of colonialism, not from sexual discrimination.[6] This older generation of Australian women composers, whose forgotten manuscripts turned up in the Grainger Museum in Melbourne, is an important reminder of those early times which must have been crucial for laying down the foundations for those who came after them, those who by the 60s were beginning to mark out vastly different musical styles from their inherited colonial models.

Unlike America, Australia did not inherit the intellectual cream of Europe during the inter-War years. Vincent Plush[7] maintains that the fashionable Stravinsky versus Schoenberg debate passed Australia by and that Margaret Sutherland, who took lessons in Paris in the 1920s, 'came home with her Stravinskian music, endured official ridicule and sought refuge in the first duty of Australian womanhood, the family.'[8] But this is only one version, and rather glib at that, of what happened. With her contemporary, Mirrie Hill (1892–1986), wife of the so-called 'Father of Australian Music', Alfred Hill (1870–1960), Sutherland forged a voice for women composers and for Australian music in general. Indeed, far from seeking refuge in her family, Sutherland composed all her life, in spite of her family duties and the handicap of her husband (Dr Norman Albiston, a psychiatrist) who was once said to have asked Felix Werder whether Sutherland was demented. That his wife had claimed she was a great composer was, in his view, a sign of madness. Needless to say, Sutherland divorced Albiston in 1948.

Margaret Sutherland struggled all her life to gain recognition as a composer. She was aware of the fact that her male counterparts had no such difficulty in establishing themselves. Nowadays and despite the difficulties she perceived for herself, she has become recognised as a composer of immense stature and significance. Roger Covell writes that '. . . it was a woman, Margaret Sutherland of Melbourne, who really naturalised the 20th century in Australian music. Long before World War II she was writing music which paralleled the new-classical reaction against romantic styles in most European or Europe-derived societies.'[9] Certainly, Sutherland was up-to-date, creating a sound-world which was reminiscent of post-Debussy, Stravinsky, Ravel and Bartók. That a woman should do this for Australian music makes her contribution, I believe, all the more exceptional.

Her First String Quartet, composed around 1939, is a case in point, for it was written when she was still married and rearing children and it displays a tonal language which would have probably appeared shocking to Australian audiences at this time. Although cast in a fairly conventional mould – four movements: fast, slow, fast, fast – it breaks the conventions it sets up. There is a tendency towards continuous growth, proliferation and development within a contrapuntal texture. The work's fluid elasticity comes from what Sutherland described as her *chant interieur*, a stream of musical ideas which insistently present themselves for crafting and refinement. A prolific composer, this and many other works from her pen, especially, perhaps, the songs, articulate a highly original and expressive style which must surely have had a significant impact on the next generation to follow in her footsteps. As Deborah Crisp wrote in 1979, 'Sutherland provided for Australian music the beginning of its own musical style. For Australian women, she provides a precedent, proving that women can indeed be creative and innovative in their music; she provides also that most essential element in the growth of any tradition: a starting point with which Australian women can identify and from which their music can develop.'[10]

Mirrie Hill, in contrast to Sutherland, lived and worked in the shadow of her composer-husband, Alfred Hill. She devoted herself to his career. He worked in the luxurious comfort of a rather large studio while she, in her spare time, did her work at the kitchen table. Despite this, it has now come to the notice of the establishment, that her music, which had not been exposed, as Alfred's had, to the outdated idioms of romanticism, possessed an originality of perspective[11] which far exceeded that of her husband. And, to this end, she was one of the first composers to address herself to finding a musical style that was uniquely Australian. Certainly, she was one of the first composers to incorporate elements of Aboriginal music in her compositions. Like Sutherland's, her output is made up of chamber and vocal works but there are a number of works for orchestra as well, dispelling the myth that women cannot write for large-scale forces.

The next composer to share in a dedication to the cause of women's participation in musical composition was Peggy Glanville-Hicks (1912–1990). The extraordinary thing about Glanville-Hicks was that, despite being an Australian by birth and in death, she was, as Thérèse Radic puts it, '. . . a major musical force as a critic, promoter and composer, not in Australia, but in America.'[12] Radic goes on: 'Though her reputation was made and widely proclaimed from the 1950s on, it was not until she returned to live in Sydney in the mid 1970s that her music began to receive the attention it deserves from her compatriots. There is now an escalating interest in her music by younger composers and performers, attracted by an assured voice from outside the mainstream, a voice now being reclaimed as Australian.'[13]

Although, like Sutherland, she wound up in the 1930s in Europe for further studies – in London with Ralph Vaughan Williams, in Vienna to learn the 12-tone and atonal systems of composition from Egon Wellesz and in Paris to be schooled by Nadia Boulanger in neo-classical methods – she ultimately rejected all the techniques in which she had been trained and began her search for a more ancient source, a more authentic soundworld which was capable of breathing life into 20th century music.

Glanville-Hicks' works of maturity, composed in the 1950s – among them the Sonata for Harp (1950), the Sonata for Piano and Percussion (1951), *Letters from Morocco* (1952), *Sinfonia da Pacifica* (1952), the *Etruscan Concerto* (1954) – take up this challenge, incorporating elements of melody and rhythm from Indian antiquity and resulting in some of her most original music. One of her best-known works from this period, reviewed well in America but not so well in Australia, is her opera (the first of six by Glanville-Hicks) to a libretto by Thomas Mann, *The Transposed Heads* (1952–3). The work was premiered in New York in 1958 and given its first Australian performance by the University of New South Wales under Roger Covell in 1970. Marilyn Bachelder has summarised the opera's Indian and West European components, suggesting that the Indian influence is represented by the repetitive motifs of the music, the use of five-note scales, drone-like accompaniments, decorated melodies, resonant octave doublings and exotic instrumental colours.[14] The Western influence she analyses as being the work's deployment of tertian and quartel harmonies, key relationships, cadences, vocal style and timbre, and prosody. Be that as it may, this opera is highly distinctive and in its way, as one critic put it, '. . . a masterpiece.'[15]

Glanville-Hicks went on to digest other exotic music from indigenous North Africa, 'Eastern' places (but, not South-East Asia) and Greece to produce what is generally regarded as her highly original style, structurally founded on melody and rhythm with harmony serving as a bi-product of these. Glanville-Hicks' oeuvre is large and spread over all the important musical genres. The titles to her works are dazzlingly descriptive and suggestive. Thérèse Radic sums up the achievements of the composer, saying: 'Peggy Glanville-Hicks was an innovative Australian composer who worked in America, influencing its new music through her opinions, concert direction and her music. She was also a woman who composed and one who disliked being termed a 'woman composer'. She believed that to be included in the general term – simply composer – was the only proper ambition and that to allow separate spheres to develop for male and female creatives would inevitably result in the women being considered the lesser group.'[16]

Against this backdrop, another group of women composers were making a different contribution, writing music for the Australian Music Examinations Board (AMEB). Nurturing this outfit with a wealth of material to keep young, aspiring performers' fingers busy, these women, who include Dulcie Holland (b. 1913), Miriam Hyde (b. 1913) – who both turned 80 in 1993 – and Marjorie Hesse (1911–1986) will be remembered for many years to come by all those unfortunates who were tortured into submitting to the rigid form of musical training proscribed by the AMEB. But it is even more unfortunate that this is almost exclusively where Hyde's and Holland's fame is located. Both women have written works in almost every significant genre, including orchestral, choral and vocal, and chamber music. Although these works are rarely performed in Australia, they nonetheless form an important link between a quasi-European tradition and that of the next composer-generation. It is to Australia's loss that these works have been allowed to slip from the concert platform.

In the last few years, however, some positive steps have been taken to repair these gaping holes in the history of Australian music. The composer, Robert Allworth, for example, has churned out as many as 18 CDs, produced on a shoestring budget under the JADE label, which feature the music of women composers. Dulcie Holland's Trio for violin, cello and piano (1944) was finally premiered to great acclaim by the Montefiore Trio at the Composing Women Festival held in Adelaide in 1991, a staggering 47 years after its completion. This performance of the Trio is featured on one of Allworth's latest discs, *Portrait of Australian Composers*, and stands as a testimony to the quality of women's composition. Earlier in 1993, in the presence of the composer, the Sydney Festival paid tribute to Dulcie Holland with a concert devoted entirely to her, featuring both her own music and music composed by others especially for the occasion.

One of these other composers was Ann Carr-Boyd (b. 1938) with a work for violin and piano on that occasion, who makes an entrance into the Australian music scene in the next generation on from Glanville-Hicks, Hyde and Holland. A successful composer based in Sydney, Carr-

Boyd also studied overseas after graduating as one of the first of two students from the Department of Music at the University of Sydney in 1960. The need for a mass-exodus of talent from Australia in the musical scene (particularly prevalent among performers) is all too much a reminder of the inherited cultural cringe – if you can't 'make it' over there, then there'd be no chance you'd ever make it back home. Since her return from England in 1967, having studied under Peter Racine Fricker and Alexander Goehr, Carr-Boyd has participated fully in a gradual, yet sometimes painful burgeoning of a now thriving and vigorous art-music culture in Australia. She is influenced by 'tradition' and interested in exploiting unusual sound combinations. This manifests itself in her music in a variety of different guises. For example, her *Music for Sunday* (1982) in two movements, is a short tonal essay which alludes to early Australian colonial music through its chirpy, salon-music rhythms and melodies as well as referring to the European baroque music heritage. Her fascination with the timbre and diatonic basis of the harpsichord in works such as *Nadir* for violin and harpsichord (1975) illustrates her ability to turn an old-worldy instrument into something quite new and fresh. Mandolins also feature in Carr-Boyd's music with a number of works composed for the Sydney Mandolins.

A few years older than Carr-Boyd, Helen Gifford (b. 1935), born, educated and currently based in Melbourne, is another composer whose achievement in Australian music is significant. Whereas Carr-Boyd explores the possibilities of timbre within traditional and non-traditional paradigms, Gifford has developed a wholly unique style out of an intense interest in the music of the ancient traditions of Asian civilisations and their application to the European-oriented musical language in which she was schooled. In her works of the late 60s and early 70s, for example, Gifford literally borrows the Asian concept of structuring material over long, non-resolving time spans while at the same time articulating a harmonic language which has much in common with the Polish composers, Penderecki and Lutoslawski, and with other Europeans such as Messiaen and Ravel.

A sensitive and highly individual composer, Gifford, like Margaret Sutherland had initially wanted to become a concert pianist. It was not until she graduated with a Bachelor of Music in 1958, having studied composition with Dorian Le Gallienne (who inspired in her a deep love of the music of the French impressionists) that she directed her energies into composition and realised it was the career of her preference. Like Sutherland, it was her first-hand experience with the European avant-garde that shaped the beginnings of this career and which has subsequently put her on the map as one of Australia's most important composers.

The Department of Music at Sydney University was an important training ground for many of the composers in Carr-Boyd's generation.

Indeed, it was Professor Donald Peart and Peter Sculthorpe who actively encouraged their young students to experiment in some of the most extreme modes of composition around at that time.

Two women composers who were directly influenced by Peart and Sculthorpe were Anne Boyd (b. 1946) and Alison Bauld (b. 1944). Anne Boyd is currently Professor of Music on her old stamping ground at Sydney University. Alison Bauld resides in London. With a career formerly in acting, Bauld has composed a number of striking music-theatre works, one of her best-known being *Banquot's Buried*. On the other hand, Anne Boyd has steered away from the theatre, composing only a few such works.

Boyd is regarded today among her peers as a significant composer in that she has made it her project to find her own distinctive musical voice from the Asian culture, including the music of Indonesia, Japan, Korea, China and so on. In an indepth analysis of one of her works, *Cycle of Love* for countertenor, flute, cello and piano (1981), I believe I have tapped into what I describe as a 'female energy' which exudes from the work. This energy – and I note, too, that Boyd would not necessarily want to claim that her biological sex is an imperative in her musical representations – is apparent because of the way in which she borrows so openly from Asia, intersecting a Christian love with Buddhist silence. Overall, *Cycle of Love* articulates cyclic and circular patterns. Unlike some of Boyd's earlier, more tonally static and meditative compositions – for example, *I crossed a bridge of dreams* and *The book of the bells* – *Cycle of Love* produces a high concentration of energy from a single source, a Korean folk tune. In turn, it becomes a heteroglossic text[17] (one which simultaneously speaks/sounds in many different voices) and it is set into a heterophonic texture. This work eludes any sense of closure. The text (translated into English from poems by 15th century concubines by Don o' Kim) begins and ends with questions and, while there is an occlusion of narrativity through songs 2 to 4, the work generally avoids the narrative form, slipping in between and through the barriers of time, dreams and love. A firm identity is never established and the music serves to reinforce the ambiguities of the text. In keeping with a notion that 'woman' cannot be defined, *Cycle of Love* is like a musical process. It seems to be always in a state of becoming.

Singled out for her exceptional idiomatic musical style, Moya Henderson (b. 1941) is another who is recognised today as one of Australia's leading composers. This, in spite of the fact that she had a more delayed beginning than her contemporaries, Gifford, Boyd, Carr-Boyd, Bauld and others in that generation, including Jennifer Fowler (b. 1939 and resident in London), Judith Clingan (b. 1945 and resident in Canberra), New Zealand-born Gillian Whitehead (b. 1941, resident in Sydney) and American-born Mary Mageau (b. 1934, resident in Brisbane).

Despite exhibiting a considerable talent for music in her childhood,

Moya Henderson chose in 1960 to enter the Sacré-Coeur Order as a nun, a decision which saw the end of her musical training for at least the next nine years. It wasn't until 1969 that she convinced her superiors to allow her to resume her musical training and in 1970 she commenced a full-time music degree, studying composition with one of Australia's leading composers, Colin Brumby in the Department of Music at the University of Queensland. In 1972 she graduated with a First-Class Honours Degree and simultaneously severed her ties with the Sacré-Coeur Order so that she could embark on a career in composition, albeit somewhat later in life than most of her colleagues.

Recognition as a composer came early for Henderson as, immediately upon graduating from the University, she was appointed resident composer with The Australian Opera during its inaugural season at the Sydney Opera House in 1973. In 1974 she accepted a DAAD (German Academic Exchange Scholarship) to study music-theatre with Mauricio Kagel and composition with Karlheinz Stockhausen at the distinguished Cologne Musikhochschule. During a three-year term in Germany, Henderson consolidated her interests in music-theatre, contributing a number of significant works, including *Clearing the Air* (1974) which won first prize in composition at the conclusion of the Darmstadt summer courses, a rewritten version of *Marxisms* (1974) – originally staged in the Sydney Opera House in 1973 – and *Stubble* (1976).

Since 1976, Henderson has been based in Sydney and works as a free-lance composer. Henderson's output, with its emphasis on instrumental and vocal music, has been prescribed by the requirements of the various commissions and fellowships she has accepted since her return to Australia. As a result, she has not produced as much music-theatre as the early signs might have indicated. Despite this, the dramatic potential of that genre has been transposed into her vast catalogue of instrumental works. From the programmatic style of *Min Min Light* and *Larrikin's Lot* (1982) to the introspective stillness of *The Dreaming* (1985); from the intense lyricism and poignancy in *Sick Song* (no 5) to the flippant irony in *Song of the Housewives* (no 2) of *Six Urban Songs: the Patrick White Song Cycle* (1983); from the distinctive counterpoint of *Cross Hatching* (1984) to the abrupt shifts of mood in *Celebration 40,000* (1987) as it pays homage to the eons of Aboriginal culture and survival, Henderson constantly engages her audience in engrossing drama. Even in her string quartet, *Kudikynah Cave* (1987) which was performed by the Auryn Quartet on its 1991 tour of Australia for Musica Viva, Henderson links herself in dramatic encounter with the cave which is hidden on the Franklin river in the rainforest of Tasmania. Her song cycles, *Six Urban Songs* (mentioned above), *Songs about Music: the Gwen Harwood Song Cycle*, (1987), *Pellucid Days: the Bruce Beaver Song Cycle*, (1989), and *Wild Card: the Dorothy Hewett Song*

Cycle (1991), honour some of Australia's great writers.

Moya Henderson's capacity to portray strong sensory images through her music makes her a very accessible composer. This is nowhere better demonstrated than in her two recent radio plays: *Currawong* (1988) describes the auditory and visual environment of native birds while advancing a kind of avian theatre: and *Meditations and Distractions on the Theme of the Singing Nun* (1990) which, in complete contrast to the earlier play, draws upon the composer's own theatrical and vocal resources, as well as those of the Sydney Chamber Choir, as they improvise plainsong fragments to provide much of the vocal music which was an integral part of the play's production.

As a composer, Henderson is deeply concerned with the society's myths and cultures. Her sounds become the symbols she uses to interpret and unravel these concerns. Her current project, in collaboration with the poet, Judith Rodriguez, is the opera, *Lindy*, based on the Azaria Chamberlain case, commissioned by The Australian Opera and due for performance in 1994. Other recently approved commissions include an ABC radio drama for voices and orchestra entitled, *Yura Yata Songline*, and a new series of *G'day Africa* pieces for the mixed chamber ensembles, Perihelion in Brisbane and Lights in Adelaide.

Though fewer in number than the men composers, the women have got Australia covered. The 80s, a 'golden-age' for composition in Australia, has seen a highly talented younger generation emerge from just about every capital city in the country and in all the important musical styles and forms. If you visit Perth, you may well hear the exciting acoustic and electronic music of Cathie Travers (b. 1959). Travelling on to Adelaide, the names Becky Llewellyn (b. 1950) and Andi Aldam (b. 1967) will be tossed around; indeed, Lights, an exciting contemporary ensemble based in Adelaide might be showcasing their music. On to Melbourne and you will be bound to run into music of a very different kind – often described as hard-edged and modernist – by Liza Lim (b. 1966) and Mary Finsterer (b. 1962). However, this is not the only style promoted in Melbourne: Judy Pile (b. 1954) and Cindy John (b. 1950) have been making a name for themselves in the worlds of radiophonic and computer music respectively while Andrée Greenwell (b. 1964) has been acclaimed for her postmodern opera, *Sweet Death* (1991), which was featured at the Melbourne International Festival. Some of the younger ones in Sydney include Caroline Szeto (b. 1956), Gretchen Miller (b. 1968) and Sarah de Jong (b. 1952) while two composers of growing distinction, Judith Clingan (b. 1945) and Margaret Legge-Wilkinson (b. 1958), represent the Australian federal capital, Canberra.

And then, there are those who reside overseas. Two exceptionally talented Australian women composers have made Germany and The Netherlands their home, respectively, Elena Kats-Chernin (b. 1957) and Barbara Woof (b. 1958), for how long we know not. And it is interesting to discover, too, composers who, from elsewhere, have made Australia their homes. If you happen to be in Devonport in Tasmania, you might just come across a relative of Gustav Mahler, Hellgart Mahler (b. 1931) who is continuing to write music very much in that atonal idiom laid down by the Second Viennese School.

For something completely different, however, there is yet another group of women composers who are at the cutting edge of the collaborative composer/performer sound-art world. Two women in particular, deserve a mention here because they have created such an unique approach to their art which crosses many of the boundaries of musical genres and related art forms. Sound sculptor and environmental artist Ros Bandt (b. 1951) won the most distinguished Don Banks Fellowship for composition in 1990 for her extraordinary work in this field. Sarah Hopkins (b. 1958), currently living in Brisbane, tours both nationally and internationally, performing her music. Over the past 12 years, she has represented Australia at many prestigious events such as the Paris Autumn Festival and the International Composers Symposium in Colorado. As a composer-performer, Sarah has developed an expansive, pure musical style which resonates with the space and energy of the Australian landscape. She composes solo, ensemble and choral music of a holistic nature which draws upon the natural beauty of the cello, voice, whirly instruments (her own invention) and handbells.

The tradition of music-making in all the significant styles and genres across the vast expanse of Australia is as much the domain of women as it is men. The composers who are women in Australia may be doing it differently from the men, but whether they are or they are not, to come back to what Margaret Mead said in the 1940s, '. . . when one activity to which each (sex) could have contributed . . . is limited to one (male) sex, a rich differentiated quality is lost from the activity itself'.[18] As the British composer, Nicola LeFanu (who has Australian citizenship through her marriage to Australian composer David Lumsdaine) remarked, '. . . in the musical world it is the men who call the tune. But it's not necessarily the men who write the best tunes.'[19]

Notes
1. See James Murdoch. 1972. *Australia's Contemporary Composers*. Melbourne: The Macmillan Company of Australia. p. 184.
2. See Sally Macarthur. 1993. Music as Lifestyle, Politics as Music: Moya Henderson. *Contemporary Music Review: Reclaiming the Muse*. London. Spring.
3. Mary Mageau. 1991. Australian Women Composers Network aiming for its own demise. *24 Hours*. December.
4. ibid.
5. Thérèse Radic. 1991. Where are the Women Composers? *24 Hours*. December.

6. ibid.
7. Vincent Plush. 1988. 'Notes from the Great Southland: The Origins of Contemporary Music in Australia' from the *Program of the Aspen Music Festival*.
8. ibid.
9. Roger Covell. 1967. *Australia's Music: Themes of a New Society*. Melbourne: Sun Books. p. 152.
10. Deborah Crisp. 1979. Australia's Women Composers. *Refactory Girl*. December.
11. ibid.
12. Thérèse Radic, from the typescript of a lecture on Peggy Glanville-Hicks delivered at the New Music Australia 1991 Festival. In Sally Macarthur (ed). *Sounds Australian*. Sydney: forthcoming. 1992. *New Music Australia*.
13. ibid.
14. Cited in Radic's lecture on Peggy Glanville-Hicks from Marilyn Meyers Bachelder. 1973. *Women in Music Composition: Ruth Crawford Seeger, Peggy Glanville-Hicks, Vivian Fine*. MA thesis. Eastern Michigan University. pp. 60–95.
15. Cited in Radic's lecture on Peggy Glanville-Hicks from the International Theatre Institute's publication. 1969. *World Theatre*.
16. ibid.
17. I have borrowed this term from Terry Threadgold, taking it from a lecture on Methodologies in Performance Analysis given at the University of Sydney on 25 March 1992.
18. Margaret Mead. 1962. *Male and Female*. Harmondsworth: Penguin. First published 1949 in the USA.
19. Nicola Lefanu. 1987. Master Musician: An Impregnable Taboo? *Contact, A Journal of Contemporary Music Vol. 31*. Autumn.

WOMEN'S CINEMA IN AUSTRALIA

Australia is one of the few countries in the Western world where women filmmakers have been supported, both economically and professionally, by a body known as The Women's Film Fund. Established in 1976, the Women's Film Fund developed as a result of initiatives taken the year before during International Women's Year. In that year, the Federal government gave a grant of $100,000 to Germaine Greer, author of the then controversial *The Female Eunuch* (1969), to produce a series on human reproduction for television. After the controversial dismissal of the Whitlam government the project was cancelled and the moneys placed in a trust for the establishment of the Women's Film Fund. For over a decade, the Fund provided assistance in the form of loans and grants to film projects supported by the five-member women's Advisory Panel of the WFF.

But Australian women had been active in all forms of filmmaking since the early 1970s – in production, distribution, exhibition, training, education and in making films. Women had formed their own film groups, begun to teach themselves the skills of filmmaking, and had held conferences and weekend workshops on the media. Women's film groups were established in virtually all of the Australian states with the largest groups in Sydney and Melbourne. The establishment of the Women's Film Fund provided crucial financial assistance and support but without the Fund women, no doubt, would still have continued to make films about women's issues. While the Women's Film Fund no longer exists, the Australian Film Commission has a Women's Program unit which organises workshops and provides an information service for women.

Women's filmmaking in Australia also has a history and a past. It certainly did not commence with the second-wave of feminism of the late-60s. From 1921 and 1933 at least sixteen feature films were either directed or produced by Australian women filmmakers – these included Lottie Lyell, Yvonne Pavis, Louise Lovely and Isobel and Paulette McDonagh. Films directed by these early pioneers covered a variety of subjects and themes: outback life; father-daughter relationships; high society; male/female relationships. Some of the better-known titles were *Sunshine Sally, Jewelled Nights, The Cheaters* and *The Far Paradise*. Those that still exist are held by the National Film and Sound Archive.

In the early 70s women's films were marked by a desire to put into practice the aims of the feminist movement, to document women's lives and to explain the basis of feminist thinking to the community. From the beginning, the women's film movement in Australia set itself up in opposition to the practices of mainstream commercial cinema. Women favoured a collective process and a co-operative model of film production. Films were exhibited to community and women's groups and discussion was considered an essential part of any screening. While today women filmmakers tend not to work in groups, but on their own individual projects, their films continue to be screened to community groups, women's groups and at film festivals where they provoke discussion and debate.

Initially, films tended to fall into two main categories: documentary or short fictional films with a strong realist basis. As women became more confident with cinematic forms and filmmaking techniques, experimental or avant-garde films began to form a third category. From the early 70s to the mid-80s a large number of films were made, covering a diverse range of subjects: women's sexuality, birth control, abortion, incest, lesbianism, Koori and migrant women, gender role conditioning, masturbation, women's history, working women and so on. However, it is important to stress that not all films made by women or supported by the WFF were necessarily on feminist topics. A number of women made films that did not seek to explore feminist politics. What was important was that women were attempting to break with tradition and enter what was, and still is, a male-dominated industry and profession. Some men were quick to respond to the appearance of feminist-inspired films and not all were happy with the new state of affairs. One was Mr B. Goodluck, a Tasmanian member of parliament who said in 1977 when commenting on a women's film festival which was supported by the WFF: 'These films are about incest, abortion, lesbians, and other obscene subjects . . . these films attack the structure of the family . . . they are just plain filth.'

A brief discussion of the short films made by Australian women directors will give some idea of the range of styles and subject matter. Jane Campion's style has a surreal quality which, combined with her black humour, endows her films with a sense of the absurd. Yet at the same time her films have a strong narrative drive and usually focus on social issues such as sexual harassment (*After Hours*), the construction of femininity (*A Girl's Own Story*) and the dysfunctional nature of familial relationships (*Peel*). Tracey Moffat's films (*Nice Coloured Girls, Nightcries*) use avant-garde techniques to present a powerful critique of racism in Australia from the point of view of Aboriginal women. *For Love Or Money*, a feature-length documentary, presents a feminist history of the place and role of women in Australia from 1788 to the advent of the new women's movement in the 1970s. Drawing on archival footage, interviews, photographs, clips from feature films and other sources, the film was made over a five year period by a women's collective. A landmark in Australian filmmaking, *For Love Or Money*, explores issues such as female transportation to the new colony, the treatment of aboriginal women, unequal pay for women, family and motherhood, abortion, Aboriginal landrights, the environment, peace, immigration. Two other important avant-garde films are Helen Grace's *Serious Undertakings* which examines the construction of 'woman' in an Australian cultural context and Laleen Jayamanne's *A Song Of Ceylon*, an erotic, confronting work about the construction of cultural and sexual identities.

A number of directors have explored lesbianism in both a political and personal context: Anne Turner (*Flesh on Glass*); Megan McMurchy (*Apartments*); Sarah Gibson and Susan Lambert (*On Guard*). In two recent films – *The Father is Nothing* and *In Loving Memory* – Leonie Knight draws on recent developments in feminist film theory to explore female fetishism, lesbianism and androgyny while Vicki Knight problematises the gaze in her two films about a lesbian detective (*Can't You Take A Joke* and *Red Label*). Jackie Farkas won the 1992 Grand Prix at the Festival of International Cinema Students in Tokyo with *Amelia Rose Towers*, a bizarre film which draws on surrealistic techniques to comment on the nature of cinema itself.

Most of the above films are in the libraries of the Australian Film Institute and the National Film Library or available for hire from commercial distributors. Along with films currently being made by women, the earlier films continue to be hired by community, educational and women's groups. Women's filmmaking constitutes a dominant aspect of feminist culture in Australia and the films produced are now integral to the running of the large number of women's studies courses that proliferate throughout the educational institutions and Universities.

Since the early 70s a number of women have either learned the necessary skills and/or graduated from the various Australian film schools and become internationally known professional feature filmmakers. These include Gillian Armstrong (*My Brilliant Career, High Tide, The Last Days of Chez Nous*); Ann Turner (*Celia, Dallas Doll*); Jocelyn Moorehouse (*Proof*); Jackie McKimmie (*Waiting*); Tracey Moffat (*Bedevil*) and Jane Campion (*Sweetie, Angel at My Table, The Piano*). It needs to be noted, however, that working in what remains an essentially male-dominated industry is not easy and a number of these directors have spoken out in interviews about the sexist structures with which they have had to contend in the course of their careers. Nevertheless Australian women directors have in the last decade produced a number of feature and short films which have achieved acclaim both at home and internationally.

Janine Burke
DRAWING THE FUTURE: AUSTRALIAN WOMEN ARTISTS

I

Women have shaped the course of art in Australia. In Aboriginal society, women are singers, dancers, artists and powerful individuals within their communities. Since the European settlement in 1788, women have been recording a particular response to their environment. This essay addresses the work of European-Australian artists.

Colonial flower painters and watercolourists sought the humble details of their new landscape rather than its heroic vision. They tracked down flowers and birds, documenting unusual or precious species.

The botanical artist, Ellis Rowan (1847–1922) was an intrepid explorer. She braved the tropical scrubs and jungles of Queensland up to the Cape York Peninsula and still further north to New Guinea, the American Rockies and many other parts of the world in her search for rare wildflowers and birds. She did this in a cumbersome Victorian costume for she never relinquished the correct attire of a well-brought-up lady. Her charm and her iron-will were equally effective as she travelled the world alone, hardy and adventurous, captivating, apparently, the bewildered and admiring people who provided her with food, shelter and other forms of assistance. In letters to her husband, *A Flower Hunter in Queensland and New Zealand* (1898) Ellis Rowan describes her adventures with a humour born of courage and determination. Her watercolours, of which she produced several hundred, are meticulous, delicate studies. A large collection of her work is on display at the **Australian National Library, Canberra**.

Adelaide Ironside (1831–67) broke with convention to study in Europe. She was the first of many artists to realize that colonial Australia did not offer the kind of education and stimulus an artist needed. A sensitive and highly strung woman, she was proficient in both poetry and drawing. In 1855 she set off to London with her mother, who proved a great support in the difficult years ahead. Mrs Ironside, a linguist, was responsible for Adelaide's education and for encouraging her ambitions. In London, Adelaide took drawing lessons from critic John Ruskin, before moving to Rome. There she was part of a community of painters, sculptors and poets. After an audience with Pope Pius IX she was permitted to copy pictures in the Vatican, in particular, Raphael's Stanze frescoes. She produced religious paintings, though hampered by poverty and increasing ill-health. She contracted tuberculosis and died in London. Though several of Adelaide's large paintings were returned to Sydney after her death, they were left to rot in a shed behind the Art Gallery of New South Wales. Her major painting, *The Marriage at Cana in Galilee* (1865) is on view at

St Paul's College, University of Sydney. *A Self-Portrait* (1855) is on view at Newcastle Region Art Gallery, Newcastle. See Jill Poulton. 1987. *Adelaide Ironside: The Pilgrim of Art.* Sydney: Hale & Iremonger.

II

For young women of the nineteenth century, painting was seen as a lady-like accomplishment, together with singing, playing the piano and embroidery. It was not to be taken seriously as a profession or a career. 'Women artists' were seen as amateurs and hobbyists and art schools were regarded as finishing schools for the daughters of the newly refined bourgeoisie.

But the late nineteenth century was also a time in Australian history when a sense of national identity fostered through cultural unity was developing. Women began to graduate from Australian universities and women's suffrage and wider social aspects of emancipation had become matters of public debate. Between 1894 and 1908 women were given the vote, long ahead of Europe, and without the bitter, violent suffrage campaigns. In these years, Australia led the world in social reform. The 1880s and 90s were decades important for the changing status of women.

At Melbourne's National Gallery School, two women students, Jane Sutherland and Clara Southern, were about to be involved in the new landscape movement, the Heidelberg School, often known as Australian Impressionism. It took its name, not from the German university town, but from the suburb of Heidelberg, north of Melbourne. In the 1890s, it was a picturesque place with river flats, rolling hills and commanding views of the Dandenong Ranges.

Jane Sutherland (1855–1928) participated in the artists' camps at Heidelberg where, with Tom Roberts and Fred McCubbin, she sketched the landscape 'en plein air'.

Sutherland's landscapes do not depict the bush as a threatening or a hostile place, nor did she share in themes favoured by her male colleagues of heroic masculine labour, of bushrangers and pioneers. While detailing the subtle colours of the countryside and capturing the peculiarly hard, clear Australian light with a light 'impressionist' brushstroke, she presented an environment of safety and pleasure.

Clara Southern's (1861–1940) landscapes reflect a prevailing interest in atmospheric effects, where the landscape at evening is a theatre for mood, mists and evanescence.

Both Southern and Sutherland were active in the art world of their day, becoming the first women members of the powerful and prestigious Victorian Artists Society council, and exhibiting regularly. However, their confidence did not extend to asking the same prices as their male colleagues: their works were sold at a fraction of the price of a Tom Roberts or Fred

McCubbin. Major works by Jane Sutherland and Clara Southern are on display at the **National Gallery of Victoria**, 180 St Kilda Road, Melbourne. Juliet Peers and Victoria Hammond. 1992. *Completing the Picture: Women Artists and the Heidelberg Era.* Melbourne: Victorian Women's Trust.

III

In the years between the First and Second World Wars a generation of women artists emerged, who were to have an extraordinary impact on Australian art.

This group, who formed part of the two waves of modernism to reach Sydney between 1913 and 1930, includes Grace Cossington Smith, Norah Simpson, Margaret Preston, Thea Proctor, Grace Crowley and Dorrit Black. They were instrumental in introducing post-impressionism and other avant-garde styles into Australia through their painting, printmaking, teaching and writing. During this period there was something approaching a real balance between male and female artists in influence, prominence and prestige.

This flowering of talent had its roots in the growing awareness of feminist issues from the 1880s and 90s. In 1920s Australia there also existed a political climate that accepted liberal, left-wing attitudes. New possibilities existed for women in image, lifestyle and career while film and popular magazines promoted the 'New Woman', imported largely from America – the 'flapper', 'career girl', 'advanced woman' or 'bachelor girl' who was sophisticated, educated and independent. Sexual licence and liberty were discussed, if not actually embraced.

For the first time, unchaperoned travel became possible for young women and many left Australia to study art in Paris, London or Berlin, staying away for many years.

Norah Simpson (1895–1974) was a seventeen-year-old art student from Sydney when she travelled to London. She met members of the Camden Town Group, the British version of post-impressionism. They provided her with introductions to Parisian art dealers and collectors, enabling her to see firsthand the work of Matisse, Picasso, Van Gogh and Gauguin. When she returned to Australia she had much to share with fellow student Grace Cossington Smith (1892–1984), including colour prints of these artists' paintings. They were some of the first seen in Australia and had a lasting effect on the art, not only on Cossington Smith, but on Roi De Maistre and Roland Wakelin. Simpson's important painting *Studio Portrait, Chelsea* (1915; on view **Art Gallery of New South Wales, Sydney**) shows the influence of vivid Fauvist colour and flattened simplified form. Unfortunately it is the only known work by Norah Simpson who stopped painting in 1926 after the birth of her son.

190

Grace Cossington Smith lived all her painting life in the same house, with her sisters, in a quiet leafy Sydney suburb. Like most Australian women artists, she had a private income: there was little money to be made in Australian art outside portrait commissions and so the story of women artists is of those privileged to have the opportunities that allowed them the time, study and contemplation to pursue their art.

Cossington Smith is Australia's greatest post-impressionist painter. For many years, she was regarded as an amateur 'lady painter' from the suburbs – attention and admiration came late. She painted many subjects: crowds, political demonstrations, Royal visits, theatrical events and landscapes but her best works are her late interiors where her gifts as a colourist are most evident.

The interiors are radiant visions of the real world, full of dense saturating light. Though fragments of living rooms and bedrooms, they are transformed by an eye for detail so acute that they encompass a whole world, personal, but very much alive. Grace Cossington Smith's work can be viewed at the **Art Gallery of New South Wales, Sydney**, the **Australian National Gallery, Canberra**, and the **National Gallery of Victoria, Melbourne**. See also Bruce James. 1990. *Grace Cossington Smith*. Sydney: Craftsman House.

Margaret Preston (1875–1963) was a prolific painter and printmaker, a provocative critic, a champion of Aboriginal art and Australian culture and, later in her life, an adventurous traveller. In 1904 she studied in Munich at the Government Art School for Women, before travelling to Paris. Her work was influenced by Japanese prints, by their decorative qualities, clear linearity and bright, flat colour. She changed the status of Australian printmaking, which had previously been seen only as an illustration to a text. Preston believed it should be an independent art form,its cheap multiples available to a wider audience who enjoyed modern art but couldn't afford an original oil painting. Preston was concerned, too, that Australian artists were too ready to adopt European styles and methods without considering Australia's own cultural tradition. She loved the stark beauty of Australian native flowers and made them subject of her work. At a time when Aboriginal art was not appreciated, Preston wrote articles drawing attention to its aesthetic qualities; she also appropriated stylistic elements and motifs for her paintings. The best display of Margaret Preston's work is at the **Australian National Gallery, Canberra**, though all state galleries show her work.

Thea Proctor (1879–1966) was an elegant and beautiful woman who, though struggling against poverty all her life, managed to present an image of enviable ease and style. She was a printmaker and a teacher and an influential tastemaker in 1920s and 30s Sydney. She was supportive of younger, more radical artists, and certainly of women.

Proctor was also a commercial artist, designing covers for fashionable women's magazines. In her watercolours and her woodblock prints, she depicted a private, feminine world of glamour and of languid pleasure. Her prints remain very popular and are available in postcards and colour reproductions at the **Bookshop, Art Gallery of New South Wales, Sydney,** and at other state gallery bookshops.

Grace Crowley (1890–1979) and Dorrit Black (1891–1951) were responsible for the second wave of modernism. In the late 1920s both studied in Paris under Andre Lhote. He taught a simplified form of cubism, insisting all form could be perceived and then rendered in geometric shapes. Crowley and Black attended his summer school at Mirmande in the south of France where they lived in the homes of local people, painting and having weekly group discussions about one another's work.

Just as Grace Crowley was achieving some small degree of success in Paris, she was ordered home by her family. For a short time she stayed on her family's country property before she fled to Sydney where she started a school of modern art. Dorrit Black, equally enthusiastic about modernism and fresh attitudes to art education, began The Modern Art Centre in Sydney in 1932.

Crowley's work would change dramatically through the 1930s as she experimented with increasingly radical composition and structure until a pure geometric abstraction resulted. Her great friend in the lonely years of experimentation was Ralph Balson who went on the same journey from figuration to abstraction. Though they did not marry or live together, theirs was a beneficial relationship of mutual support and admiration. Grace Crowley's work is on view at the **National Gallery of Victoria, Melbourne** and the **Art Gallery of New South Wales, Sydney**. Dorrit Black's paintings can be seen at the **Art Gallery of South Australia, North Terrace, Adelaide**.

Clarice Beckett (1887–1935) who produced subtle tonal paintings of Melbourne's bayside beaches and rainy, winter streets was another important figure. Living at home with ageing parents, responsible for their care and the running of a large house, she was only able to paint in the mornings and evenings, yet she left behind a large body of work that resonates with subtle atmospheric effects. Clarice Beckett's paintings can be seen at the **Australian National Gallery, Canberra** and the **National Gallery of Victoria**.

Kate O'Connor (1875–1968) though born in Perth, spent nearly thirty years living, painting and exhibiting in Paris. Her impressionist paintings with their luscious brushstrokes bring her portraits and flower studies vividly to life. Kate O'Connor's work can be seen at the **Art Gallery of Western Australia, Perth**.

IV

The Second World War changed Australian society. Many women had been drawn into the work force to help with the war effort while the men were away. The message at the end of the war was that women should resume their previous roles, give up their jobs and go home. The 1950s, while an era of great prosperity, was also one of conservatism. Women's magazines no longer lauded the independent career girl and travellers. Now the desired roles were that of wife and mother. The new wave of women artists needed to carry through the achievements of the 1920s and 30s was not forthcoming. The only major artist who emerges from the post-war years is Joy Hester (1920–1960).

Joy Hester belonged to a talented group of radical Melbourne painters. The main influences were surrealism and German expressionism, gleaned from journals and art books, because, until the 1939 Herald Exhibition of French and British Painting, few original modern paintings had been seen in Australia. Hester lived in poverty in the lofts and studios of the inner city with her husband, Albert Tucker, an articulate young painter. Hester knew the work of die Brucke. Her other influences included tribal art, the occult, modernist French poetry and the drawings of Jean Cocteau. An enormous impact came from seeing footage of the Nazi concentration camps when the camps were liberated in 1945: stark images of death and suffering, of hallucinatory nightmare faces with haunted staring eyes suddenly filled her work.

Hester chose to draw and not to paint, working rapidly, producing thirty or forty works at a sitting using ink and Chinese brushes. She also wrote poetry.

At twenty-seven, she was diagnosed as having Hodgkin's disease, a cancer of the lymph glands and was given a short time to live. Her drawings from this time, particularly the *Faces* series (1947–48) indicate hope and despair, a dark night of the soul where illumination is gained after intense experience. Though the disease went into remission for eight years, the symptoms reappeared in Hester's mid-thirties. She went on writing poetry, painting larger and more complex works until her death at forty. Her work is on view at the **Australian National Gallery, Canberra**. See also, Janine Burke. 1983. *Joy Hester*. Greenhouse Publications.

The Fifties and early Sixties were years of quiet production by women artists. French artist, Mirka Mora (1930–) settled in Melbourne in 1953 after studying mime in Paris under Marcel Marceau. She became a friend of Joy Hester's. The joyful innocence and humour of her paintings, dolls and magical animals are at one with an ebullient personality that helped enliven the dull Melbourne artworld of the 50s. More recently, she has also painted a mural which can still be seen at **Flinders Street Railway Station, Swanston Street, Melbourne.**

V

Though the paintings of Janet Dawson (1935–) in the 1960s pioneered colour-field abstraction, it was not until the 1970s with the rise of an international women's movement that 'women's art' suddenly became, once more, a decisive force in Australian art.

Women artists, especially a younger generation of 'baby boomers', brought content – political, sexual, feminist – back into art, altering forms and challenging premises of taste and methods of making and presenting art. In 1974–75 the Women's Art Movement started in each capital city as women artists, critics and curators made contact in order to discover and learn more of one another's work, taste, ideas and directions. Slide registers were started too, as a resource for contemporary art, the most extensive being housed at **Melbourne's Carringbush Library**, 415 Church Street, Richmond where it is readily accessible.

Abstract painters like Lesley Dumbrell (1941–) and Elizabeth Gower (1952–) refer to women's traditional crafts such as weaving and embroidery through elaborate patterning. Realist painter Jenny Watson (1951–) eyes Australian suburbia with critical affection while Vicki Varvaressos (1952–) attacks with painterly gusto the false and foolish advertising images aimed at women. Photographers such as Sue Ford (1943–), Mickey Allan (1944–), Ruth Maddison (1942–) and Ponch Hawkes (1946–) document the changing lives of their lovers, friends, children and mothers with compassion and humour.

Sculptor Ailsa O'Connor (1920–1979), who had been a social realist painter in her youth, created sensuous and beautiful images of women to celebrate her own return to art after many years of motherhood and work as a cadre in the Communist Party. Rosalie Gascoigne (1917–) makes sensitive sculptures from the natural environment, from twigs and feathers she collects as well as old tins and other forms of detritus; from these she created icons of beauty and strength. Ann Newmarch (1945–) and Vivienne Binns (1940–) have worked extensively with community groups, producing murals and collaborative projects that address the real conditions of women's lives and oppression while Marie McMahon (1952–) has made prints and posters which lyrically deal with domesticity and relationships between black and white Australia. In the last decade Susan Norrie, Julie Brown-Rrap, Lyn Boyd, Mandy Martin and Sally Smart have defined a feminine sensibility through theoretical and historical strategies, space, the landscape and their own bodies. Urban Aboriginal artists, Ellen Jose and Karen Casey, draw on the depths and strengths of their traditions with vigour and passion.

The art of most of the women represented in Section V is held in state gallery collections where, with regard to changing exhibition arrangements, it can usually be viewed. **The Australian National Gallery, Canberra**, is probably the best place to see a range of this work. It can also be seen at selected commercial galleries in Sydney and Melbourne. The sculpture of Ailsa O'Connor can be seen at the **Conservatory, Fitzroy Gardens, Melbourne** and **St Kilda Public Library**, 150 Carlisle Street, St Kilda.

References
Janine Burke. 1980. *Australian Women Artists, 1840–1940.*
Janine Burke. 1990. *Field of Vision, A Decade of Change: Women's Art in the Seventies.*

Merren Ricketson
THE WOMEN'S ART SCENE IN AUSTRALIA

Australian women have been working towards equal representation in the arts arena for the last twenty years. The success of this struggle is reflected in the number of women who are exhibiting across the country in a diverse range of media and exhibiting spaces.

Battles and discussions in the 70s and early 80s concentrated on re-defining the hi(s)story of art, the recognition of women's diverse artforms and questions of female sensibility. The debate was fuelled by the publication of surveys on women artists through the centuries, texts addressing the inequitable situation in galleries, and new 'ways of seeing'.

Women's Art Movements were established in most states. Seeking new avenues of expression in regard to women's practice was almost subsumed by the textual acrobatics of postmodernism. However a large number of women artists, curators, academics and writers have kept the debate simmering and have been responsible for exhibitions, publications, forums and events exploring women's art and arts practice.

Perhaps due to the difficulty women have had breaking into formal networks there is often a far more exciting, maverick, experimental quality to their work. The range of work women are doing across Australia is immense. The elitist and often gender-based hierarchical distinction between art and craft has diminished and this has benefited the many women working in multi-media while extending the parameters of accepted practice.

This has resulted in a far wider representation of women in state collections and publicly funded exhibitions and particularly in the commercial arena, which is so economically important for Australian artists who are supported by a much smaller art market than their international counterparts.

There is an ever increasing number of women who work and exhibit in the many alternative galleries, publicly funded contemporary art spaces, artist-run co-operatives and more innovative uses of space: empty shop fronts, show cases at stations, public art projects for example. Women also dominate the community arts area as both artists and administrators.

Funding bodies at both a state and national level have been instrumental in policy determination which promotes women. At the 1993 Venice Biennale, Australia was represented for the first time by a solo woman artist, Jenny Watson. While at the 'top end' of the market the situation for Australian women artists is perceived as being far better than for women artists in Europe or America there is still much to be done.

The battle now is to get similar recognition for the huge number of

Aboriginal women artists working across Australia. Statistics suggest that 56 per cent of work being produced by Aboriginal artists is by women: painting, weaving, photography, ceramics, filmmaking, printing, jewellery making and public art projects. However it is male Aboriginal artists who are receiving the greater share of exhibition and written coverage and being publicly acquired and exhibited in major Australian and international exhibitions.

Aboriginal art is possibly the most powerful aspect of the Australian art scene. There are departments of Aboriginal art in each major state gallery and museum where older paintings and three-dimensional works are exhibited alongside the dynamic work being done by a growing number of contemporary Aboriginal artists including many women. Aboriginal women artists in Melbourne and Sydney are particularly active in organising one-off exhibitions and art events. Women curators at the Museum of Victoria in Melbourne and the Koori Heritage Trust, also housed at the Museum, have established a precedent in acquiring a large body of two and three dimensional works by Aboriginal women.

There is a lively and diverse art scene in each state of Australia and a greater number of women working as curators, gallery directors and community arts officers than ever before. Alongside this are the many informal support networks that women artists establish to support each other.

In Regional areas across the country there are publicly funded galleries in major centres. The addresses are available in all tourist guides. Often large numbers of women artists are represented in these collections. It has been suggested that this better representation of women reflects the lower prices often paid for women's work which suits these galleries' tight budgets and that Regional galleries frequently benefit from bequests from artist's families.

1995 marks a year of national celebrations of women's art in Australia. Galleries, museums, libraries, community art centres and performance venues are concentrating on exhibiting women, and publishing information about the women artists in their collections. Events include seminars and conferences.

Art Almanac is an invaluable, inexpensive monthly guide to galleries across Australia. It can be purchased from most city galleries particularly the public state galleries which have bookshops. In most major cities there are free weekly papers available which list exhibitions and related events. Tourist magazines will list most attractions. Most commercial galleries show the work of women artists; state galleries have substantial collections some of which are on display and, from time to time, exhibitions of women's work are mounted. Books about the work of Australian women artists are a further useful source of information (see Resource List).

The following state by state list indicates places that either concentrate on or feature women artists and most will facilitate contact with local artists and arts organisations.

Victoria

A major Women's Art Festival was held at the **National Gallery of Victoria**, St Kilda Road, Melbourne in February 1994 including exhibitions, seminars, performance art and concerts. Major exhibitions of women's work have been held at the National Gallery of Victoria, including Aboriginal women's art, contemporary art, installations, photography, cartoons and associated events. Ring (03) 685 0222 for information on current exhibitions. **The Women's Art Register**, established in 1975, is an ever-expanding collection of slides, information folders and catalogues representing over 2000 Australian women artists, predominantly living. Located at an inner city public library, Carringbush: 415 Church Street, Richmond, (03) 429 3644 or (03) 752 5757 AH, it is easily accessible by train and tram from central Melbourne. The library holds many books on women artists and women's arts practice. **The Women's Gallery**, 375 Brunswick Street, Fitzroy, (03) 419 0718 only exhibits work by women and also holds related events. The gallery is located in Melbourne's most bohemian street where cheap cafes, artists' studios, shops selling second-hand everything and the constant street fashion parades will provide hours of entertainment. In September watch out for the Artists' Street Parade

which opens the Fringe Arts Festival. Consult *Art Almanac* for many other galleries in the area, most on tram routes. **No Vacancy Temporary Galleries** is an initiative where artists show installations designed for 24-hour street viewing. Current sites in use around Melbourne are 183–189 Collins Street; Upper level of the City Square; Administration foyer, Melbourne Town Hall; Regent Theatre Foyer, Collins Street; 671 Rathdowne Street, North Carlton; 488 Victoria Street, North Melbourne. **Craft Victoria**, 114 Gertrude Street, Fitzroy, has constantly changing exhibitions and a resource library and artists' directory representing many craftswomen. **The Victorian Tapestry Workshop**, 260 Park Street, South Melbourne (03) 699 7885, employs up to 20 weavers working on large scale commissions. Tours are available on Wednesday and every second Thursday, $4. Direct tram available. **Linden Arts Centre**, 26 Acland Street, St Kilda, has a program of constantly changing exhibitions and installations plus related activities. Linden is situated in one of Melbourne's most favoured leisure areas on the seafront, with a marina, countless cafes and restaurants, buskers, the Sunday market and galleries. Take a tram or light rail from the city. **Artspost**, 21–27 Main Road, Ballarat East (2 hours from Melbourne), (053) 33 3822 is an artist-run collective of 100 artists who exhibit in an ex-post office complete with coffee shop and warm fire, a good contact point for regional visitors.

New South Wales

Art Hotline, (0055) 29334 is a telephone information service giving weekly details of one-day arts events at a range of sites around Sydney. Sydney's buses and trains provide transport to the following galleries which all feature women artists. **Artspace**, (02) 368 1705, concentrates on innovative contemporary work and is located at The Gunnery, 43–51 Cowper Wharf Road, Woolloomooloo (a visually rewarding walk overlooking the dock area if you come from the Art Gallery of NSW). **The Gunnery** also houses the offices of the National Association for the Visual Arts; The Arts Law Centre of Australia; The Copyright Council, The Artworkers Union and The Regional Galleries Association which will provide information on the many galleries in country NSW. Artist-run spaces include **First Draft West**, Parramatta Road, Annandale, (02) 516 1957, and **Arthous Too**, 379 South Darling Street, Darlinghurst (02) 360 1716. The latter is located in the Darlinghurst/Paddington area bustling with cafes and restaurants, bookshops and commercial galleries. Darlinghurst hosts Sydney's Gay and Lesbian Mardi Gras in February/March and the outrageous Sleaze Ball in October. **Boomali Aboriginal Co-operative**, 27 Abercrombie Street, Chippendale, (02) 698 2047, is a wholly Aboriginal initiative for self-management in the visual arts showing work by contemporary Aboriginal artists including many women. **The Performance Space**, 199 Cleveland

Street, Redfern, (02) 698 7235 has a program of contemporary performance, installations, site-specific collaborations between artists created in a workshop environment and forums concerned with current arts debate. Eighty to ninety percent of exhibitors are women. **The Australian Centre for Contemporary Photography**, 257 Oxford Street, Paddington, (02) 331 6253 represents a large number of women photographers both in the exhibition program and in the Photofile listing artists. Installations, electronic imagery, artists' exchange programs, workshops and publications are all part of ACP's program. **Tin Sheds Gallery**, City Road, University of Sydney, shows a diverse range of work and can be followed by a wander through the campus of Australia's oldest university. For interesting historical exhibitions featuring women artists visit the **S. H. Ervine Gallery**, Observatory Hill, Sydney, another stunning walk which overlooks the harbour and The Rocks tourist precinct. Other areas rich with galleries and/or street life are **Balmain, Glebe** and **Newtown**.

Australian Capital Territory
AGOG, Australian Girls Own Gallery, 71 Leichhardt Street, Kingston, (06) 295 3180, shows only women artists from around Australia. Accessible by bus from central Canberra or on one of the beautiful bicycle tracks that criss-cross the suburbs. AGOG is situated in the Leichhardt Street Studios, a complex of artists' studios and two other galleries: the artist-run Spiral Arm and Studio One a printmaking workshop/gallery. **The Canberra Contemporary Art Space** has two locations: Gorman House, Ainslie Avenue, Braddon (06) 247 0188 and 19 Feurneaux Street, Manuka. Changing exhibitions and installations, performance art, soundworks and forums are part of their innovative program. The Art Space is one of many organisations housed in the Gorman House Arts Centre which comprises artists' studios, theatre and dance groups, Clarry's Art Cafe and an Art/Craft market on Saturdays and Sundays. **Tilley's**, 96 Wattle Street, Lyneham, (06) 249 1543, is a women-orientated licensed cafe that combines a women-only gallery, live music and a public events program 7 days a week. Accessible by bus. **The Drill Hall Gallery**, Kingsley Street, Acton, (06) 249 5832, shows contemporary work and can be found on the campus of the Australian National University a five minute walk from Central Canberra. Also on campus on Ellery Circuit is the **Canberra School of Art Gallery,** (06) 249 5810, which shows touring exhibitions from interstate, solo exhibitions, graduate, post-graduate and staff exhibitions associated with the art school and specially curated exhibitions. Opposite the Drill Hall Gallery is **Photoaccess**, an artist-run initiative with a strong women's perspective, exhibiting innovative two – and three – dimensional photographic work and offering photographic workshops and seminars. Look out for **Aktion Surreal**, a performance art group that performs around

the city. Other areas where galleries and artist-run spaces/studios abound in Canberra are **Braddon**, **Dickson**, and **Manuka**, check *Art Almanac* for details. For a complete change and an opportunity to experience a working rural station, visit **Lanyon**, (06) 237 5192, a half hour's drive from Canberra. **The Nolan Gallery** at Lanyon exhibits work by one of the patriarchs of Australian art, Sidney Nolan as well as touring exhibitions. Apart from this, the property is well worth a visit and close to the **Cuppacumbalong Craft Centre** which, like most Craft Centres, has substantial representation of work by women, and the **Tidbinbilla Nature Reserve** if you need a break from the city.

Northern Territory
There are many, many commercial galleries in the Northern Territory showing Aboriginal work. General contemporary commercial galleries in central Darwin worth visiting include **Sunstorm** and **Framed Gallery**. **24 Hour Art – NT Centre for Contemporary Art**, Vimy Lane, corner Gregory Street, Parap, Darwin, (089) 81 5368 has a wide exhibiting program featuring many women artists and provides information on the NT art scene, reached by bus or walking from the central city. Visit 24 Hour Art on a Saturday when the Parap markets open for tantalising food and clothing stalls reflecting the large Asian population in the NT. **Alice Springs** is also crammed with commercial galleries showing Aboriginal work. Less commercial is the **Aruluen Centre**, Larapinta Drive, Alice Springs, (089) 52 5022, which has two galleries, one showing work from the permanent collection which includes Aboriginal work while touring exhibitions from around Australia are shown in the second gallery.

Western Australia
The central arts precinct in Perth is a minute's walk from Perth Central Station where you will find the **Art Gallery of WA**, the **State Library**, the **Museum** and the **Perth Institute of Contemporary Art (PICA)**, (09) 227 6144 which has a multi-arts program of exhibitions, performance art, soundworks and installations and provides information on other exhibition spaces in WA. Situated on Central Station itself is the **Crafts Council of WA** with a shop attached with a range of works from all over the state. Close by is **James Street**, good for cafes and street life. The **Artrage Festival** can be contacted through the **Artshouse** in James Street for information on the annual Visual and Performing Arts Festival held in Perth every October. People living in Fremantle, the beautiful port town on the Indian Ocean a very pleasant half hour train trip from Perth, boast it has the highest number of artists living and working there than anywhere else in Australia. The vibrant gallery and cafe scene testifies to this. **The Fremantle Arts Centre**, 1 Finnerty Street, Fremantle, (09) 335 8244, is a

good start. There is a cafe and bookshop, as well as a number of exhibition spaces, a music program in summer, a readings program in winter and artist residencies and workshops. **The Artists' Foundation**, 8 Phillimore Street, Fremantle, (09) 335 8366, provides support services and information on all aspects of arts practice in WA. It is housed in an arts complex comprising studios, a performance space and the **International Exchange Studio**. The Foundation will provide information on regional galleries throughout WA.

Tasmania

The contemporary art scene in Tasmania is perhaps less formally developed than in other states currently, due to funding difficulties, although there are huge numbers of practising artists in most localities across the state. The state art galleries in Hobart and Launceston will provide general information as will **CAST, Contemporary Art Services of Tasmania**, (002) 243 637, which also publishes a fortnightly bulletin on exhibitions and art events throughout Tasmania. The main centre for commercial galleries in Hobart is **Salamanca Place** crowded with eateries and tourist shops. **Plimsoll Gallery, Centre for the Arts, Hunter Street, Victoria Dock, Hobart**, focuses on contemporary and innovative art, craft, photography and design in changing exhibitions by local and interstate artists. The Centre also houses the **Tasmanian School of Art** in an architecturally interesting building with access to the art and design studios. Both will provide information on the local art scene. **Arthous** and **Snake Pit** in Launceston are artist run-spaces with changing exhibitions providing contact with local artists.

South Australia

Adelaide is a spacious, well planned city where the major cultural institutions, the **State Art Gallery**, **Museum** and **Library** can be found on North Terrace. **The Adelaide Festival Centre** housing the Theatre complex and Gallery, on the bank of the Torrens River and close to the University of South Australia, is a short stroll down King William Street. At the western end of North Terrace is the **Lion Arts Centre** housing artists' studios and many arts organisations: **The Multicultural Arts Committee, Mercury Cinema, Italian Theatre Company, The Media Resource Centre, The Adelaide Fringe Festival Office, The Crafts Council of South Australia** and **The Experimental Art Foundation**, (08) 211 7505, which works to develop experimental art through changing exhibitions both within and without the gallery space, holds occasional forums and artists' talks and supports publishing projects. At the cutting edge of contemporary practice is **V *&* S Matrix**, a group that develops computer-generated artworks from a feminist perspective. Contact

Josephine Starrs on (08) 271 0137 or Francesca da Rimini on (08) 231 0070 (BH). **Tandaya,** corner Grenfell and East Terrace, (08) 223 2467, a large Aboriginal-run exhibiting space and information centre featuring work from all over Australia and specially curated exhibitions. **The Contemporary Art Centre** South Australia, 14 Parkside, (08) 272 2682, shows changing exhibitions of innovative work and site-specific installations in its internal and external exhibiting spaces.

Queensland
First stop should be the **Queensland Artworkers Alliance,** 497 Adelaide Street, Brisbane City, (07) 844 9002, which provides information on the visual art, craft and design industry in Queensland and can direct visitors to the large number of artist-run art galleries in the city and beyond. **The Institute of Modern Art**, corner Ann and Gipps Street, Fortitude Valley, 4006, (07) 252 5750, has a particular emphasis on installation, performance and conceptual work supported by a program of seminars, lectures and forums with a bias towards women artists and curators particularly those with ethnic backgrounds. **MOCA – Museum of Contemporary Art,** 8 Petrie Terrace, Brisbane, (07) 368 3228, has a permanent collection of contemporary art and a program of changing contemporary touring and curated exhibitions. Women artists are sometimes represented in the temporary gallery space, **The Loading Bay**. MOCA has a cafe and bookshop, the latter specialising in contemporary theory including many publications on women's art practice. Downstairs from MOCA is a commercial gallery, **Michael Milburn Gallery**, (07) 367 0277 representing contemporary Australian artists particularly women.

2
CITIES – COUNTRY – RIVERS

NATURE

Susan Hawthorne and Renate Klein
NATIONAL PARKS AND OTHER ATTRACTIONS

The best resource books on Australia's natural attractions are books on National Parks with pictures of the main attractions and give you an idea of the climate and landscapes. State Tourism offices are another useful source. Each of the regional sections in Part 2 gives a brief description of a few selected places of interest. For further information contact Tourism offices (each state has offices in every other state). When travelling in National Parks you should not remove or destroy plants, animals or rocks. Fire arms are not permitted. Pets are generally not allowed. Camping is usually permitted only in marked areas (read the signs on entry). There are restrictions on the use of open fires, and in summer months you should always carry a gas stove. You can't assume running water will be available, especially in dry and remote areas. Many of the areas mentioned also hold significance for local Aboriginal communities, please respect these areas and do not go into areas restricted for Aboriginal use. Places that have sacred significance should be treated with the respect you would accord to other sacred areas such as churches, mosques, temples. Most Australian native animals, birds and many plants are protected, both inside and outside National Parks. Be careful when you drive in remote areas during dusk; it is getting up time for kangaroos and it is a horrible experience when they suddenly appear in front of your car. If you are travelling slowly you may be able to stop in time.

Australian birds and animals are an important part of any journey through the Australian landscape. The lazy caw of a crow, the morning warble of the currawong or the raucous screech of the cockatoo (see Namjoshi, Reilly and Cafarella) can be heard in most parts of the country. Australian animals may be harder to see, as so many of them are nocturnal. Ask the locals in areas you are passing through, if there are any special places where kangaroos, koalas, echidnas, wombats, marsupial rats, platypus and the like can be seen; some hotels or camping grounds may have tame or visiting animals. If you do come upon them in the wild, try to be as unintrusive as possible.

Many native plants are peculiar to Australia and the overall landscape, particularly untamed bush, has an 'untidy' look about it. The Ngiyambaa people of western NSW have a word, *walu*, that describes the messiness, the untamed wildness of the Australian bush: the hanging strips of bark, the scattered leaves, the disordered look that is so very different from the artificially kempt and ordered stretches of land in other parts of the world. If you look carefully through the grasses and bark you may find tiny wildflowers or orchids in the undergrowth.

Jeannie Devitt's piece describes some traditional plant uses from Central Australia, but if you are trying 'bush tucker' do so with guidance. There are roots and nuts in some parts of the country that can give you severe diarrhoea unless they have been soaked in water for weeks! Nor do plants in one part of the country necessarily have the same properties as similar plants in other parts of the country.

If you are planning to bushwalk carry plenty of provisions and prepare well. Apart from dehydration in summer or in dry areas, you can also die of exposure in mountainous regions. A clear sunny day can end in a blizzard. Walking in the bush in Australia is dangerous mostly because of its remoteness. You cannot necessarily walk out of an area in a single day, and you can rarely assume that anyone else will pass by. For these reasons sufficient water and food is essential for more days than you plan to be away. In the summer months, snake bite is another danger. Parties of three or more are advised since if someone is bitten, the most recent advice is that the person should remain as still as possible, thereby decreasing the circulation and the speed at which the poison reaches the heart. A party of three means one can stay, and one or more can go for help. Most snakes will retreat if they hear you, you should do the same if you see them first.

A reminder to those coming from the northern hemisphere, if you get lost remember that the sun in Australia is in the north and that the stars in the sky will be unfamiliar. A star map can be an interesting and useful companion when travelling in inland Australia where, on clear nights, you will see star-filled skies.

If you are planning to travel through areas marked as Aboriginal Land, or if you wish to visit sites on Aboriginal Land, you will need to write well in advance to the appropriate Aboriginal Land Council, stating the purpose and expected duration of your visit. In some areas alcohol is prohibited and this and other requirements should be strictly respected (see Resource List).

Suniti Namjoshi
AUSTRALIAN NOTEBOOK

For Renate

There were three elements: the woman, the cockatoo, and me – a disembodied narrator observing them. The woman had a body; the cockatoo was rock, sheer white rock, flint veined with quartz; and the cockatoo was in there, neither awake, nor asleep, but probably content. The woman was standing in front of the rock face. I don't think she was praying, though in the white moonlight that might have been appropriate. She was just looking at it. I could see the bird. But what happened next wasn't really possible: wing feathers stirred. How can feathers be composed of solid rock? How can they stir? Wouldn't the rock crumble? The rock was crumbling, slivers of flint grinding against one another, sparks and noise filling the air. When the bird emerged it had a sulphur crest. So far so good. The bird bowed. The woman bowed back. Everything was seemly, till the woman and the bird began shrieking at each other. I turned away then. Mere observers have their limitations. I saw them take off. The woman and the bird? No, the two cockatoos, the cockatoo and her sister. It stands to reason. Flying women belong to the realm of myth and comic books. But sulphur-crested cockatoos racketing in the sky – that's observed reality. And I have not presumed to interpret them.

Robyn Adams
EXPERIENCE THE AUSTRALIAN FLORA!

The Australian flora offers the traveller a unique experience – the opportunity to travel into the past! The flora itself is your time machine, so with a little imagination and some attention to planning your itinerary, you can see both the vast array of modern species as well as catch glimpses of the plants which covered Australia millions years ago.

As part of your preparation you need to settle back, close your eyes and imagine the ancient supercontinent of Gondwana. If you begin your imagining at the start of the Tertiary period, about 65 million years before the present, you will see Australia fitting snugly into the Gondwanaland jigsaw, next to the future Antarctic continent, and neighbour to the other pieces of the puzzle – Africa, South America, India, Madagascar and New Zealand. Outside in your mind, the sea is warm, the winds are blowing from the west and they bring persistent rain to all the jigsaw-continents. When the rain eases and the swirling clouds lift briefly, put on your coat and take a walk. It is warmer than you expected, warmer than the present, and what appeared to you from a distance to be a jumble of rainforest greens, and a tangle of trees and ferns and flowers, begins to take form. When you look more closely the plants are not so strange to you after all. You have already met many of their families, and know some of the species through their descendants 65 million years in the future.

If you continue to watch, you will see the pieces of the jigsaw begin to move apart. First Africa, then Madagascar and India, then South America and New Zealand, and finally, if you have been watching patiently for 25 million years, you will see the Australian continent tear free of Antarctica and begin to drift northwards towards the latitude where you first found it. Keep watching, but keep your coat on! It will stop raining but it will also get colder. The lush greens of the rainforest pines and beeches will gradually be replaced by the blue-greys and blue-greens of the new indigenous eucalypts and wattles and sheoaks, and you will notice new species appearing, many of them with small, tough, pointed leaves, and unusual lifestyles. Finally, just before you open your eyes and get back to planning your trip, you look into the distance and see that the sea level has risen, cutting off New Guinea and Tasmania from the mainland, and clearly drawing the boundaries around the islands of Australasia that you are familiar with.

When Australia separated from Antarctica, the new island continent carried with it a rich and varied cargo of plants, all related in some way to the plants on the other drifting pieces of the Gondwanan jigsaw, and which over the next 45 million years made and re-made new alliances, rose and then fell from prominence, formed many new species, many new genera, and a few new families, until it reached the mix and distribution of vegetation you are about to visit.

As Australia moved northwards the continent gradually became colder and more arid, causing the habitat of the original Gondwanan rainforest to slowly contract towards the southern edges of the continent. The old Gondwanan flora was not lost, and Victoria and Tasmania offer excellent opportunities to see what Gondwanan cool temperate rainforest looked like.

In Tasmania, the Cradle Mountain-Lake St Clair National Park contains remnants of this cool temperate rainforest, and easy access can be gained from the area around Cradle Mountain (see pages 239–40). It is typified by the moss and lichen covered trees of *Nothofagus*, the southern or antarctic beech. Scattered in patches throughout these beech forests are the rainforest gymnosperms, *Phyllocladus* or celery top pine, *Dacrydium* or huon pine, and pencil pine and King Billy pine, both species of *Athrotaxis*. Some spectacular remnants can be found in the Walls of Jerusalem National Park (see page 240) but it is accessible only by foot. None of these four species are now found on the mainland, but some excellent pockets of beech forest can be found in the Otway Ranges in the south west of Victoria. Maits Rest, off the Great Ocean Road, is well worth visiting.

The main attraction of the Australian flora is the endemic flora that evolved and expanded into many of the habitats vacated by the retreat of the rainforests during the long period of isolation following separation of the new island continent from Gondwanaland. Many of the uniquely Australian species are described as 'sclerophyllous' – they have small, crowded, prickly leaves which originally developed in response to low soil nutrient availability, but were also fortuitously more drought and fire resistant and they rapidly spread as the continent became more arid.

Fire is the major regenerating influence on much of the Australian flora, and you will not travel far without seeing clear evidence of its recent passage. However, the precise nature of the role of fire in the formation of the Australian flora is uncertain, and the use of fire to manage the present day vegetation is controversial. Around 150,000 years ago, there was a gradual change from the earlier fire sensitive rainforest flora to a flora dominated by species better adapted to fire, and this trend is even more marked from about 50,000 years ago to the present. The role of the first human inhabitants in causing the increase in fire frequency on the continent is uncertain. Aboriginal Australians certainly used fire to deliberately manipulate their environment, but the scale and purpose of burning varied greatly across the continent. The impact of Aboriginal burning is best understood in the monsoonal areas of the Northern Territory, and in Central Australia, and least understood in the forests of south-eastern Australia.

Examples of the truly Australian flora can be found in the many different types of eucalypt forest, and in the heathlands, found in many regions of Australia.

Major Vegetation Types

1. The Rainforests: There are two very different types of rainforest represented in Australia. In southern Victoria and Tasmania, rainforests are remnants of the earlier Gondwanan flora, with dominant species similar to those found in New Zealand, and South America. In northern Australia, rainforests are similar to those of nearby Asia, with a wide diversity of large leaved species, and the highly specialized species including lianes and trees with buttress roots typical of tropical rainforests. All rainforests are dark, as their close tree canopies stop light reaching the forest floor, so if you want to take photographs a 400 ASA film is essential.

Places to Visit: **Cradle Mountain, Tasmania** – has good walking tracks through easily accessible rainforest. **Otways Region, Victoria** – has some excellent sites for viewing rainforest. In particular **Maits Rest** has board walks which enable a view of the ecosystem from high above ground, and a drive along **Turtons Track** should not be missed. **East Gippsland, Victoria** – board walks have been established at a number of sites which provide good view points of rainforest gullies. **Mossman Gorge, Queensland** – an easily accessible walk through typical tropical rainforest with lianes and buttress roots, and where colourful butterflies are frequently seen. **Daintree Area, Queensland** – several commercial operations provide accommodation close to typical areas of rainforest.

2. The Tall Eucalypt Forests: The dominant trees in the forests of Australia are species of *Eucalyptus*. There are well over six hundred individual species of eucalypts, and they dominate a wide range of vegetation types from the tall majestic forests in areas of reliable rainfall, to the smaller trees on the drier sites, to more open woodlands often found in areas with a more unpredictable climate. The eucalypt flowers have no petals, but the masses of brightly coloured stamens serve to attract a range of insect, bird and possum pollinators. In some of the wetter eucalypt forests *Eucalyptus regnans* (mountain ash) may grow up to 100m tall, towering over a rich understorey of wattles (*Acacia* species) and tree ferns, and with smaller ferns, vines, mosses, lichens and liverworts carpeting the forest floor. In Victoria, a drive along Turtons Track in the Otways, or along the Black Spur between Healesville and Narbethong to the east of Melbourne, will show you the kind of forest which now grows in the cool wet areas once covered by rainforest. In the south west region of Western Australia, tall eucalypt forest dominated by *Eucalyptus marginata* or jarrah, and *Eucalyptus diversicolor* or karri, can be found on the more fertile soils and higher rainfall areas. The thick understorey makes exploration of these forests difficult unless preformed tracks are used.

A wide range of eucalypt forests are found across the whole of the continent, but the exact mix of species varies greatly depending on a number of factors, including location, climate, soils, rainfall and fire history. In southern Australia, rainforests develop on sites with about 400 years without fire, and following fire eucalypt forests initially develop. In these areas most of the forest is dominated by eucalypts with pockets of rainforest on sheltered sites such as watercourses which have escaped fires.

Places to Visit: **Otways Region, Victoria** – a good road network allows exploration of an area with many accessible short walks through tall eucalypt forests. Patches of rainforest are often found within these forests. One of the tallest documented eucalypts (now cut down) was located in this area. **Upper Yarra** and the **Black Spur, Victoria** – this area forms part of the water catchment for Victoria, and tall evenly spaced trees represent regrowth from the 1939 bushfires. **East Gippsland, Victoria** – good maps and guides to this area are available, and useful to explore the tall eucalypt forests used for hardwood timber production. **Pemberton Area, Western Australia** – some good examples of tall eucalypt forest can be found in this wetter area of Western Australia.

3. The Eucalypt Forests and Woodlands: Eucalypt forests and woodlands occur over most of south-eastern Australia. These forests typically have smaller trees than found on wetter sites, and also often have a colourful understorey of wattles, peas, lilies and orchids. These species regrow rapidly following fire, and the stark beauty of recently burned patches of bush contrasts with the green vigour of rapidly regenerating vegetation. A visit to most of these drier forests will show evidence of recent burning which is part of an attempt to control bushfires which are relatively common in this vegetation, which can become tinder dry in summer.

Places to Visit: **Wombat Forest, Victoria** – a good network of roads allows easy exploration of this area. The open understorey should encourage an easy walk off the formed tracks, and a very wide variety of colourful species will be found, especially in spring. A wide variety of bird species, and abundant kangaroos will also be seen. **Coastal Forests, southern New South Wales** – eucalypt woodlands consisting of species with smooth white bark, and an understorey of primitive looking cycads are worth a trip. **Canberra, Australian Capital Territory** – the dry forests surrounding Canberra, and on Black Mountain in the suburban areas are worth exploring. They have spectacular understorey of wattles, peas, and lilies in spring, and there are a number of short well-marked walks available. **Jarrah Forests, Western Australia** – these forests are superficially similar to the dry forests of eastern Australia, but they include an even more spectacular set of understorey species. They should be visited in spring if possible. They have frequently suffered the effects of cinnamon fungus or dieback, which is often associated with hardwood timber production.

4. Heathland: Many areas of coastal Victoria and New South Wales, and Western Australia are covered by extremely nutrient-poor sands. These areas, called the sandplains or heaths, contain an extraordinarily high number of sclerophyllous plant species which are not only endemic to Australia, but often to just a small region. In particular the sandplains and coastal heaths of Western Australia have not only a very high species diversity, but up to 80 per cent of these species may be endemic. The spectacular flowers of *Banksia* are most abundant here, but the strangest plants are the tall grass trees from the family Xanthorrhoeaceae. From a distance *Kingia* and *Xanthorrhoea* look like left-over tree ferns, with their tall trunks and tufts of long narrow leaves, but the bunches of drumstick flowers of *Kingia* and the tall spear-like inflorescence of *Xanthorrhoea*, which are produced after the plant has been burned by bushfire, soon set them apart as uniquely Australian. *Kingia* is only found in Western Australia, but different species of *Xanthorrhoea* are very widely spread through Australian heathland.

Heathland can be disappointing if you visit it out of season. The plants begin to flower about August, but the best times are September and October. In heathland, species diversity reaches a peak about eight years after it has burned, and it is well worth seeking out areas which have been recently burned.

Places to Visit: **Sandplain and Stirling Ranges, Western Australia** – the diversity of heath species is highest in Western Australia, and up to 100 different species can be found in a ten metre square. The sandplain north of Perth, and especially around **Mt Leseur**, has the greatest species diversity of plants per area than any other place in the world. Spring is the most spectacular time. **Sydney, New South Wales** – the sandstone areas surrounding Sydney have large areas of heath which are easily accessible. **Royal National Park** has a number of good access roads and walking tracks. **Gariwerd (The Grampians), Western Victoria** – an area with a wide range of vegetation types including magnificent River Red Gum forests, and some good examples of heathland. **The Little Desert** to the north also has large areas of heath.

5. Arid Australia: Over 70 per cent of the Australian continent is classed as arid land, where the rainfall is low, and more importantly unreliable. Rainfall can be spread over the seasons, some years may have no rainfall, or several year's rainfall can fall in an hour. It has been described as the place where 'the creeks are dry or ten feet high'! Much of the arid zone has been modified by grazing, but after a 'wet' season, ephemeral species provide a spectacular site. After a 'dry' period, there may be no obvious plants except prickly bushes and widely spaced trees along dry water-courses. Arid zone vegetation is extremely variable and depends on a wide range of environmental determinants. In its broadest sense it can include 'mallee' – a group of eucalypts with a large underground stem which can survive intense fires which occasionally burn this hot dry region; spinifex 'grasslands' – a prickly grass covering vast areas of the arid zone with evenly spaced tussocks, saltbush – a shrub covering large areas which often show degradation due to grazing, such as on the Nullarbor Plain.

A visit to any of the more remote arid zone areas requires careful planning, and should not be approached lightly. Population centres are widely spaced, fuel and water may need to be carried, and a four wheel drive vehicle may also be necessary.

Places to Visit: **Wyperfeld National Park, Victoria** – an easily accessible reserve which includes a generally dry drainage system, and a range of arid zone plant communities. Also has good diversity of birds, and large numbers of kangaroos. **Flinders Ranges, South Australia** – easily accessible area with a range of arid zone communities, including watercourse eucalypts with smooth white bark, and native pine woodlands. Well worth a visit. **Alice Springs, Northern Territory** – more difficult access because of large distances to travel between population centres, but provides a good starting point for a visit to a truly arid area. **Nullarbor Plain, Western Australia** – a drive along two thousand kilometres of well made road from Adelaide to Perth crosses a large area of changing arid zone vegetation.

Much of Australia away from the urban areas is still covered by native vegetation, and you should be able to find small parks close to all major centres of population. Any trip will be enhanced by some brief stops to look at a flora which is very different to that now found in the northern continents of Europe.

With a little planning it is possible to visit a wide range of areas and see an enormous variety of species. If you are interested in a spectacular show of colourful flowering species, then a visit in spring (September/October) is essential. Note that most native species are protected and may not be picked without a permit. Government Conservation Departments have a wide range of pamphlets and interpretation material which is free and easily obtained from Rangers in Parks or from their Head Offices in capital cities. To fully appreciate the flora an illustrated guide to the plants of the area you will be visiting is essential. The best places to obtain regional guidebooks are from the bookshops run by conservation groups, and the major bookshops.

Useful Illustrated Books

G. R. Cochrane, B. A. Fuhrer, E. R. Rotherham and J. H. Willis. 1973. *Flowers and Plants of Victoria*. NSW: A. H. & A. W. Reed.

R. Erickson, A. S. George, N. G. Marchant and M. K. Morcombe. 1986. *Flowers and Plants of Western Australia*. NSW: A. H. & A. W. Reed.

E. R. Rotherham, B. C. Briggs, D. F. Blaxell and R. C. Carolin. 1982. *Flowers and Plants of New South Wales and Southern Queensland*. NSW: A. H. & A. W. Reed.

Jeannie Devitt

TRADITIONAL PLANT USE IN THE SANDOVER RIVER REGION

The Sandover River lies within the Central Australian arid zone. It is an area that is sometimes loosely referred to as 'desert' country. The rainfall is about 300 mm a year, falling mainly in the summer, while temperatures range from 40°C in summer (December–February) and plummet to near freezing in the winter months of June, July and August. The area includes uplands drained by the Waite and Sandover River systems. There are large expanses of woodland dominated by Mulga trees (*Acacia aneura*); there are sandy creek beds and their associated well-vegetated floodplains, some smaller areas of low ranges and rocky outcrops as well as large expanses of waterless sand plains. The sand plains are spinifex covered but may also support a shrub covering of mallee (*Eucalyptus gamophylla* and *E. pachyphylla*) and Grevillea with occasional Kurrajong trees (*Brachychiton gregorii*). Generally the area offered a diversity of productive environments to Aborigines living a traditional lifestyle. They made extensive use of plants as foods, medicines and as the source of raw materials for utensils, tools and weapons.

One such tree was the Batswing coral tree (*Erythrina vespertilio*). With its clusters of brilliant red flowers and few leaves, it is striking looking. Called *atyweretye*, this tree provides a light-weight but strong wood that was traditionally used to make wooden trays and dishes for domestic use and shields. Women still use a shallow wooden tray or *alengarre* as a baby carrier. The *alengarre* is about 60 cm long and 30 cm wide. Men carve the trays from a section of the Batswing coral tree trunk. The inner surface is carefully smoothed while the outer one is decorated with a series of narrow parallel grooves. The tray is then painted all over with red ochre before it is given over to the woman. Nowadays women place a sheet or blanket on the tray to provide a soft surface for the infant. Lying on the *alengarre*, completely covered, the baby is protected against scorching sun and flies as well as the chilly winds of a desert winter. Mothers often softly scratch the underside of the *alengarre* with their fingernails to provide a soothing sound for a sleeping child.

The seeds of the Coral tree are large and brightly coloured – varying shades of yellow, or red through to deep maroon. People collect them and string them together to make necklaces, bracelets and other jewellery or sometimes mats. These *inernte* bean strings are a common item in the tourist and souvenir shops of Central Australia.

The larger, deep wooden bowls are no longer made but were used for water and food collection. In earlier times women returned to camp carrying these large wooden bowls filled with the day's hunting and gathering returns – lizards and grubs to be cooked in the hot ashes, or perhaps loads of seeds to be pounded and ground into edible meal. At the end of a day's foraging, women would gather in small family groups to prepare food and, no doubt, to swap anecdotes about the day's hunting dramas.

One of the seeds they regularly gathered was *ntyerrme*, the seed of the Dogwood tree (*Acacia coriacea*). Dogwood trees are found on the sandy spinifex plains. The long pods contain up to 10 large pea-sized seeds and hang from the branches in bunches. A large quantity can be gathered easily in a short time. The pods are lightly steamed, either on a small grass fire or in the ashes of a larger one to split open the pod and extract the seeds.

Once dry, the seeds are more difficult to collect. Women break off pod-bearing branches, and pile the dry pods into heaps which they then beat with short, sturdy sticks. This breaks open the pods and releases the seeds which fall to the bottom of the pile. Periodically they remove the pod fragments and other plant debris. Eventually, a quantity of black, shiny seeds, each with an orange-coloured aril or cap, can be removed from the other debris.

The dry seeds were soaked in water to produce a milky, white, slightly sweet drink. The aril swells with water and comes away from the seed. Arils were thought to have therapeutic value and can be scooped up in handfuls and plastered on the body. The wet seeds were not discarded but laid out to dry prior to being ground.

Traditional methods of processing seeds into edible paste were lengthy and labour intensive. Many women now in their 40s have the knowledge and skills to process seeds although they no longer do it regularly. People very quickly adopted the white refined flour that the Europeans brought in place of the variety of tree and grass seeds they previously used. Although the processing of tree seeds like *ntyerrme* was more complicated and time-consuming than that for grass seeds, the grass seeds were so much smaller (some less than half the size of a pin head) that a great deal of time was expended gathering sufficient quantities of them. In a demonstration of seed gathering and processing, women prepared a tree seed paste at a rate of about 5.5 hours per kilogram of edible paste, but they needed almost 8.5 hours to prepare a similar quantity of grass seed paste. Given this, it is not difficult to understand the immediate attraction that flour had for Aboriginal women who otherwise had to spend so many hours processing seeds.

The processing of *ntyerrme* seeds is complex. The seeds have an extremely hard outer case which women first parched by mixing the seeds with hot soil, coals and ash. This made the seed case brittle and easier to break. But recovering the seeds form the soil then entailed further work. Women referred to this as 'cleaning' the seed. They placed the mixture of seeds and soil, ash and coals into a wooden coolamon and by deftly moving the dish in rhythmic motions were able to separate seeds from soil, or from plant debris or whatever. There are several different rhythmic patterns depending on the type of sorting being undertaken.

Once cleaned, women pound and shatter the parched seeds to expose the edible inner kernel. The mixture must then be cleaned again to remove the fragments of seed case. The final stage in the process is grinding. Using a small hand-sized upper grindstone on a plate-like lower grindstone and adding water as a lubricant, women produced a coarse wet meal from the pounded fragments. The paste they produced was eaten immediately or cooked as a small cake or 'damper'. I found the traditionally prepared seed pastes flavoursome but unpleasantly coarse and gritty. Older women said that taste was part of their early attraction to flour: they found it tasty and soft compared to bush seed cakes. Of course, it was also a lot less work to prepare.

These days dry seeds are not collected for consumption, though the green seeds of *ntyerrme* are still a favourite. However, seeds are regularly collected for sale to nurseries and seed merchants. Although not required to grind these seeds, women still work hard to gather and clean seed in quantity when the season is right. Seeds now sought include many like Gidgee (*Acacia georginae*) which were not part of the traditional food inventory.

Apart from a few prospectors, the Sandover River area had little appeal to early pastoralists. Although there were Europeans, and in some places, groups of Chinese, working at small mine holdings, the Anmatyerre and Alyawarre people of the area controlled the larger portion of their traditional lands until the 1920s. From then on, European Australians moved in, systematically dispossessing people of their traditional homelands, repeating the brutal and sadly familiar pattern of the Australian pastoral frontier: they restricted Aborigines' movements, limited access to traditional waters and ran their sheep and cattle on the best localities. Using a combination of compulsion and enticements, pastoralists exacted from Aborigines the labour necessary to establish and maintain their holdings.

Despite the undoubted harshness of the times, individuals sometimes recall those earlier days with more nostalgia than bitterness. Here, Gloria Petyarre, a woman born in the early 1940s describes her life as a young girl moving around the local area with her family.

We used to go to Athathenge [now Artatinga Station] to get rations. We used to work on the fences, making holes for the fenceposts. That White boss was very aggressive. He used to shout at us to dig the holes deeper. We were continually throwing away the dead branches, picking them up and throwing them aside – clearing the fenceline. As we cleared, we lit fires to warm ourselves.

My sisters and the others used to work. In the morning, we'd get up and eat – flour and the rations that the White Boss, Old Purvis, had given us. There was flour, jam or treacle. Then we used to go to work . . . cutting the fence lines. When the work was completely finished it would be holiday time – Christmas holiday. We'd go back and he [Purvis] would give us food. We'd put on the clothes he gave us and eat the grapes he gave us in a wheelbarrow. Then we'd go off on a holiday to Alcoota [another neighbouring station]. You could just go and get food. People would start working again straight away. The old woman would shepherd the cattle and do the milking. Then we'd go to Ankerrepwe [Utopia Station], to Alpwerrenenge [Waite River] and we'd keep going right up to Alhalkere.

Oh! Talk about bush potatoes and yams! Yes! There bush potatoes every day of the week, and emu. This was a long time ago when I was a child – there were many emus. Look at the land now, there's nothing left, it's all finished. We used to get ntyerrme [Acacia seeds] dry them and drink their juice – it was lovely! And seeds! Mulga (*Acacia aneura*), Pigweed (*Portulaca spp.*) and grasses. We'd get bags full of them. We used to go and get wild tobacco (*Nicotiana spp.*) out west from Athathenge . . . When we ran short of food we used to go back to the station – to the boss, our boss.

When I was a kid . . . it always rained, it was always green and we had bush food every day. [Now] it's changed to dry times. When lots of White people came, bush meat and other foods started to disappear. A long time ago we used to have lots of goannas, perenties, echidnas, kangaroos, emus, but there's not much now.

One food people continue to gather in quantity is the honey of the native bee. The bees are small, black and stingless, making their hives within hollow sections of a variety of trees including Coolibahs (*Eucalyptus microtheca*), Bloodwoods (*E. terminalis*), Beefwood (*Grevillea striata*) and Gidgee (*Acacia georginae*). Particularly in the cooler winter months, families enjoy trips into the bush searching for the hives or 'sugarbag' as the honey is known. It's not easy to find a hive though. The hunter stands beside a likely tree and looks carefully for the small hive entrance – a round opening of less than a centimetre diameter. Or, she may look skywards through the branches, hoping to catch a glimpse of the bees returning to their hive. Having confirmed the presence of the hive, she sets to with an axe to expose the honey cache. This might take only minutes if the tree is a Eucalypt or similar soft wood tree. If the honey lies inside a hardwood like Gidgee, it could be a lengthy process – especially if the axe is blunt! Women share the axe work, systematically removing layers of wood. All the while they discuss whether or not they're working at just the right place to best remove the honey. They may put an ear to the tree to be better guided by the buzzing of the bees within.

Once the cache is exposed everyone crowds in close to the tree, removing honey with their fingers, or with sticks and eating it on the spot. The cache has internal divisions: small yellow balls of pollen packed together, the honey in its wax sacs and the creamy-coloured laval sacs. All are edible though there is now more interest in the honey and pollen than the eggs. If the cache is large, the hunters scrape it into a container to take home. Pollen-rich honey is a highly nutritious food as well as being delicious.

One of the most accessible of the bush fruits is *akatyerre* or Bush raisin (*Solanum centrale*). Growing in sandy country, it is a small plant which grows to approximately 15–20 cm height. It has purple flowers and small, grape-sized fruits that are a sunny yellow colour. People may gather large quantities of *akatyerre* quite quickly. They tip their collected fruits out on to an open sandy patch and roll them around in the sand. The sand adheres to a greasy film on the skin of the fruits. The sand and the film is removed by gently rolling the fruits between the palms of the hand. I was told that eating Bush raisins without first removing this film will cause a headache. The fruit has a rather tart taste, akin to tamarind. As the season progresses, the fruits undergo a natural drying process on the bush. The fruits remain edible in this dehydrated state despite their less attractive brown and shrivelled appearance. Many people prefer them this way. Traditionally, women gathered the dried fruits, cleaned them and pounded them lightly with grindstones to form a pulp. The pulp was formed into small cakes which could be either stored or transported.

There are a number of edible Solanum species in Central Australia including *S. cleistogamum* and *S. ellipticum*. But a word of caution: some of these very similar-looking plants *are definitely not edible* – they will cause illness. Only try them if you're with someone who knows the plant well.

A favourite fruit still regularly gathered is *alangkwe* (*Leichhardtia australis*). Called Bush bananas in English, these fruits grow prolifically after rain and are found on vines growing on Mulga trees in woodland areas and on Blue Mallee and Red Mallee (*Eucalyptus spp.*) on the sandplains. The fruits grow up to 10 cm long, but are best eaten before they attain this size. The small young fruits are sweet, wet and crunchy and are eagerly sought when at their peak. The seed material dries out and the skin toughens as the fruit matures. Collected at this stage, the fruits are steamed in the ashes of a fire to soften and moisten them. Traditionally people also ate the leaves of the Bush banana vine. They rolled them into bundles and lightly steamed them in the ashes. The rosette-like flowers were also eaten straight from the vine.

Suggested Literature

Anne-Marie Brody. 1990. *Utopia: A Picture Story*. Perth: Heytsbury Holdings Ltd. Robert Holmes-a-Court.

Isobel White, Diane Barwick and Betty Meehan (eds). 1985. *Fighters and Singers*. Sydney: Allen and Unwin.

Suzy Bryce. 1986. *Women's Gathering and Hunting in the Pitjantjatjara Homelands*. Alice Springs: Institute for Aboriginal Development.

Dulcie Levitt. 1981. *Plants and People*. Canberra: Australian Institute of Aboriginal Studies Press.

A. McGrath. 1987. *Born in the Cattle*. Sydney: Allen and Unwin.

Phyllis Kaberry. 1939. *Aboriginal Women Sacred and Profane*. London: Routledge.

Anne Urban. 1990. *Wildflowers and Plants of Central Australia*. Southbank Editions.

Cliff Goddard and Arpad Kalotas (eds). 1985. *Yankuntjatjara Plant Use*. Alice Springs: Institute of Aboriginal Development.

Pamela Watson. 1983. *This Precious Foliage*. Oceania Monograph.

We'd like to add to this:

Thanks to Gloria Petyarre for her permission to quote.

Pauline Reilly
OF EMUS AND COCKATOOS

Australia's wildlife – not the human sort – is nothing to be scared of. Many visitors imagine that the place is writhing with snakes waiting to fling themselves at unwary travellers. This is not so. Yes, our snakes are venomous but they are much more concerned to keep out of our way. I live in the country and have seen only one snake in ten years, even though I am constantly out of doors and wandering round swamps and forests and woodlands. If you are silly enough to go wandering round at night during the summer with bare legs and no idea where you are treading, you just might be unlucky but you are in far more danger each time you cross the road.

We do not have ravening wild beasts either. No tigers, lions, wolves. Our native mammals – wombats, kangaroos, koalas – are cautious but not aggressive, even the Tasmanian Devil that looks rather frightening. Probably the only animal of which to be wary is the saltwater crocodile of the tropical regions. Keep out of crocodile infested waters and you are safe.

And you are safe with birds too – or most of them. More than 750 species visit or live in Australia. Some of them are migrant waders that breed in the northern hemisphere, particularly in the Arctic, and spend the southern summer here. They come to us in eclipse plumage, meaning that they no longer wear the brighter colours they use for display during breeding. Instead they are clad in shades of grey or browns with touches of white and black. Wader watching requires specialised skills but for those who are enthusiastic there are many good wader watching places.

Many of our birds live nowhere else in the world. The flightless emu is perhaps the best known and one that should appeal to feminists. The female emu lays a clutch of eggs, a dozen or so and admittedly rather large, each one the equivalent of ten hen eggs. After that mighty effort, she then leaves the male to do the rest and wanders away. She can even choose another if she feels so inclined. The male's task is not easy. For eight weeks, he does not leave the nest even to eat, drink or defecate. Then when the chicks hatch, he teaches them how to feed and stays with them until they are half a year old, protecting them from danger by high speed running or by a powerful forward kick if he is cornered.

The emu is related to the cassowary that lives in tropical Australia and to the ostrich (South Africa), rhea (South America) and kiwi (New Zealand). The cassowary is occasionally bad-tempered but you are unlikely to meet one as they are few in number and restricted to tropical north-eastern Queensland.

If you envied the emu with her freedom from domesticity, then feel sorry for the lyrebird. In the depth of winter, the male lyrebird spends his time singing and dancing on his mound, trying to entice any passing female to mate with him. His song is loud and tuneful and he is one of the most accomplished mimics in the world. If in the winter you visit the wet forests of eastern Australia from the Queensland/New South Wales border to just east of Melbourne in Victoria, you may hear a stream of song composed of different birds from kookaburras to thrushes to cockatoos to rosellas – any bird that happens to share the same forest. The music of the male lyrebird is enchanting and his intention is to enchant the female lyrebirds. The male that performs best is likely to attract the most females. At least she has this choice. Having made her choice and mated, she is thereafter on her own. She builds the nest, incubates the egg for nearly seven weeks – she goes off to feed each day – and then feeds the chick in the nest for another seven weeks. By the beginning of the next winter she is free of it, and promptly thinks about breeding again. The young one joins with other young lyrebirds and roams round for years before it begins to breed. Lyrebirds are not easy to see in their rugged mountain habitat but you can view them at the Healesville Sanctuary near Melbourne.

The kookaburra is one of the largest kingfishers in the world and the loud laughing chorus of a group – 'kook-kook-kook-ka-ka' – rolls on and on through the bushland, ensuring that only the hard of hearing will be unaware of their presence. Unlike the lyrebird female that appears to have a hard life, the kookaburra has a much more cosy domestic arrangement. The mated pair co-operates with nest-building, incubation and rearing of the young but they also have the help of the young of the previous year. These helpers bring food and help to protect and rear the young.

There are other smaller kingfishers, all colourful in blues, greens and rich rufous. They are widespread in different parts of the country but rarely in the larger cities.

An unusual method of breeding is undertaken by the malleefowl, unique in Australia. In the drier inland areas, both members of the pair scratch up a mound of sand with a crater in the top. They then rake up debris of sticks and leaves to fill its centre. When it rains, they cover over the debris with sand. As it rots, it produces heat, which the male keeps at a constant temperature by removing or adding sand as necessary. This is a continual duty and he must be ready to open the mound each time the females wants to lay an egg. She spends her time feeding to produce about 24 eggs laid over a period of four months. The chick hatches out deep down in the mound, fights its way to the top, rolls off into the bushes surrounding the nest and looks after itself. It is never attended to by its parents who do not even seem to recognise it as their own.

There are two other mound builders: the orange-footed scrubfowl and Australian brush turkey of the wetter rainforests. None of the three are easy to see without a guide but these are available.

If you like the sea, then you will want to see penguins. All 17 species of penguin live in the southern hemisphere. Only one, the little or fairy penguin, breeds in Australia and it is at the famous Penguin Parade on Phillip Island, Victoria, that visitors can view it with ease. Each night the lights are turned on to allow viewing of the birds as they return to land after the day at sea. They walk on land only in darkness and it is possible to see them performing all their domestic routines as if the thousands of watchers did not exist. The noise of discordant penguin song accompanies ritual behaviour and the small fluffy penguin chicks emerge from their burrows from about October to February. The parade is open every night of the year but during the time of moult – end of January for three months – there are fewer birds coming ashore. It can be quiet in early winter – May, June – but this varies from year to year. You will always see some penguins no matter when you go and there is an extensive interpretation area at the entrance to the parade. Here the whole life cycle is described as well as information about other penguins.

You don't have to go to any special place to see the brilliant parrots of Australia. Galahs, softly pink and grey, are even in some of the cities and are evident in large numbers over most of the continent, certainly in the drier parts. The large white sulphur-crested cockatoo makes its presence known by its raucous screeching. It ranges over most of the eastern half of Australia while the similar sized pink cockatoo and slightly smaller corellas (two species) cover the rest of the continent. Even larger than those cockatoos are the magnificent black cockatoos, inhabitants of forests and woodlands, but not of the dry, treeless desert areas. They draw attention to themselves also by screeching but not quite as noisily as the white cockatoos.

Rosellas and lorikeets are not as widespread as cockatoos but they are in abundance mainly not too far inland from the coast. Lorikeets fly fast in flocks and screech as they search for flowers. They eat pollen and extract nectar with their specialised brush tongues. Rosellas sound slightly more musical and have bell-like calls. They vary in colour from green to red to blue to yellow, all distinguished by their cheek patches of various colours.

One parrot favoured by people who like to keep caged birds is the budgerigar. Aviculturists have bred it in many different colours but the budgerigar in the wild state is bright green with a yellow head. It is common over most of inland Australia and is easily recognised as it flies in dense fast-moving flocks continuously uttering its chirruping contact call.

These are just a few of the 52 species of parrot that inhabit Australia, most of them to be seen with little effort.

In wetlands (swamps, lakes, rivers) waterbirds are everywhere. Only one is a swan. This is black but unmistakably a swan like the white swans of the northern hemisphere. Some of the ducks are bizarre, such as the musk duck, a carnivorous species that in display inflates a large black lobe of skin hanging beneath its bill and splashes wildly. The brolga is a large grey crane with bare scarlet skin on its head. Brolga pairs display with loud trumpeting calls as they leap into the air, bow and dance. Kakadu in the Northern Territory is famous for its waterbirds and there are many organised tours that take in this area.

Another large bird that is spectacular in display is the bustard, which inhabits drier inland areas, particularly in the north of Western Australia. The male struts with his head and tail erect while a large feathered pouch hanging from his throat almost to the ground swings from side to side, rather like a Scotchman's sporran. All the time he utters a sound that resembles the roaring of a distant lion. The male that puts on the best display, like the lyrebird, will attract the greatest number of females who then make their choice.

We have our share of small brown birds that tend to confuse birdwatchers throughout the world but we also have some that are highly coloured. Our fairy wrens are generally clad in various amounts of blue, some with purple and russet and one in black and red. The females are rather drab, a necessity for their protection as the important breeder. Fairy wrens live in small groups with helpers like the kookaburras. They may lay three or four clutches of eggs in a season and the helpers from the previous year or the newly fledged young assist with caring for the successive breeds. This co-operation in family life is as it should be.

Honeyeaters use their brush tongues, like the lorikeets, to feed on the nectar and pollen of flowers. They also eat insects and generally feed these to their nestlings. Ranging in size from10–40 cm, some are brightly coloured and most are reasonably easy to identify both by appearance and by song which is often melodious. Honeyeaters are spread throughout the continent and in New Guinea, as well as in the Pacific islands, with a few in southern Africa.

These are just a few of the birds you are likely to see in Australia. It is impossible to describe them all in this restricted space – the pigeons, pardalotes, eagles, owls and finches. I suggest that if you are keen to have some of them pointed out to you in pleasant circumstances, you visit the bird observatories where the charges are very low. These bird observatories are:

- Broome B.O., PO Box 1313, Broome, WA 6725
  (north-west Australia), (091) 93 5600.
- Eyre B.O., Cocklebiddy, via Norseman, WA 6443
  (south-west Australia), (090) 39 3450.

226

- Rotamah Island B.O., PO Box 75, Paynesville, Victoria 3880 (south-east Australia), (051) 56 6398.
- Barren Grounds B.O., PO Box 3, Jamberoo, NSW 2533 (eastern Australia between Canberra and Sydney), (042) 36 0195.

Of course, you will need bird books. To help you find the birds, read *Where to Find Birds in Australia* by John Bransbury.

Where to Find Birds in North-east Queensland by Jo Wieneke is an excellent guide to places, listing how to get there, what accommodation is available, where to buy books and anything else you might want to know. On the outside cover is written: 'No birdwatcher or wildlife enthusiast from Australia or overseas, visiting north-east Queensland should be without this book.'

For identification, I suggest any of the following. The order of preference is mine for ease of use and illustration.

Ken Simpson and Nicolas Day. 1986. *Field Guide to the Birds of Australia* (and many later editions). Melbourne: Viking O'Neil.

Graham Pizzey. 1982. *A Field Guide to the Birds of Australia* (and many later editions). Melbourne: William Collins.

Slater's Field Guide to the Birds of Australia.

If waterbirds interest you, visit either:

The Shortland Wetlands Centre, Sandgate Road, Shortland, PO Box 130, Wallsend 2287 (suburb of Newcastle, north of Sydney), (049) 51 6466; or Serendip Sanctuary, 100 Windermere Road, Lara 3212 (an hour's drive from Melbourne), (052) 821 584. At Serendip, a long-term breeding programme enables you to see brolgas, bustards, Cape Barren geese, magpie geese and many other free-flying waterfowl.

Even if no animals other than birds interest you, you really should try to see the platypus. This extraordinary animal is fur-covered, lays eggs and suckles its young with milk. It swims underwater with eyes and ears closed and locates its food of worms and water insects by sending out electrical impulses. It then grasps its prey with its bill that is shaped like a duck's bill.

Only slightly less bizarre is the echidna, the only close relation of the platypus. It also lays eggs and suckles its young but it lives on land. It is covered in spikes rather like porcupines and hedgehogs but it is not related to them.

Platypuses feed at night in many streams and can be seen at dusk and dawn if you are patient and lucky. If not, they are on display at the Melbourne Zoo and Healesville Sanctuary, and possibly at similar institutions in eastern Australia.

If you want illustrated factual stories about our animals, I suggest Picture Roo books by Kangaroo Press. I have written 14 of these inexpensive ($A7.00) books at the reading level of about eight years. They are fully researched and refereed. Animals covered so far are: Penguin, Lyrebird, Emu, Kookaburra, Galah, Malleefowl, Kiwi, Koala, Wombat, Tasmanian Devil, Echidna, Platypus, Frillneck (an Australian Dragon) and Kangaroo.

Jane Cafarella
BLOODY COCKIES!

Bloody cockies! Why didn't somebody tell me that they were the vandals of the bush? For the first month in our new home, we diligently left 'wild-bird mix' out for the birds, attracting rosellas and galahs, Indian doves, the occasional jays and a few Indian mynas, curious about the queue but disappointed at the menu. Then came the cockies.

'Look at the cocky!' I said excitedly to Greta, as I held her closer to the lounge room window for a better view. A sulphur-crested cocky, his feathers rich and creamy, his yellow crest standing up boldly, strode confidently on to the feeding tray. He turned a knowing eye to Greta and me and started tucking into the sunflower seeds at an alarming rate. I made a mental note to get the two kilogram packet next time.

The next day there were two cockies, politely taking it in turns to feed. The day after there were three. These days there are often seven or more – and that's the problem. The cocky hierarchy means that the top cockies get to eat their fill first, while the others wait. And what does a cocky-in-waiting do? Anything it likes – starting with nipping the buds off my young camellia bush.

I had wondered why my fishbone fern had failed to thrive. Closer inspection revealed that it had been a bad case of cockyitis.

As for my new polyanthuses, purchased when in spectacular bloom, I came home one afternoon and found them all nipped neatly off at the base, the leaves and blooms scattered wantonly along the veranda.

To coax the cockatoos away from the house, Rob put a feeding tray in a tree outside the kitchen window. The tray, a square base with a pot plant lid nailed to it, is suspended with rope, attached to a cuphook on each corner. To fill it, you haul down the rope. The trouble is, when a full-grown cocky lands on it, the tray becomes a cocky trapeze. Round and round the tree it whizzes, with the cocky hanging on to the rope with its beak, and on to the tray with its claws, looking like a kid on its first merry-go-round ride – not sure whether to throw up or smile. Some cockies are smarter than others. For the cocky trapeze, they bring a friend, each sitting opposite the other to balance the tray. Other cockies are really dumb. Like the one that keeps trying to cut the rope with its beak.

And other cockies are just . . . plain cocky – like the one that hung upside down from the guttering outside the kitchen window last week to get a good look at me, standing at the kitchen sink (as usual).

Our friend Bevan says that the Aborigines believe cockies are lost souls – people reincarnated in a kind of bird-like purgatory. I think I agree. There is something almost human about them, which is why, like humans, they become destructive when they are bored.

A neighbour says not to worry – these cheeky vandals are not locals; they just pass through at this time each year, rampaging and pillaging on the way. I hope she's right. Until then, living here is like living in a giant aviary, except that we are in the cage.

I had visions of putting Greta in the pusher out on the veranda to sleep on balmy summer afternoons, while I read a book and sipped a gin and tonic – but now I am afraid the cockies would walk all over her. After all, they are walking all over me.

Laurene Kelly
A Piece of Tasmania

We all learn in school that the last Tasmanian Aboriginal, Trucanini who died on 8 May 1876 was the last of her race. It was almost boastful in our textbooks that we had caused the extinction of a whole race in less than eighty years. The blood on this island, spilt from the massacres, still haunts the spirit of the island. In less than seventeen years of her life, Trucanini had seen her mother stabbed to death, her sisters abducted, her stepmother kidnapped, her uncle shot, her fiance murdered and her own self raped and abused by the invading white men. Trucanini was so named after a salt bush, *Atriplex cinerea*, growing on Bruny Island, where she was born.

The original Tasmanians have probably been here for forty thousand years, with up to sixty-two tribes with distinct boundaries, many different dialects and formed in all, nine major tribes. There are upwards of five thousand Tasmanian Aboriginals today, fighting for land rights and self determination. Many live on the Furneaux group of islands, to the north east of Tasmania. It has been predominantly the women who have kept their culture alive, many of them having survived the assimilation policies of the government. Even today when the annual get together occurs at Oyster Cove, in the South of Tasmania, families meet each other for the first time, even though they may well know of the existence of relatives through stories that are passed on in the great oral tradition of the Aboriginal people. On Bruny Island there is a Trucanini Lookout which is in the shape of a cairn, as a monument to her tribe. Today the Aboriginal Provisional Government has a strong voice in Tasmania, a state that still denies Land Rights to its indigenous people. They have occupied several sites and made claims for the land that has been stolen to be given back. In 1991 they occupied part of the Rocky Cape National Park in the North West of the state. On Flinders Island where many Aboriginals were taken they have made claim to Wybaleena, a place where many were buried when they succumbed to white men's diseases, like starvation.

A Land Rights Bill was presented in our Parliament in 1991, which was passed in our lower house but defeated in the upper house. The Government of the day denies that there are any Tasmanian Aboriginals and refuses to grant even the most basic Land Rights, let alone enact any legislation.

I was born on Tasmania, this 'bloody' island, and spent my formative years growing up in the south of the island. We are an island now, yet 10,000-12,000 years ago we were joined to the rest of Australia by a narrow land bridge. In some ways I'm glad we are separated from the mainland of Australia, it has meant for some species of fauna survival, rather than extinction. We have some of the last remaining tracts of wilderness in the world. Unlike the continent of Australia, Tasmania is a maritime temperate climate which is generally conducive to the development of forests. In the higher rainfall areas of the central highlands and the west, rainforests predominate, although treeless habitats are frequent on waterlogged soils. The east coast is mostly drier with more open eucalyptus forests. Of the 900 or so flowering plants native to Tasmania about 300 are endemic. Many of the endemic species are found on mountain plateaux. Our flora, overall, is closely related to that of mainland Australia. Our alpine flora has close affinities with the mainland, New Zealand and southern South American Alpine floras. The southern beeches (*Nothofagus spp.*) are still present as scattered forests in Australasia and South America. Myrtle beech (*N. cunninghami*) is a dominant rainforest tree and deciduous beech (*N. gunnii*) is a subalpine small tree. Nothofagus fossil pollen records in these areas and in Antarctica extend back to the age of dinosaurs. Some of the prominent and characteristic plant communities include button grass plains, which are extensive on wet and infertile soils, mainly in the south west, native pines, which are often present within rainforest and alpine communities. King Billy (*Athrotaxis selaginoides*) and pencil pines (*Athrotaxis cupressoides*) occasionally form forests up to 30 metres in height in elevated valleys and on subalpine plateaux. Both these species are also found around mountain tarns. Pencil in the Central Plateau and King Billy further west and south. All the pines above Lake Dove at Artists Pool and at Hansons Lake in the Cradle Mountain National Park are King Billy. It also occurs in rainforest as an understorey as can be seen in the Ballroom Forest near Waldheim, in the same Park. The Huon Pine (*Dacrydium franklinni*) grows in low lying damp areas in the west and south west. Most of the mature trees of this species have been cut down. They take hundreds of years to grow, and some of those cut have been aged upwards of three thousand years. During the Vietnam War, hundreds of thousands of these trees were used to build huts in Vietnam for Australian soldiers. When they left they burned them so as the Vietnamese could not use the resource. There is one stand of mature trees left in the Truchanas Huon Pine Reserve.

Tasmania is an incredibly beautiful island despite the efforts of the Europeans to destroy that which was so different from their own environments, although many equate the Cradle Mountain area with the fjords of Norway. The colonialists, afraid of the wide spaces tried to turn the land into a copy of the Europe they had left behind. Driving through the countryside you see farmlands and townships that please the European eye for their conformity. Not only did people invade but also plants like gorse, blackberry, Scotch thistle and hawthorn. Driving down the Midland Highway you see paddock after paddock of Scotch thistle growing like regiments of the British army. You ask yourself, is this a cash crop? The answer, no. We have turned what once were magnificent eucalypt forests into wasteland.

True wilderness can be found in the Central Highlands and the South-West of Tasmania. To see this wilderness, untouched by man is a true gift to the soul. After the man-made world of regular shapes and straight lines, to see the perfection of mother nature in her pristine state revives beauty and hope and makes all the fight against patriarchy well worth it. Unlike other remaining wilderness in the world, there are not the same hazards, like insects that could give you a life threatening illness. You just need to be well equipped for all kinds of weather, including blizzards. Advice can be given from Outdoor shops on equipment that is needed for bushwalking in wilderness. 27 per cent of Tasmania is National Parks. There are several books that give walking times, maps and general guides of what to look for. In all of these parks photography, drawing, writing and meditating are enhanced by their natural beauty and remoteness. This is the wholly unaffected beauty of nature, a rarity in this greedy world.

In less than 200 hundred years, 75 per cent of rainforest and 50 per cent of dry sclerophlyl forests have been destroyed. There is quite a strong conservationist base in Tasmania, represented by about 17 per cent of the population. Many of these people have moved here from other states in Australia for the slow and relaxed lifestyle. We are still fighting battles on many fronts, including trying to prevent the logging of the last remaining temperate rainforest in the world: the Tarkine Wilderness on the West Coast of Tasmania. Multinational mining and forestry companies are determined to rape and ravage what they can before they are stopped by popular opinion and more knowledge. The Aboriginal people are never consulted on these decisions. Last year they were trying to prevent flooding of sacred sites in the West, but the Tasmanian Government threatened them with all the cost involved in a lengthy court battle. They had to drop their claims as it could well have run into the millions if they had lost. A whole past has been flooded in what now is a hydro scheme and also a recreational lake for fishermen. The victory of the Franklin River in the early eighties spurs the fight on for remaining areas of wilderness, though not pristine because of logging in the last century, they are still unique ecosystems that white man does not and cannot understand, except in terms of dollars. We have no railway system in Tasmania for passengers, just for dead bodies.

> I get a fright in the night
> when I hear the trains go by
> It is because they are carrying bodies
> carrying bodies, bodies of trees
> they are murdering in the night
> and in the day,

233

> our trees, our spirits
> the death trains rattle by.

I wrote this when I returned from South America in the early eighties and it is still happening today, and the worst thing is that most of these trees go for woodchip. These magnificent trees, hundreds of years old, going to make paper to throw away. Most of them go to Japan and each Tasmanian subsidises their export. It's criminal but aren't all the activities of multinationals?

Another feature that struck the colonialists was the unique species of fauna. The Tasmanian Tiger (*Thylacinus cynocephalus*) believed now to be extinct, created hysteria and was accused of all sorts of crimes against white man. It used to roam throughout Australia but was thought to have become extinct about a thousand years ago, because of the introduction of the dingo from South East Asia about 5,000 years ago. It is believed the dingo came to Australia with the fisherpeople who came to trade with the Northern Aboriginals. Because the land bridge was submerged by this time it never got to Tasmania, which meant at least two of the species survived here. The dingo is a pack hunter, whereas the Thylacine and the Tasmanian Devil (*Sacrophilus harrissi*) are solitary animals. They believe on the mainland of Australia, that the dingo out competed with these animals for food, so those species starved into extinction. These species could have easily become extinct in Tasmania, as well, not because of the dingo, but white man. The Thylacine and Devil were accused of destroying the invaders' animals, sheep and cattle, so they instigated a bounty system. Thousands of these species were shot, trapped and poisoned. In fact, many believe the Thylacine is extinct. They also suffered from introduced disease that came with the exotic species, like cats, dogs, sheep, cattle and fowl, brought to the island. The last known Thylacine died in the Hobart Zoo in 1935. One of the women I work with believes it still exists and she has been searching for over ten years. Prior to working with her, I believed they were extinct. I felt what had happened to the original people, also meant a four-legged creature stood no chance against the barbarians. She has convinced me that it could well still be out there in remote areas. Her search is restricted by lack of funds, even though she has appealed to all sorts of bodies. Many men have been funded in the search and have come up with nothing. Because of their draining of funds from the Australian Conservation Foundation and the World Fund for Nature, there are no more resources to commit. Trudy (the woman) is a bush woman who grew up in the area where I now live and work, and I think if anyone will find it it will be her. It is not for it to be captured, but for it to be protected. The Smithsonian Institute in Washington, USA, has already built an enclosure for its subsequent study if found. Not if she finds it, no way!

The Tasmanian Devil almost became extinct in the 1930s and would have had they not been protected in 1942. It is considered common now with estimated numbers of between 50,000–100,000. They are very timid animals, rarely seen in the wild. I work with these animals at the Tasmanian Wildlife Park. The uniqueness of the Tasmanian Devil, its difference from any other animal, made the myths and almost satanic proportion of this animal akin to other hysterical reactions. Fortunately the wilderness of Tasmania, which indeed is its claim to fame, allowed the animal pockets of resistance that allowed it to survive. Though common now, a number of species that are considered extinct, rare or endangered on the mainland of Australia are considered common in Tasmania.

Tasmania can be nature itself. Inspiring, awesome, our own presence an acceptance of how perfect it all can be. I worked at the Tasmanian Wildlife Park, near Mole Creek for five years. The Wildlife Park is a wonderful place. Well, this one is. Most of the animals and birds are injured directly or indirectly by man. We rehabilitate, raise orphaned young and take excellent care of those that cannot be released.

Most of Tasmania's fauna is nocturnal. An ethical Park, like the Tasmanian Wildlife park will allow you to see many species, that otherwise you may well only see in a photograph. We have been breeding koalas, non-native to Tasmania. They are an endangered species and I believe what we have been doing will eventually be of benefit to the survival of the species. I have seen many European women shed tears when they meet one face to face. Especially ours, as they are specially Tasmanian. Softer and thicker, some would say! Because of our cooler climate, they have adapted with much thicker fur than their mainland Victorian and South Australian counterparts. Other species live in Queensland and New South Wales. The further South you go the bigger they get. All of ours have Aboriginal names and they are truly amazing animals. One of the things I have really appreciated since working with various species, like wombats, kangaroos, possums is that the social order they established for their survival is so removed from our own. That is not to say that rape, murder and assault don't occur in the animal world. It is the social order, that is important. In most species, the females live in groups, old, young etc. There may be one or two males who look out for the group. They do not dominate the females, but co-exist and protect from wayward males. It is predominantly quite peaceful in the animal world, that is until Oestrus. Generally speaking this biological function, which does not occur in all females, can be pretty torrid. A young female Forester Kangaroo, coming into her first Oestrus can suffer from many males' harassment. The only defence she has against an unwanted pregnancy, is by being able to prevent penetration. This, of course, does not make the abuse any easier. Generally speaking

235

though, the females manage to control their society with minimum disruption. Once the female does conceive the harassment ends. We call the kangaroos the gentle giants. Some of them stand taller than humans and they have great dignity. In some of the National Parks, you also have the opportunity to see some of our larger species in their natural environment. There are many beautiful spots that you can visit and mostly get away from others. It is often a strange feeling for those living in densely populated places to be somewhere they can shout, scream, enjoy the beauty of silence, except birdsong or the splash of dolphins as they break the water in their dance.

If you are looking for Women's ventures in Tasmania it can be a little more difficult. It is more a place women come to get away from it all. Sometimes the safety of women's communities can make you immune to what is called oppression or discrimination so that the edge of the battle is absorbed into a safety that means the horizons become unexplored and that comfort can be created and if you step out into a xenophobic, sexist, racist community that lives in a visual paradise, it can sharpen one's wits and make it well worth the visit.

Apart from the uniqueness of Tasmania, in its pristine beauty, it remains one of the only places left in the western perimeter of mind control, that makes homosexuality illegal, but the Act itself makes all sex illegal. In spite of this it is a place once you have visited, you will always want to return to. Two weeks is not enough. Give yourself time. It can hide itself well. The Office of the Status of Women, in the phone directory is a good information service. Up here where I am, at Moles Creek, there is a woman who runs a caving business who will do women-only tours. Wild Cave Tours. There are women in Hobart, the capital city, who have a Wild Women bushwalking group. Hitchhiking is an experience that will be very different from what you may expect or what you may desire. Most of Tasmania's fauna is nocturnal, but most humans aren't. You will get a lot of early nights, and read a lot of good books. Accommodation is best sought in your backpackers hostels. If you arrive in Devonport on the ferry from Melbourne, there is the Radclyffe House hostel for women only, where you can get your bearings. If I am still here at the Tasmanian Wildlife Park, I will give you my knowledge of Tasmania, if I'm not it is still worth the visit, to see our different nature and an island paradise.

Dianne Simmons

WALKING IN THE WILDERNESS – TASMANIA

There are few places in the world where women with a moderate level of
fitness can experience and enjoy a safe but challenging 'wilderness'
experience. The island state of Tasmania has more than half a million
hectares of pristine land, with no settlements or facilities, and protected in
several National Parks and World Heritage Areas. These areas provide
opportunities for wilderness walking for periods ranging from a few days
to several weeks. Access to most walking tracks is simple to arrange, as
there is regular transport from major cities and airports throughout the
summer period (December to March). Good route guides and maps are
available for the most popular areas.

Women have been walking in Tasmania from the earliest days of
European exploration, when Lady Jane Franklin and her companion Miss
Stewart travelled overland from Hobart to Macquarie Harbour in 1842.
From the 1930s, many women have walked in the wilderness of Tasmania,
and all-women groups are often encountered. If you don't think that you
have the experience to safely walk in Tasmania, there are a number of
companies who will provide guides and equipment to small parties, and
arrange extended trips to most areas.

No wilderness walks are easy – they all need a careful approach and good
planning. In most areas vegetation is impenetrable beyond the formed
tracks or major routes, and there are no rapid escape routes to 'civilization'. Little has changed since Sir John and Lady Jane Franklin travelled
'on foot, over watery marshes, nearly impracticable swamps, through
tangled forests, across precipitous mountains, boisterous torrents and
flooded rivers'. It is not uncommon for walkers to be alone for a week
without any contact with another group – this is both the attraction and
the hazard of wilderness walking.

With a few simple precautions, wilderness walking can be safe. All
wilderness areas are isolated, and as help may be several days away, all
parties should be equipped to be completely self sufficient for at least a
few more days than the length of the trip planned. A good first-aid kit is
essential, and even minor injuries such as blisters may become serious if
they slow the progress of the group. All snakes in Tasmania are venomous,
and should be avoided at all times. Snakes are shy creatures, and if walkers
always watch carefully for them, and avoid them if they are sighted, they
pose no real danger.

Weather in Tasmania can change rapidly and without warning, and the
major hazard is hypothermia or exposure. The highest peaks are only about
1700 m, but weather can be very wet and very cold, with severe snow

storms at any time of the year, including mid-summer. All areas include long stretches of extremely muddy tracks in wet weather, and walkers can expect to have wet feet for much of a trip. All groups should walk within their capacity, and be equipped with strong boots, waterproof coats and overpants, warm clothing and a good quality sleeping bag kept dry in waterproof storage bags. In extremely poor weather, it is often safest to STOP and simply wait for one or two days for the weather to improve. In recent years, several people have lost their lives as a result of hypothermia, and it is ALWAYS a danger. Don't forget the sunscreen either – the weather can also be sunny and clear for weeks at a time, especially in February-March !

Note that most wilderness areas are designated 'Fuel Stove Only', and NO camp fires may be lit.

The Standard of Wilderness Walks

Easy Walks – You are likely to meet other groups, huts are generally available at regular intervals (though tents must be carried in case huts are full), route finding is easy and tracks are generally well formed and avoid steep slopes, with bridges on all creek crossings.

Moderate Walks – These walks are physically taxing due to long distances or difficult terrain. There are likely to be other groups in the area, but it is possible to see no one for several days. There may be one or two rough shelter huts, but tents will be required most nights, in reasonably sheltered camp sites. Tracks are usually rough, though well marked, and they will have sections which are steep, rocky or muddy. Some creek crossings may have log or wire crossings, or an aerial cableway or 'flying fox', though wading may sometimes be necessary. Crossings may be difficult after heavy rain.

Hard Walks – You can expect to meet few parties, and will need to be completely self-sufficient for at least seven days. There are no shelter huts, and the few sheltered camp sites are small, with space for only a few tents. Routes generally follow obvious land features such as ridges, but route finding may be difficult, and some off-track walking may be necessary. Good navigation skills are essential. Any tracks will be rough and poorly formed with many sections which are very steep, rocky, or muddy. There is rarely any assistance with creek crossings, and many streams must be waded. Many crossings may be difficult, or even impossible after heavy rain.

Classic Walks in Tasmania
The Overland Track. Easy.
Location: Cradle Mountain – Lake St Clair National Park.
Access: Cradle Mountain in the north, or Derwent Bridge in the south.

Time: Allow five days minimum, but seven days gives time for exploration of the area.

This is one of the most popular extended walks in Tasmania. In spite of the large number of walkers each year who use the 'Overland Track', it has a feeling of remoteness combined with spectacular scenery, and gives a taste of wilderness walking. Tracks are well marked, and huts with toilets and heating are located every few hours along the track. All groups need to carry tents in case huts are full. Some parts of the track cross high passes, and snow is possible at any time of the year. Side trips to peaks and lakes off the track, or to Pine Valley and the Labyrinth, are well worth the extra time required.

Commercial companies also run guided trips through this area, and use private huts which have additional facilities. There is considerable controversy about the ethics of commercial enterprises within National Parks, and walkers using these companies are not well regarded by other walkers.

The Walls of Jerusalem. Easy.
Location: Walls of Jerusalem National Park.
Access: Via Mole Creek and the Fish River.
Time: Area can be visited in three days, but five days allows for some exploration of the area.

This area provides an opportunity for relatively easy walking in a spectacular area, which has only a few formed tracks, and several historic huts. Walkers should always be prepared for poor weather in this exposed alpine area. Tracks are marked by foot pads and occasional stone cairns, but even in light falls of snow, track markers are quickly obscured. The alpine vegetation allows some off-track walking, but good navigation skills are essential. The Walls of Jerusalem can be combined with a day walking down the untracked Mersey River to a series of waterfalls in the southern end of the Cradle Mountain – Lake St Clair National Park.

The area is generally quite open, and the Pool of Bethesda or Dixons Kingdom (which is near Pencil pines believed to be hundreds of years old), make good bases for exploration of the area.

The South Coast Track and Port Davey Track. Moderate.
Location: South West National Park.
Access: Cockle Creek, Melaleuca Inlet (light plane) and Scotts Peak.
Time: Scotts Peak to Melaleuca Inlet four days minimum, and Melaleuca Inlet to Cockle Creek six days minimum.

The South Coast Track is generally well graded and in good weather, it is a relatively easy trip. However, the length of the trip (about 70 km), the lack of any huts (except at Melaleuca Inlet), and the difficulty of creek crossings in poor weather, make it a serious undertaking. There is a rough and steep climb over the Ironbound Range which may be difficult in poor weather. In wet weather parties may need to wait for creek levels to fall before crossings can be made safely. However, the track passes a mix of vegetation including open forests, rainforests, and open button grass plains interspersed with beaches, and provides a varied and interesting walk. Light planes can be used for access to Melaleuca Inlet if time is limited.

The Port Davey Track is generally easy, but it is now less frequently used due to increased access by light planes to Melaleuca Inlet airstrip. The track is well graded, and passes through some fascinating areas around the base of the Western Arthur Range, past Mt Rugby, and across Bathurst Harbour.

Dinghies are located either side of New River Lagoon (South Coast Track) and the Bathurst Narrows (Port Davey Track). Sufficient time should be allowed for these crossings (one to two hours depending on tides and weather), as unless there is another party crossing at the same time, several crossings will need to be made so that a boat can be left on either side.

Rest days at some of the beautiful and isolated beaches on the South Coast Track are recommended. A trip from Scotts Peak to Cockle Creek covers some 130 kilometres, and takes about two weeks. This is a very good introduction to long distance wilderness walking.

Mt Anne. Moderate.

Location: South West National Park.

Access: Condiminion Creek from the Scotts Peak Road via Maydena.

Time: Three days allows for a trip to Mt Anne, and exploration of the Mt Eliza Plateau.

Mt Anne has an easily recognised profile from many areas of the South West National Park. A relatively easy climb to the High Camp Hut below Mt Eliza paves the way for a steep climb over boulder fields to the Plateau, and on to Mt Anne. Mt Eliza and the surrounding Plateau provide good views of Lake Pedder impoundment, which was formed as part of a hydro-electric installation, Lake Judd below high, sheer cliffs, and to good views of most peaks in the south west area. Beyond Mt Anne, the track is poorly marked, and very exposed. Many sections require pack-hauling, and a climbing rope should be used by most parties.

Frenchmans Cap. Moderate.

Location: Franklin – Lower Gordon Wild Rivers National Park.

Access: Lyell Highway near Derwent Bridge.

Time: Four days minimum.

Frenchmans Cap is only a few kilometres from the Lyell Highway, but it is located in some very steep and rough terrain which can result in a hard trip in poor weather. The peak has a distinctive profile from many areas in South West Tasmania, and its white quartzite face can be seen from as far away as Cradle Mountain. Part of the track covers some of the route used by Lady Jane Franklin and her party in 1842. The Franklin River is crossed by a 'flying fox', and the Loddon River crossing is by a large log. Crossings can be dangerous and should not be attempted during high flows. The climb to Barron Pass, and from Lake Tahune to Frenchmans Cap is well marked, though very steep and rough.

The track is usually extremely muddy on the Loddon Plains, unless the weather is very dry. There are comfortable shelter huts at Lake Vera and at Lake Tahune.

Western Arthur Range. Hard.

Location: South West National Park.

Access: From Scotts Peak Road via Junction Creek or the Huon Track via Geeveston (aptly referred to as the Yo-Yo Track).

Time: Allow at least seven days minimum.

This is a serious walk for experienced walkers only. A traverse of the Range is only about 25 kilometres, but it is physically taxing, and requires good route finding ability over very rough terrain. Most parties use the standard approach routes at either end of the Range, and there are no easy ways off the range once the traverse is commenced. Route finding in this exposed area is difficult in poor weather, and parties should be prepared to wait at more sheltered sites for weather to improve. There are no huts on the Range, and campsites are very limited in size, accommodating only a few tents. A high proportion of parties do not complete the trip because of the notoriously poor weather in the area.

Federation Peak. Hard.
Location: South West National Park.
Access: Easiest route is from the Scotts Peak Road via Junction Creek, or the Huon Track via Geeveston, and then from Cracroft Crossing to the Eastern Arthur Range.
Time: Allow seven days minimum.

Federation Peak was first climbed in 1949, and this spectacular peak with its characteristic tooth-shape remains the ultimate in wilderness walking in Tasmania. Nancy Shaw was in a party which pioneered the route which resulted in a first ascent of Federation Peak in 1949, and Nancy Wilson also reached the summit in that year. Route finding can be difficult, and the rough cairned track is often very steep and difficult. All parties need to be fit and experienced. Some rock-climbing experience is an advantage, and most parties will need to pack-haul in some areas along the Four Peaks. A climbing rope is recommended for the final exposed ascent to the summit. For groups with no rock-climbing experience, the view from the Devils Thumb and Hanging Lake makes the effort well worthwhile, even if the summit is not reached. Parties need to be well equipped to cope with poor weather and have tents suitable for extremely exposed camp sites.

Further Reading
J. Chapman. 1990. *South West Tasmania*. Melbourne: J. Chapman.
J. Chapman and J. Siseman. 1990. *Cradle Mountain Lake St Clair and Walls of Jerusalem National Parks*. Melbourne: Pindari Publications.
K. Collins. 1990. *South-West Tasmania: A Natural History and Visitor's Guide*. Hobart: Heritage Books.
H. Gee and J. Fenton. 1978. *The South West Book*. Melbourne: Australian Conservation Foundation.
J. Luckman. 1951. *Ladies First: The Tasmanian Tramp* Vol.10. pp. 27–29.
R. Rankin. 1989. *Classic Wild Walks of Australia*. Brisbane: Rankin Publishers.

Susan Hawthorne and Renate Klein
THE NORTH AND EAST

Brisbane
Growing at a fast pace, Brisbane is Australia's third largest city and there has been a huge expansion of building in the business centre as well as in the suburbs over the last decade. Alongside that expansion has been a comparable burst of cultural activity in all the arts. Each September the Warana Festival brings together its own mix of writers, artists, theatre, opera and music. A sub-tropical climate, Brisbane has the advantage of a comfortable year round climate. But it is not a beach city – for that you need to travel either south to the Gold Coast and Surfers Paradise or north to the quieter Sunshine Coast. From Brisbane you can drive right up the coast through Rockhampton, Townsville and Cairns. The coast is dotted with numerous islands, many of them resort islands. The coast of Queensland is well-populated, (and it's a long drive up this coast), but inland it is drier and huge tracts of thinly populated land predominate. If you are travelling along the coast, check if it is safe to swim between October and May, as stingers (deadly jellyfish) are common in coastal waters during this period. (This also applies to parts of NT and WA.)

Cairns
Cairns is becoming a major entry port for many overseas visitors attracted by the Great Barrier Reef, Daintree Rainforest and tropical holidays. Accommodation in Cairns varies from a large selection of backpacker hostels to expensive resorts on the coast and on nearby islands. Cairns has a vigorous arts community, as has nearby Kuranda on the Atherton Tableland, which you can reach on the historic train that passes through spectacular scenery. If you don't go by train, the station is worth a visit just to see the pot plants hung from the rafters. There you can visit the huge Barron Falls, as well as the nocturnal house where you'll get a chance to see fruit bats, sugar gliders and possums and all the other animals you are bound to miss seeing at night. Driving north from Cairns will take you to Port Douglas, where a gay resort, Turtle Cove, has recently opened, or you can go inland to Silky Oaks and fall asleep to the sound (rather noisy) of the rainforest. Further north takes you through the Daintree Rainforest or inland and north to Cape York. These are remote areas and you should plan your trip well in advance and carry sufficient water and food for one to two weeks in case of breakdown (see McLellan).

245

Daintree Rainforest

On the southern end of the Cape York Peninsula is the Daintree Rainforest. Soon after you cross the Daintree River you enter the World Heritage Area. This rainforest is one of the few virgin rainforests left anywhere and until the Cape Tribulation Road was built in the mid 1980s it was impossible to drive into this area. Now with the road in there are an increasing number of beach resorts developing along this coast where the rainforest comes down to meet the sea. The Cape Tribulation Road is a mixed blessing. The region is now accessible, but there are dangers that the run-off and silt from the road will have long-term destructive effects on the reef just offshore. It is an area of immense beauty and like all rainforest areas the bio-diversity is one of its great values (see Llewellyn). You should not swim in the rivers of northern Queensland which are home to salt-water crocodiles. You may lose your life. Obey all warning signs regarding crocodiles, even if you can't see anything. A few years ago a woman died in the Daintree River. But worth taking are the river cruises along the Daintree that provide you with a sense of the richness and immensity of this region.

Cape York Peninsula

The northernmost point in Australia, Cape York is a rugged beautiful area, parts of it rainforest. You need a four-wheel drive to visit this area on your own, or there are tours with four wheel drives that you can join. You can also fly in to the Wilderness Lodge on the tip of Cape York from Cairns. This is the northernmost point on mainland Australia. Rainforest and quiet beaches look north to the Torres Strait, where you will find Thursday Island, as well as other islands populated by Torres Strait Islanders, whose Melanesian cultural traditions can be found in the work of writers such as Elsie Roughsey: Labumore and of Ellie Gaffney. You can also buy recordings of the music of The Mills Sisters (*Frangipani Land*), whose irreverent harmonious songs have become a hit with world music festival audiences around Australia. At Lara, at the southern end of Cape York, you can visit the largest outdoor rock art gallery in the world. The Quinkan paintings can be visited either with a tour, or alone if permission is obtained. The children's books by Percy Roughsey and Dick Tresize will give you a good idea of what to expect and some useful background to the stories (see McLellan, Llewellyn).

Great Barrier Reef

Along the Queensland coast there are many places to see the reef. It is relatively close to the shore just north of Cairns and a number of tour operators have day trips to the reef. Usually they offer a chance to go snorkelling on the reef, some offer scuba diving, some have submerged or glass-bottomed boats from which the reef can be viewed. The sight of a huge clam opening, or the complexity of brain coral, or the darting brightness of a tropical fish is one that you will remember forever. And if the boat you take goes out to a cay, you are also likely to share the beach with thousands of seabirds. A day on a boat can make you terribly sunburnt, so take 15+ block and a hat with you. Remember Australia is near the ozone hole, and even cloudy days can be high UV days. (See also Llewellyn for more on coastal islands and McLellan.)

Hinchinbrook Island
Lying almost midway between Cairns and Townsville (see McLellan), and just offshore from the town of Cardwell, Hinchinbrook Island is a National Park island. It is possible to bushwalk the entire coast of the island or you can stay at the (fairly expensive) Hinchinbrook Island Resort. It offers cabins as well as tree houses. The cabins are close to the sea, hidden among the trees; the tree houses are more recently built and look out over the trees to the sea. There is no television or telephones in the rooms, just the sound of waves breaking on the shore. From the resort you can take boat rides to the mangroves or you can walk along beaches deserted except for the occasional curlew hunting crabs.

There are a large number of islands to visit. Hinchinbrook is low key and quiet, as is Heron Island, further south and on the reef. Each island has its own character. Some are inexpensive and more in keeping with ecotourist ideas; some are enormously expensive and exclusive. Others are primarily resort islands not dissimilar from the Bahamas or other resorts. Some have a culture attractive to young holidays makers, some cater for families, others are quieter escapes for overworked executives (again the tourist centres will have information).

Dorrigo National Park, NSW
Inland from Coffs Harbour and Bellingen (see Arianrhod), Dorrigo is the southernmost tropical rainforest you can visit. A boardwalk takes you on a walk at treetop level from which you can view the many birds. Dorrigo borders on agricultural pastures, and gives an idea of what the area would have looked like before the land was cleared. As with most Australian National Parks there is an informative visitors' centre with a slide show and quality food is available from the kiosk.

Oodgeroo Noonuccal
SUMMER

Living on Minjerribah (Stradbroke Island) is beautiful all year round.

Minjerribah is situated about sixteen kilometres from mainland Australia, off the bayside township of Cleveland, near Brisbane, and is the grass-root home of the Noonuccal tribe.

I welcome summer's yearly appearance here. To awaken to the dawn of another day, listening to the happy twitter of baby birds in their nests.

The first call of the kookaburra at five o'clock in the morning and then again at six o'clock is better than any man-made awakener. Truly they have earned the title of 'the Bushman's alarm clock'.

The early calls of the kookaburras and their young trying to copy them are a delight to hear. Young kookaburra chicks have to learn to laugh; they are not born laughers. I have discovered that, like all children, some are fast learners, some average and some slow.

Before dawn breaks, the storm bird is calling to his mate. After mating they seek out a ready-made nest where the female can lay her eggs. Usually the friar-birds are the victims. After hatching the storm bird's chicks, the friars become very angry and do their best to throw the baby storm birds out of their nest. This pattern is repeated every summer.

By nine a.m., the bush is alive with the call of the cicadas, and the melodious voice of the thrush can be heard as she and her mate flit from branch to branch, eating their breakfast of golden orb spiders.

There is a rustle of dry leaves and I know old man goanna is sneaking through the undergrowth in search of a victim.

Carpet snake stealthily climbs the high pine trees in search of birds' eggs. The battle for reproduction ensues, as crows join together to peck him off his perch and away from their eggs. Their cries of anguish echo and re-echo through the tall pines.

All creatures welcome the electrical storms, for they energise and strengthen the land.

To walk the low tide in search of oysters and quampies (pearl shell) is an experience rewarded by the feast when they are cooked on the open fire.

Going to the outside beach, where the Pacific Ocean washes daily the thirty-six kilometres of white, sandy beach. Doing the eugarie (pippi) twist in search of the fat shellfish lying just beneath the rolling, shore-bound waves.

Fishing from my flat-bottom three-metre aluminium dinghy for summer whiting and bream around the mangrove trees. Rowing over to check the dilly pots for blue-claw sandcrabs.

Taking my dogs for their daily swim in the placid waters of the great sea spirit, Quandamooka (Moreton Bay). Watching their efforts at trying to catch a fish.

Marvelling at Nature's way of working with the moon to bring us the high three-metre tides.

The gathering of seaweed washed up on the beach after a strong westerly blow to fertilise my garden.

Going swimming in the warm waters of Brown Lake, three kilometres inland.

Watching the beautiful colours of the sunset as the sun disappears over the western horizon.

When night appears to swallow the last of the daylight, I hear the heavy growl of old man koala claiming his territorial rights. His mate is busy teaching their young one how to climb from limb to limb, from tree to tree.

Revisiting Myora Springs as it empties its tumbling waters into the Bay. Lighting a small smoke fire to keep the mosquitoes and sandflies away.

Catching my breath at the beauty of the cork tree in flower, their long branches of deep green leaves contrasting with their clusters of mauve flowers.

Hearing the fruit bats quarrelling in the tall gum trees as they suck the honey from the gum's cream-puff flowers.

The boo-book owl calling his mournful call of 'book-book – book-book'. He is our message bringer. He also protects us from the white spirit owl of death.

The sea-curlew calling from the mud flats at low tide.

The summer rain beating out a tune in monotonous repetition during the big wet. The dry sandy soil welcoming its cool contact.

The pine trees losing the last of their smoky blooms, as a bird lands on their green branches, shaking the heavy pollen into the air so that, to the naked eye, it looks as if the pines are on fire.

The deep, almost indigo blue colour of a cloudless sky. Night brings stars into focus and I marvel at the bear, the evening star, the saucepan, the milky way, and I remember the Aboriginal legend of the seven sisters.

When the moon has grown to full size, watching the nocturnal animals and night birds going about their nightly business.

Comes morning, and a willy wagtail chatters and darts about, catching the flying insects coming from the smoky pines. The bronze-wing pigeons strut about, puffing out their chests, looking for seeds on the ground.

All these things do not happen every day or night. They come after many years of my watching and learning from the Earth Mother and her beautiful creations. I spend my spare time listening and learning about her beautiful balance of all living things.

I am sad when I see the cane toad hopping all over the land, having been brought to the Island under the bonnets of the four-wheel-drive cars. The tourists, who, in many cases, act like terrorists, dropping their rubbish over the land and bespoiling the beaches.

My anger at their fear on seeing a snake and killing it. Their mad rush across the island, bringing death to kangaroos, wallabies, koalas and bird life. Their young people stealing mainland cars and abandoning them in out-of-the-way bush tracks. Their irresponsible habit of partying on the high cliffs at the far end of Minjerribah, at Point Lookout, sometimes ending in tragedy for some of them as they fall to their deaths from the high cliffs.

Watching the dolphins riding the waves from those same cliffs, swimming with the surf riders, quietens my anger and leaves me with another type of sadness, a kind of uneasy peace. I wonder whether all the human race will ever learn to live in peace and harmony with the Earth Mother and her sea spirits.

I visit Blue Lake, the spirit lake of the Noonuccal Tribe, to meditate, to pay my respects to our long-departed dead, whose bodies were placed on rafts of paper bark, set fire to and pushed out into the middle of the lake, so they could sleep their last deep sleep in the arms of the water spirit of the lake's deep waters.

I visit the last of our remaining middens, piled high with the long-ago discarded shells and bones, now overgrown with shrubs and ferns. My anger rises again as I notice the roads made by the miners, which cut deep into the last of the middens. I have been told this is not desecration, that this particular exercise is called progress.

I watch the life-savers at Point Lookout guarding the summer visitors from harm. Feeling deep sorrow when they risk their lives to bring back to shore a lifeless body that was once a happy, laughing human being. Summer brings with it the laughter, the tragedy.

The heat of the summer morning air disappears with the arrival of the cool afternoon sea breezes, blowing themselves from across the Bay.

The ti-trees' heavily scented blooms become decorated with the beautiful coloured lorikeets, screeching their happiness and well being from the swamp lands.

Last summer I saw a sad pelican riding the waves close to the shore on the outside beach. He was guarding his dead mate being washed back and forth by the rolling surf of the incoming tide. I wondered how she had met her death. Was a speeding car racing along the beach responsible? I really couldn't tell. A great sadness overtook me and I walked away wishing I had the ability to stop some of the sad things that happen during our summers. I find a large pile of eugaries (pippies) above high-water mark, their shells opened and gasping for water. I take them back to the surf, knowing most of them will die. Knowing, too, some thoughtless human being had dumped them in their hurry to get home. I rationalise, they won't die in vain. The seagulls and eugarie birds will appreciate the unexpected feast.

Watching the sunrise from the outside beach always brings an overwhelming calmness within me. The ball rises out of the horizon and records its reflection in the Pacific Ocean.

Overseas liners stand out against the skyline, making their way to the Port of Brisbane. I note the rubbish that has been dumped overboard, coming slowly in on the incoming tide, pieces of plastic, bottles and tin cans decorate the white sands. I found a discarded syringe once, lying in a tuft of grass. I swept it up with a piece of plastic and dumped it in the industrial bin.

On the Bay side of the Island, the beautiful sea eagles have built a nest high up on a large gum tree. They sit on the mangrove trees proud and free. I count twenty pelicans cruising along outside the mangroves.

When I take my fishing gear to the beach they come paddling in closer, waiting from me to clean my catch and throw the gut into the water. As I move back to the land, they come squabbling in, competing with each other for the gutted remains.

The summers of Minjerribah are movements of actions, and all living things are our reminders of the Earth Mother's balancing of her realm.

Only man, through his greed, disrupts, destroys, maims and kills her balance. How many more summers will Minjerribah have to endure before man learns to live in peace and harmony with her elements? When will he ever learn that Earth was created for all living things?

The rocks of the Island are her sentries. They are mute reminders that they are her temples that we have inherited from our Rainbow Serpent, our Earth Mother.

We, her children, know it is our duty to take care of her creations and pass them on when our time comes to return to the loving arms of our Earth Mother.

Therefore, we know, too, we cannot own the land – the land owns us. All seasons are precious gifts to all living things to be shared with all.

Oodgeroo of the tribe Noonuccal
(formerly Kath Walker)

Ruby Langford Ginibi
THE FENCING CIRCUS

Texas, Bonalbo, North Star, Nindigully, Thornby Station
We found an empty hut on the riverbank outside Texas. I set up camp and the two men went to work on the sawmill at Yetman. When I went across the footbridge into town for supplies, I was in Queensland and when I came back to the tent I was in New South Wales.

I fished in the river for yellow belly perch, using mulligrubs (like a witchetty grub but smaller) or worms for bait. The grubs and worms I found in moist places under cow dung. I had a handline wound around a coke bottle and I cast out into the early morning light. The perch took the bait quietly and if I was lucky I'd catch two or three, about ten inches long and good eating. Early in the morning there were also plenty of ducks. I had a .22 rifle and when I had shot some I waded into the cold water and swam out to get them. It was getting towards winter. Across the river and behind me were herds of piebald and skewbald horses. There were the times I had to myself – the men gone to work, the kids still asleep – and I sat on the bank fishing and thinking about my life.

My mind was always turned back to home in Bonalbo, and how content I was there. Sometimes I wished I'd never left. But then I would never have had my adventures, I told myself. Knowing how to sew trousers was one thing, but knowing how to survive in the bush and be able to sleep under the stars, that was another thing.

We stayed at that camp for six months. Bill was eight, Pearl was seven, Dianne was six, Nob was five, Dave four and Aileen three. I'd bought exercise books and textbooks in town and I sat them on the riverbank and taught them to read and write. On days when it rained we sat in the hut and told each other funny stories, and when the rain stopped we took buckets and went out to collect mushrooms. Texas mushrooms are as big as saucers.

Sometimes I felt like a mother and other times it was like I was the kids' big sister, still a kid myself and playing with them for the day, waiting for the real mother to come home and take charge of us all. And the real mother was me, but where had all these children come from so fast to change my life so much. The days when I felt old and responsible I would look at the kids as separate beings, I'd think about the differences between them, and about their personalities. For instance, Billy was an animal lover. Pearl was a mother hen. I would think about what they'd be like when they grew up.

One weekend I asked the men to teach me how to drive the truck. For some reason I could reverse it better than I could go forward, and when I almost backed it into the river they called the lessons off. But I'd picked up the basics and later when I got in the Hudson car I drove it easily.

When there was no more work at the sawmill we packed up and left for Toowoomba, Gordon's old town. The Darling Downs was like a huge painting and we drove through acres and acres of wheat – a rusty colour, then gold, then pale yellow, according to the stage of ripening. It was September and we could smell Toowoomba before we saw it. In the town there were blossoms everywhere.

We stopped for supplies and then pitched the tent beside a creek on the outskirts of town. These days we'd be called fringe dwellers but in those times we were just bushies, and plenty of people lived like that, poor whites as well as blacks. The men left early each day to find work in town. I should have realised this place was Gordon's old stamping ground, and one day he didn't come back.

I applied for a job at the hospital laundry, after getting work references from Marty and Jim to say they'd known me for fifteen years. The hospital was on a hill overlooking the school on the opposite hill. I looked out the laundry window and saw my two children playing in the schoolyard.

With the money we earned between us, we bought new mattresses and pillows and clothing for the kids. Things were going fine, then one Friday night Gordon was at the door. I mentally kicked myself for the way my heart lifted when I saw him, that long frame (like my father), those eyes. He said he'd given up the drink. 'You and the kids are all I've got.' He let out a breath. 'I don't want to be on my own any more.' I invited him in and he sat in the kitchen talking to Peter. They were glad to see each other again, despite whatever it meant about me and what I might decide to do.

I went out into the backyard to think. He did look sober. He was the father of my kids. A part of me still loved him. I must have wanted to believe him, because I went inside and heard myself explaining to Peter and beginning to pack. I think now I mustn't have given myself a hard enough time yet and wanted more trouble, more drama. Who can tell. Peter said he understood and waved us goodbye with a low sad look. He hugged Gordon who he always regarded as an older brother, his mate for life.

Gordon had a job to go to on a property at North Star near Goondiwindi. We said our goodbyes to Midge and Doug. What I didn't realise was that I was two or three months pregnant to Peter, too late for feeling sorry for myself. I didn't tell Gordon. I didn't write to tell Peter.

We called in at the homestead where Gordon was told he'd be night ploughing and sowing, then we went on to the outer station house where we were to live. It had big verandas all around. There was only scattered furniture here – the kids had beds and we slept on the floor. A new hole was being dug for the bush toilet and I had to watch the kids so they didn't fall in.

This place was very lonely because the only time I saw Gordon was at night when he'd finished work. In the day he went out in the boss's jeep and fixed fences and did station hand work. The ploughing had been done so next he harrowed the ground and then started night sowing. He was working fifteen-hour days. When the kids were asleep I went out to the veranda to look for the light of the tractor so I could feel some contact with the world. Sometimes I made a billy of tea and walked down to where the light was, and he'd stop for a while. I sat on the tractor and we yarned about ordinary things – how long he thought the job would last, whether any mail had come for us at the homestead. We never had permanent jobs or houses, so were always thinking ahead to when this one would pack up and always feeling a bit insecure.

I wrote to Midge every week and sometimes at weekends we went to the pictures in Goondiwindi. We saw mostly westerns – 'High Noon' with Gary Cooper, or Roy Rogers and Gene Autry pictures. As we drove to town we saw crowds of Kooris walking the ten miles in from the mission at Boggabilla. We loaded as many as we could in the car and gave them a lift, you can fit thirteen people in a Hudson if some are kids. I used to think it was a long way to walk just to see a movie.

Not long after the wheat sowing was finished Gordon had a letter from Peter saying he had a fencing contract and that he was coming to see us. He turned up in a Ford Customline sedan, the truck had been repossessed. The men fell into each other's arms, the kids jumped on Peter, calling, 'Chub, Chub'. He held me briefly and patted the swelling at my waist. He didn't ask whose baby. Neither had Gordon.

The next day the men decided to paint the cars. When we pulled into Nindigully where the job was, we looked like a travelling circus – Peter's car was red, blue and yellow, and Gordon's was blue and white. I got out of the car, put the kids on the ground and stretched my legs. The fencing circus had arrived.

Nindigully was a bush pub, a petrol bowser and a shop beside a small bridge on the Moonie Creek. Gordon stayed at the pub and sent Peter and me and the kids to set up camp at the property about ten miles away. First we stocked up on tucker and called at the homestead to see the boss who said he'd bring a sheep out later on. We were to do three miles of eight-foot-high boundary fence.

We pitched a tent between two dams, we'd use one for drinking and one for washing in. The kids went off and came back to report they were getting nipped. Yabbies in the dam, good, I liked to have curried yabbies as a change from sheep and damper, though at the moment the idea of yabbies or any other food made me nauseous, I had morning sickness. I kept looking out for Gordon because if he didn't turn up and I had to build a fence while I was pregnant I wasn't going to be too delighted with him. Late in the afternoon the boss came out with the sheep in his ute. He looked at Peter and me (I was standing up pretty straight by then) and he looked along the line of the paddocks where the fence would be and saw his fence and went off happy.

There was no sign of Gordon, so Peter and I had the job of killing the sheep. I put the chops and the lamb's fry in the meat-safe, that was tonight's dinner, and I corned the rest in a kerosene tin. The kids collected wood and got a fire going for me. I unpacked the camp oven and made a stew for tea.

Early next morning we drove up to the fence line with a waterbag and some cold cooked meat and bread for lunch. Still no sign of Gordon. Looks like we had to do this job ourselves. Peter tied netting from the old fence to the towbar, and I got in the car and took off at high speed. That ripped the old fence netting and posts right out of the ground. I kept doing this until I had it all down.

Billy and Pearl did the marking – we had to dig holes for straining posts every ten chains. Then came the iron posts which had to be rammed into the ground, then the running through of the plain wire, and last barbed wire through the top. It cut our hands pretty badly.

By eleven o'clock in the Queensland heat I'd ripped the sleeves out of my dress and dipped a towel in the dam and put it on my head and it was held in place with a man's hat. When the heat was too great I told the kids to sit in the shade or some trees, then when the day's work was finished they cooled off in the dam while I cooked tea.

Some days I was too sick with my pregnancy to work and I stayed in the camp. The kids played around outside, the fence was left to Peter. I was lying on the mattress one day when I heard the kids running and screaming, 'Snake, snake, Mum.' I jumped up and went to where the snake was, I could see it in the long grass, its forked tongue going in and out. I grabbed an iron fence post and bent the end by belting it on a log. I approached the snake, the fence post raised, and when I got to within hitting distance, it ran up a tree. The kids started to laugh at the way I was sneaking up on it – it wasn't a snake but a huge goanna.

I had to restore my dignity so I got some meat and string and showed them how to catch yabbies in the dam and later I made a curry. The next afternoon I heard Peggy Sue barking at something and went to look. 'Bunning,'[1] I said to the kids, 'look its quills are up. Get me a waddy,[2] quick.' Pearl came running with a stick and I hit the porcupine hard on the head. Now to get the quills off this fella, you need a kero tin of boiling water and one tin of cold. You dunk it in the boiling water to loosen the quills, then in the cold. Hold it by the legs on a log, and use a tom-axe to knock the quills off. Cut it open from the neck to the belly. In the neck are two kernels, like gallstones, where the taste of the ants goes. Take these out or else when you cook it the meat will taste of ants. Gut and wash it. The flesh is pale, the colour of pork. You bake it in a camp oven and the skin cooks like a rind, like crackling.

There is another way you can remove the quills, if you don't have kero tins for water, and that is to throw the porcupine into an open fire. It swells up and the quills burn down, but then you have to pull the butts out, and the better method is to dunk it in water.

I cut up potato and pumpkin and baked them beside the porcupine in the camp oven. I made the gravy. A baked dinner called for bush sweets, so I made a scone mixture and boiled doughboys. The porcupine was a feast and after we had the doughboys with Golden Syrup (cocky's joy) poured over them.

Between Peter and me and the kids marking for us we did three miles of fencing in three weeks. I think it was a record. Sometimes we started while it was still dark and worked by the hurricane lamp and the headlights of the car. This was so we could escape the heat of the day and mostly we didn't finish before nightfall.

When we were short of groceries I put the kids and Peggy Sue in the car and headed for Nindigully. I was speeding along the boundary line and some roos were hopping along in front of me. The kids called, 'Look at the roos! Look at the roos!' Peggy Sue jumped clean out of the window and brought one down and by the time I screeched to a stop and reversed she nearly had its leg taken off. She was very protective of the kids and when they yelled out, she'd thought the roos were going to hurt them.

Just as the job finished and we were packing up camp Gordon drove in. 'Where the fucken hell have you been,' I said, 'on a binge again? Thanks for all your help.' I could see he was sick as a dog from the grog, and he was lucky I only tongue-bashed him, I gave it to him though. Serves you right, I thought, I don't have any sympathy for drunks, and I went on packing.

We went from one fencing job to the next – Toobeah, Talwood, Bungunya, Daymar.

On the way to St George we called in to a garage on the outskirts and got yarning to a bloke called Clem Jollie. Our reputation had travelled ahead of us – when he heard we had a contract to fence at Thomby Station he loaned us a tractor, posthole digger, crowbars and spades. Thomby Station was about seventy miles out on the Moonie Highway, so we stocked up on tucker, placed it in the tin bathtub on Gordon's roofracks, and the fencing circus was on its way again.

It was a huge property – the boss had a private airstrip and a store, and the boundary was fifteen miles from the homestead. We followed the boss in his ute to the fenceline, Gordon driving the tractor and Peter driving Gordon's car and me with the kids and camping gear in Peter's car. It was rough ground and very bumpy.

This job would last about three months and we were roughing it. We pitched the tent and put the mattresses inside. Gordon was well enough to kill this sheep. The kids and Peter rounded up wood for the fire. The boss had brought drinking water in two forty-four-gallon drums, along with the sheep. The men had bedrolls and slept in the cars or on the ground near the fire, the kids and I slept in the tent.

That night we were woken up by wild pigs. They could smell the guts of the slaughtered sheep and had come into the camp. The kids slept through all the noise. Our cars had spotlights and we could see the tusks on the boars. We kept the .303 handy, but Peggy Sue chased them into the scrub. They came into camp every time a sheep was killed.

Next day on the fencelines we could see this job was going to be harder than the last one. The ground was covered in gilgais, deep holes which would fill up when it rained and which made the fence go up and down unevenly. Gordon drove the tractor with the posthole digger and Peter and I lifted the poles in and rammed them down with crowbars. I told the kids to play close by and I kept watch for snakes. I killed four or five a day but they weren't poisonous ones.

A week went by and I went with Gordon to the homestead store. We packed the food in the tin bathtub on the roof-racks. By the time we got back to camp it was raining and the gilgais filled with water. I stripped the kids' clothes off and bathed them there, then I washed the clothes because the rainwater lathered well and the water in the drums was hard bore-water. I spread the clothing on bushes to dry and years later standing over a washing machine in Alexandria I saw the image of my earlier self squatting over a gilgai – how I'd had two completely different lives.

The following day we broke a part of the tractor and the boys had to go into St George to get it. I expected them back about nightfall, but there was no sign of them. All I had to do to get myself really anxious was to think – I'm alone in the bush with six kids. There are snakes and wild pigs around. I'm fifteen miles from the homestead and seventy miles from town. There's a car here, but I don't know the way to the homestead, there are tracks going off in all directions. If anything goes wrong, that's it.

I sat on a drum all night stoking the fires. In the distance I could hear the shitringers (Queensland stockmen) rounding up cattle, whistling to their workdogs, the crack of the whip. A curlew called out with its eerie sound.

In my people's way curlews are a spirit bird warning of death. The last thing I wanted to think about. Another bird I couldn't recognise called mew, mew like a crazed cat till it chilled my bones. In the dark I heard the soft thudding of roos and just before daylight an owl went hoo-hooo-oo. I hadn't slept at all but I was glad to see the sun and go about my chores. I convinced myself the boys would turn up by tea time.

The second night was worse. I seemed to hear every noise magnified, every sound in the bush was going through my body. I held my hands over the baby inside me. I could hear the continual hum of a motor and nothing arrived. When daylight broke I hadn't slept again and went about my chores like a zombie. I had this image of myself sitting on a drum with a .303 listening to wild pigs grubbing in the ground and an endless parade of roos thudding by.

About dusk the third day the men came into camp. Gordon's car had broken down. 'Never again,' I said, 'if anything goes wrong again, me and the kids are going too. You're not leaving us out here alone.' I didn't tell them about the night noises and how I thought I was going mad. I laughed about it later, but in a hysterical sort of way.

This job lasted three months and it was as hot as Nindigully. My face felt like it was peeling off in layers. Every day I'd leave the fenceline early and go back to camp to cook tea. When we ran out of bread I made ashes damper or fried scones, and when the meal was ready I banged on a pot to call the men in. Every day in the heat one of the kids would remember what they'd be having in town – 'Ice-cream,' they'd say, or 'Pineapple juice,' and they'd roll on the ground groaning and giggling.

The day came to pack up. We looked along the fence, the heat haze above the wires, and said, 'Well that's done, let's get to town.' The kids were jumping all over me which started Peggy Sue off and all the way to Clem Jollie's place the kids wriggled and slapped each other and sang songs about town and the silly things they'd do. We hadn't been out of the camp for eight weeks, we were all burnt, and with the tractor and two cars piled up we looked a sight in that empty country. 'Goodbye,' I said to the fence, waving an arm out of the window.

We picked up our pay and drove into St George, paid Clem Jollie what we owed him, and on to the shops. This town was a mecca of civilisation to me, look, here was a dress shop – I went right in. I needed a new dress. Halfway into the shop I saw myself in the long mirror, close up. Here was a pregnant woman with blistered hands like a man's, her face peeling like flaky pastry and black, she started black, but her arms were BLACK and the hair ginger. I stared at myself for a long time and then I bought a sleeve-less cotton dress and went outside. I hadn't been in town for so long I was lonely for another woman to talk to, so every woman I passed I said hello, hello, just to hear them talk to me.

Notes
1. Porcupine (echidna)
2. Stick

Gillian Hanscombe and Suniti Namjoshi
LONGITUDE 151° 55′E LATITUDE 23° 26′S

On Heron Island, herons haven't understood that they're allowed to belong to distinct species; grey and white pair at random, and yet their offspring remain unmixed. Is it the sea: now jade, now turquoise, now far in, now right out, but always working? On Heron Island, the pisonia trees haven't understood that dead wood is dead. They drink too much, their limbs break off; then green leaves sprout from their broken limbs. Is it the rule of birds, the predominance of wings; or the scratch of bird feet in the undergrowth? The pandanus palms haven't really understood that their function is to protect the rest of the island – they grow where they like. Perhaps it's the noddies, who crowd their branches, and who haven't understood that when the sun goes down it's time to sleep. Or is it the rails who scurry about and ignore the signs written in English?

On Heron Island, rock and sand partake of one another. Coral turns to sand; sand turns to rock. And live coral is as hard as rock, now covered by the green silk sea, now open to the glint of the sun. Watch where you walk: the reef breathes, and ridiculous baby sharks have wedged their heads between rocks or corals, certain that since they cannot see, they cannot be seen. If you stare for a while, a black ray flips out of the water. Just for the hell of it? Or for breeding purposes? Or to get rid of mites? Was it really there? Or in this place is imagining conjunct with seeing?

Does the island exist? It lives, and therefore exists, in the stored information of greedy brain cells, in the search and grasp of soft corals, in the secret manoeuvrings of bivalves and sea cucumbers, turtles and fish. Here you too are a creature, and memory matters. The sea slaps and licks the island's edges. The sea makes and unmakes it, over and over.

Betty McLellan
WOMEN IN THE TROPICAL NORTH

The city of Townsville, often referred to as the 'capital of the north', has a very active and energetic women's movement.

Situated in the tropical north of Australia, Townsville has hot, humid summers (December, January, February) and unbelievably beautiful winters (June, July, August). A visit to Townsville any time between May and October would almost certainly guarantee you near-perfect weather. And the women of Townsville are ready to welcome you whenever you choose to come!

With a population of 120,000, Townsville is not a small centre by Australian standards. In fact, it is the second largest city in the state of Queensland, and one of the largest provincial cities in the country. Because of its geographical isolation, however, many residents feel it is one part of the country that is often overlooked by state and federal governments. True, compared with larger cities and wealthier rural areas, the north and west of the country often appear uncared for. But it is that that gives Townsville and regions further north their uniqueness and charm. The advantage of having been neglected by governments and developers is that this part of the country has been allowed to develop naturally. There is a rugged feel to it and a natural, unspoiled appearance which causes backpackers and other visitors from all over the world to refer to it as an 'undiscovered jewel'.

An important feature of the Townsville region is its large indigenous population. While many of the original inhabitants of Australia, the aborigines, live side by side with white families in the suburbs, some live in predominantly aboriginal communities, each governed by its own aboriginal community council. The community closest in proximity to Townsville is the Palm Island aboriginal community, situated off the coast, north-east of Townsville. Any white Australian or overseas visitor wishing to travel to Palm Island must first obtain permission from one of the community's elders.

The following are some snippets of information designed to give you an overview of the city of Townsville, and to tempt you to pay us a visit. Situated on the east coast of Australia, Townsville has a long stretch of beach where people swim all year round. Its location on the coast has also lent itself to the development of a large port facility which services ships from many parts of the world.

It is also a university city with James Cook University catering for both Australian and overseas students. The Arts are also an important part of the city's life. Performances by any of our local theatre companies are well worth seeing, but special mention must be made of WINQ (Women in North Queensland) Theatre Group. Townsville's local dance company, Dance North, has risen to national and international fame, and if you are fortunate enough to visit when Dance North is performing, don't miss it.

Another feature of Townsville is the Cotters Market in Flinders Mall, open from 9am till 1pm every Sunday. If you are here on a Sunday, whatever else you do, make sure you visit the market.

One of the simple yet really enjoyable things to do any day of the week, is to take a leisurely walk through the city heart and admire the tropical landscaping of the Flinders Street Mall. While you are there, be sure to stop in at the Perc Tucker Gallery where you are always assured of a feast of talent from local and non-local artists.

Those who enjoy good food will be delighted by the variety of restaurants, cafes and coffee shops in the city. For lunches, I recommend The Metro Eastside, 235 Flinders Street (in the block just east of the Mall), Cafe de France in Northtown on the Mall, and Seva's Coffee Shop, at the corner of Sturt and Stanley Streets.

For evening meals, my favourite restaurants are Jun Japanese Restaurant, 436 Flinders Street, where the Japanese cuisine is superb. A five-minute drive west from the city heart will take you to The Taste of India restaurant (279 Charters Towers Road), which offers both Indian and Persian menus. The atmosphere is casual and the food delicious. Then, a five-minute drive north-east of the city will take you to a casual little French restaurant where you can dine cafe-style on the sidewalk or inside the airconditioned restaurant. You will find the food at Le Potiron (71 Eyre Street, North Ward) delicious and reasonably priced.

There are several good bookstores in Townsville, also. The one that always has a large stock of feminist literature, fiction and non-fiction, is Mary Who Book Shop, 155 Stanley Street in the city (about two doors down from Seva's Coffee Shop).

Women's Activities

Because of the geographical isolation of northern centres from the rest of the country, many feminist women have felt cut off from the kind of feminist scholarship and action that seemed to be happening in the larger southern cities. In response to such feelings of isolation, we have worked hard over the years at creating our own feminist community.

In 1984, a group of Townsville women met to discuss the need for a Women's Centre, a space for women only, an information and referral centre, a place where women could meet for study and discussion, a centre for planning social and political action. A decision was made at that meeting to look for a suitable location in the heart of the city, and each woman present pledged to pay $20 per month to cover the rent and other expenses. At last, we had our own women's space based on feminist principles.

After about eighteen months, we obtained government funding, and the women's centre is now operating as the North Queensland Combined Women's Services. We found larger premises in one of the suburbs, and now employ five workers who provide counselling and support to women in need. The centre has a 24-hour telephone counselling service to women, is a referral point to the Women's Shelter for women escaping from domestic violence, provides rape crisis counselling and support, and generally exists in the community to offer women any kind of help they may require.

While one of the functions of North Queensland Combined Women's Services (the Women's Centre) is that of being available to help women in need, that is not its only function. It is also a place where groups of women meet for fun, personal development, skills sharing, feminist action and so on, and where individual women drop in for a cup of tea and a chat.

A very popular activity organised by the Townsville Feminist Collective and held at the Women's Centre is 'Gertrudes – A Salon for Women'. Modelled on the European 'Salons' early this century where artists and writers (including Gertrude Stein) met to share ideas, offer support and inspire each other to greater heights of creativity, the aim of Gertrudes is to provide a place where women can come together and share women's knowledge and creativity. On the first Friday evening of every month (March to November), Gertrudes features a woman who is invited to share her work/talent/interest with all who attend. It's a wonderful celebration of women.

We hope, when you are visiting Townsville, that you will drop in and meet the staff at the Women's Centre. They will have information about any women's activities, women's theatre, women's study weekends, etc., occurring during your stay. The address is: 50 Patrick Street, Aitkenvale, Townsville, and the telephone number is (077) 757555.

For those interested in checking out other women's services during their visit, Townsville also has a well-established Women's Shelter with an excellent reputation for service to women and children. The Shelter can be contacted through North Queensland Combined Women's Services on (077) 757555.

Also, for visitors interested in women's health services, Townsville has recently opened the Women's Community Health Centre in the heart of the city, offering health information and referral. The address is: 35 Sturt Street, Townsville, and the telephone number is (077) 716867.

Palm Island aboriginal community also has a women's centre. Again, permission must be obtained to visit the community. Any woman wishing to visit the women's centre on Palm Island should first phone the centre on (077) 701226, and speak with one of the women elders.

Further north, there is the Cairns Women's Centre located at 7 Miller

Street, Cairns, Qld, 4870, phone (070) 519366 and also the Tablelands Women's Centre located at 15 Beatrice Street, Atherton, Qld 4883, phone (070) 913369. Women are always welcome to drop in and spend some time.

If you are visiting our region in August, you are in for a real treat! Every year, in August, the Winter Institute for Women is held in Townsville. A month-long celebration of women! Courses, seminars, forums, panels, lectures, weekend workshops, etc. It's a wonderful feast of feminist scholarship and discussion, together with lots of fun and laughter and music and friendship.

If you can come only for a short time, then aim for the second weekend in August, because that's when the Winter Institute's weekend workshop is usually scheduled. This event is always the highlight of the month's activities for those who can attend. It is a live-in workshop held at one of the Camp and Conference Centres in the Townsville region. Sometimes we go to tropical Magnetic Island, just off the Townsville coast, and other times to beautiful Crystal Creek, about 64 kms north of Townsville. Information can be obtained about the Winter Institute for Women by phoning (077) 726060, or by writing to PO Box 688, Townsville, Qld 4810.

Tourist Activities

Magnetic Island For a really inexpensive holiday adventure, take the ferry from Townsville to Magnetic Island – beautiful, natural, peaceful, an absolute delight. The ferry ride takes only 20 minutes (each way) and costs $15 for the total trip. The different parts of the island are identified by the names of the bays. You'll get off the ferry at Picnic Bay which is the most commercially developed bay on the island. If you walk along the sea-front mall at Picnic Bay, you'll be impressed immediately with the island's casual, laid-back atmosphere that beckons you to relax and enjoy the feeling of being alive.

Sometimes small groups of friends from the Feminist Collective go to Magnetic Island and spend a day together, swimming, walking, relaxing, eating, talking, laughing. It's a wonderful place to be together with other women.

While most islands stretched out along the east coast of Australia are dominated by expensive, resort developments, Magnetic Island remains relatively unspoiled.

Of all the bays on the island, (Picnic, Nelly, Geoffrey, Arcadia, Alma, Radical, Florence, Arthur, Horseshoe), the favourite with my friends and I if Florence Bay. We love it because it's beautiful, quiet, peaceful and still in its natural state. We love it, too, because we fought hard to keep the developers out. A few years ago, our City Council was considering giving permission for a huge resort complex to be built there, an action which

would have ruined its natural beauty forever. Many of us rose up in anger at the thought of such desecration. We organised and demonstrated and wrote letters, and the end result was that permission was not granted to the developer. Florence Bay is close to our heart because we feel we saved her, and she continues to show her gratitude by giving us hours of happy, peaceful times, every time we visit.

The most inexpensive way to move around Magnetic Island is by bus. You can buy a day-pass for $6, which allows you to get on and off the buses as often as you wish all day long. Some of the bays, however, are not serviced by the bus company because the roads are not suitable, and can only be accessed by car or bike. Florence is one of those bays. Most people going to Florence Bay hire a mini-moke (a small car used mainly in seaside communities). The cost is around $35 a day and they hold four people. Of the bays accessible by bus, the most popular for swimming and picnicking is Alma Bay.

Tropical Rainforests Just north of Townsville, there are some lovely rainforest areas where you can enjoy walking along well-marked rainforest tracks and swimming in cool mountain streams. Nestled at the top of Mt Spec National Park is a little village called Paluma. Be sure to visit the Pottery Studio, the Craft Gallery and Rainforest Shop, and then treat yourself to a delicious devonshire tea at the Ivy Cottage. For those who want to stay longer than a day, there are camping areas and some reasonably priced units called Mist Haven Rainforest Retreat.

As you drive up the coast further north, you will come to Cairns which is a very popular city with tourists because it is the gateway to the northern rainforest areas, Cape York Peninsula, the Atherton Tablelands and the Great Barrier Reef.

About 110 kms north of Cairns will find you at the Daintree River. World Heritage listed area, this is one of the most scenic regions in the whole of Australia. A cruise on the Daintree River is a must, because it will provide you with views of the magnificent tropical rainforest and mangroves. Also, you will be introduced to some of the 200 species of fish, to the crocodiles that can sometimes be seen sunning themselves on the water's edge, and to the magnificent birdlife of the area, including jabirus, egrets, flycatchers and kingfishers.

Cape York – at the top of Australia
Cape York Peninsula is the sharp point of land on the north east corner of Australia. You can drive yourself (preferably in a four-wheel drive), go on a Safari tour with a tour operator, go by cruise ship from Cairns, or fly. It's a vast land mass begging to be explored.

Accommodation at the Pajinka Wilderness Lodge is in comfortable,

266

reasonably priced cabin-style units set amongst beautiful gardens. Pajinka Lodge is unique in that it is operated by the Injinoo Aboriginal Corporation. 'Pajinka', in Cape York Creole, the language of the Injinoo people, means 'this place'. To obtain information, write to Pajinka Wilderness Lodge, Box 7757, Cairns, Australia, or phone (008) 802968.

The Injinoo people say 'Pass time you bin ya, Pajinka gor me'ke you com bak gan', which is Cape York Creole for: 'Once you come here, Pajinka – this place – will call you back'.

The Atherton Tableland A special treat awaits you on the Atherton Tableland, west of Cairns. Whether you go by road to any of the towns on the tableland (Atherton, Yungaburra, Mareeba, Malanda, Kuranda), or take the famous train trip from Cairns to Kuranda, you will be amazed at the breath-taking views.

If you take the train to Kuranda, look for the twelve-person carriage drawn by clydesdale horses. This service is owned and operated by a woman called Karen who meets the train every day and takes tourists on a sight-seeing tour around Kuranda. You may get on and off the carriage anywhere on the route. Make sure you meet Karen. She enjoys helping women make their visit to Kuranda a memorable one.

There are many beautiful places on the tableland – like Lake Eacham, Stoney Creek, and Barron Falls. Reasonably priced accommodation can be found in caravan parks and cabins all over the tableland, but there is one very special place where women from all around the world love to stay when holidaying in Australia. I refer to Witchencroft Women's Guesthouse, which is on a landscaped five-acre organic farm situated in a forested valley 6kms. from the township of Atherton.

Witchencroft is owned and run by Jenny McLean, whose brochure describes her very affordable accommodation like this: 'The guesthouse has two private self-contained rooms named "Hazel" and "Frances" after my grandmothers. Each is a double room overlooking bush gardens and providing you with modern kitchen and ensuite facilities. Meals are flexible. Self-cater or enjoy our delicious vegetarian cuisine featuring home-grown produce.'

Jenny also offers personalised tours to 'help you experience the wet and dry areas of Australia's Tropical North. Tours include combinations of four-wheel drive adventures and bushwalks, depending on the time of year and your interests.'

If you would like some help in planning your visit to the Cairns area (which includes the Daintree rainforest, the Atherton Tableland and the Great Barrier Reef), this is another service Jenny offers. Write to her: Jenny McLean, PO Box 685, Atherton, Australia, 4883, or phone her on (07) 912683.

The Great Barrier Reef One of the seven natural wonders of the world, the Great Barrier Reef can be accessed from several places on the northern part of Australia's east coast. Sunlover Cruises leaving Trinity Wharf, Cairns, boasts it will give you 'the total reef experience'. Out of Townsville, Pure Pleasure Cruises leave daily from the Great Barrier Reef Wonderland wharf. Once out at the reef, you may choose to go swimming, snorkelling, scuba diving, or you may prefer to view the reef from glass-bottom boats. Whatever you choose, you will be amazed at the colour and beauty of the reef's underwater life.

Those who can't afford a cruise to the reef, or haven't the time, may prefer to visit the magnificent Great Barrier Reef Wonderland Aquarium in Townsville. On Flinders Street, within walking distance from the Flinders Street Mall in the city heart, the complex includes a Museum, the Omnimax Theatre, several shops and food outlets, as well as the Aquarium.

Conclusion

We look forward to welcoming you to Australia's tropical north. Townsville's feminists believe in working hard to change the status and experience of women in a world that oppresses and ignores us, but we also believe in rest and recreation.

We hope you'll include Townsville on your Australian itinerary. When you come, be sure to contact the Women's Centre on (077) 757555, and let us know you are here. We would love to meet you and assist you with your travel.

Robyn Arianrhod
Northern New South Wales

The Rainbow Region

I'll never be able to think less than passionately about the Rainbow Region, that fertile, subtropical area of northern New South Wales between Bellingen and Murwillumbah, so I asked a friend for a more unbiased view of it. She recalled the relaxed, unhurried atmosphere, and the joy of sitting in the sunset eating superb fruit bought at one of the many road-side stalls in the region. Then there's the air, she said: a luscious blend of eucalyptus, earth and flowers. She remembered swimming in secluded rivers, she remembered the miles of sandy beaches and the acres of banana plantations. She remembered that she felt really free there, really at home on the road in a green and inviting land.

A striking aspect of the Rainbow Region today is the legacy of the alternative lifestyle experiments which took place in the 1970s, a legacy that is evident to the traveller in the architecture[1] and ambience of the region. Thousands of people have moved there for a better life over the past 20 years, and many towns which were economically depressed before the 'hippies' discovered them now have community schools, solar technology industries, art galleries, naturopaths, cafes, health food shops, holiday farms, bed-and-breakfasts and self-contained cottages built in the 'alternative style.' There are walks and four-wheel-drive expeditions into the rainforest that are advertised in the local tourist brochures; yet before the 'hippies', the 'new settlers', the 'alternative lifestylers', the 'drop-outs' (as they have been variously called), there was very little local appreciation of these forests. Indeed, the new settlers fought long and hard battles to save the forests from logging, and to raise public awareness of their environmental and cultural importance. In particular, the battle to save Terania Creek (near Nimbin) was long and expensive, but ultimately successful, for the environmentalists; new settlers in the logging town of Bellingen fought to save the beautiful Bellinger River,[2] which once was deep enough to be a shipping port, from silting up as the surrounding forests were logged. Their efforts were less successful, although they contributed towards the general increased public awareness of the economic importance of preserving the environment.

The Rainbow Region is not just beautiful, fascinating and relaxing, it is magical. Because of the alternative lifestyle communities which still exist in the region, there is a palpable sense of freedom about the place – a sense that one really can try new ideas, live new ways, explore new lifestyles. This is enhanced by the fertile landscape and the subtropical climate, which effortlessly seduce one to relax and slow down! The scent of the place – the rich, damp earth, the fragrant flowers and the smell of the eucalypts in the early morning or evening dew – symbolises this spirit of freedom, as it evokes an awareness of the magic of the land, and invites abandonment to subtropical sensuality!

Nimbin: The Heart of the Rainbow Region
I took what I considered to be a giant leap towards freedom in 1976, when I moved to Nimbin, which, with its shopfronts painted with rainbows during the Aquarius Festival of 1973, was the heart of alternative Australia, the heart of the Rainbow Region.[3]

In 1993, the Nimbin Aquarius Foundation held a twentieth anniversary festival. The alternative spirit is still very much alive in Nimbin today. Indeed the 1991–92 Summer edition of the *RACV-RAASA Accommodation Australia*, describes Nimbin as a 'small town with alternative lifestyle community.' It goes on to say, 'bush walks, scenic drives. Nimbin Rocks (3km SW) . . . date back to the time when the Mt Warning volcano was alive. Best viewed from the Uki-Nimbin Road.' In the 1970s, one of the most beautiful and symbolic things one could do was to watch the sunrise from Mt Warning, in order to see what were reputed to be the first rays of the new day to touch mainland Australia.[4]

The community where I lived in 1976, at Tuntable Falls which is about 10 km from the Nimbin village, had been conceived (at the Aquarius Festival) three years earlier.[5] I knew I was giving up financial security and conventional respectability when I gave up my fledgling career to move to Nimbin, but I felt I was about to gain my freedom. I spent weeks after I arrived, just sitting in the sun by the creek, thinking about what my colleagues would be doing at that very moment, their lives ruled by time-tables – other people's timetables – while I had broken free of the habitual and the expected, and had chosen to just sit there by this lovely creek and contemplate choice in a timeless paradise!

I was delirious with freedom and music, and with the way the full moon looked after a cup of local mushroom tea. The landscape of the area around Nimbin dazzled my city eyes, with its flame trees and the Nimbin Rocks in the late afternoon sun, and the pockets of rainforest . . . and the nearby Terania Creek rainforest that we later helped to save from logging. (You can now visit the officially named Protesters' Falls, which are at the end of a short walk through a strange and beautiful palm forest.)

Alas, by the end of 1976, I felt that a Nimbin tribe of really free people did not seem to be evolving. It was said that the Nimbin Rocks were sacred to Aboriginal people, but that the Aborigines only ventured into the region for ceremonial occasions. Perhaps it was true, and the Aborigines were right – that this beautiful area should be kept for sacred purposes, not for everyday living. In 1977, I moved to a wilder, more isolated area,

270

in the New England gorge country, about 160 km inland from Coffs Harbour.

New England: Wild Beauty amidst the Devastation

New England may once have been an appropriate name for this area (which specialises in producing superfine wool), but I have never been able to see any resemblance between this dry, devastated country and England. The few trees that have not been ringbarked or chopped down are dying from a disease known as dieback.

If you go off the main roads into the gorge country, however, the land is wild and spectacular and relatively untouched. This is the wild, isolated country which taught me how to be 'alone', how to belong to the land rather than to people. This country feels mysterious, solitary and ageless. There are secret stands of primitive grass trees amongst the stringy barks; there are the harsh and irreverent screechings of cockatoos and the eerie, mournful cries of crows. From the ridges you can look down at a river soundlessly winding its way past ancient rocks and twisted she-oaks, and feel that you've seen eternity. This land is not soft and beguiling like the Rainbow Region, nor is it harsh and threatening; it is impassive. It is like a pagan goddess: it will provide and it will consume. It is neither merciless nor merciful. Like the universe, it is.

The region where I lived has not been protected as a National Park, and, in their inability to look to Aboriginal methods of drawing sustenance from the land, white men[6] had tried to clear the steep and fragile slopes for their cattle. But they did not obtain dominion over this land. Their descendants ended up selling it to a group of hippies, and later they marvelled at the vegetables that were grown in the organic, virgin soil, and at the native grasses which survived drought when their own pastures did not.

I see this land as Mother Earth's triumph over man, as the Australian landscape's triumph over foreign ideas of what it should be. When we moved onto the land to live, apparently the first white people to do so, the locals were incredulous: to them, it was 'tiger country', and there were rumours that a black panther, presumably escaped from a circus some-where, sometime, – along with wild bulls and dingoes – lurked in the gorges. There were also reports, from further down the river, of UFO and big-foot sightings.

Once, I did actually see a strange black animal that looked like a panther as it loped off into the distance. (I regret that I did not see a single dingo, however, though the neighbouring sheep farmers complained of them.) I did find the land otherworldly, but safe, not malign. Once, however, a group of us were camping for a few days on another area of the property, when we found evidence – in the carcasses of small animals with only their throats bitten out, in strange footsteps in the night, and in strange eyes beyond the firelight – of an unusual, perhaps fierce, creature. Was there an ordinary explanation for the evidence we saw? Had we tracked the thylacine, the apparently extinct, almost mythical Tasmanian tiger? Or was this a totally otherworldly creature?

Our imaginations had been stirred by the magic of the ancient starlight and the legends we were telling around the campfire, so we invoked protection by keeping a bonfire burning all night. In this wild, isolated land, one's belief in the ordinary is easily dislocated!

The hissing-snarling sound of a possum in the night in such a place is at first utterly chilling. There was nothing otherworldly about the possums where I lived, however. Bushwalkers know that possums are adept at sneaking into tents at night and stealing the most treasured edible treats. I lived in a little house which we built, complete with a wood-burning stove and two water-tanks, for $70, thanks to our scrounging for second-hand and discarded materials. We had a set of tin cannisters with tight-fitting lids which you pulled off to open. Possums can compress their bodies so that they can fit through amazingly small spaces, and one possum used to squeeze inside and go through all the cannisters until it found the sesame seeds.

This country is most accessible to the traveller at the New England National Park near Ebor. It's a long time since I've been there, but I remember the marvellous view from the lookout across the valleys of the Park, then across the river flats some 1600 metres below, to Bellingen, about 50 km away. One day, I'd love to walk through the Park and along the Bellinger River to Bellingen. The New England National Park has an area of 29,985 ha, and contains World Heritage listed rainforest and fast, snow-fed creeks. It's about 2 hours and 15 minutes' drive from Coffs Harbour, and is about 85 km east of Armidale. (The Cathedral Rock National park is 77 km east of Armidale, and the scenery is quite different from that in the New England National Park, being dominated by giant boulders and naturally sculptured rock formations; wedge-tailed eagles, cockatoos and grey kangaroos abound.)

Dorrigo: Rainforest out of Time and Place

Needing an escape from the tensions of our community, two of us decided to head for the coast for a few days. All of a sudden, after driving through the flat, dry New England tablelands, we found ourselves in a whole new world of beautiful, green, undulating country. This was the Dorrigo Plateau, and the country became more amazing the further east we drove. Suddenly, the road wound past a mysterious, dark, old forest. It was rainforest, astoundingly out of time and place perched there at the edge of the relatively barren New England tableland. It is now World Heritage listed as part of the 7885 ha Dorrigo National Park. Now, too, there are board-walks across parts of the rainforest canopy, from where you can see the birds and the views and the trees. You can also, nowadays, take a horse-drawn carriage trip through the pretty Dorrigo farmland and into the rainforest.

But at that time, it was 'undiscovered'. To me, it was simply a beautiful landscape of panoramic views, misty, mysterious rainforest, and rolling green hills, a gateway to a whole new country. The drive from the Dorrigo plateau, at the edge of the New England tablelands, down nearly 1000 metres to the Bellinger Valley, is just a delight. A waterfall tumbles down to the side of the narrow, winding road, and, glimpsed between the trees, the views across the hills and valleys are beautiful.

Once down the mountain, the traveller enters the lush, tranquil Bellinger Valley, and the Dorrigo plateau appears in the background as a row of blue hills guarding this new, green paradise. It is remarkable the difference 1000 metres makes to the climate and landscape, for once down in the valley, the climate is subtropical. You can follow the Bellinger River for many kilometres as it meanders up into the forest or through lush farm-land to lovely little places with evocative names like Thora, Darkwood, Fernmount and Promised Land. But on that first, magical day, we did not know of those hidden treasures, and we kept on driving towards the coast. We never made it to the beach, however, as we became entranced by Bellingen.

Bellingen: Subtropical Paradise
Beautiful Bellingen – frangipani-strewn footpaths, people swimming in the river in the middle of town, colourful new settlers, beautiful, old shop-fronts (a rarity in rural Australia), and grand, old camphor laurel trees. Sometimes on summer evenings, the whole sky would darken with thousands of flying fruit bats. No wonder we fell instantly in love with the place.

When I arrived in 1978, Bellingen was alive with colourful new settlers and visitors from all over the world. As a result of the efforts and interests of the new settlers, visiting speakers came from near and far to give talks and seminars on permaculture, appropriate technology, sustainable economics, alternative education, playbuilding theatre, and so on. A focus for all this activity was the Community Centre, which housed the Library, the Neighbourhood Information Centre, the Environment Centre, and also provided a venue for concerts, dances, pantomimes and meetings.

Later that year, activities funded by a government scheme to help un-employed youth develop their creative and professional skills led to a flowering of creativity in Bellingen. Music flourished, and was a key factor in the integration of new settlers and 'locals', for the young members of both groups flocked to the Friday night dances at the Community Centre. Some of the young locals ventured into the Community Centre by day, too – initially against their elders' wishes – in order to learn to play the guitar, or to work on the fabulous (unfunded) *Maggie's Farm* open-access north coast magazine.

Prototype wind-generators and solar ovens[7] were made by some of the unemployed young people at the Community Centre. Community groups came from all over the state to see the alternatives in Bellingen – in the Community Centre projects and in the surrounding alternative communities. Women had a lot of power in the alternative community in Bellingen, and perhaps that was partly why there was such an emphasis on communication, both within the alternative community itself, and between it and the local community. There were many articulate women among the new settlers; some of them formed their own communities, for music, or for the exploration and development of their own strength and skills, in order to challenge the sex-role stereotyping that confronted women when they attempted to live economically self-sufficient or independent lives.

As so often happens in human groups, however, there were disagreements in the new settler community. Some people resented all the attention Bellingen was receiving and wanted to keep the tranquility of their new life, fearing that publicity would destroy their peace (as it did to some extent in Nimbin). Eventually the Community Centre was pulled down and an era closed.

I left New South Wales at about that time; it seemed as though once again, the alternative dream had died. Now, however, there is a mainstream pride in the architecture – both historic and alternative – in Bellingen. Some of the old buildings, such as the Old Butter Factory and the Yellow Shed, which were disused or in disrepair when I lived there, have become tourist attractions, for themselves and particularly for their wares – arts and crafts, plants and recycled building materials. Artists and craftspeople work in the Old Butter Factory, so it is alive with people as well as goods. Bellingen now has a reputation as a centre for art, and there is an Art Gallery upstairs in the historic, grand, old Hammond and Wheatley building, which was just a lovely old dry goods store when I lived there. The Bellingen market, held on the third Saturday of every month, is a must – for both the arts and crafts, and for the colourful new settlers who come in from the hills with their wares and their music.

Bellingen is still beautiful and interesting. The Bellinger River is delightful, and although it's no longer as deep as it used to be, there are still parts of it in the forested hills that are deep and clear and secluded. The road from Thora to Darkwood winds through hills and forest and criss-crosses the river many times. The road along the Kalang River to Kalang is also an adventure. I lived near the Kalang River, and I remember my winter morning ritual, in that mild, subtropical climate, of sitting in the sun under a mandarin tree, eating the magnificently sweet fruit, and sometimes swimming in the river. In the long summers, I swam every day, and ate only raw food; I felt the healthiest I've ever felt.

The land around Bellingen is bountiful and fertile, and it has an unusual combination, in Australia, of subtropical warmth and abundant water. I used to spend hours standing at the water's edge, feeling that I was a heron or a reed, feeling part of the river. Occasionally, I would see a snake, but it would always dart out of my way. (In Nimbin, however, there were huge, lazy carpet snakes, which initially terrified me until I was reassured that they were non-venomous – although there were rumours about their ability to crush their prey! People used to treat them as pets, because they kept down the mice, and they had beautifully patterned markings.) With its greenery and its rivers, Bellingen really is something of a promised land. Apparently, the latitude of this region produces more than an almost perfect climate and relative lack of dangerous wildlife, in the coral reefs and other marine life off the coast around Coffs Harbour.

Coffs Harbour: An Underwater Treasure Trove

Coffs Harbour has taken ecotourism to heart, and has some beautiful but environmentally sensitive resorts. There is the Solitary Islands Marine Reserve, a place that has only relatively recently been 'discovered' by tourists and travellers. The latitude of the Reserve (30° from the equator) is such that the southern temperate waters meet the northern tropical ones, and the result is a marvellous diversity of marine life from both regions. There are dolphins, whales (between May and August), turtles, sharks and abundant colourful tropical fish and coral. The reef here is probably the most southerly occurrence of coral around mainland Australia.

From Dreamtime to Today

I do remember the beauty of the beaches around Coffs Harbour, especially those away from the crowd at Coffs Harbour itself. I also remember the 1980 live-in protest to save Middle Head beach from further mining of mineral sand for use in the nuclear industry. This protest was important for its training sessions on non-violence, for the associated Beach Walk project in which a group of environmentalists walked the beaches of the entire north coast, recording their environmental state and status, and above all, for the meeting between the white tribe of environmentalists and two local Aboriginal tribes, the Dhungudii and the Gunbangerii. Middle Head beach had been an Aboriginal meeting place since the Dreaming, and the unity of the black and white tribes on this issue was,

I believe, a major though little-known achievement in Australian history.

Much was achieved in Australia (as elsewhere in the world) by the environmental protests of the 1970s and early 1980s; well-coordinated and well-informed protests such as those at Terania Creek, Middle Head beach, Washpool (described in a tourist brochure as being two hours' drive from Coffs Harbour, and containing 'the rarest of rare, rainforest wilderness'), and the Franklin River in Tasmania, led to the proclamation of many National Parks and World Heritage areas. The environmental concerns and identification with the land that informed the alternative lifestyle and environment movements in Australia were very largely moulded – at least subconsciously – by the Australian Aboriginal perspective that people are guardians of the land, and have a responsibility to protect it, rather than to exploit it as though it were a non-living and infinite resource. The Middle Head Aboriginal tribes only joined in with the whites when they were convinced that the greenies believed the Earth to be a living being. (Many ecologists also now believe that this is so!)

The Aboriginal attitude to the land has been encoded in an ancient web of taboos, legends and laws born of at least 40,000 years experience of living on this continent. Most white Australians, including myself, and indeed, (what a cruel irony!) many dispossessed Aborigines, do not know enough about this ancient knowledge; many of us romanticize it, or otherwise misunderstand it, in our ignorance. Yet we are extraordinarily privileged in this country – despite all this ignorance, and despite the human blood that was shed on the land during an ignoble history of cruelty to Aborigines – that the land still speaks to our spirits. It seems that this continent is so old, that despite 150 years[8] of white misunderstanding and mismanagement of it, despite two-thirds of our forests having been destroyed in that 150 years, there is still enough wildness here to speak to the soul.

Unfortunately, the gains made in terms of legislated protection of the environment during the last decade, are being eroded by the present New South Wales government. The following is an extract from an article by Ned (Aldan Ricketts) which was published in the *Nimbin News*, January–February, 1993, p.26.

An alliance has been formed between North Coast environmentalists and Koori[9] people of the Bundjalung Nation. The Bundjalung Nation is the traditional territory of the Koori people of the Far North Coast. The Alliance represents a new era of cooperation in which Koori people and environmentalists can work together to preserve aspects of our heritage that are sacred to us all.

This is really inspiring news, which makes me want to head on back to the Rainbow Region. And then there's the climate, and the scent of the place, and the softness of the air on one's skin . . .

Notes

1. In the late 1970s, the NSW Labor government (thanks largely to the late Planning and Environment Minister Paul Landa and to the work of community groups such as the Homebuilders' Association) began to introduce radical new zoning and building regulations to accommodate the new settlers. This meant that environmentally sensitive hamlets (where some facilities were shared) could be built in rural areas which had previously been designated farm land, and 'new' building styles and materials (such as A-frames and mud-bricks) could be used. Thus 'homebuilders' could provide their own homes without being tied into the building industry, with its high costs.

2. Apparently, an early cartographer made a mistake whose consequence is that we now have the Bellinger River and Bellingen town!

3. The history of this fascinating time and place is currently being collected and preserved in the Rainbow Archives, which are housed in the Mitchell Library in Sydney.

4. Mt Warning is between Uki, 37km north of Nimbin, and Murwillumbah, which is not far from the New South Wales-Queensland border.

5. For an informative account of the genesis of the Tuntable Falls community and many of the other Australian alternative cultural experiments of the 60s and 70s, see Peter Cock. 1979. *Alternative Australia*. Quartet: Melbourne. For more spontaneous accounts, written as the events were unfolding, see back-copies of *Nimbin News* (which is still being published), and old copies of other alternative magazines from the region, notably *Maggie's Farm*, in the Rainbow Archives. This Community is now closed, and like most such communities, does not welcome tourists or any visitors who are merely curious.

6. I use this word deliberately.

7. Now a commercial alternative technology company has set up in Bellingen, and, along with other such companies, in other north coast towns as well. There is also the highly successful and ideologically sound Rainbow Power Company in Nimbin.

8. For example, the Bellinger Valley was first discovered by white settlers (the first new settlers!) in 1841, when loggers discovered the great stands of cedar that used to be there.

9. An Aboriginal word for some of the original inhabitants of Australia, often used to include all original peoples of Australia, but most frequently used for those from South East Australia.

At sea
Tuesday 31 May
Dear Caro

The boat is little short of rough, and I don't mean the weather. The passengers are Australians. Also cheerful. But it did blow last night with big waves.

We called into Lizard Island today and I lay on the beach in hot sun, swam over the coral and then took out some glasses and flippers later and looked at the coral. It was not very coloured; fawn, cream and dark. The water was sensational. Clear, clear; like melted warm ice.

Audrey, a passenger, and I walked down the beach round the bay to some rocks, found some oysters and cracked them open and ate them. Next time I go ashore I'll take a lemon.

Wednesday 1 June
Dear Caro

We are heading north and coming now into Farmer Island which is another uninhabited island. I lost my new straw hat overboard yesterday. A shark has been seen this morning beside the boat.

Thursday 2 June
Dear Caro

I have been in a wonderful forest. Not an underwater one, but this morning we were taken ashore to the tip of Australia at Cape York. There, across a wide beach I found a track into tall trees, vines, palms and things I hadn't seen before. I felt very moved. This lovely land.

This morning we had a wonderful sight, Caro, a moon rainbow. They are very rare, found only in the tropics. It wasn't a rainbow round the moon, which we have at home, but a full rainbow, rather silver and grey and luminous right across the horizon. The captain saw it first and pointed to it and said it was only the second one he'd ever seen in his life.

Friday 3 June
Dear Caro

We are coming into Sherrard Island. The sea is neither blue nor green, but something in between. Not turquoise, though. Thursday Island has truly turquoise water. A sad and beautiful dry, dry island. There are a few rough stores in the unpaved main street with Islanders wandering around or sitting on steps, chatting. Some schoolchildren ran and jumped among dust, playing so happily in their lovely dark pink cotton uniforms. As I walked down the street back to the wharf I looked down at my old sandals and thought of all the miles they've gone and how many dusty tracks and polished city streets they've been on. Travel's an inflated thing with a barnacled underside.

Later

I've just been to the most beautiful island. Sherrard is just a dot surrounded by coral. The most wonderful shells. I got huge clam shells and many cowries and others I don't know. Pink and red and green and dark shiny grey. I filled a hat and the top of my bathers, then my towel. I saw a stingray slither away in the clear water just before I stepped on it. It was pink. A sea eagle's nest is there in the only tree. Thick grey sticks with big gulls wheeling overhead.

Part of the island, and one could walk round it in ten minutes, is a grey bleak coral graveyard. I was told it was from crown of thorns infestation, but Kel, who has worked with scientists on Green Island, the central and most affected island of the whole Barrier Reef, says that when the islands form the coral begins to die as the sand builds up on one side. So it may be that.

I saw a bright blue starfish lying in the water. The size of a hand.

Saturday 4 June
Dear Caro

Betty is here bathing her foot in hot water, Dettol and then applying hot compresses. Her husband dropped a live shell on her foot. She's taken a piece of shell out this morning and been up half the night with the pain. Coral micro-organisms are in the water and they poison wounds. Col showed me his scars to prove it.

We are surrounded by beautiful low hills of islands. It is all so soft, pink, hazy, blue and very, very romantic. Combe Island is where we stop today.

On land
Trade Winds Hotel, Cairns
Sunday 5 June
Dear Caro

Land. Lovely land. I clutch things as I walk past. My body thinks it's still at sea.

Oh, the many beautiful things I've seen. Yesterday on Combe Island, a pelican rookery. Big white eggs simply lying about in the sun. The pelicans gently rocking like boats at moorings out at sea. They build no nests, simply let the eggs lie among the sand and green vines.

I put my swimming goggles on and swam round looking at coral with small fish, exotically shaped, darting everywhere. This island moved me so much I was close to tears. Perhaps it was the pelican's eggs. I felt so privileged.

A dozen or so islands were visible around us most of the time. We saw turtles swimming like brown helmets in the sun. Then dolphins leaped out of the water. No bait is used for these fish, just a silver lure.

Cairns/Daintree
Tuesday 7 June
Dear Caro

Heaven is a rainforest. I was surprised to see that this huge area is not just rainforest. There are farms, tea plantations, orchards, camping areas, motels, cafes, even an art gallery, and many roads.

We went to the protest place. A most curious church has been built there from stone and canvas and branches. It is called the Church of the Molecule. On the walls are some press cuttings showing the people buried in earth up to their necks to stop the bulldozers. Tears came to my eyes. I just hate thinking about it – their faces look so sad and desolate, tormented. I signed the petition kept there to get World Heritage listing for the forest.[1] That, you see, will stop the Bloomfield road going through. The protesters say the runoff from the road will harm the reefs and will allow the plague of dieback, which is through Australia now, into the rainforest. They say, too, it will let feral animals have better access and so increase. Even if none of this proves to be true, and it is after all, supposition, surely it's not worth the risk for any road. A rainforest needs more than seventy inches of rain annually. I didn't know that. There are great palms like round fans. A figtree I saw was two thousand years old. Dozens of great ferns weighing tons hung from it. It was really a garden in itself.

Originally this tree was a strangler fig. They fasten onto a big tree and finally kill it. Then, having risen to the sky on its buttressing, they have strength to stand. The original tree dies and the fig, if it continues, becomes a cathedral fig. Sounds like some marriages I know.

At Cape Tribulation there is a lovely bay where the bus stopped for a picnic. I had a swim and walked around the bay to the mangroves. Speaking of mangroves, we passed many crocodile habitats. Estuarine crocodiles are there in their thousands but I didn't see any. Didn't really want to.

I saw bright blue fruit lying on the ground. A woman who sold shells and postcards told me it's called casuary fruit. Poisonous to humans. Only the cassowary bird eats them. Blue and red fruits are usually poisonous, Caro. Don't touch them. But red apples, cherries and plums and purple grapes are of course exceptions.

At Cape Tribulation the foliage runs right to the beach. Wattle is in bloom all along, waving yellow over the sand. This land breaks every rule.

Near a mountain comprised entirely of marble with some foliage draping it, I saw islands floating in a bay glittering in the sun, with Cairns tucked in at the water's edge; little white dots far away. And everywhere are butterflies. The bright blue Ulysses, the brightest blue imaginable, jewel-pale. Fish too, white ones with black stripes that disguised them in the glassy water and only the shadows of tiny waves on the yellow sand to hide them.

Lawn Hill National Park
Friday 10 June
Dear Caro

Darling, paradise is here. I've just had a swim among blue waterlilies in a green river.

Lawn Hill National Park
Sunday 12 June
Dear Caro

The stars are fading. The birds are just beginning to call and to net the stars. They are folding up the chiffon scarf of the Milky Way and putting it behind a red hill until tonight. Such stars, Caro. Imagine a starry starry night. Imagine another. Imagine a third. Put them all together.

This is a place so beautiful it almost defies description. The deep river is lined with pandanus on both sides. Behind that are cabbage tree palms and great figs with the fruit sprouting from the bark. Bowerbirds of a kind I haven't seen come and eat and drop the fruit in the water, where tortoises snap it up. All around are high red cliffs and beyond them is the desert. There are Aboriginal paintings on the cliffs. Some of great antiquity.

Yesterday just before dawn the eight members of this group walked up a big red outcrop of rock called the Stack, and that is just what it is. A stack of red rock rather like a high sandwich. We watched the dawn come up over the cliffs then down, shining on the water, reflecting the cliffs.

The forest through which I began running to catch up with the group is really awesome. Suddenly I stopped and thought, 'Why am I running through all this?' It was so quiet. Just the occasional crunch and rattle of a palm and then birds. I think Eden was like this. The garden, and outside beyond the cliffs and the river, the wilderness. We travelled for hours and hours in the four-wheel drive ten-seater through miles and miles of spinifex, turpentine and bulldust. Whole waterfalls of red dust ran down the back window. It's utterly blinding.

I stood for a while in that place by the river and walked slowly on and watched how the sun lit up all around the Stack and out beyond to the plains with chalk-white gums dotting the spinifex. We had eggs, bacon and sausages and toast for breakfast. Before that I swam naked alone among the waterlilies in the happy belief that there were no crocodiles.

282

Lloyd took me for a walk to a natural spa upriver. Caro, do you remember me saying I couldn't understand how in Treasure Island you could dive into a cave through water into safety and air? Well, that is almost what we did there. The spa is from a small waterfall built by the limestone deposits building up. It drops into a rock basin. Behind the waterfall is a small cave. If you go under the fall, there you stand with the water shining and pouring in front of you, this thick veil of water, and behind it we stood laughing. Back through rocks and spinifex.

I went up the river in a small yellow canoe with Lloyd up through the tall red cliffs, letting the boat drift from time to time. Such silence. Profound as death, but so beautiful. Up past the waterfall where we lugged the canoe up a portage into the higher part of the river. I wanted to see what was round each corner. I was told then that there were plenty of crocodiles in the river but they were harmless because they were freshwater species. Immediately I wanted to see one. We rowed on and on until the river was blocked by pandanus palms. We pulled the canoe into the bank and walked on and found another spa. We jumped into this, yelping like children. It was such an untouched secret place. I got out and stood on a log, watching a small red-tailed lizard basking in the sun.

On the way back I asked whether we could row over and see another small cave. It was just a lift in the rock about half a metre above water level. We peered into the dark and two eyes shone straight back at us. A crocodile. I rowed backwards so fast. Lloyd, telling the story, says he was rowing forward, but my strength took us backwards. Indeed I turned the boat around, which I didn't think I knew how to do. As we rowed back I felt hypnotised by the silence when we drifted from time to time. It seemed like a cathedral with no one else in it. Death, I think, is to float forever on a boat through great cliffs of rock on a green river through blue waterlilies with the peace of a cloudless sky above.

Just before dusk we pulled into the mooring. I set off to see the Aboriginal paintings through the palms round the base of the Stack. I ran because we were to leave before eight next morning and so it was my last chance to see them. There they were. Arches and circles and curious patterns, rather like the footprint of a Dr Scholl's sole massage sandal. On one side was a deep pool where, according to legend, lived the Rainbow Serpent, one of the great mythological Dreamtime creatures.

On the way back two kangaroos hopped away through the palms. A small grey snake lay curled on the track. I hopped through the spinifex to avoid it.

We had drinks before dinner and played a game I invented where everybody described the image or artefact of the day. A sort of show and tell. Such things as case moths, rocks from Riversleigh, the memory of a great jabiru flying across the river where we stopped for lunch on the first day, the crocodile, a flight of rainbow lorikeets, the bowerbirds feeding the tortoises, and so on. In the midst of this, a world authority on bats arrived to tell us about her work on the fossils at Riversleigh. She's Dr Sue Hand, about twenty-five, small, dark and vivacious. Bruce, a fellow guest on this safari, showed her a rock. She launched into a description of it, and he asked her to write down what she said. This is what she wrote:

Stromatolite = structure produced by cyanobacteria (used to be called green algae).

These bacteria are the oldest known forms on earth. Some are older than 3.5 million years. Some, under very specific conditions (e.g. high salt concentrate in oceans at Shark Bay in Western Australia and the Bahamas) grow to one metre across and two metres high.

They were very important bacteria because they produced oxygen (as a by product, or help produce) the ozone layer to filter the lethal UV rays so other organisms (e.g. plants) could get a start on earth.

I was mightily impressed by her. Bats, she said, are pollinators of trees. Where whole colonies have been wiped out it is now found that such trees, crucial in some areas, are also dying. The boab tree in Africa is a case in point.

It only served to show what you already know, Caro, and that is that none of us can be made too aware that the earth is a very fragile little system and we interfere with it at our peril.

We had damper for dinner with fresh fish, boiled potatoes and fresh corn on the cob. The Canadians went bananas over the damper. Time was it used to be called cockies' joy. They fed it to their employees with treacle or golden syrup because it was so cheap. Poor people ate it in the Depression. Now it's yuppie food, the tourists' delight. But it was good.

Dawn is creeping away with a blush. The light is beginning to hit the white trunk of a big gum and light the cliffs. Many gums are in blossom and the creamy flowers fall in bunches on the dry ground. Little grey-and-yellow honeyeaters drive themselves on in orgies all day.

Dingoes called in the night. They howl but cannot bark. The first night they seemed to be yelping like puppies. Lloyd said that the dingoes make a noise like a bunch of bloody blokes having a few beers and a good time.

Mt Isa
Tuesday 14 June
Dear Caro

Just a short note. I am off to Riversleigh in an hour.

This time I will get the clothes right. On the last trip the others had safari clothes from army surplus and I wore a sundress, which was a little incongruous.

On the way home I saw a flock of emus and a dingo. I've never seen either in the wild before. The emus were glossy, with looser dark grey feathers than I had seen in zoos.

All day we passed cattle trains which are trucks with two or three trailers double-decked and full of cattle going to the Cloncurry market. One had turned over and a field of bones, dragged, I suppose, from the road, was all that was left.

I will miss the feel of dust in my nostrils, I thought to myself as I rolled over in bed last night. And what's more, I meant it.

Riversleigh Station
Wednesday 15 June
Dear Caro
Shirley, the cook for this camp, is behind her serving bench under the gums with a pannikin of tea. Tracey, a Black American from the film crew, is standing beside her eating beans from a tin plate. She and I have been given tents in a prime position side by side on the river bank. Peter, one of the Riversleigh volunteers, has asked if I want to go for a walk to see a sea eagle's nest.

The Riversleigh volunteers are seven men and women who answered an advertisement in a magazine for people to help the scientists dig and bag the fossils. They pay their own expenses. The fossils are taken back to the University of New South Wales. They are then put in a vinegar bath which dissolves the surrounding limestone and frees the fossils. The method was invented there for this find.

The flies are getting bad so I must stop and get the holy Aerogard.
Later
Shirley has just taught me how to use ashes instead of Bon Ami to clean pots and pans. I remarked on how dry my skin was from the limestone river water and she told me she uses Dove soap as a remedy. Jean Shannon on the camp last week told me that fat, that is, dripping, and sugar are good for cleaning and smoothing hands. Also that milk mixed with lemon juice is a good skin cream. So I pass these things on for you to try if you wish.

Riversleigh Station
Friday 17 June
Dear Caro
It is now eight o'clock in the morning. I've just had a swim: steam is coming off the river. (The air is colder than the water early in the day.) Also, I'm getting better at canoeing.

This fire is warming my feet. Shirley is filling up a deep pot with river water from a big jam tin with a lip made by bending the edge to a point.

It is to cover a great haunch of corned beef. About ten kilos, she says, and because she has no bay leaves she says she will put in a couple of gum leaves, but I am not certain she isn't pulling my leg. In goes half a cup of sugar and a quartered bush lemon and on goes the lid of foil with a cake stand across to keep it down. We had this the first night I camped last week with cabbage, boiled new potatoes and pumpkin with a parsley sauce. Really it was memorable, the meat was firm but tender and not too salty.

Recently I was struck by something Victoria Glendinning said to me. 'I think Australia is a paradise of physical perfection . . . if I were twenty years younger I would live here.' And truly it is so.

Yesterday, coming back from the visit to Lawn Hill, I saw more emus, many wallabies, kangaroos and a black dingo. The dingo was rounding two calves with a cow rushing at him every now and then as he prowled remorselessly round and round. Finally the cow got the calves back to the other ten or so cattle nearby, who at once formed a circle with the calves in the centre. But still the dingo slunk round and round. Lloyd said, 'Cheeky bugger, that one.'

Later

Lloyd has just taken me out to the site of the fossils. We got about ten stromatolites for me to take home as gifts. They look just like buns and it's perfectly all right to take them as they have no special rarity.

Note
1. Daintree is listed as a world heritage area, and the Bloomfield road did go through despite protestors' efforts.

West / North

Susan Hawthorne and Renate Klein
The West and North

Perth/Fremantle

Perth is the most isolated capital city in the world (see Jolley). Set on the beautiful blue Swan River, one of the most striking features is the huge array of wildflowers you'll see in and around the city. Kangaroo Paw of various colours line some streets, and if you drive out of Perth make sure you stop the car and get out to look at the flowers you'll miss otherwise. The bio-diversity of plants here is legendary, so take the time to see it. The city of Perth is still relatively small, the buildings do not tower as they do in Sydney, Melbourne and Brisbane. Like many other Australian cities there is a Pioneer Women's Garden located in King's Park. For art and culture Fremantle, Perth's port, has been restored and is filled with shops, arts venues and historic sites. You'll also be reminded that this was where Australia won the America's Cup, when an Australian yacht beat the Americans at their own game. You can take in the four-hour walk of Fremantle with its sixteen points of interest. The Energy Museum has a large section on old household appliances, such as heavy irons and old stoves. Perth's Arts Festival is held to coincide with Adelaide's (March in even-numbered years) and although some of the international guests will visit both, Perth, with its considerably larger Aboriginal population, turns on a very different festival and in recent years has made the most of its proximity to Asia. From Perth you can easily drive into the Southwest corner (see Caddy), or to Margaret River, where you might catch up with the Bushtucker Woman, Helen Lee. But if you're planning to drive else- where (particularly inland) be prepared to travel on isolated roads and travel with provisions. The distances in Western Australia are enormous.

Darwin

Always hot, and in summer humid, Darwin has a long history of multi- culturalism with its large Aboriginal and Asian populations. Darwin is closer to Indonesia than any other Australian city and this is evident in the cultural mix of the town (see Kapetas). Darwin's Festival takes place in April, a sunny month that ushers in the dry season. More a town than a city, Darwin is a starting point for many four-wheel drive and adventure tours. Litchfield National Park with its waterfalls and iridescent green grass during the wet season is the nearest point, but Kakadu with its Aboriginal art (especially Obiri Rock), and day tours to see crocodiles and other wildlife, is more frequently visited. If you go at the end of the dry season (October) you will see huge flocks of Magpie Geese, especially in the wetlands near Coinda. As with Western Australia, take account of the distances before you set off. North of Darwin are Bathurst and Melville Islands, home to the Tiwi people. The islands can be visited as part of a tour. Tiwi design T-shirts and fabrics are available in some shops in Darwin, with a specialist shop at the airport that also sells bolts of fabric. In northern Australia (WA, NT and Qld) you should not swim in estuarine waters as saltwater crocodiles attack humans. In the freshwater rivers, it is possible to swim even in the same place as Johnson crocodiles (freshwater crocs) which do not attack humans. Estuarine crocodiles may look slow moving but they move quickly on both land and water. Always check with the locals first.

Broome

Situated on the north west coast Broome is a town of contradictions. Originally known for its pearling industry, Broome feels like a mix between a cosmopolitan city and and small town. With a population under 20,000 it is nevertheless a cultural mecca for the people of the surrounding region. Magabala Books, an Aboriginal owned and run publishing house is based in Broome and at the Kimberley Bookshop you feel as if you've walked into an inner city bookshop. Aboriginal owned art co-ops and galleries are also open to visitors. The main street has a selection of restaurants and cafes reminiscent of Melbourne's Brunswick Street. For accommodation you can choose from a range between backpackers hostels and the luxury Cable Beach Club. Whether or not you stay at the Club, you should visit Cable Beach, a wide white sand beach that has one of the largest tide variations anywhere in the world. At low tide Cable Beach can be quarter of a mile wide (almost half a kilometre). If you are in Broome between April and October at full moon you'll be able to see the 'stairway to heaven' as the moon rises over the Indian Ocean. If you are driving north, south or east of Broome, carry water and food supplies, as this is a very remote and thinly populated area. There are some direct international flights into Broome from Singapore.

Margaret River

Margaret River is famous for its wines and there are several other points of interest also. Ask for Helen Lee, the Bush Tucker Woman, at the boatshed at Margaret River. You can paddle downstream to limestone cliffs and caves, where Helen Lee will tell you local Aboriginal legends and introduce you to a selection of traditional local foods. At Margaret River you can also go on a Leaps and Bounds adventure for women, run by Ricky Coates. There are also guided walks through the karri and jarrah forests.

Seven Spirit Bay, Cobourg Peninsula, NT
The trip to Seven Spirit Bay is an adventure in itself. The day we went a tropical storm was brewing. The trip begins with a flight in a light aircraft, which must pass over some stunning scenery, but the bumpy flight we had through rain-filled clouds was bearable only because of the skill of the pilot. The plane lands on a dirt runway with nothing but bush surrounding it. Here a four-wheel drive vehicle picks up the passengers and ferries you along rough dirt roads to a beach. A couple of dinghies take you out to the boat moored offshore. No doubt the sea can be calm, but it can also be windy and rough. We bounced from wave to wave with dolphins around us and certainly felt we deserved the holiday that was to come. Seven Spirit Bay has won awards for its design, culinary finesse and its eco-tours. Each hexagonal room overlooks the sea and the semi-outdoor bathrooms are amongst the most original designs I've seen. Various tours to beaches (including reefwalking), paperbark swamps, and forests are offered each day, or you can explore the beaches and walks nearby. A couple of huge goannas (quite harmless) visit the saltwater pool or wander around the garden near the central building.

Keep River National Park, NT
Not far from the border of WA this park is not well known, but is extraordinarily beautiful. In among the rocks that form the central attraction to the park are a number of Aboriginal paintings. (Some parts are restricted.) The rocks have wonderful forms, eroded by wind and water they are one of nature's works of art. There is a delineated campsite, but hotels are many miles away.

Bungle Bungles, Purnurlulu National Park, WA
You need a four-wheel drive to get into the park or you can join a tour company (Wildwise, a women's tour company organises tours there from time to time). Getting into the park is a long and rough drive and the park is closed from 31 December until Easter. It is useful to fly over the Bungle Bungles before going there in order to get a sense of its immensity – you can do this from Turkey Creek, Halls Gap or Kununurra. From the air you can see the beehive coned rocks, striped in orange and black and you can follow the course of Piccaninny Gorge with its palms perched precariously in the rocks. Back on the ground you face a choice of two directions when you enter the park. If your time is short go to Echidna Chasm. This is the most most extraordinary rock formation. From the carpark it is a short walk to the beginning. As you walk between rock walls look up at the ever decreasing width of the chasm. Eventually you can walk no further as the rock closes in. Cathedral Gorge and Piccaninny Gorge which are reached from the camping ground on the other side are

also spectacular, but the walk through Piccaninny Gorge takes eight hours and you need to carry sufficient water to stay overnight. A minimum of one litre per person per hour is essential all year round. You may see goannas, and you're bound to see bustards, corellas and perhaps black cockatoos. The arid regions of WA, NT and SA are where you are most likely to see the black cockatoo with its bright red and yellow tail plumage (see Reilly). The campsites here are not only beautiful but offer running water nearby. Parts of the park are restricted to Aboriginal use.

Hidden Valley National Park, WA

One kilometre from the centre of Kununurra, visit this park on your way through. A couple of short walks through the rocks is like an introduction to the places you might go on to visit. A circular chamber of rocks looks out over Kununurra and is particularly beautiful at sunrise or dusk. Kununurra is a good place to stock up on supplies if you are driving and planning to go bush (the Kununurra Supermarket has everything!). Driving in arid country it is more useful to carry tinned foods as they are already wet. Dried foods such as rice and pasta are useful, but they use up precious water in the cooking. You should carry a good supply of tinned foods, drinks and plenty of water just in case you get stuck somewhere (e.g. bogged in sand or mud) where there isn't any water. A week's supply is the minimum; two weeks for some areas (such as the Tanami Track). Two eskies (ice boxes) are essential if you are travelling in hot, dry, remote areas – one for fresh fruit and vegetables, which will last two to three days in an esky; the other should be filled with a solid ice block (which can be bought from most petrol stations or supermarkets) and drinks – you'll long for something cold in the middle of the afternoon. Tea brewed in the mornings and poured into empty bottles is a refreshing warm drink for when your ice has melted! A block of solid ice should last one to two days, while a bag of crushed ice will last about half this time. If you are travelling to very remote areas let the local police know your itinerary and expected arrival date, and report in when you reach the other end.

Gibb River Road, Emma Gorge to Windjana Gorge

The Gibb River Road can be reached either from Derby in the west or Kununurra or Whyndam in the east. This description follows the route from east to west. Get a good map of the road before you leave. The Kimberley is vast and much of its remain inaccessible. The Mitchell Plateau (see Grace) is accessible from the Gibb River Road. The four-wheel drive guide to the Kimberley (see Resource list) has detailed descriptions of all roads, tracks and landmarks. The road is passable all through the dry, but may become impassable in the wet. Check with locals if you are driving between December and April. Emma Gorge and other parts of El Questro Station are worth seeing, and make a good first stop along this scenic route. Here you can see gorges, swim in idyllic hot thermal spring pools at Zebedee Springs, and you can have a guided tour around the station. At Emma Gorge you can stay in comfortable tent accommodation, or luxury suites at El Questro Homestead and eat a gourmet dinner, or you can camp elsewhere on the station for $5.00 at the time of writing. Travel the road at your own pace; what is most breathtaking is the extraordinary expanse of horizon and sense of space which is uniquely Australian. Don't miss Bell Gorge if you're in a four-wheel drive (which you'll need). Bell Gorge is a magnificent waterfall and waterhole and is safe to swim in – though you might see a Johnson crocodile eyeing you or a goanna sunning itself on the rocks. The road through the King Leopold Ranges gives magnificent views of the surrounding country and there are many possible side trips to gorges and swimming holes along the way. The final attraction along the road is the ancient Windjana Gorge, with its screeching corellas, Aboriginal rock art, and eerie ancient reefs. If caveing is an interest, then a visit to Tunnel Creek will be rewarding, but be prepared to walk through waist high water in the dark. As elsewhere in northern Australia, road surfaces can change within minutes. A wide dirt road can quickly become a river and you will need to react instantly to these changes.

The Pinnacles, WA

About halfway between Broome and Perth are the Pinnacles. These are peculiar stalagmite-like growths in the open air (see Hawthorne, 'The Great South Land'). From postcards you assume that these formations probably cover a few metres, but be prepared for acres and acres of them, from tiny ones just beginning to grow to others that tower over you.

Susan Hawthorne
THE GREAT SOUTH LAND

The Pinnacles at Nambung National Park, Western Australia comprises a large landscape of extraordinary rock forms. They were first sighted by early Dutch navigators who thought they were the ruins of an ancient city.

The Australian Adventure (1988)

The listener speaks

A traveller stayed here at the Herberge last night. I sat and listened as he told stories to my father and anyone else who would listen. He drank ale and as the night drew on the stories became more and more fantastic.

He had been to places that I had never imagined, even in my dreams. But he said that they are real, that they do exist. He told tales of forests dripping with mist, of flowers bigger than a man's head, of buildings so massive that it takes a day to walk around the perimeter. He said that instead of narrow cobbled streets there are footways encrusted with sparkling jewels – ruby, sapphire, emerald. But even more fantastic were his tales of the Great South Land – they now call it New Holland – which, he said, is no other than the fabled land of Atlantis. And, he said that he saw the ruins of the Atlantean civilization with his very own own eyes.

The observer speaks

It was a bright day with the sun sparkling on the water and the sky overhead like the blue domes of the infidel. We had been following the coast for a week or more and though we had taken shelter in a cove here and there along the coast we had seen nothing to indicate a kingdom or a civilization of any kind. Then as we sailed along a stretch of coast in the vicinity of latitude thirty, the fellow in the forecastle cried, "City ahoy."

We, none of us, believed him. But we pulled in nearer to the land and dropped anchor (we had our guns manned in case of aggression). We moored in a shallow bay a few hundred strokes from the shore, remaining overnight, half expecting the people of the city to come out in boats and welcome us.

The unseeable speaks

The ghosts come from the west following the track of the wind. They wait. They sit and dream and wait for the sun and the moon to set. Then they are coming to us over the water from the west. These ghosts from the Land of the Dead must be very old. They are unlike the other visitors who come from the dreaming places beyond the sea. Their extremities are pale, like the feathers of old cockatoo. Elsewhere they are adorned with coloured feather-skin. They are stiff-legged and they leave the strangest of tracks. Their feet have no partings. They move in strange ways, standing stiff-legged or lying on their backs.

They come out of the west and make fast fire magic. They touch our earth and walk around our country ignoring our ways, crossing tracks, scattering their tracks in ways we have not seen – even the eldest of our people knows no stories of ghosts such as these. They do not carry out the usual practices. They do not follow our maps. They carry off parts of our mother. They take hot stones with them, they break and damage the places left to us by other dreaming spirits.

With neither spear nor boomerang, animals fall down dead. Angry spirit shouts go up and the animals die.

They do not seem to hear us. We squat nearby, just beyond their range – all day. We sing dreaming songs, but they do not seem to hear us. Except one, who came near, who spoke gibberish and who fled when we approached him.

The moon dances, waiting. They walk to the west from their camp. They climb into their boats and follow the clouds to the west. The earth is quiet again.

The observer speaks

At sunrise I went up on deck, and there before my eyes were the golden pillars. Thousands of golden pillars. The captain was there too, with his glass. He passed it to me, I could hardly believe my eyes. As each man looked he gasped at what lay before him. Line after line of golden pillars.

We discussed how we should protect ourselves as we went ashore, since any king with such wealth would surely wish to protect it.

We agreed after some time that we would go ashore in groups of three. The first three were excited at being chosen to be the leaders, but there was fear in their eyes as they left. We watched as they stepped from the boat and approached the gleaming pillars. All was quiet. I went in the second group of three. We landed unharmed and tried to catch up with those ahead of us. Others followed.

We walked forward into what might have been a forest of stone pillars (alas, they were not solid gold after all). The area of the ancient city – for it could be none other than that – was huge. A winding track wove between the ancient foundations of the city.

That night we discussed how it might have been that the city was destroyed, what had happened and how long ago the disaster had occurred – for why else would anyone desert this wondrous place with its vista of green India sea? The place was utterly deserted and appeared to have been for eons. As we talked, our imaginations wandered through the possibilities. We agreed that some giant wave must have destroyed everything and everyone. Perhaps the city was once even bigger than the remains we saw.

The next day we set out, again in groups of three, to draw a map of the ancient city. It was so vast and complex of design that by the end of the day we had covered a mere fraction of it. Our captain was intent on doing this, so that we could return to Holland with a map of our findings. He assured us that the king would send us back better prepared for further explorations.

But to return to the ruined city. Such a city it must have been. Such an extraordinary civilization. The design was beyond anything I had ever seen before. Our mathematician, admittedly more accustomed to mapping latitude and longitude, turned himself to the task of deciphering the pattern of the city. He said that if it resembled anything, it resembled the pattern of the stars in the sky.

We found no sign of habitation, no sign of living beings, no king. Only our shipboard fool reported he'd seen naked men and women bedaubed with paint and feathers, but when we went to investigate, there was no one and no trace of anyone. I think he must have seen ghosts or his imaginings had run riot. He said too, that he had heard singing and the sound such as might be made by a giant buzzing bee, but none of us heard a thing. He had his moment of glory in entertaining us with a ridiculous story about a hopping mouse as big as a man!

After making the maps and after searching and exploring in the area we returned to the ship and set sail. It is a land of eternal sun and one day I would like to go back and see if there might be a people such as we found in other places. But none of them could have built such a city. Unenlightened and dispirited savages as they were.

The city we saw could only have been built by a civilization so old and so sophisticated such as the one Plato writes of. His Atlantis was a city of light (just as this one was) and built on geometric principles (such as those reflected in the stars). This, I am certain, is, or rather was, the city of Atlantis. It is the land we have dreamed of, the land we have all known about in our minds for millennia. But we are too late, too late to speak with those enlightened inhabitants of the past.

I am sure that at one time it was encrusted with gold, but only the pillars have withstood the winds of time. They remain, the skeleton of humanity's pinnacle of achievement.

The king speaks

This fabulous story you tell me Sir, what is your proof? This map is mere marks on paper. Any fool could concoct that. And judging by your shipboard fool, and the outrageous stories he has told to my fool, I would suggest that this tale you tell is entirely fabricated. No one else tells such stories – giant hopping mice and swans that are black! What do you take me for? A fool? And how would this Plato know? He's dead. A lot of use. Maps, marks on paper, stories told by fools. They are nothing. I want to see some real evidence of this place. Where are the jewels, the gold, the real things of conquest. A city's not much good if it doesn't have any inhabitants. Ha ha. I tell you what. You go and talk to my cartographer. Tell him your story and show him your map. Tell him to put the city on the map and call the place New Holland. At least if it's worth anything we'll own it. But I'm not wasting my gold in sending you back there.

The listener speaks

New Holland. How lovely. How fresh, not like this Old Holland. That place where the sun shines on vast plains and gold shimmers before your eyes. The Great South Land, yes, surely it must be. Or else the world would topple over, top heavy. And with so many people here, there must be just the same number there – somewhere. God likes symmetry and beauty and geometry.

Oh, to sail out beyond these narrow canals, these constricting streets, these eternally grey skies into the world of sun and sea (even a raging sea) and space. I would go there on this thin thread of hope to start life anew, to start a life that I do not know in advance. What strange adventures would befall me, Hilde? What wondrous sights would I see? Oh, for motion and for light, I would do anything. Anything.

Perhaps there are kings there still, and queens and princesses, girls like me. How I would like to talk with them, to have them tell me their history; to tell them about this world. About the rain that is so constant, about the small cozy rooms and the talk over ale and how I first came to hear of their civilization. A traveller, I would say, passed by and told of you.

I have been looking at the cartographer's newest map. He has drawn in the land described by the traveller. He has drawn Zephyr blowing the ships towards the west coast of a vast and amorphous land. And there, right on the coast, is the single city. The city is labelled Atlantis. The land mass has written, in ornate calligraphy, 'New Holland'.

I want to go and see it for myself.

July

Dearest X,

I write to you as promised. You who want to know my every feeling, my every thought. You who cannot make this journey with me, but who want to understand. I have arrived here in this small city which balances on the northern margins of Australia, closer to Asia than it is to the south of the land mass. Here in Darwin with 60,000 locals, and a few other tourists and travellers like myself.

There is the unmistakable scent of frangipani in the air. The liquid fragrance of the white and deep red flowers wafts through the louvred windows and the hot darkness. I sweat profusely and my hand catches on the paper as I write. It is evening, but early yet, and the heat of the day has not yet passed. At first I was exhausted by its intensity. The sun is high overhead all day. The light blindingly bright. The sky powerfully blue. So many strong impressions, and I have only been here a week. X, this place is so different from home that I barely know where to begin, or how to make you understand.

I came here wanting to see the desert, the wilderness, you know, crocodiles and lizards, that sort of thing. I expected oh, I don't know what I expected any more. To have my senses and my knowledge of myself stretched, I guess. And that has happened, but too quickly. I find it hard to focus clearly.

Perhaps I should just tell you about the week sequentially and let you find the images that suggest the truth.

The airport is like airports everywhere, you wander about, wait too long for your bags, read the ads for rent-a-cars and trips you can take. You wait just long enough to forget your anticipation, and then, suddenly, you are outside, and everything hits you. The heat, the way the air is really clear and yet your breath is caught, perhaps by the unexpectedness of heat after the journey's airconditioning, but more than that, some immensity, some sense of the air being infinite. And you're wearing summer clothes, but somehow you are already hot and exhausted and uncomfortable and wanting to shower and lie down in a cool place, or at least change into something cooler.

Taxi to the hotel the agent booked back home. The driver tells me it is 34 degrees. It seemed warmer. The hotel is too expensive, but I only booked for the first two nights, just long enough to catch my breath and look around for something more my style. Upmarket there are the usual 5 star hotels, but I wanted backpacker's rates, so now I have no airconditioning, just an overhead fan, and a room in an old house built up on stilts. It's clean, and freshly painted, and the garden is magic. Papaya trees, bananas, hibiscus, bougainvillea, vines whose names I don't know, and two huge shady mango trees to sit under through the heat of the afternoon. The woman who owns it is Greek. She lives next door. Sometimes she brings over plates of bits and pieces she has cooked. She comes from Kalymnos. Remember that summer we went to Rhodes? Well, she was there that summer. Visiting family back home. So we talked about the *ekklesias* we've both seen, the ikons, the markets, the problems with the touristas, everything.

But I have forgotten. I meant to write everything as it happened. So ... the hotel was modern, you know, the same as exists everywhere, bars and coffee shop downstairs, restaurant in the garden with umbrellas. I had a room looking out across the harbour. And the harbour is part of the unexpected. It is beautiful. Cliffs of sandstone, green lawns, trees and then the most brilliant blue ocean. And the light in the water shifted all through the day from turquoise to tourmaline to ink. I have found out that it is the tide that brings the changes, but more of that later.

Darwin is a small place. Only sixty thousand people, the guide book says, but looking about at the markets last night, it seemed that everyone of them had come from some other country. I asked someone about it and was told that there are people from more than seventy nationalities living here. All under this huge unchanging blue sky. There is so much of it. Somehow you never escape it. Even inside the room, for the light enters everywhere. I keep digressing, X. But perhaps you will be able to make something of that too ... the way the place keeps invading my head.

Well, the first morning I wandered about the town, you know how I am, always needing to get my bearings, always needing to know the place and sense of things like a cat. But there wasn't much to see. A quiet mall, tourist shops, cafes, a couple of art galleries. No one hurries. No one dresses for business. Not one woman in a suit, not one man in a tie. (I've seen a few since, but elegance seems very much the exception here.) Most of the office buildings are airconditioned, but the heat when you step out soon persuades you that the only way to dress is casually. I found one great coffee shop, (our sort) where there's a great deal of talk, artists, travellers, notice boards and posters. Called the Roma Bar. And saw a poster for the Women's Embassy there. Went across the road and upstairs in this tiny office cluttered with books and posters, and was made very welcome by the woman there. Got all kinds of information. They only open once a week so I was lucky to find someone there, but they have an answering machine for women's enquiries. Seems that they are the only source too, for the woman told me that government funding for women's issues is constantly being withdrawn. Same the world over, isn't it?

Well, by the time I left the Embassy, I just wanted to lie down and sleep. Jet lag, heat exhaustion, call it what you will, it lays you out the first few days. But I wandered down to look at the backpacker accommodation. There was one huge complex, multistorey, next to the bus station, but I decided on a small place. Wanted the garden, and not too much conversation. (I forgot to say that the streets are full of young travellers, and senior ones. The young ones are from all over the world, but the old ones all seem to be Australians who come on coach tours 'to see the real Australia', as one old man told me by the South Alligator River.) I wonder, X, what the other Australia is like? Anyway, I was glad to learn I'd chosen the real one.

I booked a room, and went back to the hotel and stretched out flat and slept till nearly midnight. I couldn't believe it. Me sleeping so long. There wasn't much point in going out after that because I had booked a two-day camping trip to the Kakadu Park which left at six the next morning. I wanted to see the wilderness, didn't I? (Though I'd suggest to anyone else who thought of coming here that they plan to spend the first few days in Darwin on the beach or sleeping by the pool at their hotel until they acclimatize!)

But not me. Up before dawn and sitting in the back of a Toyota 4-wheel drive, hurtling through the darkness, half way asleep like everyone else in the van. The soft darkness is silky and warm, hypnotic. I stare hard through the window trying to make out my wilderness, trying to stay awake. And then without warning this huge pink fluoro sun floats out of the forest. That woke me. It was like nothing I have seen before, light as ether, in the lavender light, riding the rough grey treeline, watching or rather, it seemed to be mildly contemplating the earth, and what this new day might unfold.

My fellow travellers were as stunned as I. After the first exclamations we fell silent. The tour guide said that he could never live anywhere else. That this sun and the ancient sandstone of Kakadu are in his bones. That he aches for it when he goes away. The rest of us reflected on its size and the immensity of the power it might develop through the day, and how small and subordinate we were beneath it as we flew along the highway.

The forest is not remarkable. Straggling black-trunked trees, silvery yellow grass once two metres tall, but bent now, dead from lack of moisture, for the rain only falls in what they call the Wet season, (between December and March). Apparently the monsoons sweep across the Kakadu plain flooding it with water so that the grass grows madly for a few months and then dies, so that at this time of year, green is a colour unknown except around the waterholes and rivers.

Our first stop was to take a boat up one of these rivers to see the remarkable sight of crocodiles leaping metres out of the water to catch dead chickens thrown to them by the tour guide. I was astounded for as we moved up river we saw several of the monsters lying in the hot mud among the mangroves looking so huge and cumbersome and evil, not blinking an eye, with such a somnolent weight upon them that one could not imagine them doing more than slip slowly into the water to float in silence waiting for their prey to come to them.

And this was just the beginning of my wilderness experiences. Everything out there had dimensions I could not have foreseen. A tree that seemed from a distance to be filled with flapping white rags became a tree on which a whole colony of white egrets sat. Why that tree and not any other? There were anthills like the tiny tenuous growths of stalagmites, and others which were huge mounds of rocklike earth reaching skyward, their orientation north-south like sign posts. But signs of what? And what are meanings of the rock paintings? Oh, they are all nicely explained by the guides and the little notice boards, but there is something not quite real in the translation. A sense that Aboriginal meaning is not captured at all.

We camped in places that seemed so alien, despite the shower blocks and notice boards, that I felt present and absent at the same time. There are strange spiky plants that explode bright red fruit onto the path before you; there is the constant enervating sun above you all day; there are magnificent rock formations, coloured like postcards; deep cool waterholes with

signs warning that fresh water crocodiles are at home. (The guide tells us it is fine for swimming though, because it is only the salt water monsters that attack humans.) But who can be sure? Nothing is certain here. Everything seems both ancient and ephemeral at the same time. At one moment the horizon is sharp, blue violet against an azure sky, the bitumen road stretching eagerly towards it, and then suddenly the road disappears into a haze of dust, or the horizon melts into mirage until orientation, both geographical and metaphysical, seems impossible. It is a landscape of metamorphosis.

I came back into Darwin bewildered and dazed and wanting to go back, or come home. The heat, the humidity, the flies, the dry land where everything crackles underfoot are all strange. And the emptiness and timelessness. I came here to find a wilderness, a landscape untouched, ancient. I have found it but it is not at all what I had expected. There is something unreachable, unavailable there, to the European mind.

So I came back to Darwin and drank many strong coffees and not a little wine, and went dancing. But I can still hear the dingo at Graveside Gorge hoop hoop howling in the night. This city is perched on the edge of the wilderness and yet its people go about their lives without even looking over their shoulders to see if the bush is creeping closer. And yet, to me, it is clear that there are ancient patterns re-establishing themselves while the tropical tides slip sluggishly in and out of the harbour and the sunsets pour brilliant colour across the western sky. But I am only a tourist. And so I do the things that are arranged for us.

I go to the marketfair on Thursday at sunset in the parklands next to Mindil Beach. There are sellers of crafts from Southeast Asia, local crafts, massage booths, flower sellers, didgeridoo sellers and players, fortune tellers . . . it's wonderful! There is food from every nation and thousands of people, some sitting under the coconut palms dining by candlelight with their friends, some on the beach watching the sun set, others wander up and down between the stalls, talking, looking, flirting or dancing to the music from the buskers and the bands. It feels like the whole world has met for a fair. The atmosphere is heady and warm. I sat for ages smiling and nibbling roasted nuts watching everything, and then the sun went down suddenly, the inky silk sea, and well there was a band, and some young women invited me to join them. So what can I add? That there is something about a tropical night and the scent of frangipani?

It seems I am back where I started with the wafting of frangipani across the warm evening air. The overhead fan flops lazily, X, and I am weary too. I close this letter with love.

Your travelling friend.

Heather Grace
NATURE RULES, OK?

I

We drove the sixteen kilometres from the mining camp to the end of a dirt track. Then we had to walk. We had been told to look for bits of plastic yellow tape tied in trees. Squinting into the sun's glare we followed these scraps of yellow across a dry creekbed and a grassy plain. The air was still, hot and humid. We were sweating. We had forgotten to carry a waterbottle. There were small stick-figure paintings under an overhang of rock at the far side of the plain. We stopped to rest, wondering how much further it was.

We trudged along a gully blackened by fire. Flies were thick and sticky. I voiced doubts about going on. Suddenly we were at the top of a gorge. In the distance, at the far end, there was water falling, from one level to the next. The bits of yellow tape led us to the top of a break in the cliff wall, where a jumble of boulders and rocks provided a way down. It seemed to take ages to reach the bottom and across to the water at the far side. We fell in. After the swim we saw the eyes of freshwater crocodiles, watching us.

We boiled the billy and drank weak black tea. Then we explored. The walls of the gorge were orange, red, white, grey and brown. The waterfall we saw from the rim fed the pool where we swam. Almost underneath the falls, but away from the drift and spray, there was a painting on the rock of an upside-down man. We followed the wall around and found an opening to a narrow breakaway with sheer sides. The pool at the bottom was dark, deep and spooky. Across the other side of the gorge there was a third pool almost enclosed by rock, and a cave at the far end, full of logs left by floods. We remembered the crocodiles and did not swim across the pool to explore it.

Near where we had climbed down into the gorge there was another cave, with a sandy floor. Paintings filled the back wall of the cave, overlapping one another: figures, fish, and outlines of hands. We camped there.

I woke in the night. My friend snored. Underneath my foam sleeping mat the sand was cold. I was afraid. I had heard stories of snakes sliding into beds for the body warmth. The fire had burnt low. I added wood. The painted wall came to life by firelight. I looked at the paintings and the fear left me. The land was friendly. People had lived there for thousands of years.

The next morning we explored some more. Where the river left the main pool it ran through rocks. There were house-sized boulders at the foot of orange cliffs. The water was clear. My friend had brought a handline for fishing and caught bream. Further on there was a patch of sand by the river, and tall paperbark trees sweet with nectar. Underneath them the ground was slippery with dead leaves. We lit a small fire and cooked the fish on the coals. A pheasant coucal's call echoed around us. Lizards scuttled through flood debris, over leaves and rock.

We found a wall of the gorge overgrown with vines and creepers. Behind them were large paintings of kangaroos. Near the cave where we camped there was also a horizontal painting of a figure. It fitted in the space between an overhang of rock and a ledge.

I spent the hottest time of the day lying on this ledge in the shade. My friend walked further down the river.

The rock was warm, smooth and comfortable. I watched green ants glueing leaves of a tree to make a nest. I listened to the far hush of water, cries of birds, the movement of lizards. I thought about silence, the city where I had lived for some years, our control of nature, the Aboriginal people I had seen in Kimberley towns. I thought about the events which had brought me to this place.

We had been travelling across the continent, from the south east to the north west. Chance encounters in caravan parks had encouraged us to go to Mitchell Plateau, in the north Kimberley. Waterfalls and gorges, people said.

There was a mining camp at Mitchell Plateau. It was doing feasibility studies for bauxite mining. We stopped there and asked about work. There was none. And the gorges were not for us, we were told. Those tracks needed a four wheel drive vehicle. We only had a two wheel drive. We could get to the coast, though.

We had imagined golden beaches. What we found were mangroves, sandflies and silty brown water. On the second day we saw a saltwater crocodile on the mud below our camp. One sighting was enough. We packed the car and left.

At the mining camp I was offered a job as cook's offsider. What convinced us to stay was that we would be able to use a company four wheel drive vehicle to explore the area on our Sundays off. We worked at the mining camp for six weeks, until it closed for the wet season. We saved Mitchell Falls until last. The caretaker at the camp reluctantly let us have a vehicle for two nights.

I had no idea, as I lay on the rock beside the painting, how much Mitchell Falls would change my life. At the time I was happy just to have seen the place.

I must have slept. When my friend came to find me the sun had dropped below the top of the gorge. He had caught more fish.

That night we went down to the river and hunted for cherrabin, a small freshwater crayfish, by the light of a torch. It seemed the stars were singing, or was that the water, running through rocks? We caught three cherrabin, enough for a taste. While they cooked on the coals of our fire, we talked about staying another day. We decided against it. If we did not return the vehicle when we had said we would, the caretaker would come to look for us.

We started early to beat the heat. We filled the billy with water. It slopped all over the place, despite the lid being jammed on tightly. We reached the vehicle without needing a drink.

II

The Kimberley is an area of Australia bordered by desert to the south, the Northern Territory to the east, and sea to the north and west. It covers an area of more than 420,000 square kilometres, and is larger than the states of Victoria and Tasmania combined. There is a central plateau area, including Mitchell Plateau in the north, large river systems in the east and south, and open grasslands which peter out into desert. 350 million years ago part of the desert was a warm shallow sea edged by coral reefs. These reefs are now the limestone outcrops and ranges along the southern edge of the central plateau. There are caves both here and in the sandstone country to the north which have sheltered people and animals for thousands of years.

The climate and vegetation range from subtropical to tropical. Rainfall varies from 1400mm in the north, around Mitchell Plateau, to 350mm in the south. Almost all of it falls between October and April, which is known as 'the Wet', or cyclone, season. Non-Aboriginal perception has two seasons: 'the Wet' and 'the Dry'. Various Aboriginal groups distinguish five, six or seven seasons, according to weather changes and sources of food.

The best time for visitors from cool climates is in the middle of the year when it is winter in the south of the continent. Our winter is like a southern summer and is short. July is the surest month. June and August can be cool as well. Temperatures range from 7 degrees overnight to 33 or 35 during the day. The sky is mostly blue. If there is winter rain, it is slight. The boab trees are leafless and grasses yellow. The air has great clarity. Sound travels a long way and stars are bright.

If you miss the coolest time of year, August to October is still bearable, although there is less water in the rivers and waterholes. The sky is still blue, but hazy with smoke and dust. Winds from the desert are gusty, creating whirlwinds, or willy-willies, which lift leaves and rubbish high in the sky. Trees begin to shed leaves out bush or, with increasing temperatures, have a spurt of growth if they're in watered gardens. Grasses are bleached, and people start hoping for an early wet season.

In the late hot dry season, from October to December, clouds build in an aching white-blue sky. Trees are thin and there is little shade. Mangoes fruit, boab trees flower and begin to leaf, and grasses are sparse. The increasing humidity thickens the air with frustration and waiting. The dollar birds arrive from the north in November. Termites cap anthills. Honeyeaters and flycatchers stay close to human habitation and cool themselves in sprinklers. Temperatures are between 16 degrees overnight and 45 during the day. This is the season when tempers fray. If we're lucky we get the first fierce electrical storm for the rain year.

My favourite season, if we get good rains, is the Wet. We can have a week or two of soft grey sky. Humidity is high. Temperatures are between 20 degrees at night and 38 or more in the day. Everything comes alive. Trees and grass are green. Dragonflies and butterflies appear. A constant drone of cicadas fills the air. Rivers flood. Sometimes roads to the north and south are cut.

One estimate of the present Kimberley population is 28,000. This means a density of 666 people per 10,000 square kilometres. 45% of the population is Aboriginal. Of the non-Aboriginal population, most have come from elsewhere – 'down south', 'over east', or overseas.

People live on cattle stations, in camps, in outlying communities, and in the six main towns. The towns are connected by a thousand kilometres of the Great Northern Highway.

Of the three larger towns Broome is the biggest and most popular. Its beaches attract many tourists. The town has a semi-tropical air, cooler than any of the others and humid. The sea is a brilliant blue against a red soil in town, or yellow sand on the beaches. There are a couple of cafes with great coffee, an excellent bookshop, and an outdoor movie theatre.

Seen from the air, it is hard to imagine why anyone would live in Derby. There is a clump of buildings on a peninsula jutting out into the mudflats of King Sound. On the ground, it is flat and hot and sandy. It is a good place to buy supplies – the cheapest for food in the Kimberley – and friendly. Derby has always been a service town, and has the biggest hospital in the region. Tourist information sheets call it 'The Gateway to the Gorges'. The Gibb River Road, the alternative route to the East Kimberley, starts from here.

East of Derby is Fitzroy Crossing, a small and spread-out town on the Fitzroy River. Just out of town is Geikie Gorge. There is a boat trip you can take up the river between white and gold limestone walls. Further east again is Halls Creek, an old goldmining town on the edge of the desert.

Northwards, at Kununurra there is a freshwater lake surrounded by rocky hills. The birdlife is fantastic. There are few places in the Kimberley where you can see line after line of ducks in the evening sky. The Great Northern Highway ends at Wyndham. The town is at the foot of a hill called The Bastion. From the top you can see red escarpments, mudflats, and the mouths of five rivers which drain into the purple waters of Cambridge Gulf.

If you choose the Gibb River Road instead of the Great Northern Highway, be prepared for some spectacular country, dust, and a corrugated road. There are plenty of tours which can get you out there. If you have your own vehicle, you will need to carry plenty of food, spare fuel and water, and it is wise to get off the road if confronted by a roadtrain carrying cattle. The turn-off for Mitchell Plateau is 420 kilometres from Derby, or 250 kilometres from the Wyndham/Kununurra end. From the turn-off it is another 230 kilometres to Mitchell Plateau.

III

I have been reading a book called *Arctic Dreams*, by Barry Lopez.[1] You might wonder how ice and a long dark winter could relate to a place of heat and light. But much of what he says about the Arctic Region can be said of the Kimberley. I came across these words:

Our obligation [to the land] . . . becomes simple: to approach with an uncalculating mind, with an attitude of regard . . . To intend from the beginning to preserve some of the mystery within it as a kind of wisdom to be experienced, not questioned. And to be alert to its openings, for that moment when something sacred reveals itself within the mundane, and you know the land knows you are there.

The series of events which first took me to Mitchell Falls seemed like chance. Sometimes I think nothing is accidental. My friend and I went away and came back three years later, in our own four wheel drive vehicle. We worked on cattle stations and at Mitchell Plateau mining camp as caretakers. We walked out bush several times.

Much has changed in fourteen years. The mining camp has gone, although the company keeps an option on future development. There is an easy walking track to the top of the Falls, which follows the small creek we crossed after parking the car. Lots of people visit. Some find a way down into the gorge, most are happy to be at the top. The Aboriginal people whose country it is have moved back and live at the old mining camp site for part of each year. My friend and I separated and he has gone east.

There are many gorges, many sacred and magical places like Mitchell Falls, in the Kimberley. Some have tracks to them. Others are accessible only by walking, boat or helicopter. Some are on cattle station leases, some in Aboriginal land.

I now live near Derby. Accustomed to a more temperate climate, many non-Aboriginal people find living here a struggle, a trial of strength. But it is this rule by nature, the fact that it is clearly we who need to adapt, which keeps me here. Heat, storms, floods, cyclones and the insect hordes are a constant reminder that we are just human animals on the surface of a planet amongst the stars. I have not travelled the Gibb River Road for some years, but it is enough to know that those places are there. And each time a pheasant coucal calls, green tree frogs chant, thunder cracks open the skies and the rain plays Brahms on my roof, I know that the land knows I am here.

Note
1. Barry Lopez. 1986. *Arctic Dreams*. London: Picador.

Elizabeth Jolley

A SORT OF GIFT: IMAGES OF PERTH

Perhaps there is something invisible which a person is given early in life, a
sort of gift, but the giver of it, not expecting any thanks, is never given it.

My father liked what he called a splendid view. He would dismount
from his high bicycle and, parting the hedge, he would exclaim on the
loveliness of what he could see. We would have to lean our bicycles up
against a fence or a gate, scramble across the wet ditch and peer through
the rain-soaked hedge at a sodden field or a dismal hill hardly visible
through the rain mist. But first something about his bicycle. This may
seem irrelevant but perhaps it is necessary to say that the bicycle was
enormous; twenty-eight inch wheels and a correspondingly large frame.
He collected the parts and made it himself, and once, when it was stolen
he went round the barrows and stalls in the Bullring market place in
Birmingham and bought back all the parts as he recognised them and
rebuilt it. I mention this because it shows something of the kind of man
he was.

We had to ride bicycles too. When I was six I had a twenty-four inch
wheel with hand brakes, left and right, back and front respectively.

'Never use the right hand brake before you use the left,' my father said.
Excellent advice of course but my problem then was that I was not sure
about my left hand and my right. The back mudguard had small holes in
it for strings which were meant to keep a lady's skirt from getting caught
in the spokes. I was terribly ashamed of these small holes and wished I
could fill them in with thick paint or something ...

The reason that I mention all this is because I believe that my own love
of what my father called scenery or a splendid view comes in part from the
bicycle rides he insisted upon. We had to go with him. The bicycle rides
through the rural edges of the Black Country in England were his relaxation and pleasure. We stopped frequently while he studied gravestones
in small overgrown cemeteries and explained about lychgates. He told us
about turnpike houses and about towing paths and locks – those mysterious sluice gates so powerful in altering the water levels in the canals. My
own love of the quality of the air comes too, I realise, from my father who
often simply stood at the roadside enjoying what he declared was fresh air,
unbreathed air. He marvelled at the beech trees in the fenced parklands
of the wealthy. He paused before fields and meadows explaining about
the rotation of crops and about fallow fields. He was inclined to make a
lesson out of everything. To him health and learning were the means to
a particular form of freedom and the bicycle was the way in which to
achieve these.

I developed the habit in my letters to my father of describing in detail the places where I lived and through which I journeyed. Wherever I went I was always composing, in my head, my next letter to him . . .

My mother, who loved order, cleared up her house as she moved steadily into old age. Before she died she had, in a sense, tidied up, thrown away and burned up her household so that nothing remains of my descriptions posted home every week during all the years.

There are people for whom the details of landscape, the rocky outcrops, the particular hollows grown over with soft mosses, the groups of ancient trees and the little paths, unchanged from one year to the next, do not provide much excitement. Scarcely noticed, these things are not carried in the memory. Such people are capable of going for a walk and not really seeing anything of their surroundings, rather like the concert goer who does not really hear or feel the music and does not know afterwards whether a symphony was being played or a string quartet. Similarly, people have been heard to remark after crossing the whole world by ship that they haven't had a decent cup of tea since they left home.

To travel to Western Australia by ship is to receive images in advance. Being told, a few hours away from the coast of Britain, that it was necessary to place the legs of the dining table in tin cans of water to prevent the ants from demolishing the meal before the family could get to it presented an unusual picture of Western Australian furnishings. Added to this the fact that stockings and 'underclothes' had to be kept in screw top glass jars because of the ravenous ants, still unsatisfied after clearing the dining room or kitchen tables, gave another unusual image and the suggestion of an entirely different way of living. Would the glass jars be stored like jam on open shelves, labelled and dated?

Our arrival in Perth in 1959 was a short time after the official opening of the Narrows Bridge. This requires elucidation for the majority of Australians who have never had the privilege of visiting Perth. A glance at a moderately large scale map will show that the modern Perth is divided into two by the Swan River. An encyclopaedia will reveal that the original Perth was placed well on the north bank of the river and that the southern parts developed later and soon acquired an independent existence. At first there was no bridge across the river between the traffic bridge at Fremantle and the Causeway at the eastern limit of the town. Whatever it may once have been (and I have heard it described as a bush track covered all over with a species of wild lily) the Causeway became, in fact, a bridge. This lack of bridges seriously inconvenienced north/south traffic but it had a much greater bearing on the local mythology. At parties in 1959 people were still describing the smell of the stagnant water before the river was reclaimed for an efficient road and bridge system. The claim was also made that gentlemen wishing to call on young ladies in the evening used to strip off on the northern bank and swim to the south bank holding their clothes above the water. It was further widely reported that business men in Perth set up their chosen secretaries in discreet apartments in South Perth. Whatever the truth is in these stories South Perth now preserves no signs of its shady past. Another story told to the new arrival was of the sports' mistress of a respectable school for girls who, being an ardent swimmer, used to swim every morning across the Swan River and back before breakfast. She was said to have declared that any shark venturing up the river as far as Claremont would never attack a lady.

The garden suburbs of Perth now, like any other garden cities in the world, lacking these earlier legends, are clean and well watered and, most of the time, incredibly dull.

The suburb, so littered with people and yet empty of life, sometimes suggests that the people who live there have no real feeling either for their surroundings or for each other. It is true the lawns are shaved and clipped and water is drenched religiously over everything. You see it every day, white spraying mists leaping and dancing, an endless ballet, the choreography extending across the gardens and the street lawns. Street lawns? To the newcomer the street lawn makes a great impression. Perhaps these grassy verges need a chapter to themselves. They are the carefree owners of box trees, chopped and trimmed clear of the overhead electricity and telephone wires. The grass is sometimes a deep, springy, dark green buffalo grass carefully nourished and mown repeatedly;

sometimes the grass is of a weaker kind, sparse on the bleached sand, neglected and, at times, lavishly covered with the brilliant yellow flowers of the cape weed. Perhaps a word about the cape weed. Picturesque as it is, where the cape weed grows nothing else can grow. It is fleshy and tenacious, smothering and spreading to the size of Victorian (the Queen, not the state) dinner plates. It is attractive on a picture postcard but detestable in reality. Some street lawns are endowed with a prickle grass vicious to the bare foot. Dogs enjoy street lawns and people park their cars on them (the lawns not the dogs).

'Will you have it on your virgin strip?' the man delivering firewood asked me once. Deliveries of sand are dumped on the street lawns, also garden loam and, more recently as older houses are being pulled down and replaced by more modern models (though we do not have the Bavarian mountain hut yet), all kinds of building materials including a particularly rugged, unwieldy, freshly quarried stone. Builders, plumbers and carpenters are a floating population in the suburbs and can be seen, at intervals, taking their rest time under the box trees on the street lawns. Their lunch wraps are often a sort of decoration.

Every morning the sprinklers make water snakes in the dust. The fragrance of this water on the dust is sharp like an anaesthetic. There is too the smell of petrol and of dogs' dirt and of empty champagne bottles, of scented groins and burning toast. Sometimes there is the sweetness of cut grass drying in little brown ridges. Then there is the aromatic scent of the yellow broom and of roses and of a lemon, bruising slightly, as it falls. The spindles of rosemary, straggling by a gate post, brushing the legs of people as they pass, add their fragrance to the Chinese privet and the datura – those long white bells whose perfume can lift the passer-by into a temporary forgetfulness.

The letter boxes, exposed to the street, reveal their owners' intentions; battered rusty tins nailed to rotten posts or often something galvanised and durable. Occasionally there is a home-built edifice bulging with mortar and crawling with snails. Many are imitations of art, a fortress, a windmill, a ceramic boot, a gnome, a goddess – her belly gaping conveniently for newspapers. Some letter boxes have tiny slits or lopsided lids or lids broken off and hanging rough and sharp and sad. Some are never cleared and some houses do not have one at all. At all times of the day, inhabitants can be seen wandering with vague steps across lawns and down paths to peer with hope or fear into these strange contrivances. Many make several such pilgrimages as the postman on his bicycle does not always keep to a fixed time.

To anyone accustomed to hearing letters fall with the soft thud of promise on to the floor inside the front door, the letter boxes in Western Australia are indeed remarkable.

In an area between the railway line and the sea there are certain places, a bend or a gentle rising of the road, from where it is possible to see the sea. Serene blue surprises in glimpses between the trees and the houses. This smooth blue sea, beyond immediate reach and yet visible from time to time, seems to meet the sky in a quiet gentleness only possible in dreams. And dreams are necessary in the suburbs . . . For the lonely or the heavy hearted the neat streets with well kept lawns, brick and tile houses with closed doors, blank venetians and drawn curtains, as in other parts of the world, seem to be unpeopled and without exuberance of any sort. In other words, they seem to be the most sad and depressing places to be in, especially on a Sunday. And, now that the fashion for high brick walls is coming in, escape is essential. Perhaps the imagination can come to the rescue and a mulberry tree be inhabited by people having a mulberry fight, arms, legs, faces, hair and clothes purple-red with mulberry laughter. Or, at a given time every afternoon, at a certain time of the year, a shepherd complete with lamb and crook appears on the roof of the house next door. A trick of light and shade and chimney? but a Blessing all the same. A woman, unseen by anyone else, takes a slow walk every morning pushing a small girl in a push-chair and, almost at earth level, is teaching her the world which is at her feet, stones, twigs, pavement, hedge, flowers, tufts of grass, gate posts and scatterings of gravel. A postman plans to tamper with the mail and a travelling salesman hatches a plot to burn down the house of one of his customers . . . The suburb offers a great deal . . .

From another direction, this time approaching Perth from that small distance possible from the west in Western Australia, the road fringed with shivering nodding grasses follows, high up, the curve of the Swan River. On some days the stillness of the shining water seems to hold in restraint a hidden power. It used to be said (another of those legends) that you could walk across the Swan at any point. Anyone who has foolishly lost an outboard motor will tell you that this is not true. Across the wide saucer of water the city lies in repose as if painted on a pale curtain. Often in the mornings it has a quality of unreality as if no life with all the ensuing problems could ever unfold there. In comparison the large cities left behind in other parts of the world seem, with the incessant nightlong pulse and beat and roar, to have no rest.

The mood of the river can change very quickly. Is it possible to hear an image? Something unforgettable is the screaming and complaining of a flock of black cockatoos as they fly low over waters changed by gale and heavy rain. One of the questions I am asked from time to time is, has it made a difference to my writing coming to live in Western Australia? And what would my writing be like if I had stayed in Britain. There is no answer to the second question, I am unable to answer it. To the first, of course, there is a difference. Until I came to Western Australia I had never seen or heard a flock of cockatoos. These marauding birds, heralding a mysteriousness unfathomable to us, fly low, almost breasting the choppy waves of the river swollen with rain storm and purple brown with top soil washed down from the vineyards in the Swan valley. As the cockatoos disappear the rain bird calls, little phrases of bird notes climbing up in among the flame tree flowers brilliant against the dark clouds. Drops of water quiver on the fencing wire and the thin narrow leaves of the eucalypts tremble. To come to this country is to come to foreign land.

How can I be the same person after the flight of the cockatoos? The images of Western Australia on arrival made and continue to make an impact. They serve, too, to sharpen the images from the places where I was before.

Can air be described as an image? Can it really be as my father used to think it was? Fresh and unbreathed?

It seemed, on my first visit to the vineyards in the wide sand plain through which the Swan River flows (close to Perth) that the air there was light and clean and softly refreshing. The sweet fragrance I discovered came from the flowers of the beans growing between the vines. Later, I was told, the stalks would be ploughed back into the earth. The road through the vineyards was crossed then by sandy tracks and there was a fig tree standing in a sandy patch just back off the road. A rough trestle table stood under the tree and some scales hung in one of the lower branches. Behind the golden tranquillity which seemed to drop from the heart of the fig tree there was a small shabby weatherboard and iron house. The wooden planks of the table were piled with melons and the sweet muscat grapes.

This place, after a great many years, is still there. Whenever I pass the place now, though I am unable to see it as I saw it the first time (it is always hard to recapture something exactly), I never fail to feel again a deep excitement. I gave the place, on my first visit, to my character, Uncle Bernard. I caused him to think it would be his.

There was a time when writers, some writers, felt they had to deny their regions. But it is in the very place where you live and walk and carry out the small things of living that the imagination, from some small half-seen or half-remembered awareness, springs to life and goes on living.

I never thanked my father for giving me the gift of looking. I was never able to show him the places which he would have liked very much. I could only describe them for him first in my letters and later in some of my fiction. I do not regret that I never thanked him because he understood that some things do not come back to the parent from the child.

Caroline Caddy
SOUTH-WEST WESTERN AUSTRALIA

Western Australia covers one-third of the lowest and oldest continent in the world. Most of the population of one million is concentrated in the south-west corner and Perth, its capital, is the most isolated capital city in the world.

The south west is geologically stable. With no volcanic activity for millions of years to renew essential minerals, the soils are not fertile compared to younger lands. This factor, along with low rainfall and isolation from other gene pools have bred a unique flora and fauna.

Because of this startling difference from the European landscape, native plants and trees were often cleared and replaced with more familiar species by the early pioneers. Though we can see the beauty of our indigenous plants now, there are none that are an economically viable food source. This was a major difficulty faced by the original settlers.

What are miles of swimming beaches now were a barrier of sand with no deep water ports except at Albany in the south. Perth and Fremantle are built on sand and limestone. There is so much sand that the early colony was described as the place of 'sand, sin, sun and sore eyes'. The sin refers to the fact that it began as a convict settlement and the sore eyes to conjunctivitis transmitted by the ubiquitous bush flies.

The Swan River which flows through Perth, rises as creeks far inland and spreads out on its flood plain below the Darling scarp, then narrows again to gouge its way through sandstone ridges at Fremantle. Many old buildings such as the Roundhouse (the first gaol), the Maritime Museum and the Fremantle Arts Centre are built of this easily worked stone.

The Fremantle Arts Centre is a centre for the arts in Western Australia, though it was once a women's asylum. It now houses artists' workshops, galleries, a bookshop and a coffee shop. The bookshop sells a wide range of WA literature as well as the many titles published by Fremantle Arts Centre Press. These include novels, poetry, and books of local and historical interest. If you are interested in the difficulties faced by early pioneer women, look for books on the Bussel, Molloy or Bellanger families. Sally Morgan's book, *My Place*, tells of her discovery and acceptance of her Aboriginal heritage and Albert Facey's *A Fortunate Life*, is a fascinating account about growing up in the inland wheatbelt country.

Fremantle has a large ethnic population and seafood in the Greek or Italian style is the specialty of many small restaurants. Visit the fish markets and have a feed of fish and chips, with vinegar and salt, no tomato sauce or mayonnaise for a real Australian experience.

317

Perth is a thriving but relaxed city with old convict brick buildings interspersed among the modern. Kings Park is just west of the central business district. It is situated on a sandstone bluff and overlooks the river and city. Visit the War Memorial or the Pioneer Women's Memorial then take one of the many wildflower walks. Spring and early summer is the wildflower season and practically all are unique to WA. The kangaroo paw is our state flower and can be red, green, yellow or black. Around Perth they can have a red stem and green flower and bear a strong resemblance to a kangaroo's hind foot. To see real kangaroos take a ferry ride across the Swan River to the zoo in South Perth.

The Swan River is estuarine and moves with the tides. In summer it thrives with prawns, salt water fish, jellyfish and even small sharks. It narrows quickly as it reaches the foothills of the Darling Ranges, where deposits of loam and hot dry summers produce good red wines.

The Darling Ranges are an escarpment, the edge of an ancient plateau that forms the bulk of southwest. The ranges are rich in bauxite, much of which is mined for aluminium. The mining is carefully monitored and topsoils replanted. The jarrah eucalypts which make up most of the forest are slow growing and valuable for the hardness of their wood. They can withstand termites, immersion and marine borers. Large areas of forest were cut down and sent back to England as ballast and then used to pave the streets of London.

A trip into the hills east of Perth will take you past the Katherine Susannah Pritchard House. Katherine was one of our early writers and her home is now preserved as a community arts and writing centre. Visitors are always welcome. further up you can stop for a drink at the Old Mahogany Inn. This was once a staging post for the Cobb & Co. coaches on their way east. It is now under the care of its first woman licencee, Mary Arnold. A drive through the John Forrest National Park will show you jarrah trees, grasstrees and cycads, a species of ancient palm. All of our WA flora have adapted to grow on poor soils. They make good garden plants but must not be over fertilized. Species of eucalypts are valuable plantation trees in California, Middle-East countries, Africa and India.

An exit road from the Park comes out near Parkerville. Try a meal at the Judge Parker Bistro in the old Parkerville Hotel. The proprietors, Rebecca and Margaret Foster, know the area well and can guide you on to an interesting afternoon.

At one stage of its geological history, the south west of WA went through an upheaval in which the whole plateau was tilted and depressed towards the south. This is seen in the way coastal estuaries get deeper the further south you go. Bunbury, one of the largest centres outside Perth, is situated two hundred kilometres south on the Leschenault Inlet. Between

December and March you are sure to get a feed of fresh crabs from the stalls along the inlet.

Because distances between towns in WA are so great, bus tours or hire cars are the best way to get around. Many people also hitch-hike, but this limits you to the larger highways and roads, and most of the best sights are quite a distance off the main roads with little passing traffic.

Cape Naturaliste is literally the corner of the continent. Here you can see the meeting of the Indian and Southern oceans. From here on, the coast that has been limestone begins to push out headlands of granite. The karri forests begin here. Vineyards, wineries, wildflowers, caves and surfing beaches make this area popular with visitors.

Much further along the coast and more isolated is the Walpole Inlet. On the way to Walpole the road passes through the logging town of Pemberton and thick forests of karri, the tallest flowering plants in the world. The local craft shops specialize in pieces made from the local wood.

From here to Walpole is one hundred and eighty kilometres with hardly any human habitation. About three-quarters of the way there, you will come upon Crystal Springs, a tiny garage that is never open. The road winds through deep karri forests near the coast, and though you can't see it, if you stop on a still day you can hear a soft deep roar of the surf in the distance.

As you approach Walpole, the karri becomes interspersed with rugged coastal jarrah and redgum. These sections are lower and make the karri sections stand out like great domes. Walpole is a tiny logging and farming town famous for the fishing on its deep inlet (the deepest in WA). There are many drives and walk trails in the area that are bursting with wild-flowers, usually in September/October. A good example is The Valley of the Giants, between Walpole and the town of Denmark. This is a scenic drive about fifteen kilometres long, that winds through tall karri trees and rivers. The population of Walpole is not more than five or six hundred but local women keep a craft shop going most of the year.

If you are interested in making contact with women in any country town, ask for the CWA (Country Women's Association). This association was started in the early part of the century to help women overcome the problems of isolation. Visitors are always welcome at meetings. Try to get hold of a *CWA Cook Book*. They are full of old Australian recipes and amazing/amusing household hints.

Between Walpole and the town of Denmark is Peaceful Bay and Greens Pool. Both are wide bays with white beaches and areas where granite promontories and boulders protect clear pools of shallow green water. At Greens Pool you will see some oddly shaped boulders balanced on hills above the beach. These and others can be glimpsed along the coast from the highway – all created when glaciers melted after the last great Ice Age.

Denmark is an idyllic, environmentally aware town situated on the Denmark River. Denmark was named by a team of explorers sent to map the area, who thought the scenery reminded them of that country. Sample some wine or view local art work at Goundrys' Winery and the Mary Rose coffee shop. Jassi Skin Crafts, run by Judy Woods, manufactures wool and sheepskin products. Her specialty is fleece-lined Ugg boots which she distributes nationwide, but you can get them factory direct here. Take a drive out to the Scotsdale gallery for quality local works in wood, oils and water colours. Barbara Bennet is a printmaker who sells her prints and runs workshops from her gallery home on Lights Beach Road.

At Ocean Beach, visit the wildlife sanctuary started by the late Iris Anderson. Her family runs it now, caring for injured and orphaned kangaroos, wallabies, black swans and other local animals.

Denmark has two alternative lifestyle communities: the Cove and the Wolery, that are well integrated with the town. Keep a look-out on local bulletin boards or ask at the Tourist Bureau as the Cover, in its lovely karri setting, is often a venue for concerts or participating arts events.

About sixty kilometres to the east is Albany, the first area to be settled in WA. The main reason for this settlement was to lay claim on the western half of Australia. The town nestles between two granite tors, and cliffs form most of the coastline. A drive out through Torindirup National Park will take you to the Gap and Natural Bridge lookout.

The Gap is a deep gash in the high granite cliffs. If you study the walls of the Gap and the formation of the Bridge, you will see how granite erodes into huge, roughly square blocks known geologically as 'cyclopean masonry'.

The whaling station at Cheynes Beach was active until the early eighties. The old station is now a museum dedicated both to the whalers and the animals they hunted. Along with the factory itself, one of the last whaling chasers has been beached and can be inspected. There is an excellent natural history of whales with a display of skeletons. The skeletons were taken from whales that had died a natural death, as every part of the whales taken for processing was used.

The old Post Office and the Court House (still in use) are made of granite. If you have a look at the entry arch on the Court House, you will see that is an example of an eccentric arch. The large, wedge-shaped blocks get smaller towards the left side and spiral slightly back like the inside of a shell.

A major attraction of Albany is the Brig Amity, a replica of the original ship that carried the first settlers and all their worldly goods (victuals, pianos, sheep and cattle). Next to this is the old jail and the Residency

Museum, originally the home of the first Governor of WA.

Housed in a building nearby is the optic from the old lighthouse that was used on Eclipse Island until replaced by an automatic light. The lenses have been reassembled and rotate on a bath of mercury as when in use. The new building that houses the optic sweeps up at one end to accommodate its great size. It makes an interesting contrast against the old jail walls topped with broken bottles, the barbed wire of the day.

Anette Grant is the director of the Vancouver Arts Centre. It is named after the French explorer who also lent his name to Vancouver Island half a world away in Canada. The centre was once a hospital and Anette has a full-time job organizing exhibitions and workshops in its old high-ceilinged wards.

One of the oldest industries in Albany is the woollen mill. It manufactures pure merino wool blankets and over the years has been a mainstay of full and part-time employment for local women.

The Closet Shop and Amity Crafts carry a range of handcrafted wood, pottery and artworks. Jo Sharp sells her marvellous pure wool sweaters and cardigans through these outlets. She keeps a team of knitters busy with her innovative designs.

Don't forget while you are on the south coast to step outside at night and look up. The southern hemisphere looks straight into the centre of our galaxy and there are many more stars than in the north. You may be lucky and catch a display of the Aurora Australis. Sometimes only a red glow to the south, sometimes deep red curtains across the sky.

The trip back to Perth up Albany highway will take you through typical wheat and sheep-farming country. Three small towns punctuate the four hundred kilometres. Some people find the great distances in Australia tiring but distance is in some ways the essence of Australia. Meet people, admire the tangible landscape and on the way from place to place feel the phenomenon of distance. Take it in the way the eye takes photographs for us that we can call back in our mind's eye. Later you will call up this feeling and without words or photographs be able to experience Australia again.

Susan Hawthorne and Renate Klein
THE SOUTH AND CENTRE

Adelaide

The Adelaide Arts Festival (held in the first weeks of March in even-numbered years) is the oldest and most prestigious in the country. The Writers' Week which takes place in tents in parkland alongside the Torrens River attracts huge audiences who gather to hear many of the best international and Australian writers. Adelaide has a reputation for innovation and has hosted many extraordinary talents such as Bessie Head, Keri Hulme, Alice Walker, Sara Paretsky and others. Adelaide is quieter than Melbourne or Sydney, with wide streets and a grid of terraces that helps the visitor keep their bearings. Norwood, North Adelaide and Glenelg are suburbs where you'll find feminist organisations. Vitalstatistix, a women's theatre company, performs regularly in Adelaide. A drive through the Adelaide Hills to the wineries and rather old fashioned German towns is an easy half day or one day trip. Further afield is the extraordinary Coorong, a haven for waterbirds, especially huge flocks of pelicans, among sand dunes and lakes, and a long drive north will take you to the remarkable Flinders Ranges, beyond which is the desert. South Australia is the most arid state in Australia and if deserts fascinate you, South Australia can offer salt lakes, hot springs, stony and sandy deserts, as well as the underground opal town of Coober Pedy.

Alice Springs, NT

The heart of Australia, geographically and symbolically, Alice Springs is situated inside the ring of the MacDonnell Ranges. Alice Springs has the largest Aboriginal population of any Australian city and is a major centre for Aboriginal art. There are several Aboriginal owned and operated galleries in Alice Springs (see Ricketson), as well as others that are not. Ask the locals for information on this. It rarely rains in Alice Springs but during the winter months (May to September) it can be very cold at night time, and the temperature may drop to freezing point. Alice Springs still has the feel of a country town about it and if you are planning to drive in any direction out of Alice Springs you should carry water and other supplies. It is the starting point for tours, or self-drive touring to Uluru (Ayer's Rock) and Katatjuta (the Olgas). Mt Helen Gorge in the MacDonnell Ranges has a hotel that was, until recently, run by two women, and the nearby Pine

Gap installation has been the site of feminist demonstrations against nuclear defence installations in alliance with local Aboriginal women's groups. Alice Springs is also the starting point for Desert Tracks (see James).

Flinders Ranges, SA

A day's drive north of Adelaide or west of Broken Hill is the spectacular Flinders Ranges. Most visitors start at Wilpena Pound, (where there is a camping area) surrounded on all sides by mountains. The walk to Mary's Peak is long but rewarding. From the top you can look out over the Pound and westward to the snake-like spine of mountain ranges and beyond to the saltlakes. Allow a day for the climb and the return. Wallabys, galahs and the ubiquitous crow will probably share your campsite. A week in the Flinders Ranges is well rewarded by driving right around the park, with perhaps a visit to the Hot Springs that entrepreneurs in the 1930s planned as a health cure (but the water is highly radioactive and you shouldn't drink it or swim in it). Then head north to Arkaroola where you can take tours to out of the way places such as the Needles. Sacred Canyon, outside the Ranges near Wilpena Pound is well worth a visit. Some of the roads in the area are not often used, so take supplies with you. The Flinders Ranges is a terrific place to see kangaroos and emus in large numbers, but avoid driving at or after dusk – that way you'll avoid hitting a kangaroo with your car. If you must drive at these times, be watchful; reducing your speed will also reduce your chance of collision.

Coober Pedy, SA

If you head north from the Flinders Ranges the road will take you near to Lake Eyre (how near will depend on the season and the rainfall over the previous six months). Lake Eyre (Katitanda), covering 9300 square kilometres, is the largest inland lake in Australia and has a catchment area of 1.3 million square kilometres. Out in the middle of the desert you can see vast flocks of waterbirds, perhaps a thorny devil (a lizard) or a dingo. You can drive into the National Park from here. Here and elsewhere between the Flinders Ranges and Coober Pedy you can see miles and miles of salt encrustations. A sandy road takes you on to Coober Pedy, a town that is largely built underground. The houses have ordinary frontages that then disappear into the hill, like hobbit dwellings. Even the Catholic Church is underground and worth a visit (see Jones).

Witjira State Park, SA

This is a very remote area and you need to be well stocked with food and water for dry conditions. Stop at the Pink Roadhouse in Oodnadatta and pick up an annotated map, you may also want to inform the police of your itinerary. Witjira State Park is a hundred kilometres off an already deserted road. Even a four-wheel drive can get bogged in the sand or the mud along this road, so travel well-prepared. Dalhousie Springs is the purpose of this detour. The thermal springs here are the result of water travelling underground from Queensland for three to four million years! The warm water, palm trees and the accompanying screech of galahs is a truly Australian experience. If here, or elsewhere, your vehicle becomes bogged, or you break down and can't fix it, stay with the car. DO NOT WALK for help. Many people have died from heat exposure walking for help. Providing you have sufficient supplies you are safer staying where you are, even if it is out of the way (this is the reason for leaving your itinerary and expected arrival date with police). From Witjira you can travel out into the Simpson Desert, BUT YOU SHOULD NOT DO THIS WITHOUT LONG AND CAREFUL PREPARATION. You will need maps and guide books with a lot of detail.

Nullarbor, SA to WA

If you like driving, then take off across Australia on the Nullarbor Highway. It is flat and often straight and best travelled with a companion who can share the driving. You can visit the deserted cliffs – the Bunda Cliffs on the easter stretch and the Baxter Cliffs in the west – and beaches of the Great Australian Bite and there are huge underground limestone caves that can be explored with some tour companies. Sinkholes – such as Koonalda Cave and Abrakurrie Cave – provide entrances to these caves.

Uluru and Katatjuta, NT

Many tourists to Australia come to see Uluru (Ayer's Rock). It has become a symbol of Australia and, though a stereotypical view of the rock may seem overdone, being there, seeing the rock from a variety of vantage points especially in the early morning or at dusk is a very different experience. Take the Liru Walk (enquire at the Park headquarters) which is usually led by a couple of Anangu women, perhaps accompanied by their children, who will point out traditional food along the way, how to use some of the plants medicinally, and how implements such as digging sticks, spears and spear throwers are made. Aborigines do not believe the rock should be climbed. Bear this in mind before you make your decision. Katatjuta (the Olgas) is a forty-five minute drive on the most amazing orange dirt road from Yulara (the accommodation complex near Uluru, where you can camp or stay in five star luxury). It is a complex of beautifully rounded rocks that warrant many days of exploration. Follow the walks on the local maps through the labyrinth of rocks. Visit the Valley of Winds where you feel the awesome immensity of the rocks and their history (see James).

Rosemary Jones
THE DOG FENCE

Everyone went to the races, except us.

We drove out past the race track and the beer drinkers sitting in the dust, and women sitting on the edges of eskies wearing wide-brimmed hats and sandals, and fly nets from the Miner's Store. Past the cars painted in Aboriginal colours and a cluster of people who sat on the mound outside the race track. we went past the race track and missed the Coober Pedy Cup and the Mintabie Maiden and the children's egg and spoon.

Everyone tells big stories up here, wild bush stories, mining stories and Aboriginal stories. But this hardly rates as a story, it doesn't amount to much because there are the locals and the tourists; a tourist can hardly scratch the surface, and to be a local you've either got to live for years in the Umoona Community, or a dug-out cut deep in the side of Tom Cat Hill, or on North West Ridge in Frank the Painter's Road – I don't know what he paints, maybe he sits with an easel propped up against an air shaft mixing a palette of dusty/rusty colours, dangling his legs over the rock face and painting sunsets, or maybe he paints and plasters the insides of dug-outs. Or you've got to live in Potch Gully with the only recently bitumenized road in town, and there's a story to that bit of bitumen too. You can tell Frank the painter isn't on the local council or his road might be all smoothed out flat with freshly rolled bitumen.

Or you've got to live in a house with an air-conditioner, your opal-cutting machine on your kitchen table ready for use, with your life's work in tapestries, painstakingly stitched in petit point, world-class tapestries brought from Europe, each framed and worth several thousand, covered in drapes to keep out the dust, glorious compositions waiting for a buyer in the middle of the desert. Glorious juxtapositions of life as it once was, and as it is.

But we went past all that, through the opal fields and past a shimmer of mullock heaps in the heat, the blowers lined up like exotic sculptures in blues and reds and greens and yellows as if ready for an esoteric outdoor exhibition, or a carnival.

Past the mine shafts where a stone takes four seconds to hit the bottom and you know there are bodies out here, anonymous bodies with strange tales to tell, chucked down there just as the warning post indicates – with a figure upside down, its hands flailing and its hair on end, stiff with fear.

Past the caravans and the tiny sheds with no air-conditioners, and men with dust in their hair and women with children on their hips, past them, and out to the Breakaways.

Great wedding country, the Breakaways, where the wedding of the decade took place between the flying doctor and the flying nurse; they had a marquee, and a pig on a spit, and oh it was the talk of the town.

Weird-coloured country with eerie yellows and browns and black blending into the prickle bushes. An eerie cluster of bird holes stuck in the yellow rock face – as if ancient creatures still live there, rather than birds. Eerie chunks of left-over ranges thousands and thousands of years old, deathly quiet, too quiet for a wedding you would have thought.

Through a couple of gates then, and along the dog fence. The longest fence in the world. The dingo fence, the one that shouldn't have a hole in it anywhere, not even big enough for a dog's paw. The dog paw fence.

We drove along the fence looking for things to collect, like a couple of wildflowers to stick in a honey jar even though it wasn't the season, or some fencing wire to train geraniums, or a star dropper or two to hold up the wire to train the geraniums up a rickety fence, in the front yard of a dug-out. We kept our eyes peeled for moon rocks – glinting brown-rust, moon-rust rocks, except that we weren't on the moon plain, we were by the dog fence near the moon plain.

Or the plain of moons, we thought, and imagined hundreds of small desert moons dancing on the flat earth at night as the moon-rocks dreamt themselves into the next hundred years. It would have made a good photograph, if we could find them, if we could capture the moon out of the sky and make it into a thousand little moons tap-dancing with silver desert feet.

We wondered about the dog paw inspector, the dog fencer on this Sunday afternoon, out on a Sunday afternoon drive along the longest fence in the whole world.

What did he or she look like? Sure, she wore boots, and maybe, we said jesting, a cork hat and a truck full of star droppers, just what we needed for the geranium training. And maybe one of us could keep her talking while the other reconnoitred round the back of the truck and prised out a couple of those droppers . . . we had real visions of the dog paw inspector. She, (though probably in this neck of the woods it was a he), could have been lining up the Toyota through binoculars, anticipating our arrival . . .

But, just our luck, we found a roll of old wire lying next to a roll of new, ready for a patch-up job, so we reckoned that the dog paw inspector, as we now rather fondly called him or her, must be in close proximity – except it was Sunday and surely a fencer didn't have to work on a Sunday, so we threw the old wire and a couple of star droppers into the back of the four-wheel drive and headed off.

About half a kilometre down the track, just as the Mintabie Maiden was getting into gear, and bets had been placed, and people were into the next dozen of Victorian Bitter, and children had fallen flat on their faces and broken their eggs, we came across a vehicle, stuck at the bottom of the hill, well not exactly a hill but a bit of a dip, in the middle of the track.

Hello, hello, we said to ourselves, and left our vehicle running in case there was going to be trouble; odd things could happen in the bush we'd decided, and I peered across into the window, only to discover a man slumped at the wheel.

And you can believe this or not, but he was wearing a cork hat though not one of the corks was moving, and he held a map in his hands, and neither of them was moving either. Not so much as a twitch. He wasn't dead because he was dribbling a bit of saliva. On the other hand . . .

We tapped on his window and perhaps more genteelly than the occasion required, asked if he was all right. We asked politely as Sunday drivers should, and yet again, until eventually he came round just as we were contemplating dowsing him with a water bottle.

He was the dog paw man, our vision personified, the dog fencer with a late night behind him and probably another one to come. Logs and other fencing accoutrements lay in the back of his truck, which we eyed, we confess, rather longingly.

And that was our good samaritan deed for the afternoon because he'd been dead to the world in the middle of a potentially dangerous spot in the centre of the truck.

Luckily we didn't have to put him in the back of the Land Cruiser and take him to hospital, which boasts another bitumenized road in the town, or radio the recently married flying doctor and flying nurse, because we had a little bit of evidence in the back – the old wire, and the star droppers, and he might have got hot under the collar about that with a late night behind him, and what with missing out on the Coober Pedy Cup and the Mintabie Maiden and the egg and spoon, and all that high-spirited community caper.

So we headed home through the moon-rock, rust-rock, which glinted and sheened in the late afternoon silence, and the prickle bush like mustard, coloured the land into strange shapes. We headed home with the dust in our eyes, ingrained in the seams of our hands.

If you could write a story about this land, about this portion of it, you could make more riches than digging for opal, more than that particular quest entails, more than the amount you might spend on explosives and other mining equipment, more riches than film crews. Oh yes, they come up here a lot and hold up the traffic when they want a bit of quiet at the end of the main street to film a bit of action in a tinny old tin shed. And leave a burnt-out bus somewhere on the fields as a reminder to the locals of Mad Max country, and a brief blaze of glory for those who were extras for a couple of weeks. Or they have daily plane drops of oysters and prawns and sit under the recently built hangar for a film about the end of the earth, some of them scoffing caviar, hardly aware that on the other side of town things are different.

But yes, if it came down to it, you could make enough money for a couple of dug-outs and everything you had your eye on in the Miner's Store; you could afford the occasional fresh fish, the big sardines sitting in buckets of ice on the counter, or sides of meat – you could make enough to hold a barbecue a week in a dry creek bed. You could make enough to fly back to Adelaide or up to Alice, or buy a night of shaslicks at the best nightspot in town before it got blown up early one Sunday morning. And you could go to the annual screening of the dilapidated drive-in with the sign that says – No explosives please – and have your photograph taken and enlarge it to hang on the wall of your newly plastered dug-out. And if you did happen to find opal, a huge pocket of it in the back of your dug-out, you could quite happily afford the explosives to blow your house to smithereens and go and live somewhere else.

You could sit and watch idle sunsets, and polish zebra rocks you'd collected out beyond the moon country to your heart's content; you could step out every evening into nights you have only ever dreamed about, with moons as fat and waxy as giant pearls, or as apricot as summer, or as lush as lovers sitting, perched kissing, on the sandstone ridge; you could head off to the suddenly bulging lakes after the town's been flooded with torrential rain, and swat the flies; or peer across the lake beside the unfamiliar lap-lap of water, at black swans and every kind of parrot and the wedge-tails, in pantaloons (they always wear pantaloons in brown and white), biding their time on tree branches – if you could write about it, if you could get a pocket full of stories as big as a good opal find, and cut and polish them until they gleamed like black opal. You could even wear black opal.

But first, you've got to find the story, like a miner, in the dark. Like miners in the first dark without ropes or ladders – by the light of a tin candelabra in the deep of a shaft. You've got to lift the lid, looking for women in the desert with tales that would make your hair fall out, or your eyes go limp; with tales of fear, and of courage – women who mine, who use explosives, women who noodle on the top of mullock heaps, their eyes filled with grit, their boots spilling with white dust, women who cook and scrub and clean while their men sit drinking in the clubs, women who bring up their children and watch them leave for the city, women who found businesses and set the pace, women who look for ways out of here, women who are violated; tales with sad, harsh songs of the potency of the desert earth; tales with the lilt of wildflowers, of egg-yolk daisies and the blaze of crimson sturt peas.

I told you you wouldn't get a story this time. A tourist snap-shot instead, camera round my neck.

Diana James
DESERT TRACKS – PITJANTJATJARA TOURS

Nganyinytja:
*Ngalya pitja ngayuku ngura nyakuntjikitja. Manta nyangatja
milmilpatjara! Ngayuku kamiku tjamuku ngura iritinguru. Pitjaya! Pina
ala, kuru ala, kututu alatjara!*

Come and see my country. This land is sacred! This has been my grandmother's and grandfather's country from a long time ago. Come with open
ears, open eyes and an open heart.

This is the invitation of Nganyinytja, a tribal elder, initiate of the Elder's
Law of the Pitjantjatjara Aboriginal people of Central Australia. She and
her extended family welcome visitors who genuinely want to learn about a
way of life that has enabled these people to live in harmony with this
desert country for thousands of years.

Nganyinytja and her husband, Ilyatjari, have developed a cross-cultural
tour in conjunction with Desert Tracks, a small tour business in Alice
Springs. Desert Tracks provides the 4WD vehicles, camping equipment
and guides to convey visitors the 600 kms from Alice Springs to Angatja.
This is Nganyinytja's homeland community on her traditional lands
south of Ayers Rock.

Desert Tracks is the only tour group presently given permission by the
Pitjantjatjara people to enter their Freehold Title Lands in South Australia.
It is a privilege and trust that we respect and are careful to abide by their
conditions. These include the prohibition of alcohol on the lands and
compliance with any restrictions on the use of cameras or access to sacred
areas.

This is a form of ecotourism or low-impact tourism that focuses on
experiencing the local culture and the desert environment on the terms of
the traditional owners of this land.

At Angatja, the tour leaders and instructors are Nganyinytja and Ilyatjari.
We are all students in their unique open air college. We come to listen,
watch, participate and learn.

What makes this Angatja experience more than just a superficial look-
see tourist trip?

Unlike the majority of visitors to Central Australia, participants do not
alight from luxury air-conditioned buses, snap a few photos, buy some
artefacts and then retreat back to the insulated environment of the bus and
hotel. Rather, they camp on the ground under the clear desert night skies,
no bathrooms, no daily showers, no tents – just the bush and the warm
companionship of the Aboriginal people whose daily life they are sharing.

Getting There

Our groups leave from Alice Springs in air-conditioned 4WD vehicles. The first day is spent driving 300 kilometres on bitumen highway south from Alice Springs, then west towards Ayers Rock. We leave this highway after Mt Ebenezer and follow dirt roads for the next 300 kilometres. These take us through cattle station country, then into the Pitjantjatjara Freehold Title Lands. Permits are needed from this point. Apart from the majestic bluff of Mt Conner the scenery has been ochre, red sand hills covered with low scrub and spinifex. Soon we approach the blue Musgrave Ranges. Stands of mulga trees and Desert Oaks become more common.

Once through these hills we stop and gaze across the undulating plain to the Mann Range, in which nestles our destination, Angatja.

As the sun turns the evening sky gold, we arrive at Angatja. We are warmly greeted by our hosts Nganyinytja and Ilyatjari. They show us where to camp and explain how a traditional camp would be organised. The sleeping areas are segregated into single men's and single women's sleeping areas, married couples find their own space.

Beds are individual swags or bedrolls, consisting of a mattress and sleeping bag encased in a cocoon of canvas that wraps under and over the person. Desert nights can be very cold, frost is not unusual in June and July, so swags need to be warm. The swags are then positioned inside a windbreak around a central fire. Desert people live close to fire at all times, it cooks their food, provides warmth and lights the dark. Fire is precious and always tended well.

Western visitors need to adjust to a new pace of life. Sitting in the sand or red dust around campfires, enjoying the communal cooking, story-telling and cups of tea. There is no fixed schedule with activities happening at specified times. The Aboriginal people decide when and where to gather food, this varies according to the season. Nganyinytja sets the pace and teaches in her way. People are encouraged to learn by observation and imitation, using all their senses, not just asking questions.

We spend from three to five days at Angatja attending Nganyinytja's College. An outline of this course and the major 'Tjukurpa' creation story and Law, that is taught at Angatja is briefly described herein.

The Learning Begins

Food gathering forms a major part of daily activity for Pitjantjatjara people. The desert environment is not an easy place to survive in, it requires great skill and knowledge. The men and women have divided this task, they each hunt and gather the foods most accessible to them. Women are restricted by their responsibilities for young children while the men can range further and faster in search of larger game.

Tour visitors are usually separated into male and female groups to hunt and gather traditional bush foods.

Nganyinytja teaches women's Law related to the gathering and preparation of these foods. Women were responsible for the collection of most of the food that formed the staple diet. They gathered large quantities of edible grass seeds, which were winnowed and then ground into flour. A woman's flat portable grinding stone and the smaller rounded grinder were as important to her as a man's spear and spearthrower were to his hunting. Areas that were frequently visited, often near water, had permanent smooth depressions on suitable large rocks. These have been made by women grinding flour there for thousands of years.

Vegetable foods commonly gathered include wild tomatoes and onions; wild fruits including figs, plums, coconuts and quandongs. Honey from flowering grevilleas and honey ants provides the only source of sweetness in their diet. Women also hunt smaller game like lizards, witchetty grubs and rabbits.

Ilyatjari takes the men off to hunt kangaroo, emu and rock wallaby. Nowadays, this hunting involves the use of Toyotas and guns. The traditional skills of tracking, sharp eyesight and a steady aim are still important.

The method of killing and cooking the kangaroo is prescribed by Law. The kangaroo was the creation ancestor who travelled through Angatja and around Australia giving different languages to each group of Aboriginal people.

Activities that everyone participates in as a group are: the making of artefacts carved from local wood; the telling of major creation stories of this region; the singing and dancing of traditional song cycles. Visitors are encouraged to join in where appropriate.

Our time with Nganyinytja and her family is full, we all have much to learn and much to share. It is the Pitjantjatjara sense of humour and thorough enjoyment of life that makes living and learning with them so much fun. Beryl Blake, a tour participant, remembers her first meeting with Nganyinytja:

I could have listened to her for hours, she had such grace and dignity and a strong pride in her people's traditions. Nganyinytja spoke with a soft serious voice which would break suddenly into a sparkling smile as she shared a joke with us. Any feelings of reserve on our part quickly dissipated.

Learning the Law – Tjukurpa
Central to Aboriginal understanding of the Land is the Tjukurpa – this includes the Creation Stories and the Law. It imbues all their activities with spiritual significance. There is Tjukurpa related to their daily hunting and gathering; their dance, song and stories; their painting, carving and making of utensils and weapons.

The Creation Beings who fashioned the Land gave the people this Tjukurpa. It is continuously renewed by Aboriginal people's telling of the stories, singing the song cycles and performing the ceremonies. The Tjukurpa is alive and a vital part of the people and their Land today.

Visitors to Angatja are told the Tjukurpa of the Ngintaka Man, the giant perentie lizard-man. He travelled from his home near the Western Australian border to the camp of another lizard tribe, near Oodnadatta, in search of a special grindstone.

Nganyinytja briefly outlines the story:

Ngintaka Tjukurpa alatji – paluru ngura parari nyinangi tjiwa wiya, paluru tjiwa kurakuratjara nyinangi munu paluru mai wakati rungkaningi, munu rungkara uninypa uninymankula ngalkuningi.

This is the story of the Perentie Man – he was living in a distant place without a grindstone, he only had a very poor quality grindstone and he was trying to grind the seed from wild pigweed, and he was having to eat these rough seedcakes.

Munu paluru kulinu: 'Ay, tjiwa kutjupa ruulmananyi, ruultjinga rungkani ngura parari.' Munu kulira paluru mapalku anu ngura kutjupakutu. Munu paluru ankula nyangu, tjiwa palunya. Munu mantjinu, munu kutitlura ngalya-katingu.

And he thought: 'Ah, someone is grinding, there is the sound of grinding coming from a long way away.' And having heard he quickly travelled to that other place. And he travelled and travelled and then he saw that other grindstone. And he took it, he stole it and carried it back to his camp.

As the Ngintaka travelled he created many landforms in the Musgrave and Mann Ranges and he vomited up many different kinds of grass seeds and vegetable foods as he went.

Visitors travel in the bus along the trail of the Ngintaka between Angatja and Tjanmatapiti. As we twist along the dirt track, the Aboriginal women sing this song:

'Ngurakutuna wipuwani wipuwani tjarpaku.'

'I (Ngintaka) am travelling towards my camp sweeping my tail from side to side.'

The bus swings from side to side following the winding road. The singing and the motion transport the travellers to the Dreamtime. One feels like a small mite on the back of that gigantic lizard's thrashing tail.

One visitor, Anne-Marie Cousteau, said of this experience:

'You begin to understand, very deeply within yourself, what the Aborigines mean by the "Dreamtime" – the time when those fantastic beings walked the Earth. As you listen to the stories, you begin to realize the Dreamtime is still today. We saw the Aborigines rub the rocks out in the bush so that the Dreamtime would stay with them.'

The rocks that she saw rubbed, are at the spot where Ngintaka man vomited up the 'parka-parka' (mistletoe berries). He left his skin there on the rocks so that people would remember what he had done for them. There is a line of several rocks with distinctive circular indentations on them that look exactly like perentie skin markings. These have not been drawn by people. The Pitjantjatjara say it is *Tjukurpa puliringu* – the creation spirit has become stone. The Ngintaka man chose to become stone or other landforms at places where he stopped on his travels.

Visitors are taken and shown some of these sacred places so that they will, *kulira wanantjaku tjukurpa* – follow the Dreaming and learn. They are taught verses of the song cycle and the dances that correspond to Ngintaka's actions at these places.

The rocks at the place of the *parka-parka* vomit, are rubbed prior to rain to ensure the abundance of these edible berries. These increase ceremonies are part of the way Aboriginal people care for the Land. They put energy back into the animals and plants of their environment, they actively recreate the food sources necessary for their survival.

The Ngintaka story and the specific song stanzas and dances that are taught at Angatja are not secret sacred information. Nganyinytja and her family have consulted the wider Pitjantjatjara and Yankunytjatjara community and made sure that all the information they teach is public. Visitors may then pass on what they have learnt to the rest of the Australian and the world community.

Farewell to Angatja

Visitors are reluctant to leave this warm Aboriginal family. Nganyinytja opens her heart to all who come, they become part of her extended family. She smiles widely and says this now stretches around the world. People of widely different cultures, languages, religions and ages come together and rejoice in their common humanity. This aspect of her work is very important to Nganyinytja. She believes that world peace can be achieved on the basis of greater cross-cultural understanding.

It is hard to say goodbye, but the friendship shared is lasting.

Uluru National Park

We complete our tour with a couple of days at Uluru National Park, Ayers Rock and the Olgas.

Apart from their spectacular beauty these areas are part of the traditional hunting grounds of the Pitjantjatjara and Yankunytjatjara people. Nganyinytja walked here from Angatja as a child and knows where the water sources are and the supplies of food necessary for such a journey. Her people are custodians for song cycles that cross this country.

The base of Ayers Rock is alive with evidence of the Creation Beings and we can follow the paths of two main stories there.

Uluru and Katatjuta (Ayers Rock and the Olgas) are seen with deeper understanding by people who have just experienced Angatja's Bush College. The Aboriginal spiritual significance is alive and meaningful.

Desert Tracks Tours

Ten and seven day tours run from April to October every year. Tours depart from and return to Alice Springs in the Northern Territory of Australia. All equipment, swags, food, entry permits, camping fees, tuition fees and transport is provided. An information booklet is sent to all participants prior to departure.

Enquiries and bookings
    Desert Tracks
    PO Box 8706
    Alice Springs, NT 0871
    Tel. (089) 50 5411
          (089) 52 8984
    Fax. (089) 52 8686

Barbara Tiernan

DESERT WOMEN

They are extraordinary, these women of the desert. They stride through heat, spinifex and searing sand apparently without noticing the lacerating and scorching. Their skin is dry, weathered, not distinguishably black or white – at least not in the terms I'd understood back in the city – but a sort of leather coloured brindle. It was a while before I learned that this meant something.

I'd come to Central Australia with a handful of arts administration skills prepared to manage a major arts centre in Alice Springs and, as it happened, prepared for little else; my skin was white, my hands soft, my head full of ideas about cultural integration. I'd come on a three year contract.

What my middle-class, city-centricity ignored was that neophytes like me had passed through in their hundreds since the Territory was opened up by the Stuart Highway. Some of them desperadoes, most of them do-gooders, some simply with nowhere else to be.

It was the women who told me, not in words, how to shed my soft skin for something more practical and useful – they left me alone – ignored me and waited for me to weather.

These were women who came variously for holidays or with partners or for their careers . . . and stayed.

Women like Di Byrnes, Jill Scott and Sandra Kline who, as young nurses just graduated from a major city hospital, went to Alice Springs looking for adventure and found it soon after setting up a tourist lodge at the base of (then) Ayers Rock. When a crazed truck driver ran his Mack at full throttle through the crowded bar of the lodge, these women were well placed to deal with the horrific casualties. After a brief stint as boarding house proprietors in town, the women 'went bush' again to revive a rundown lodge at breathtaking Glen Helen Gorge. The fire that burnt the place to the ground in their first tourist season didn't stop them trading from makeshift bough shelters and rebuilding with salvaged materials to create new buildings in the architectural style unique to the Territory. The floods usually come around Easter and twice these women sat on top of a nearby hill and watched their belongings washed down the Fink River in mighty gushes and roars. They stocked up and started again. They're still there.

Then there's Rosie Kunoth Monks, some still think of her as Jedda – the role she played as a beautiful, young woman in the Chauvel film. A passionate advocate of 'dry' Aboriginal reserves or town camps as they're called, galvanised the local women with such success that almost all of the settlements are now alcohol-free some patrolled nightly and monitored by groups of women organised by Rosie Monks. It was Rosie who revealed some of the 'women's business' of the area – concerns previously unknown to the non-Aboriginal population and which helped change forever the town's consciousness and attitude to the 'Aboriginal drink problem'. She's still there.

Diana James, a contributor to this book, will tell you about Nganyinytja's tireless pursuit of reconciliation between white and black through education and access but I want to tell you about Diana herself. Separated suddenly from her husband and left with three young children to raise, Diana took over her ex-partner's part of the business and ran it herself. Doesn't sound too hard? It's just that this business involved running safari tours to some of the remotest parts of the Australia – marketing the tours, supervising supplies, driving the vehicles, cooking and caring for tourists more used to air-conditioned buses and ensuites than dusty, windowless 4-wheel-drives and holes in the ground for a toilet. Diana operates out of Alice Springs but spends most of her time in the desert. She's still there.

There's Kaye Kessing, artist, writer, designer and poet. Came from Adelaide as a young teacher via the remote settlement of Amata just to 'have a look'. Some twenty years later Kessing began to understand earlier than most, the devastating effects that introduced species like cattle, horses and camels were having on the desert's unique flora and fauna. Devising and painting a series of oil canvasses charting the loss of desert animals, Kessing took to the road performing and exhibiting in the country's capital cities in between creative spells back home in Alice Springs. She's still there.

The roll call is endless – hundreds of women we don't hear about but some like Sara Henderson, author of *From Strength to Strength,* who inherited a debt-ridden cattle station from her philandering husband and made it a success, burst into our lives with their stories of triumph over adversity and become the new heroines.

Most of these extraordinary women have been around for years, quietly and often in spiritual as well as geographic isolation, simply doing what they do.

Back in the city, my hands have gone soft, my skin more white. I'm again aware of the difference in people's skins – not the brindle colour of the bush – and I miss the sense of sameness under the skin. I miss those women too . . . I envy their endurance and weathering and their still being there.

Tania Lienert
Growing Up in Woomera

Upon entering Woomera village – now open to travellers after many years as a closed town – the first thing that strikes you is rows and rows of empty flats, three storeys high, sunset-red brick, with broken or boarded-up windows. In the centre of the village you come across a huge military plane, mottled green, and an array of rockets and missiles in the Missile Park.

Both the flats and the missiles signify the essence of growing up in Woomera, 780 kilometres north of Adelaide in SA, as I did until I was fifteen. I was born there in 1966. The flats were built for the hundreds – perhaps a couple of thousand in its heyday – single men who worked on the range; and the missiles gave the village its purpose – the Woomera Rocket Range established after World War II by the British. Most of the single men came out from England to work and never married, living their entire working lives in what, to me now, seem like dog boxes, up in the desert hundreds of miles from civilisation. Upon retirement they were forced to leave, most moving to the little coastal towns further south.

As a child my sisters, friends and I roamed without fear across the bush, the donga, the stoney gibber plains with red earth and saltbush. It probably started with walking home from the football – the oval was out of town across the donga with a great hill of rubble we used to play on. My mother took us to the Black Caves for picnics down the creek from the football oval, and later we went there alone and ventured further: down to the treatment works lake where my grandfather went birdwatching when he visited; out to the fenced piece of bush where my girlfriend Maria's horse was kept; and beyond. There were the inevitable walks around the village – a square mile set out in a grid – and it was too tempting to head for that hill or down to that creek rather than stay on the boundaries, especially past the forbidden zones. As I grew older I would walk out bush alone.

More exciting were the weekend barbecue trips or tennis club picnics. We'd travel past the gibber plains to any sandhills, rocks, interesting geological formations or Aboriginal rock paintings, patches of scrub, hills or salt lakes. Occasionally the lakes would fill and we would paddle or swim in them and at one, Lake Richardson, even go for a ride in someone's boat. We'd bring home little fish (the ones that have eggs that lie dormant in rocks for years in the desert until the rains come) to watch in the fish tank until they inevitably died. Cow manure collecting for the garden was a treat – we'd gather friends for a picnic, and with Mum, drive out into the station country where one cow grazes every square mile on stations millions of acres in size. Cow pats would transform the red sand or clay into earth a little more fertile for growing things in the garden. Never, even as we marvelled at the rock paintings, did we think of the Aboriginal people forced to move from their land out of the Woomera Prohibited Area which seemed to cover most of South Australia and half of Western Australia on maps in the 1960s and 70s.

Long hot days and nights at the local swimming pool were a delight, as was mucking around the tennis courts on balmy summer nights while Dad played. Night-time socialising was the thing to do when daytime summer temperatures reached 50 degrees Celsius.

What we were blind to was the militaristic way of life and its celebration. When you grow up knowing nothing else you think this is all there is. Hence living in a town in the middle of the outback – with no Aboriginal people, a young population of white English, Anglo-Australians and Americans (with the odd Afro-American or Latino working in the military), arranged in heterosexual nuclear families or sent there as (presumably) heterosexual single men – is ordinary. There were no old people, no unemployed people, few single women, and no tourists as the town was closed. Friends or relatives could visit only if you filled out a form for them and met them at the guard gate, where adults also had to show a security pass every time they came and went. Then the boom gate would be lifted to let you drive through. Keys had to be organised in advance for those weekend picnics and cameras and binoculars left at the guardhouse. Again, these were unquestioned facts of life, as were police checking up on us as we lit the barbecue or went for walks or played games out bush.

Nor did we question the glorification of American culture that went with the presence of the US military base Nurrungar just outside the town from 1968 on. We knew the Americans were better than us and just accepted it. We also accepted that if there were a nuclear holocaust we would be the first to die. This was a privilege and something to boast about. There was at least one red alert for such a possibility when I was a child, but as Mum told me years later, she didn't want me to worry about it at the time.

In hindsight I am horrified at how we were taught US history and culture at school because the American children at the school had to pass a citizenship test on their return to their home, but very little Australian history. What we did learn included the glorification of the Maralinga and Emu Field atomic bomb tests, on which Woomera personnel worked in the 1950s. This was mostly through the work of surveyor Len Beadell, who wrote *Blast the Bush* about his experiences and who came back to the village on speaking tours often. Part of our future, we also believed, lay in the discovery of uranium ore in 1979 at the nearby Roxby Downs station. This promised us all jobs – I was going to work there – and a future for Woomera itself at a time when the Rocket Range had all but closed. This was not to be, as a whole new town, Olympic Dam, was built at the mine site.

Nurrungar's role, too, is fading in the absence of the Cold War. While the superpowers and Australia search for other threats so the military has something to do, there is talk that the base will pass to Australian control soon. The Maralinga tests have had a Royal Commission enquiring into them and there are few markets for Roxby Downs' uranium. In the meantime, Woomera village remains very much a little American town in the Australian outback, sustained by the US military budget, facilities provided for those in the services sent to such an isolated posting; but with a much diminished population: 1200 or so compared with 8000 in the 1960s. So the people live in a cluster in the centre, the outer flats deserted, too difficult to demolish, the empty houses transported away and sold for holiday shacks and the sites bulldozed, only the kerbsides and concrete footpaths and bitumen roads remain. In between the donga has reclaimed what once were house and garden sites. I can still see my name which I painted on the footpath outside our house as an errant child – a long-term reminder of where we lived.

And with family and friends gone there remains little reason to return now, except for pilgrimages, or the Nurrungar protests organised by the Peace Action Collective in Adelaide to send the American military home and give the land back to the indigenous Kokatha people; there remains the possibility of high school reunions and facing schoolmates with me now a protester, an anti-nuclear peace activist and a lesbian! How could such a place have bred such a woman? Forever I am grateful for the efforts of my mother Lorraine, sent there to teach in the 1960s, married and stayed for 17 years, then moving to the city when I was sixteen so all her daughters could go to city schools after I'd had one unhappy year at boarding school. This move saved us from the otherwise likely scenario of marrying an American and leaving to live in the US, or staying in Woomera forever in service jobs with few prospects for careers. In childhood it was special, but now it is a place to visit and marvel at.
Flinders Ranges, February 1993

Postscript
As I reflect on this piece and look at photos at home in Geelong, Victoria, I sit in my loungeroom with red earth and rocks collected from the donga before me. It reminds me of one of my most enduring memories of my childhood – that of Dad trying to make the backyard safe for us to play in. This meant getting rid of the saltbush that might harbour snakes. For years he mowed, slashed, dug and burnt it. Always it came back. Now when I return periodically to that site, the house is gone and the saltbush reigns. I am sure that this place must return to red earth, rocks and saltbush. I work and wait for the day when the whole of this Woomera Prohibited Area might, as Australian folk singer Judy Small writes in her song 'The Futures Exchange' (from *One Voice in the Crowd*), once again belong to Dreaming.
Geelong, April 1993

Finola Moorhead

MISS MARPLE GOES TO AYERS ROCK

A Performed Reading
Slides of Central Australia showing two grey-haired women on holiday.
Music. Slides of press cuttings of Lindy Chamberlain 1980–85. Taped
Chant:

There is a tent. There is a tracksuit. There is a blood stain on the tracksuit. There is no baby in the crib. There is a sleeping bag. There is a barbecue. There is a camera. There is a man at the barbecue fire. There is a
can of baked beans. There is a bus of tourists. There is a red road. There
is the Rock. There is a camera case. There are two boys. There are the
folks from Tasmania. There is a hurricane lamp. There are as many
Gideon Bibles as there are rooms in the motel. There is a huge night sky.
There are suddenly hundreds of Free The Dingo T-shirts. There is fear.
There is a dark-haired woman with fastidiously feminine taste in clothes.
There are many photographs. There is an article which claimed the Rock
did it because Rocks can, as Hanging Rock did it to some young girls on
St Valentine's Day, 1900. There is something to be desired in the way the
mother conducts herself. She didn't cry at the right time. There is a tall
fair husband. There are religious beliefs. There are accusations against the
particular religion itself. There is a massive campaign of self-defence on its
part. There is a supposition that the baby's name was 'Sacrifice in the
Desert'. There are young mothers who know what it feels like to want to
kill their kids. There is no charge of infanticide in the Northern Territory.
There is, however, a murder charge. There is a new pregnancy. There is
separation of mother and new daughter. There is a change in the mother's
clothes. There is an unexplained fear. There is an appeal to the High
Court. There is no corpse. There is the Aboriginal tracker. There are half-
tame half-shepherd dingos. There was a bull terrier in Carlton, Victoria,
which ate a baby. There are the Northern Territory Police. There are four-
wheel drives galore. There is adult blood on the upholstery. There is a
tracksuit at the dry cleaners. There is a forensic expert from Adelaide.
There is an English one, or two. There is a female forensic expert from
New South Wales who now works for the Northern Territory. There is a
pair of scissors. There is only a mean time eleven minutes for her to have
done it. There are drag marks in the sand. There are magical caves in the
huge red Rock. There is a hanging-on-to rope on Uluru. There is a baby
gone. There is a snipped baby singlet. There is no canine saliva. There is
mystery in the air. There is a trial of forensic science. There is a dark-
coloured baby dress. There is mythology in the press. There is no matinee
jacket. There is baby's blood in the camera case. There is a question

341

whether the reagent solution could conclusively prove it is foetal haemo-globin. There are horrific imaginings of how and why she did it. There is a widespread religious campaign to free Lindy. There was a dingo destroyed. There is the private eye team. There is no defence of insanity. There is an expensive forensic campaign finding in four other Holden Toranas out of forty a spray of the substance called Dufix HN 1081 which looks like spurted blood. There is no mention of a third person. There is a woman in jail. There are hundreds of people giving money to prove her innocence. There is a new tourist development at Ayers Rock. There is also a piece of paper which says this national park now belongs to three tribes of the Dreamtime people. There is a woman in jail who makes her own clothes.

Journey of Madge,
A Poetry Reading
A hot coming we had of it,
Celia Marple and I
Just at that time of year
Hot days, bitter nights and the winds
Moaning through the sands and desert oaks.
The bus broke down and the coach captain
Swore foul oaths as the vehicle lay deep in the bulldust.
The outback stations like sore thumbs
On the sandscape, the spindly windmills,
And the dusty blacks guzzling beer
The white men filthy and cursing
And pissing off in old Holdens, and wanting their liquor
And women, though few were to be seen.
They must have taken gins beside embers of bushfires
In the night. And the locals unfriendly and charging high
     prices:
A hard time we had of it
On the Centralian coach tour.
We preferred travelling by day,
Sleeping in snatches,
With the voices of the willywag women
Singing in our ears, at night, saying
That this was all folly. Go home whites.

Then we saw the dawn across the Olgas,
Such beauty rendered Celia and I speechless for a day
As we sat apart from the others under three low trees.
We swore we saw a wild camel for a moment
But it disappeared.

Then we came to the motel at Ayers Rock
A few blokes were playing poker at the bar door
And there were empty stubbie bottles everywhere
Pathetic ignorant and boozed were the conversations inside
But we slaked our thirst
And pitched our tent at evening in the caravan park
Finally there; it was (you may say) satisfactory.
There's been such a hullaballoo about that time and place,
Since, yet, I remember
Our supper, and we would do it again, but set down
This set down
This: were we led (we felt led as if fate dictated
Our decision) all that way for
Birth or Death? There seems to have been a Death,
Certainly, but as Celia said we have evidence only
Of a Disappearance, and absence of the baby and no doubt.
Celia and I thought different theories; like Birth for me,
Really. I am not the same. I don't bemoan the hard and bitter
    agony
Nor the sympathy I felt for both beast and beauty
(For the mother had such pretty dresses)
I am reborn in an ancient dispensation
With an alien people clutching their desecrated gods.
I should be glad to die as Celia died,
Convinced of the power and truth of the Dreamtime.

Miss Celia Marple's Narrative

Performed as a lecture with a pointer and a large board displaying Celia
Marple's drawing of the caravan park, bush and Ayers Rock.

There is one culprit in this whole case and it is Evil. I chose a place outside the caravan park to scribble and sketch my thoughts and observations
of the whole affair. I know it is my last case, now. When Madge first suggested the trip my trepidation was tinged with excitement. Premonition
was it? I couldn't refuse to come for it would have meant I lacked the
courage to pursue my fate. I, with my pendulum, have been at the scene
of many deaths, murders most of them, for it seems to have been my lot
to have Detection as my main passion and commitment in life. The Holy
Spirit has guided me to arrive at just and true conclusions and it has
provided me one simple singular aid – my tiny crystal pendulum. With
this I detect the flow of good and bad energy through the living being of
creation.

In detection, it is necessary to believe in the endless battle between the
light and the dark forces of the universe(s). Then in deed and effort to

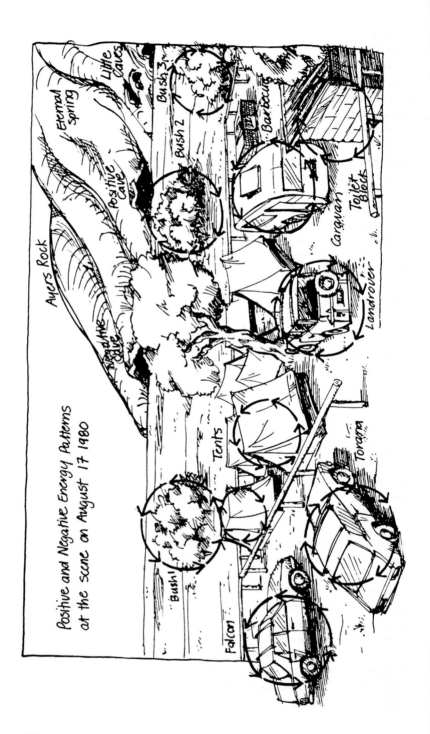

Positive and Negative Energy Patterns at the Scene on August 17 1980

Ayers Rock

Eternal Spring

Little Caves

Bush 3

Bush 2

Positive Cave

Barbecue

Negative Cave

Caravan

Toilet Block

Landrover

Tents

Bush 1

Torana

Falcon

fight on the side of good. The genre would be nothing at all without the overall intention of the detective to do good – to seek not financial rewards, not honour and respect from the world or the media but, rather, justice – to see the real culprit sent to whatever punishment justice has to offer. Sadly, many sentences and judgements are ill-advised, either inadequate or too harsh. However, it is not a part of my passion or talent to fight on that front. It is beyond my control.

All through my long life I have felt that in this land of the Holy Spirit, Terra Incognita, I would be led into the Centre and there I would take my life. Or, more accurately, It, the land, the Holy Spirit, would finally relieve me of the burden of constantly doing for others with little gratitude, misunderstanding mainly being my reward. But belief is belief and we carry on.

It was to be our holiday. Biannually we take a bus trip together, a couple of old spinsters with time on our hands. We had been everywhere else so I suppose we had to come here, yet some strange eerie feeling commenced immediately on our booking the seats. I was afraid and yet I knew we must go on. I think Madge, in her way, also felt somehow grasped by fate and sent in a certain direction for I saw in her frown a queer determination as if she saw something I did not. I called it her 'star in the West'.

Anyway, we came and the events of August the seventeenth occurred. It seemed quite simple at first. The magistrate, later, said the native dog had done the deed. There were, however, little problems, loose ends which didn't seem to tally. Grasping these loose ends, the prosecution tied them into a case and had the first inquest's findings reversed by the second.

My hand is useless as an artist's tool but you will see on my scribbling a view of the caravan park and the Rock. There are a few vehicles and tents, caravan and the toilet block. Between the park and the Rock there is a distance of about five miles; no, it is not that far, but it's a reasonable walk. It was in this bush that I made my most interesting discoveries. The caves in the Rock's face are another story in terms of negative and positive power. The entire region is immensely powerful, my pendulum could hardly contain itself. I have gone over the whole area sifting and making assessments.

Much of my life has been spent considering Evil. It is not rational yet it appears rational. It defies generalisation while inviting it. For example, in the first case it appears rational because it is materialistic and, in the second, it invites a generalisation such as all dogs are bad or all blondes are goodies and dark-haired women are to be feared, and defies an equivalent generalisation of itself, such as all men with a mean and nasty demeanour are rapists with the truth that some quite handsome men and pleasant social types have hearts (or souls) as black as soot. It takes such a thing as the pendulum operated with humility to the divine and good purpose to actually decide one way or the other; sometimes.

Let us suppose that the drawing I've done is as the caravan park was on the evening of the seventeenth. Only two of the many tents conveyed to the pendulum good vibrations. These are the Lowes' and the Chamberlains'. The Holden Torana and the landrover also sent the pendulum on the clockwise course. The Falcon station-wagon and the caravan gave negative vibrations and the toilet block positive. Because there was such an over-whelming predominance of anti-clockwise motion, I was forced to check the trees and the bush, because there is always the possibility the deeds occur because the place itself is Evil and likely to cause human beings to act uncharacteristically. In such a powerful place as this, dominated by the huge sandstone monolith of Ayers Rock considered by the original peoples to be a god and by scientific Western geologists to be quite a phenomenon, it is highly probable that at some time or another a horrific blasphemy or many little blasphemies could have taken place to turn it into a place to be avoided.

I found, however, that this was not so. The power of the Rock was extraordinarily balanced and well left as a sacred place by the Aborigines. Any punishment this particular god dealt to those who believed in its divinity would be quick and fair. So the culprit was mankind, not the spirit world.

My suspicions that a ghastly injustice was about to occur were aroused by just such accusations towards the spirit world. We were there. We heard the gossip and so did every interested Australian because the media was here with its huge inquisitive nose to the ground. A miniature coffin had been found in the home at Mt Isa and a Bible underlined in a way that one interpretation might have indicated some Satanic motive and the baby had had its last medical examination in a black dress and someone had dredged up biblical proof that Azaria, an odd name to the Australian tongue, really meant 'Sacrifice in the Desert'. I deduced that mischief was afoot in just this stirring up of superstitious feelings in a public so usually indifferent and apathetic about such immaterial things.

In fact, their very materialism gave weight to these weird and wonderful coincidences that they in themselves did not deserve. They could only be explained with imagination and compassion and these qualities – virtues – seem less delectable to a mass than the inexplicable, the mysterious. So, in my little investigation, I dismissed these 'proofs' as useless and purely psychological and relevant only to a parallel phenomenon; the extreme, nay, universal interest this incident aroused.

My attention turned to what really had happened. The loose ends. I kept in mind the incredible desire of the Territorians to exonerate the semi-native dog, the so-called dingo, when, on their stations, they would have no qualms at all about shooting a marauding canine beast. There is to the south the dingo fence which these same types consider a necessity. Madge and I on our trip to Western Australia stared into the eyes of a suffering emu stuck in that inhumane wire barrier. We watched it die.

An insane fever grew in the community around here. Nurse Downs was nearly hysterical with it – such excitement she'd never had.

My pendulum has told me that there was little human sympathy to be milked. It is necessary to have some kind of moral geiger counter lest one spend too much time with the wrong type.

I sought the owner or driver of the landrover – the ranger. This man had shot the half-tame half-shepherd dingo within hours of the disappearance of Azaria. He, unfortunately, could not hear my questions. He thought me a silly old maid. Still, I knew his vibrations were fundamentally all right.

The Aboriginal tracker, Daisy, was taken with my trinket. She saw me squatting on the ground in the bush I've marked bush '2', fascinated by the huge rightwise circles the little crystal on the string was making. She showed me where she had tracked the drag marks to – stones. The dog walks lightly on stone – no more marks. There we were both mystified. I brought out my diviner. It hurled itself in the opposite direction. By this time, Daisy was nodding sagely at its antics. There was some quite conscious human Evil here. Not far away, eventually, they found the tot's clothes apparently snipped by scissors.

This was, indeed, a loose end if one were to consider the mother herself innocent, as my pendulum indicated I must. My friend left me quite suddenly and she did not walk back toward the settlement.

Real Evil. It is one thing to murder directly in person with passion or malice aforethought. It is quite another, having found some savaged clothes, having not murdered anyone yourself, to tamper with the evidence in such a way as to imply a murder had taken place and point the finger at an innocent being. Quite peculiar motives came to my mind for this was the most bizarre aspect of the whole affair. Let me be cautious and say – hypothetically – somebody or bodies had found the baby clothes in the sand and deliberately taken scissors to them and strewn them about or left them under a rock. If this were so, did it mean, therefore, things had come to such a pass for the Territorians that, maybe without a body for evidence, they would not succeed in getting a conviction? A body they possibly knew to be consumed – a murdered baby's body? And why did they need a conviction so badly? Or perhaps it was the work of a mischievous imp. There is a strain of madness in the white men in this area. One need only be around for a while, even a short while, to notice an accepted level of insanity. As Madge would say, we – whites – should not be here.

The forces of Evil were already generalising: the dark-haired lady, the inscrutable, the witch must be burnt and tried on any evidence at all; all dogs are good. Indian wolf-boy stories are, no doubt, true, and Romulus and Remus drank hound's milk. The truly wild canine is more likely to suckle a defenceless human babe than eat it. But all dogs are not good. There are mad dogs and sane dogs; bad dogs and good ones. Half-wild feral beasts having learnt no lore in the native pack or the indigenous environment, having an innate distrust and knowledge of human beings who have cast them out and fed them irregularly, are likely to scavenge where they can. What disturbed me most was this unknown human element that would disguise the evidence of the animal's destruction and create evidence of a human's, and yet I grew convinced that this had happened.

I began to doubt my own sanity, as we had spent many weeks in this uncomfortable atmosphere of suspicion, of speculation.

My despair becomes impossible to bear as I hear the progress of the trials. Justice has given way to spurious science and prejudice. The legalistic gymnastics of the Queen's Counsels are a damnable indictment of their profession where such scurrilous tactics of persuasion are left free to whip the innocent and the just pedants with scorn and sarcasm.

So many courts of law indulge themselves getting huge salaries to puff and pant and pander to legalities and technicalities and inhuman practices that I find myself in an invidious position. All my arts and talents of inspired detection are absolutely worthless if their results are always to be thrown into the sausage machine of the legal profession – which, even if it retains some good intentions, is so structured as to be time-wasting, ridiculously expensive, awfully circuitous and, in the end, relatively tooth-less as far as worthwhile and fair punishment goes. There is no point in my going on.

I gaze at my crystal. I must follow the Holy Spirit now and walk west until I drop and die as I lived, just another old bag of bones. Maybe out there I'll meet a strange fair wolf-girl – but now I am being fanciful. I am old and have no use for hospitals with their life-support systems. If I have any choice at all in the illusion of my own freedom it is to refuse. In this case, now, to refuse to continue living.

Darkness.

Susan Hawthorne and Renate Klein
THE SOUTH AND EAST

Canberra

Australia's capital and only inland capital city, Canberra is a designed city (see Dowse). It's a city that femocrats have made a home and the location of the Office for the Status of Women. The Australian National Gallery has some wonderful work by Australian women artists in particular, the most extensive collection of Margaret Preston's work. Canberra's festival month is March (every second odd-numbered year) when the Word Festival is held. From September to October Floriade draws visitors wanting to see a profusion of flowers. One of the central meeting places for women in Canberra is Tilley's, where you can eat and be entertained. Whatever Canberra lacks in charm may be found in the nearby Brindabella Ranges which offer a variety of bushwalking tracks, mountain drives and gang gang cockatoos.

Sydney

The harbour is one of the highlights of Sydney, and your trip will be incomplete without a ride on a ferry across Sydney Harbour. If you do this you will also see both the Opera House and the Sydney Harbour Bridge, both of which have become central icons of Sydney. Grace Cossington Smith and Margaret Preston have both captured the beauty of Sydney in their art (see Burke). Sydney is rich in culture and nightlife. The annual Mardi Gras held each February/March has made Sydney famous as the Gay and Lesbian Party Capital of the world. International Women's Day, March 8, in Sydney as in other cities and towns around Australia is often a focal point for events that focus on women as well as a march on the Saturday morning nearest the day. The Sydney Festival (in January), Carnivale (in September) and Australian Feminist Book Fortnight (every second September in odd-numbered years), are times when you can hear and see the best of Australian women's arts. The National Lesbian Festival takes place in Sydney or one other capital city each year. Theatre, films, readings occur on a regular basis. In particular, look for readings at Harold Park Hotel and the NSW Writers' Centre. Watch out for events listed in *The Entertainment Guide* (also called EG) in Friday's *Sydney Morning Herald*. The Jessie Street Library, the Mitchell Library, the NSW State Art Gallery and other institutions have collections of women's works (manuscripts, books, paintings and other visual arts), and Sydney's theatres increasingly stage work by women. The inner suburbs of Sydney are where you will find the most feminist events and activity, in particular Glebe, Lilyfield, Annandale, Leichhardt, Balmain, Newtown, Erskinville, Marrickville, Petersham and Rozelle. You will find other pockets in the suburbs bordering Oxford Street and east to the beach suburbs of Bronte and Bondi. Sydney is also a starting point for magnificent bushwalks in any of the nearby National Parks, in particular the Blue Mountains, a short drive west of the city.

Melbourne

Melbourne claims to be the cultural capital of Australia and in recent years has set its vision on making this more and more self evident. Theatre, comedy and publishing are central to Melbourne's cultural life, but you will also find feminists who prefer horse racing – the Melbourne Cup, held on the first Tuesday in November is frequently an excuse for a barbecue or party – or even football (Australian Rules takes over Melbourne's radio waves every weekend throughout the winter months from April to September). Like Sydney, International Women's Day, Australian Feminist Book Fortnight and Melbourne's International Arts Festival (held in October in 1994 and thereafter in early November) provide a focus for cultural events; others can be found in Melbourne's *EG* (in every Friday's *Age*). Melbourne is renowned for its parks and beautiful old buildings, a walk in the Botanic Gardens, or along the Yarra River (especially the area near the Boathouse in Fairfield), or a boat ride along the Yarra give the visitor a sense of Melbourne's character. For a different view, Brunswick Street in Fitzroy, Lygon Street in Carlton, The Victoria Market, Chapel Street in Prahran and Acland and Fitzroy Streets in St Kilda among others will show another side. Restaurants (and the best coffee in the world), arts venues and a huge array of shops line all these busy streets. The inner suburbs again are where you will find feminist organisations, in particular Fitzroy, Carlton, Clifton Hill and Northcote and to the south Prahran, South Melbourne and St Kilda. Outside of Melbourne there are significant feminist populations in the towns of Daylesford, Hepburn Springs and Castlemaine. From Melbourne it is a few hours drive to the snowfields, the national parks of Gippsland or the Great Ocean Road to the west.

Hobart

Hobart is Australia's southernmost capital, located on the Derwent River and with the backdrop of Mt Wellington. Hobart was the first Australian city to build a casino and Wrest Point Casino is one of the city's most advertised attractions (there are casinos in all major Australian cities now).

The Sydney to Hobart Yacht Race which begins in Sydney on Boxing Day (26 December) and ends in Hobart several days later brings Hobart to national attention each year. The Salamanca Festival, held in November each year, has developed a reputation for intellectually stimulating debate. (See Edmonds on its feminist cultural history, also Kelly and Whitebeach.) Hobart is a starting point for tours to Southeast and Southwest Tasmania, while Launceston in the north and middle of the island is the starting point for Cradle Mountain (see Simmons).

The Great Ocean Road, Vic

Geelong is the starting point for visits to the western coastal region of Victoria. Geelong has a vigorous women's community. A visit to Pakington Street in West Geelong will take you to Colari Gallery and Bookshop where you may hear readings by women on some weekends, or an exhibition of women's art. Not far from Geelong, the town of Drysdale commemorates Anne Drysdale, who built a stone house on land she squatted, where she and her companion Caroline Newcombe, lived. The house, Coriyule can still be seen. From Anglesea to Warrnambool the Great Ocean Road hugs the steep cliffs high above the pounding sea. The road passes through holiday towns, with long almost deserted beaches in between. You can visit the Otways, famous for its untamed bushland and native birdlife. Keep your eyes open for the colourful king and queen parrots, as well as the sulphur crested cockatoo and the galah. Some of the camping grounds in these towns (such as Wye River) overlook the sea. At Port Campbell walk down the cliff face at Loch Ard Gorge and on to the beach (there are steps). Visit Thunder Cave where you can listen to the roaring of the ocean as though it were some vast force inside you. And look down into the green water of the Blow Hole which has burrowed its way inland. If it is Easter you can attend the Port Fairy Folk Festival and listen to the diversity of music, and perhaps you'll catch Judy Small, or Betty Little, or one of Australia's many women folk artists in concert. If it is September, drive on to Warrnambool and attend the events taking place as part of the annual Warrnambool Women's Arts Festival.

Wilson's Promontory, Vic

On the way to Wilson's Promontory you can visit Philip Island to see the fairy penguins come ashore at sunset. In summer, expect to share the show with thousands of others. Wilson's Promontory is a popular camping holiday site and there are permanent tents, caravans and cabins available. If you want to get away from the crowds then head off on the round trip bushwalk beginning with Sealers Cove. If you allow about four days for the walk you will pass through a range of ecosystems, including sclerophyll forest, beaches and dune scrubland. You'll possibly be visited by the local wombat at Sealer's Cove, so hang your food above ground. If you hear a loud heavy breathing noise in the night here or elsewhere, it's probably just the possums. If you don't do the walk, visit Squeaky Beach and hear the squeak of your footsteps on the sand. Gippsland is also the base for a range of women's activities. In East Gippsland there is a Rural Women's Festival each year. To find out where it is contact the Women's Health Centre in Sale. In 1993 a Lesbian Camp was held.

Central Victoria
There are many towns in this region that are popular with visitors. Daylesford and Hepburn Springs are famous for their spa baths, cafes and historic buildings. Not far away is Blackwood where you can follow a bushwalk following horizontal water races, based on the surveys made by a Frenchwoman, Madame Pauline Bonn Ford, in the 1850s. Shaw's Lake to Sweet's Lookout follows one of these water races.

Maria Island, Tas
Off the east coast of Tasmania, Maria Island is lovely to visit in the summer. There are no cars on the island and the only buildings are relics of a nineteenth-century settlement built with convict labour. The main camping area is shared with wallabies, cape barren geese, and curious possums who will rip holes in your tent if you leave apples and the like in corners. There are several walks you can take up to the peak, or to beaches further afield. But you'll need to carry food and water with you as there are no shops.

Australian Snowfields, Vic and NSW
Extending from Mt Baw Baw in the south, just an hour outside Melbourne to Kosciusko in NSW, skiing in Australia is quite a different experience. For downhill skiing the developed resorts of Mt Buller, Mt Hotham, Falls Creek, Mt Buffalo (all in Victoria) Perisher, Smiggins Holes, Charlotte's Pass and Thredbo (in NSW) give a range of skiing options. The official skiing season begins on the Queen's Birthday Weekend (nearest to 12 June) and ends in late September. Australian ski-fields on the lower slopes run between stands of snowgum – broadleafed, squat trees with ghostly silver-grey foliage. Cross-country skiing is also popular and there is access to these areas from most of the downhill resorts. In addition some areas are restricted to cross-country skiing, among them are Mt Donna Buang, Mt Bogong and Mt Townsend. The high country is a cool place to visit during the heat of summer when you can stand near a waterfall, take a horse trekking tour across the Bogong High Plains, bushwalk the tracks near Mt Kosciusko, or drive the scenic, but rough, road from Cooma to Suggan Buggan and the Snowy Mountain River in Gippsland. The high

country can turn unpredictably cold, even in summer. It takes only one blizzard to die of hypothermia. BLIZZARDS CAN AND DO OCCUR EVEN IN MID-SUMMER, so make sure you have warm and waterproof clothing (see Simmons, Bellamy and Whitebeach).

The Riverina, NSW

The country bordering the Murray and the Murrumbidgee River plains in southern NSW comprises the Riverina. A rich agricultural area, the produce is as varied as the country. North of the Murray, from Griffith to Leeton and Narrandera is the Murrumbidgee Irrigation Area, an area where soft fruits, grapes, rice and sunflowers are grown. Further north, where it is drier, the land gives way to sheep, wheat, oats and barley farming, with occasional pockets of cattle, lucerne, sorghum, millet and other cash crops. In the western part of the Riverina the land is flat, parts of it covered with stands of native pine, the callitris (also common in the Flinders Ranges). To the east are Tumut in the mountains and the Snowy Mountain Hydro-electric scheme, and Lake Hume near Albury where you can go boating and waterskiing. In Wagga Wagga you will find readings to attend run by Wagga Wagga Writers Writers, and Charles Sturt University may be hosting some cultural or scholarly event. The Murrumbidgee and other rivers are safe to swim in, providing you take the usual precautions of not diving into unknown waters, keep an eye out for snags (branches just below the water's surface), and fast currents. In Wagga and other places there are river beaches.

354

Rosa Safransky

BLUME, THE BORGIA OF CHAPEL STREET

I'm not crying about Felix's wedding. I don't know why I'm crying as I walk from one end of Orchid Street to the other. It will take a million years before I set foot in Horowitz Wedding Receptions again. The bridal couple go straight to Hawaii after the wedding. Honolulu has one of only four kosher restaurants in the world pure enough for Felix to eat at. The other three are in Detroit, Chicago and New York. He can get food poisoning!

I'm crying not because the glare from my father's suit outdazzles the spotlights on the ceiling or because my aunt Blume is inspecting the hems, sleeves and linings of the wedding guests with a magnifying glass. Why she needs a magnifying glass when her x-ray vision will do and why does she ask questions when she already knows all the answers, like who will be the father of my sister Sylvia's future children.

'I wish I'd bought a fly-swatter' Sylvia says.

The seating arrangements at the table for the desperately unmarried are a tribute to Blume's devious match-making skills. Felix's wedding speech is even piped into the toilets where a framed portrait of a bride smiles vacantly at a peach coloured wall. Does Felix really have to thank Blume for getting up before dawn every day of his life to clean the house? Or his bride's cousins for being his bride's cousins and his aunt for being his aunt and his cousins for being his cousins? Felix's best friend turns to Sylvia and says,

'I didn't know he had any.'

It's all Blume's fault. Blume is to blame for the twenty-five year feud where Emil tore the light sockets from the wall and 'Maurice of Paris' went kaput. People don't lock themselves in rooms and write about their aunts for nothing. I'm going to denounce Blume in the Melbourne Town Hall. She's going to make headlines in all the Sunday papers, every green luminous sequin. Fat, scaly, Blume the prune. Blume is the world expert on boiled chicken and the fastest tongue in Chapel Street. Blume has survived all my murder attempts. Even the mirror on her prized Russian birch dressing table refused to crack when she looked into it and when her cutlery somersaulted to the ceiling after I hypnotised it, Blume left the dinner table without a scratch. My father and Blume are always locked in hand to hand combat over the family dress factory. Blume's guerilla tactics could net her a job in the Defence Department. Her sabotage skills are the type that de-stabilise governments. Machiavelli could take lessons from her. Blume, the Borgia of Chapel Street. One day my father swears, he will drown Blume in one of her saucepans of rendered chicken fat. Till then, he heaves a theatrical sigh, he has no option but to put up with her.

It's always been like that. Why did my uncle Emil marry Blume and produce my cousin Felix, the dentist? An active death wish. My mother's family is prone to bouts of suicide. When a relative discovered he couldn't have children, he gassed himself. Which relative? No-one knows.

'Why not adopt?'

'He preferred to stick his head in the oven.'

'Well there isn't much time left. The way this life's been, the next one can't be much worse.' Emil laughs as we embrace in the carpark outside the Prahran market. What's in the brown paper packages he's always carrying? Heroin? Cocaine? Marijuana? No wonder Emil's always floating. His feet never touch the ground.

'How's Sylvia?' Emil asks.

Emil thinks Sylvia's still in plaits but she's a middle management executive who takes sailing lessons. My sister Sylvia and the yacht alone on Port Phillip Bay and Yup-Yup, her depressed labrador, the product of a broken home.

'Has Sylvia got a boyfriend?'

'Do cats miaouw? Do birds fly? Thousands. How's Felix?'

'Good news!' Emil's face lights up, 'Felix is getting married. Don't worry, there's no engagement party. He's already bought the house. Anyway, it wasn't love at first sight. She's a dental technician, he's a dentist. And her two brothers are doctors.' What, Felix is marrying them too?

'Mazel Tov!' I congratulate Felix, my mouth stuffed full of cotton wool. He switches on the drill and detonates my upper right molar. Instruments of torture protrude from every drawer. A 3-D poster of a tooth with terrible gum disease is stuck to the door. Who cares if Felix is a drug pedlar? He's dealing in synthetic drugs. He's growing plastic marijuana on the front lawn. My mother should never have given him that chemistry set for his bar-mitzvah. Felix's bar-mitzvah. While my father prowls around the house like Napoleon on Elba, my mother, Sylvia and me step into enemy territory, the Zelig's flat. A chemistry set is handed over, fruit bon-bons and roasted almonds are passed around. The torture session over, we leave. A week later, Felix blows a hole through the Zelig's ceiling. It collapsed on them while they were watching TV. Emil grabs Felix and drags him through the smouldering ruins. Blume wails out the front window, down the back staircase, onto the street ten floors below.

'Lay one hand on my treasure's head and I'll jump!'

'J-U-M-P!'

Felix locked himself in the bathroom. Emil called the fire-brigade, up went the extension ladder and Felix and the fire-man leaped through the flames into a net strategically placed in the middle of the street. Is it any wonder Felix became a dentist?

If only God would strike that photographer pushing that video camera into my face, dead. A piano accordion plays while the bride stands stiff with fear. Candles under the wedding canopy beam like lasers. The canopy is in the carpark of Horowitz Wedding Receptions. Why get married there? It's kosher. Six rabbis dance. Men do handsprings. Musicians play. Men dance one circle, women the other. The rabbi, a whale of a man, sits in front of a bread loaf, the size of a whale.

'At least Felix isn't gay,' my father mutters.

I'm crying because my mother and Emil have embraced. It's taken twenty-five years. Emil's hand trembles in mine as Blume sends us one of her search and destroy smiles. Does this cameraman work for the Gestapo? Is he taking x-rays? Are those floodlights probing into the pores of my skin really necessary for Blume's Happy Snaps? Each time I choke my tears back, more come racing out. He's even filming Emil wandering in a daze around the dance floor. Emil's face is pale and he looks as if he's in shock as Felix and his bride execute the wedding waltz. Can that be a waltz? Felix is wearing 18 pound boots. His legs are stiffened by steel struts. He picks his new wife up like a feather and straps her to the banquet table. His eyelids are coated with wax, a black line contorted by wire clamps opens as if it were his mouth. Felix kisses his bride and the banquet table slowly rises to the ceiling. 100,000 megavolts charge through her veins. One look at Felix and I can see the Dark Side of Dentistry. And that wedding cake. Why did Blume ask the caterers to do it in black? Felix produces a scalpel and slices right through it.

The cake was poisoned. It had to be the cake. Emil's heart stopped beating. It just gave up. There isn't a single tear on Blume's face. Her face is a mask. But is this Blume's house or Castle Dracula? It's just suburbia, not Transylvannia. Blume stands in the kitchen with the toaster and the bright blue concentration camp number on her arm.

'Emil Zelig was a quiet man,' Rabbi Wolfberg says, 'he loved his son and his wife.'

Was that why Emil rarely left the factory and disconnected the phone to boot? Emil wasn't quiet, he was invisible. His head trembled in the same way as my mother's. In looks they could have been twins. My mother walks beside Blume and Felix. Her head is covered in black lace. We walk to the grave, everyone in step together on the hard clay soil. Emil and my mother escaped from the Warsaw Ghetto and survived the war together hiding in the Polish forests. After we migrated to Australia, we all lived in the same house for six years. In the factory I always ran to Emil for a chocolate frog and a Coca-Cola. I still remember the factory, squeezing in between the dresses, then launching myself across the room, using the dress rack like a scooter. The factory was split in two. Downstairs was my father's territory, the non-smoking section, upstairs belonged to my uncle and was officially, the smoking area. The mantel radio talked and talked. Sometimes it sang. Smoke swirled around Emil's head as he bent over his patterns, straightening layers of fabric before he switched on the electric cutters and dynamited through them. Ash fell from his cigarette holder onto the scraps that covered the floor. Ash burnt holes in the red vinyl and coated the collection of ancient Coca-Cola bottles on the table at the top of the stairs. Dust and spider webs covered the wallpaper peeling off the walls. Dust covered the window looking onto the street. When Emil got engaged to Blume, the party was held in our dining room and the food was set out on card tables in my uncle's bedroom. Shortly before he moved out of the house, Emil solemnly presented me with a table-tennis set. But Rabbi Wolfberg doesn't have time to chat. He's in a hurry. He has to speak faster. His driver's got the engine running. A line forms at the graveside. The mourners express their condolences and kiss Blume and Felix. I can't kiss Blume. I avert my face from hers. My father's cap is jammed down tight over his forehead. His eyes are wet with tears. Sometimes I see Felix jogging along Elwood beach at night. He runs silently past hot dog stands, gelati trucks, youths with glistening muscles, girls in skin tight bathing suits with permed wet hair dancing in loose ringlets around their necks. Felix was married for eight weeks then went back to Blume. I don't write about family trees, I write about twigs and splinters.

Sara Dowse

CANBERRA

Canberra is a curious place. I have lived in Australia's capital for twenty-three years now and I still find it something of a paradox. The beauty of its natural setting seems at odds with the weighty angularity of many of its buildings. Official Canberra has been starkly European and male, but frequently this has been offset or, indeed, subverted by opposing forces. These are often not as readily visible as the phallic monuments that tend to dominate the skyline, but they are there. The first white explorers were unsure whether there were any natives in the region. Not a single Aborigine was encountered but signs of them were evident. Since then the tribes have gone. But their hidden legacy is everywhere: in the softly undulating hills; in the huge moths that they hunted that swarm down from the mountains each November to discombobulate the lighting and the air-conditioning in the brand new parliament house; in the campsites discovered in the region; in the names of streets and suburbs and the name of the city itself.

The Aborigines of the region were the Ngunawal, the Ngarigo, the Wiradthuri, Walgala, Kurnai and Birdhawal. The name Canberra is said to come from *nganbra* – the Ngunawal word for the region, which has been translated as 'meeting place'. Corroboree Park in Ainslie, one of Canberra's inner northern suburbs, is said to mark the spot where local tribes gathered annually, so some find the name particularly appropriate for the site of our present, parliamentary gatherings. But Corroboree Park is situated in a hollow between Mount Ainslie and Mount Pleasant, and some say that *nganbra* actually means 'resting place', the space between the earth's two breasts.

The site of Australia's capital was chosen in 1909, eight years after the six British colonies came together to form a nation. The parliamentarians who chose the site had little appreciation of the Aboriginal heritage of the region, or its womanly orientation. It is only comparatively recently that we have come to know something about the culture of the local people. One of the most striking of its features is how it reverses some of the oldest symbols of European patriarchy. The source of life is the earth, not the sky, or a supernatural being which resides in it. The sun that warms the earth is female, the cold moon is male. In the origin myths of southeastern Australia it is the earth who gives birth to man, who then, in the shape of the eaglehawk takes an emu for his wife. The emu bears the crow: the crow and the eaglehawk are the two great male totems, each vying for the sacred emu.

It is interesting that Australia's founding fathers took the emu for their own. She leans with a proud puffed chest on the left, or sinister, side of the Australian coat of arms, smiling across the decorative shield at the better-known kangaroo. You see this coat of arms frequently in Canberra: it graces the government stationery and many public buildings, including the old 'provisional' parliament house built to accommodate the move from Melbourne in 1927 and the new one, built for the 1988 bicentennial anniversary of British conquest. This coat of arms, a quaint anachronism hung over from the Crusades and Europe's feudal patriarchy, is ubiquitous, so hardly noticed. But I have been watching the emu. How subversively female she is, with her large eyes and long slender legs under her wide feathered skirt. Sometimes she has a stern look, at other times a cheeky smile, and she has come to symbolise for me the hard-won conviction that everything in this world harbours the potential for its opposite.

Against all odds, women have provided much of the spirit of this city of office towers. Its name is even pronounced the way it is because of a woman. Neither its spelling nor its pronunciation were fixed until 1913, when an official naming ceremony was held on Camp Hill, near where

the old parliament house now stands. At noon on the 12th of March Lady Denham, wife of the British viceroy, opened a small gold case, removed the slip of paper inside and read out in a clear, aristocratic voice to the assembled dignitaries, 'I name the capital of Australia Can/b'ra', and so it has been ever since. This is what appears in all the history books. What they don't say is that Lady Denham was a rather unconventional young woman for her time and station. Only in the most exclusive circles was it known that the viceroy's wife was a smoker; and the gold case, a gift to her excellency from the nation, was in fact a cigarette case.

The world-wide competition for the design of the new capital was won by the Chicago architect Walter Burley Griffin. The Griffin plan was distinguished by its sensitive regard for the terrain and an attempt to depart from the strict grid plan that characterised many modern cities. It relied instead on a series of arcs and circles intersecting a central triangle. Despite the passage of time and Griffin's differences with the government in the early days of the capital's construction, the plan has been largely adhered to. The lake created in the centre of the city by damming the Molonglo River over the summer of 1963–64 was named Lake Burley Griffin. There are those, however, who claim that the design was not the work of Walter but of his wife, Marion Mahony Griffin, who was also an architect. There is no way of proving this, but on the evidence it seems probable that the work was at least a collaboration. Certainly the drawings that won the competition were hers, and they are on display at the Regatta Point exhibition centre on the shores of the lake.

The lives of women in the early days of the capital have never been adequately recorded, though women were significant in establishing a community out of a group of disgruntled public servants and their families who were transferred from Melbourne when parliament finally moved here in 1927. The provisional parliament house on the slope of Camp Hill was ready, as were the two secretariat buildings, West Block and East Block, that were to house the public service. There was little else. One commentator reports that these settlers, who compared themselves to the convict immigrants of 1788, lived in houses that looked to an early resident 'like toy bricks on an open plain', or in government hostels that were run a bit like boarding schools. For some time the sale of alcohol was prohibited in the capital territory. The absence of alcohol may have contributed to an emphasis on family life, but local women write of the difficulties of other kinds of absence. Government-supplied houses were small, cold and lacking in the kind of amenities women find essential but are often overlooked by male planners. Everything – gardens, schools, libraries, baby health clinics, theatres, cinemas had to be built from scratch. At least one woman ran English classes in her home for the large number of European migrants who came here after the war. An active chapter of the National Council of Women was instrumental in securing milk for the schools, I'm told, and conducted a survey into housing needs which led to design improvements in government-supplied homes. After a time the city which had been considered a hardship post became a pleasant, even privileged place to live in, and Australians outside Canberra began to envy and deride what they saw as its comfortable insularity.

The suburban ethos lay at the heart of the city. People lived out rigidly defined gender roles. These were institutionalised in the policies and practices of the principal and dominant employer, the Commonwealth Public Service. Of course, many women worked for the government: their services as clerical workers were in great demand in this booming white-collar industry. But legislation underpinning the public service and the regulations flowing from it ensured that most women occupied low-status, low-paid, temporary jobs. It wasn't until 1966 that the infamous marriage bar requiring all permanent female employees to resign upon marriage was lifted.

After that women began a slow if problematic climb up the hierarchy into the senior ranks of the service. The lifting of the marriage bar and subsequent reforms in the 1970s and early 1980s significantly expanded women's career prospects in government service. This process was accelerated by the rapid development of special women's bureaucratic machinery.

The Australian experience of feminist interaction with the state merits special attention. In the fifteen years between 1972 and 1987 there was a proliferation of various forms of women's bureaucracies at both state and federal level in the Australian federal system. The impetus came from the groundswell for social change that brought in a Labor government in 1972, the first of its kind in 23 years and, in retrospect, probably the most reform-minded federal government in Australia's history. The fact that this election coincided with the revitalisation of Australian feminism is significant. This particular conjunction – between the burgeoning of the second wave of feminism on the one hand and the coming to office of a democratic socialist government on the other – was unique, and was to shape Australian feminists' attitudes to the state and influence Australian feminist strategies for years to come.

Canberra was at the centre of this. Because of its proximity to parliament and the relatively easy access to its members, the local women's movement was extremely active in the lead-up to the 1972 election. Members of the local Women's Electoral Lobby, an organisation set up nationally to capitalise on politicians' fear of the volatility of the women's vote, played a key role in interviewing sitting members and publishing the results. The Australian Labor Party had traditionally polled poorly among women, who were believed to be more conservative than the male electorate. But the

1972 campaign made Labor stalwarts think this could change. In April 1973 a Canberra philosophy tutor, Elizabeth Reid, was appointed the first women's advisor to an Australian Prime Minister. The following year machinery was set up within the prime minister's department in West Block to provide additional administrative support. This early unit also developed a policy advising capacity and began monitoring all government policy for its impact on women. Within two years a network of women's units in key government departments was established, with the prime minister's unit at its head. This special type of machinery, designed to integrate feminist concerns and insights with the development of mainstream policy, has been the peculiarly Australian contribution to the public administration of women's affairs.

The model first devised at the federal level had been subsequently replicated in every state and territory, and has survived several government changes. It has proved remarkably effective for initiating and maintaining a range of government services for women – child care, shelters, information services, health centres, rape crisis and domestic violence centres – perhaps unparalleled in the world. And this at a time when the public sector generally has been contracting.

It is an impressive achievement, which is attracting attention among feminists and students of public administration outside Australia. But over the last decade the ideology of economic rationalism has bitten deeper into the public service, and 'femocrats', as these feminist bureaucrats have been dubbed, have felt increasingly uneasy. Australia has had a long-standing tradition of public sector enterprise and support. As long as this tradition held it was generally agreed, even among women who believed that femocrats themselves might be co-opted, that substantial benefits for women could be gained by operating through the state. But this tradition has been systematically eroded, and femocrats find themselves working harder and harder for what can be described at best as minimal and at worst as doubtful outcomes. As the state's aims have become increasingly antithetical to feminist ones the femocrats' dilemma has sharpened.

At the same time the visibility of women has grown, owing in some measure to the efforts of femocrats themselves. The cultural landscape has changed, so much so that it is hard to remember when you never heard a woman read the news, never saw a woman drive a bus, or lead a political party. Yet this was the case as little as fifteen years ago. These are not the sorts of things women talk about much around the tables at Tilley's Cafe in the inner northern suburb of Lyneham; they are taken for granted. Much as Tilley's itself is, now that the community has accepted it. But even five years ago, this special cafe which was set up to provide a safe, comfortable yet lively alternative for women wanting a drink after work without being hassled by men, was the subject of raging controversy.

Today, having made its point, it is open to men as well as women, but it is still a bar where women predominate.

There are other ways in which women broke ground in Canberra. Because of its peculiar concentration of well-educated, independent women and the high female participation rate, certain themes have been played out here sooner than they may have been elsewhere. The problems of the corporate woman, for example, juggling career with family responsibilities, were encountered by women earlier here due to the creation of new government positions in the 1970s. Likewise, single employed women choosing to have children seemed at one time to be a Canberra phenomenon. The range of services combined with the relative compactness of the city made a new set of options possible. These, in turn, threw into high relief a whole new set of problems. As the 1980s proceeded these issues began to be expressed in the wider Australian community as women began playing a more dynamic role in the arts.

Post-feminist? There are those here too who like to think that since so much has been done there is little more to bother with. As a writer I am the last person to say that cultural manifestations are unimportant, but they can be misleading. While increasing numbers of women are assuming positions of leadership and some are entering occupations once considered the preserves of men, and women of my daughter's generation have vastly different aspirations and expectations from those my contemporaries had in the 1950s and 1960s, a closer look leaves me feeling less complacent. Though something like 70 per cent of the new jobs created over the last eight years have gone to women, most of these have been casual, with no security, benefits or opportunity for advancement. Because of the central arbitration system, Australian women are closer to reaching wage equity with men than their sisters overseas, but women here still earn only three-quarters of what men do. The contraction of the public sector, where many women have found full-time employment in the past, is seriously affecting opportunities and conditions. And though it is hard to know whether better facilities for coping with rape and domestic violence are responsible for an increase in their recorded incidence, or whether additional stresses of changing roles are leading to an escalation of these crimes, their viciousness and the frequency of their occurrence gives pause. In Canberra alone, which some might view as a kind of middle-class suburban paradise, half of the police calls are for domestic violence and these are the calls the police themselves consider the most dangerous.

The conclusion to draw from this is that for all our gains, real change, lasting change is not going to be easy. We may never go back to the discrimination and repression Australian women suffered a generation ago; our consciousness has been raised too much and there have been too many legal changes promoting our rights. But the economic doctrines that currently prevail threaten to undermine the material basis for our advancement. Drastic government funding cuts are affecting schools, hospitals, universities and other key institutions and programs which have assisted women over the past twenty years. After the advent of self-government in 1989 we in the Australian Capital Territory have been affected by a drastically reduced local budget and, for the moment, a government that is not as sensitive to issues of social justice as it could be.

But I am not disheartened. People here as elsewhere are becoming disillusioned with the politics of greed. With greater awareness of the importance of things like the environment and a tradition of a caring public service, Canberra's special qualities will be increasingly appreciated, and more of us will be working to preserve them.

For all my attempts, it is not possible for me to be objective about Canberra. The light, the lake, those hills are part of me now. For someone who twenty-three years ago had been used to the bustle of big cities, at times my attachment has been hard to explain. Yet when I think of it Canberra has been the place where horizons opened for me, and perhaps its very newness, the thing that some people find disconcerting, has been its attraction. It has been the setting for innovation and creation – in my personal life, in my political engagement, and in my writing. But this feeling of newness, the sense of a tabula rasa, is of course illusory. I only have to look closely again at the coat of arms I mentioned in the beginning to remember that this city like any other has a wealth of associations, many stretching deep into the unrecorded past. I see the emu and the centuries of otherness which she suggests, and sometimes I even imagine she is winking.

Kaye Johnston

THE REVOLUTIONARY NATURE OF LESBIAN ORGANIC GARDENING

Lesbians who develop community, practise lesbian feminist politics, involve themselves in caring for the environment, produce wholesome food and happy animals, can establish a way of life which fits in with the natural environment rather than exploiting and destroying it, and offer heteropatriarchy a model for social change. This is a grass roots model, encompassing a number of ideas which can be practised by lesbians, who are at the margins of society. It is revolutionary because it can shift the status quo. Heteropatriarchy can consider the examples set by lesbians who combine the above areas – feminism, environmentalism, animal liberation, building lesbian community and culture, and even population control. This is not just socialism or eco-feminism, it is more: it is an assemblage of ideas which work together to form a coherent value system.

Heteropatriarchy already has to consider environmental aspects for sustainable development. The profit motive hasn't changed, but the ability to create profit in environmentally damaging ways is reduced. It becomes more profitable to be sustainable. Heteropatriarchy can be transformed.

Our own experience can be seen as an example of how ideas develop when put into practise. We developed Moonraker Farm as an organic/permaculture farm,[1] but we did not set out with a definite plan in mind. We did work according to a set of specific values, and we have become aware that our work is based on five broad principles, which constitute our own integrated political value system.

The farm now produces more food than we can manage, and we have made lesbian feminist friends throughout Australia and all over the world. We have had the enormous satisfaction of being able to put our beliefs into practice. The process itself is important: learning by observation over time, making mistakes, and learning new ways.

Since 1985, Andrea Lofthouse and myself have developed Moonraker Farm as an organic/permaculture farm, and many lesbians from all over the world have come to visit and to work here under the 'Lesbians On Organic Farms As Helpers' (LOOFAH) scheme. They come to meet Australian lesbians, to observe our lifestyle, and to learn about organic gardening. In return, we hear the lesbian news (current oral herstory) from Germany, Britain, the US, etc. Andrea and I have become part of a global network, the aim of which is to build and maintain a visible lesbian culture. It is exciting to realise that we are part of a continuous revolutionary movement.

We bought Moonraker Farm in 1985 after searching for three years, unsure of what to look for. We didn't plan to develop land by growing traditional crops or running animals. Our aim was to leave the city – the pollution, the crowding, twenty years of full-time work and burnout.

We left Sydney in 1984, but before we moved to the farm, we lived at Austinmer, north of Wollongong, for 18 months. On our large block of land, we started a vegetable garden, and kept chooks, ducks and geese. But there were problems. A neighbour complained to the local council about the noise of the geese. And we managed to fill up the suburban block in no time. We knew that we had to find something bigger and more rural.

We looked at everything for sale in Kangaroo Valley (on the South Coast of NSW). It had been a favourite place of mine for many years. It has the security of mountains all round, lush green grass, forests, and a mystical quality which is enticing. We nearly drove the estate agent crazy. We considered: five acres with house, five acres with no house, 100 acres with water and no house . . . Finally we settled for 37 acres/15 hectares of steeply sloping land, facing north west so that it gets full sun all day, and with a spring of pure water.

Behind the house, the land slopes steeply upward towards the east, most of it covered with re-growth eucalyptus with pockets of rain forest and red cedar. It had been cleared by previous owners, and used as a dry run for cows.[2] The soil is volcanic, and is rich in minerals and organic matter – perfect for horticulture.

Along with the farm came the lease of a cafe in the town of Berry which is on the Pacific Highway near the coast. The cafe provided a cash flow during the time we were deciding what to do with the land. We took over both cafe and farm just before Christmas, 1985. We were very busy.

When we moved in at the farm, we found ourselves in charge of three cows, and some ducks and chooks[3] in a broken-down poultry house. On our first night, we were woken by roosters crowing at three a.m., perched underneath our bedroom. So the first job was to repair the hen-house and train the chooks to use it. We added more cows, some horses, some sheep and a goat.

Andrea had already had some experience of living in the country, in Victoria, when she had kept chooks and grown vegetables. I had never lived in the country and had no farming experience. I grew up in inner city Sydney. My parents did keep chooks and grow vegies, in St Peters, just after the war, and I learned about self-sufficiency from them. But later, when we moved to the western suburbs, chooks and vegies were considered 'not nice'. People in suburbia grew exotic ornamentals.

On the farm, we discovered a large area which had once been a vegetable garden. When we moved in, it had been covered with weeds two metres high. We also came upon a huge grapefruit tree after two years of slow clearing, our reward for copping all those nettle stings! The goat did the initial clearing for us, and then we would do one small section at a time, using newspaper and roofing iron to smother the weeds.

Every day, we took the vegetables and herbs we grew to the cafe, for salads in summer and soups in winter. Some customers thought the salads were weird. One man asked me if the radicchio leaf was from a coral tree! Most customers appreciated our efforts to use home-grown produce, including bush tucker[4] like lilly pilly fruit, flowers such as borage, and many different kinds of mint. Some were curious, and this led to lots of discussion. I began potting herbs and other plants to sell at the cafe.

I read everything I could on organic gardening. We developed an interest in permaculture, which is particularly suited to hilly areas, as we had little flat land which could be cultivated. We planted many fruit and nut trees and other perennial edible plants, designing the food areas around the chooks and ducks. We built chook runs which doubled as vegetable gardens. The chooks clean up after the annual vegetables, eating insects and fertilising in the process. Meanwhile, another run is shut off from the chooks, and prepared and planted. There are five of these runs in constant rotation. In the duck and geese compound, we planted an intensive orchard with a permanent undercover of living mulch, consisting of insecticidal plants like fennel, parsnips, radishes and nasturtiums. Fences went up everywhere, providing vertical spaces on which to grow passionfruit, chokos, beans and snow peas. During the whole year we grow nitrogen-producing legumes.

Since 1990, the farm has been certified as an organic farm by the National Association for Sustainable Agriculture Australia (NASAA).

For three and a half years, we managed to run the cafe as well as the farm. We would have days off in the middle of the week, except in the school holidays. And we employed women to work with us. But we did most of the organising, cooking and cleaning. Andrea also continued to work on the second edition of her book, *Who's Who of Australian Women*, while I studied Horticulture at Wollongong Technical College. We both also worked as part-time teachers at the local TAFE[5] college.

We agreed that living in the country was wonderful. We had no regrets at leaving the city. We had fresh air, ample open space and great natural beauty around us, enough work, and an income. But we missed the network of feminists and lesbian feminists from Sydney and Wollongong.

In Sydney, for example, we had belonged to the Sydney Women Against Rape Collective (SWARC). In April 1983, we participated in the SWARC demonstration in remembrance of all women raped in wars. Along with 167 other women, we were arrested just before the 'official' (i.e. men's) Anzac Day[6] march, and charged with 'serious alarm and affront'. For some years after, SWARC women continued to march on

Anzac Day in memory of women raped in war. Those were exciting times.

In Wollongong, we were part of the Wollongong Women's Performing Group (WWPG) with, among others, Sue Edmonds, Cathy Bloch and Ruth Thompson. As a collective, we all developed, wrote and acted in women-only shows.

However, we eventually developed a network in the area. Our involvement with WWPG continued with women's music nights at the cafe. These music nights have been described as a form of lesbian feminist community development. On these nights, we would close the cafe to the public, and put up a sign saying 'Private Function'. Some of the general public obviously couldn't read. Despite the notice, they would still wander in on their way from the pub,[7] looking for a hamburger. They would then be persuaded to wander out again, never knowing why there was no food for sale, and wondering why the shop was packed with women!

Many women performed, read poetry, sang, played music, put on skits.[8] Some were well-known, like the singing group, 'Mixed Bag' (Sue Edmonds and Lioba Rist). But for many it was their first performance. Among the most memorable items for me were Vegetable Liberation and The Siege of Susan – An Opera (both written by Andrea, myself, Lynne Dooley and Lynne Keevers).

We also helped establish a lesbian support group in Nowra. We met a wide network of country lesbians. Our social life expanded and we no longer felt isolated.

Our Lesbians On Organic Farms As Helpers (LOOFAH) scheme also helped overcome our isolation. The idea started when we were visited by two lesbians from Minnesota, who came and stayed at the farm. In exchange for our hospitality, they did some work for us and looked after the farm while we took a break in Sydney. This useful exchange gave birth to the LOOFAH idea. We advertise it regularly in *Lesbian Network*,[9] and we have had a stream of lesbian visitors ever since. The LOOFAHs give us three hours work a day in exchange for accommodation.

Enquiries about LOOFAHs, and lesbians visiting under the scheme, come from all over the world. Two Scottish lesbians heard about us from friends who wrote to them from the US. They came straight from a northern winter, and struggled to work in our unaccustomed summer heat. They insisted on wearing long sleeves and more clothes than necessary to protect themselves from our insects. One day, while clearing weeds, they were frightened by an equally frightened bandicoot[10] mother who jumped out at them clutching her baby. They came running to the house exclaiming that they had been attacked by 'wee beasties'.

A Canadian lesbian carpenter wrote asking if she could bring her cat.

I had to write back and tell her that her carpentry skills were welcome, but not the cat! We had enough animals of our own, and the cat would have had to spend a long time in quarantine. It seems that many North Americans are unaware of how far away Australia is, and even where it is.

One woman who visited us from Leeds had seen our LOOFAH advertisement in a copy of *Lesbian Network* in England. One of the tasks she helped us with one night was to disengage an eight foot long diamond python from around the neck of a chook. The next day she carried it across the creek for us, in a hessian bag, and released it in the bush. I'm sure she'll never forget the blood-curdling screams – both mine and the chook's.

Since 1990, we have held an annual festival at the farm. Artists, such as Suzanne Bellamy, exhibit and sell their work. We are entertained by the Swing Sisters, a local women's jazz band. We conduct guided tours of the garden and explain the permaculture system. One feature of the 1991 festival was a 'Grand Parade' of prize-winning farm animals and visitors. The 'Parade' was a rather strange one, because prizes were given for the animal who looked most like its owner, and the prizes had to be given back! Over one hundred women attended in 1991 and in spite of bad weather, nearly as many in 1992.

From early 1992, a monthly lesbian writers' group has met at the farm. Our aims are to get published and to support each other. The highlight of the day is the literary lunch to which we all contribute. We eat on the verandah in the sun, overlooking the flower garden.

Andrea and I sometimes dream of an easier life, with fewer animals, and without the constant struggle with the jungle-like growth which threatens to engulf the house. We would also like to live near the sea. But every year more species of fruit and vegetables become available, with the promise of yet more next season. This encourages us to continue, as do the positive reactions we get from students, LOOFAHs and visitors when we explain Moonraker Farm.

Notes
1. Permaculture is a holistic approach to living, where sustainable systems are designed to reduce energy inputs and damage to the environment. Animals, plants and people live together in harmony in systems that are economically viable. Organic Gardening is gardening without synthetic pesticides and fertilizers. Traditional principles of gardening are followed, such as crop rotation, companion planting, composting, and creating healthy fertile soil full of earthworms and micro-organisms.
2. Usually rough, hilly country not suitable for dairy cows but used for raising a few steers or calves.
3. Australian slang for chickens
4. Phrase originally derived from the Aboriginal people, now generally used, for food gathered from the wild, not cultivated.

5. Technical and Further Education; adult education college where students study trade subjects or complete their education.
6. Australian and New Zealand Army Corps. This day commemorates Australia's part in several wars. Militaristic ceremonies and marches take place all over Australia; a day of maudlin machismo, drunkenness, and myth-making and re-writing of the past.
7. Slang for hotel; main function is sale of alcoholic drinks.
8. Short comedy performances; short plays.
9. National magazine for lesbians which aims to disseminate information of relevance to lesbians and provide a contact network for them.
10. Australian marsupial, furry with a long snout.

References

Margaret Barrett. 1986. *The Edna Walling Book of Australian Garden Design*. Melbourne: Anne O'Donovan.

P. Bennett. 1984. *Organic Gardening*. Sydney: ANZ Book Co.

J. Cheney. 1985. *Lesbian Land*. Minnesota: Word Weavers.

M. Cheney. 1975. *Meanwhile Farm*. California: Les Femmes.

J. French. 1989. *Organic Gardening in Australia*. Sydney: Reed.

Sarah Hoagland. 1989. *Lesbian Ethics*. California: Institute of Lesbian Studies.

G. Lawrence. 1987. *Capitalism in the Countryside*. London: Pluto Press.

E. Mavor. 1974. *The Ladies of Llangollen*. Harmondsworth. Middlesex: Penguin Books.

Bill Mollison and D. Holmgren. 1984. *Permaculture One*. Queensland: Tagari.

Bill Mollison. 1984. *Permaculture Two*. Queensland: Tagari.

— 1988. *Permaculture: A Designer's Manual*. Queensland: Tagari.

— 1991. *Introduction to Permaculture*. Queensland: Tagari.

Dale Spender. 1982. *Women of Ideas and What Men Have Done to Them*. London: Routledge and Kegan Paul.

P. Watts. 1991. *Edna Walling and Her Gardens*. 2nd edition. Melbourne: Florilegium.

I wish to acknowledge the help and support freely given by Andrea Lofthouse in the production of this article.

Suzanne Bellamy

THE CREATIVE LANDSCAPE

I began my creative work life under the influence of radical feminism and the city. Both of these great forces in the 1970s nurtured many Australian women artists and writers struggling with the eternal paradox of creative freedom and commitment to political change. The city – in my case, Sydney – the anti-Vietnam war movement, the birth of women's liberation, extreme youth and an internationalist perspective, all tended to obscure any real consciousness of being 'Australian'. In practice, this meant for me a busy life as writer, artist, activist, teacher, working on women's liberation papers in Sydney, speeches, campaigns, posters, theatre, the fight for women's studies in the universities, the fight against rape, violence, and all the prisons of patriarchy. With very little money, one could survive, living in the tailend of a smug prosperous economy, freed from the expense of fashion and appearance by our new ideas, high on a marvellous optimism. The city was the locus for much of this, looking out to the rest of the planet more often than either inward or over one's shoulder to the earth I stood upon.

My mother had been born in Cobar, a rural copper town in the central west, from a long line of domestic servants, with uncertain and untraceable bloodlines and little control over their lives. Her mother packed her off to the city when she was twelve to work in the new factories, and she never looked over her shoulder after that. The heat and dust, no water and cruel men – these were all my mother told me about. Even today, in her 80s, she holds on to her urban life with a passion, uncomprehending of both her daughters, who live in the bush. I realize now that forgetting the past is my family's motto, making my own quest seem to them like sabotage. Amnesia and secrecy – a dubious inheritance.

A great change came towards the end of the 70s decade as I focused more deeply on my inner voices than the demands of the political community. Our collective visions of freedom and the end of patriarchy had led me to desire something more interior, something which might touch the chaotic core of my spirit, and unmask, for me at least, the stranger I harboured. Simple as it seems, I longed for the land, for more creative focus, less people, and a documented journey in words and clay free from ideologies.

I resigned my job at the University in 1979, travelled extensively in Europe and the USA in 1980, and by 1983 I had left Sydney to set up a clay and sculpture studio in the country. I had no idea what this would bring, beyond almost immediate relationship strain. Within three years, two lesbian partnerships broke under the difficulties of this experiment.

My commitment to staying with the journey inward was greater than all else, more fierce than the loss of human companionship and aloneness. Some force was unleashed which left my friends bewildered and my self out on the wild shore. I trusted only the land, the healing energies which opened up to me, my own spirit and the relentlessness of the process. From 1986 I lived alone on the farm, with my companion animals and the wombats, echidnas, snakes, kangaroos, tortoises, goannas, lizards and birds who approached and shared their territory. I made pots about them, gardened, cut wood, wrote in my journal, learned printmaking and chainsaw sculpture, walked and endured a journey of recovery.

It was very hard, cold, harsh and unrelenting. I would never have chosen it quite like this but I came to see it as a gift of life. We women of the late 20th century have been called to live out mysterious and miraculous lives, as wounded healers, ancestors of the new time, the time of our visions. Living day to day was anything but heroic, and my small ant-like steps kept me humble and grounded. Only now can I see the spiral force which, in taking me in and down, then spun me out into connection with other women and the planet, more forcefully than could have happened ten years earlier. How had this come to be?

Like many young artists, I had harboured a romantic fantasy about living for a time in a 'foreign' culture – a Greek village, the south of France, somewhere in the Aegean perhaps – somewhere strangeness in everyday life could shock me into knowledge of my own shape and my own voice. I dreamed of somewhere where I couldn't speak the language, where the community was indifferent to me. And then it happened, not in Greece or France, but near the village of Bredbo, NSW, Australia, a most unromantic destination. As a lesbian artist in the bush, I could not have been more alien, more unable to speak the language, than there. My test of exile began.

As a traveller in the landscape, I had already written about what I saw as our alienation from the land. In 1982, when this was written, it was deeply felt, but I was still an outsider looking in.

Women are so truly dispossessed. We have no sacred sites left, no landrights, no connection with place – and yet I feel a passionate connection with the Earth, and seem to be remembering. There are places in Australia and other countries which feel like my sacred sites, places where I feel timeless, overwhelmed by deep erotic connection, places which have flowed through my fingers into my work. I have stood and known of our connections with another time, another way of being, a deep nurturance – massive symphonic Silence.[1]

I found the door into that Silence at Bredbo, on the Strike-A-Light Creek, in a solid old farmhouse built by settlers and sheep farmers in the 19th century. I was a stranger among strangers, although at certain points we found a meeting. Two great bushfires helped to level us, as my neighbours and I did what was required to save the bush. And then there were the memorable Open Days I decided to hold, when the farm people mixed with the spikey-haired city dykes from Canberra and Sydney. They bought pots, sculptures, lavender and sage plants, scones and cups of tea. I loved these days, marvelling at how people only ever see what they want to – shearers just not seeing women holding hands or kissing, country wives buying my porcelain shells never once mentioning they were more like vaginas. And so, over the years I earned a grudging respect as I struggled with the water pump on the creek, survived the devastating locust plague, built greenhouses and had tomatoes earlier than anyone else, fired huge gas kilns into the middle of snowy freezing nights, collected a vast array of bones, feathers, wood and rock, walked long distances alone across everyone else's land with my dog, came and went and came again, staying ten years, longer than anyone expected.

Only once did I try to make a major creative bridge between me as a woman artist and those agricultural people. In 1988, the village of Bredbo celebrated its Centenary, at the same time as the Bicentenary of the whole country. I was deeply critical of the national celebrations, which were insensitive to the prior claims of indigenous peoples (dispossessed and almost eliminated), and the rural communities were blatantly racist. At the meeting to plan the village Centenary, I raised the question of the indigenous people of the area, only to be attacked and shouted down by

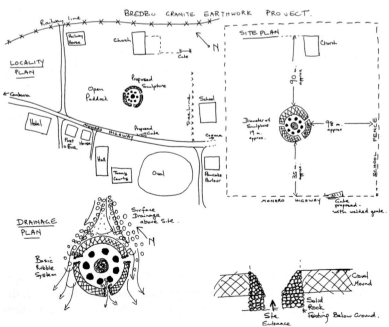

375

angry fearful landowners. I already knew the depth of feeling from an earlier battle, having spent time helping an archaeologist who was surveying the local area. Her research findings proved conclusively that there had been continuous aboriginal settlement for thousands of years in the district. The land where I was living was on an aboriginal walking track between a healing stone circle and a series of axe quarries producing stone tools, to the south. Certain property owners refused permission for surveys by the archaeologist, and she backed off, thinking it wiser to wait than have spiteful landowners bulldoze important sites.

I persisted in questioning the Centenary committee, and then proposed an Earthworks project. Miraculously, a group of local farm wives and country women supported me, and promised to make their husbands help with cranes and tractors. I designed a healing stone circle with earth mounds and standing stones, using local granite, to be constructed on a site in the village – a sheep paddock sloping down from the tiny Anglican church, rising up, as it were, from the past, challenging the Christian imposition.

I imagined a sculpture which tried to integrate at a ritual level the over-laying cultures, the archaeological realities of the place, to combine openly the elements of what had happened to the land. Along with the drawings, my written submission to the regional Council stressed the tradition of the most ancient form of public sculpture, involving patterning with arranged rock form sand earthmoving – combining the old European megalithic monuments I had seen in my travels, with what we knew of indigenous forms from scholarly sources. Like Virginia Woolf's Miss LaTrobe in *Between the Acts*, I watched with disbelief as the project was accepted and grew, on paper, through committees, through Council, through the Regional Engineer . . . Some of the very old people of the village came forward. One very old man, a beekeeper, winked at me and whispered: 'This will bring the rain back.'

It grew and grew in our minds, each seeing what we wanted to – and then, suddenly, it was over, stopped. Despite our base of village support (or because of it), higher authorities denied us the use of the land itself, public land. Like the mythic Avalon, it stayed in our imagination.

Initially disappointed, I soon realized it was remarkable in having gone so far. Perhaps beyond that point, our differences would have risen up. I had learned a lot, about negotiating for public earthworks, about large machinery, community yearnings, and about my own great well of inner resources as an earthworker. Nothing was wasted, and the story seems to me not yet over.

Through the 1980s, I continued to exhibit and travel among women's communities, peace encampments, the 1985 Nairobi Women's Confer-

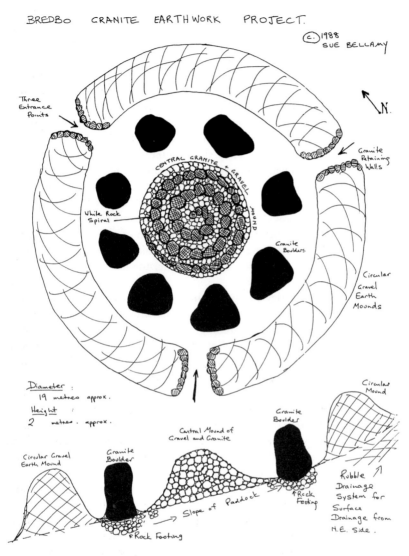

BREDBO CRANITE EARTH WORK PROJECT.

© 1988
SUE BELLAMY

Three
Entrance
Points

N.

Granite
Retaining
Walls

CENTRAL GRANITE + GRAVEL MOUND

White Rock
Spiral

Granite
Boulders

Circular
Gravel
Earth
Mounds

Circular
Mound

Diameter :
19 metres approx.

Height :
2 metres. approx.

Granite
Boulders

Central Mound of
Gravel and Granite

Circular Gravel
Earth Mound

Granite
Boulder

Granite
Boulder

↑Rock
Footing

Rubble ↗
Drainage
System for
Surface
Drainage from
N.E. Side.

Slope of Paddock

↑Rock Footing

ence, lesbian festivals and conferences, spiritual gatherings. I sold my
pots, prints and sculptures to women, held workshops, told stories, and
found a way to connect as a travelling country woman, helping, as I saw
it, to build the Trade Routes of a diverse Women's Culture. It seemed that
I lived on a re-emerging map of the world of women, no longer a dream,
with journeys, places and stories seeded into my imaginative spirit. When
I came back to my farm studio, I started making great boats carrying large
groups of women. The first was called *Going to Africa*. Then there were a

series of animal boats, elephant, reptile, birds, dragons, and finally the largest boat, a great wooden barge and sail, with a deck full of porcelain figures and objects, exotic women carrying books, instruments, artefacts, boxes, scrolls, fleece, statuary. I called this work . . . *And We Hid Our Secret Knowledge, Even From Ourselves.* Like an ancient dynamic artefact, this journey-boat came alive in my life. I felt I began to meet the women on it, scholars, artists, holywomen, storytellers, musicians, archivists, navigators. These boat women, my spiritual ancestors, had gathered up into the secret recesses of my ancient memory the key ideas and forms of a pre-patriarchal heritage. They floated upon the sea of my amnesia, waiting to return. Their mythic presence found a way of seeping into my everyday life with ease.

Some moments of clarity in my work thrill me, alter me, encourage me to live, to be alive now. But there is a parallel story – equal and opposite. The inward journey, the reluctant deconstruction of my psyche, had other destinations, more cruel and hideous to see. This was the story of how we had lost our minds, of how I had lost mine, the narrative of patriarchal hate of women and the earth.

I kept making my clay and porcelain figures: animals, earth, water, trees formed the bedrock of trust, while simple actions spun the thread – walking, sitting, listening, watching, making solid things. The tortoise became my main spirit companion, tough shell, soft protected heart. I carved her over and over again, on clay eggs, on the backs of clay women. Birds also participated, holding my terrors lightly in their feathers, appearing again and again in clay as giants in serious conversation with tiny women. Birds also give direct messages, and it was through this time that I opened to these other worlds of thought and image. Looking back from this place now, I would say that I endured a nervous breakdown of half my brain, while the other half fed my animals and made the pots. It was a thrilling and appalling time.

Out of its wake came new ideas, a new sense of self, still fragile but very alive. In a city I would have been taken away, but on the land where no one could hear me shout my rage and scream my memories, I was safe. Old spirits came to my fire, old women watched over me. They spoke simply, dispassionately, that this was not tragedy but mystery, being revealed.

From this experience I learned to trust my creative self as a problem solver. How affirming to look up from confusion and see another part of my self walking towards me with it all worked out. I knew then absolutely that for me, the exploration of non-verbal forms, the visual surreal, held the key to healing, renewal and action. And just as this process can work in my solitary life, so too could it be possible on a larger map, into deep past. Who are these women who sail towards me on their barge, who are these great spirit protectors, what is this mass of memory stirring in our nightmares like an awakening planet of secrets? The old women remind me, again – Mystery not tragedy. Hearts mending, not breaking. Take the long view.

This is true also of radical feminism which moves like the glacier, erupts like the volcano, sweeps away old forms like an earthquake, builds like the tidal wave, travels with the core heat of a comet. It is the language of artists, writers, visionaries – those who combust and prosper at the beginning of change, those who pick up the seeds. In preparing for a new century, I feel good about these seeds, I feel in fact that I am a seed, a scattered seed among many.

I am sitting writing this today, in 1993, having just left my home in Bredbo. A hard and necessary transition has begun, learning about a new place, gathering confidence and resources to build an earth studio by a new creek, with platypus in her depths. There's always another beginning.

I marvel at the continued shared visions of women globally, in great numbers, all discordant with patriarchy. That is our common ground. We have a generative spirit, which builds pictures and shapes in our brains and its heartcentre. This is our Mythic Potency. I feel that, even if we all died tomorrow, we have begun something marvellous. Out of a century of bloodlust, global wars, genocide and racism, eco-madness and environmental crumbling, mass media psychic numbing, rape, sadism, torture and despair – quite a list – we still meet, work, nurture, grow, remember and tell, explore and create. It is the unlikely privilege of my generation to go the whole journey, beyond naivety, past despair and on towards the Old Laughing Women, my old relations, my inspiration. You never get to see them, they are so old they can hardly move now, just wrinkles really. They sit like big old boulders, cared for in all ways by others, and they mostly laugh. You never get to see them – you hear them. They say to me that a day comes when I see all that has been done to women, to animals, to the planet – all of it I see clearly, fully, with a steady unshockable eye – and I know that it still didn't kill us, that life is greater than death, and you never give up when you're just about to win. Storytellers are like that. What can you do but love them.

Notes
1. Suzanne Bellamy. 1982. 'Form – We Are the Thing Itself'. In *Third Women and Labour Papers*. Adelaide: Third Women and Labour Conference.

Helen O'Shea

COUNTRY HALLS AND DEBUTANTE BALLS

Drive anywhere through white Australia's farming districts and you will find scattered settlements marked out by roadside signs and public buildings: the school, the church, and the hall. With the rationalisation of schools and churches in rural areas, the hall is often the only one of these buildings still in use.

As the focal point of a district's social life, at which communal celebrations take place, the hall is a centre for folklife. Its role has diminished considerably since the 1960s which brought, on the one hand, better access to towns and cities, and on the other, home entertainment such as television and video. Yet even in districts where the severely depleted population can scarcely support communal functions, people still regard the hall as essential to their sense of community and their sense of identity.[1]

What is the history of these halls? A close look at the building might reveal the official title of Mechanics' Institute or, in New South Wales, School of Arts, in deference to the movement, imported from Britain during the nineteenth century, which sought to foster a more highly skilled and educated workforce by providing technical education for the working man. In Australia, the mechanics' institutes were established in the major population centres from 1827, and the movement flourished until the depression of the 1890s, by which time there were over four hundred mechanics' institutes in Victoria alone.

Settlers in newly opened-up rural areas continued to build public halls well into the twentieth century, and in 1972 over three hundred were still in use in Victoria. Local historians have noted the central place of the hall in the life of a rural community, recording with pride and pleasure both the cooperative work that maintained it and the communal activities held there.

Country towns have their band halls, church halls, halls for the Country Women's Association, the Scouts, the Returned Services League, the bowling club, the racing club and the Masonic Lodge. In rural areas, however, there was usually only one hall at the heart of a district. It was used for official functions: as a polling booth, a church, a temporary school; for meetings of civic organisations such as the progress association and fire brigade; and by sporting clubs and charities for fundraising activities which included dances, concerts and balls. At all these public gatherings, everyone in a district was literally on common ground, and almost always, people were invited along by public advertisement, rather than by private invitation.

Until the end of the 1960s, when the local dances were dying out, debutante balls were organised by church parishes, hall committees and charity organisations, and was popular even in quite small rural districts. The ceremony retained something of its earlier meaning as a celebration of a young woman's sexual maturity and availability for courtship. At sixteen or seventeen, most country debutantes had left school, and their debut was the first of a number of dances to which they wore their white dress. In the 1980s, however, most deb balls were organised by schools for their students. There was no longer any relationship between 'coming out' and being allowed out with boys, and the deb dress was rarely worn again. Despite this, the debutante ball remains the social event of the year in many rural communities.

The Timboon Debutante Ball was to be held on Friday, 12 May. Ada Henderson, the trainer, was happy for me to go along to their Sunday evening practice. At 7.35 on Sunday evening the deb set was already at work in the Timboon Hall.

'The girl gets full attention from the start!' Ada's voice pierced the gloom at the back of the hall as she shepherded each couple through the descent from centre stage, the stately procession and the presentation to the guest of honour. The girls smiled self-consciously as they practised the curtsey. Some buckled awkwardly, others swayed or flapped their arms; only a few could sink gracefully into the submissive gesture. There were fifteen debs, and it all took a long time in the draughty hall.

'On Thursday night I want all girls to wear their white petticoat,' Ada instructed the class. That night most of them wore calf-length skirts with blouses and windcheaters, but a few had on the petticoat as well, so they could get used to swinging their long, hooped cage. The girls were breaking in their new high heels, too. One girl had dressed defiantly in black: a short, tight skirt and fringed, high-heeled suede boots.

There was a break of five minutes while the boys claimed their hired suits, which had just arrived in the foyer. The girls herded into the Ladies while the boys crowded around, laughing excitedly at the long black tails. Although they admitted that it was probably more fun for the girls, the boys were enthusiastic about the Deb. 'Some people say it's sissy, but it's not!' Two of the boys remembered to be cool and stood apart from the others, sharing a smoke.

The next evening I visited one of the debs, Kylie Eade and her parents, Cliff and Lorraine. Kylie talked about the Deb and how she came to be doing hers.

'I just thought it would be interesting to do, because my sister didn't go in it and I thought, oh, it might be a nice thing to do . . . I'm doing it for enjoyment: the fun of going and being part of it. It's been good. Learning to dance and making mistakes, that's been fun.'

Kylie giggled when she recalled how she had found her partner. 'Oh, well, my friend, it's her brother, and she just said, oh, he'd do it, and I thought, oh yeah! But then one day I went and asked him, and he said yes! I already knew him. His name's Scott. I think he was pleased to be a deb partner. It's his first time doing it . . . He even asked me if I'd do the Belle of Debs – that's the one after you've been presented, the second sort of deb thing.

'At school we talk about it all the time . . . We don't describe our dresses, we just say what's happening with them, when we're getting them. It's a bit of a secret. I haven't really told them exactly what mine's like. I want it to be a surprise.'

Kylie's eyes shone as she described her dress in a breathless rush. 'It's made of crystal organza with satin underneath it, the sleeves are rucked above my elbows, sweetheart neckline, there's sequinned flowers around the neck and at a bit of the back, the skirt is full with scallops and there's a layer of organza coming down for a frill underneath that, and that's about all. There's pearl buttons, and pearls around the neckline and waist, and underneath there's a petticoat with – what is it? – that net stuff, tulle.

'On Friday it's traditional to take the day off. No one goes to school in Year 11; all the girls get ready. My hair's getting done at two o'clock, and my make-up at five, then I'm going down to school, so I'll be there about six; then we get dressed, and the photos are taken. Mine are at seven-thirty, then the group one about eight o'clock, I think. And then we get over to the hall, and get presented at nine o'clock.

'My sister is going to help me dress, because I can't get the buttons done up! My family, Mum and Dad and my brothers and sister, are going to see me. My aunt and my nana are going, and probably another aunt and uncle and some friends that don't go to Timboon.

While Kylie was speaking, her mother worked away quietly in the kitchen. Now Kylie sat listening while Lorraine explained her part in the Deb.

'I took her in to practice the first night, and then her partner's taken her in ever since. You're not allowed in to watch them, so if you've got nowhere to go, you've got to sit in the car for two hours . . .

'The frocks, well they can be as expensive as you want them to be. Having the frock made works out a lot cheaper than buying it. Kylie's frock was $375 in the shop, that was cheap, and to have it made has cost a hundred and sixty for materials and I don't know how much for the making of it, because I'm doing something in return, but probably it wouldn't be a hundred dollars to make it, so it does work out a lot cheaper, to have one made. But they vary in price, you can get them over a thousand dollars. One boy we know, he partnered a girl . . . what was it, fifteen hundred dollars! But it had imported hand-made lace or something on it.

Well, they knew that that was imported hand-made lace, that's what made the frock expensive, but nobody else knew that it was that special lace. It was just another lovely frock. And this is why sometimes I don't think it's worth maybe going to that expense. . . .

On Thursday, with only one day to go, things were getting frantic at the Timboon Hall. A team of women was hard at work in the kitchen, folding red paper serviettes in intricate origami shapes. They reckoned it would take them all day. Lorraine Eade was helping set up the supper room with trestle tables covered in butcher's paper, red candles, place cards. The men were in the hall, carting around huge gum branches, fiddling with the sound equipment, lifting pot plants onto the stage, climbing a ladder to hang the paper moon. The committee's press release described the scene as 'an Australian bush setting at night, featuring kangaroo paw, tree ferns and gum saplings.'

Between directing vacuum cleaners and delegating tasks as more people arrived to help, Marg Ryan explained the fundraising function of the deb ball.

'The profits raised at the ball are divided between the two schools, the consolidated school and the high school – probably between two and two and a half thousand dollars. The high school are asked to donate cakes, and primary parents are asked to donate sausage rolls, or make a cash donation. One parent club does the sandwiches.'

The next evening I put on my good black dress and drove over to Timboon with the tape recorder, camera and notebook. At the high school Kylie was getting ready in the domestic science room. A full-length mirror was propped next to a poster promoting 'Heart Food': lean cuts of meat and other wholesome fare. The cooking counters and sewing benches were cluttered with hairbrushes, make-up and lacy white gloves. 'Scott gave me a red rose!' she confided, lowering her mascara-laden lashes.

It was time for the group photo in the school hall. The photographer swiftly arranged the deb set on the stage, the boys standing at the back and the girls ranged in rows by height. All wore their white gloves. At the centre sat Ada, beaming with pride in her electric blue dress, the young attendants nestled at her feet. Everyone looked at the camera; everyone smiled, radiating anticipation.

Then the girls were wrapped to their necks in bags, like exotic butter-flies retreating into drab cocoons. Kylie explained that the bags were sheets, with elastic at the top and bottom, to protect the dresses on the way over to the civic hall. A few minutes later everyone crowded onto the school bus. They laughed and waved as the bus pulled away through the puddles in the schoolyard.

Hundreds of people crowded the hall: the attendance was larger than

the population of the town. Family groups sat along the sides, young people, mainly girls, stood at the back, some in taffeta party dresses and lashings of make-up. The old-time dance enthusiasts had turned out, too. There were cameras everywhere. At nine o'clock the official party entered and was seated; the Master of Ceremonies went to the microphone, and Timboon's thirty-fifth debutante ball was under way.

The first act was a tease. The flower girl and page boy performed perfectly. The little boy held out his gloved right hand to support the little girl as they stepped out slowly in time with the Metrotones. When they reached the official party, Matthew bowed and Melanie stepped forward to curtsey, taking a posy from the basket she carried and presenting it to the Guest of Honour, Miss Victoria Fundraiser. As the pair returned to their bower on the stage – a cane couch set among the gum boughs and potted ferns – the audience applauded, murmuring indulgently.

Now for the real thing. Each debutante in turn walked beside her partner to the front of the stage, music rippling behind her, applause greeting her from the floor, while the MC introduced her and announced her pedigree. She descended the stairs carefully. Each girl had her left hand over her partner's; her right hand held a posy with streaming red ribbons. Each girl smiled self-consciously as she walked slowly in time to the music, her full skirt bobbing and rustling. As the pair approached the guest of honour, the partner bowed while the debutante moved forward and curtseyed low. She stepped backwards then (one girl straight onto her partner's foot, but he didn't even flinch) and the couple moved off to take up their positions for dancing.

Girls at the back of the hall stepped forward to photograph their friends, then drew back to whisper their evaluations of each deb's dress and presentation. The family groups applauded every deb, but as their own daughter appeared, each family lit up as if under a spotlight; then anxious nudges gave way to smiles of pride.

All this was recorded by Dave Stanton, the baker at Cobden, who stood on a chair with his video camera. Last year he sold fifty copies of the tape.

At the top of the supper room was one long table for the official party. Another for the debs and their partners ran down the centre of the room, with smaller tables for groups of ten parents spaced around them. The MC welcomed us and introduced Melissa, the deb chosen to cut the cake, which was an impressive edifice decorated like a wedding cake with thick, white icing.

When the speeches and the supper were over, the debs made their way through the crush to join the dancing in the hall. Like brides, they danced with their fathers, while the deb partners danced with their mothers. Some of the fathers whirled their daughters proudly, but others looked uncomfortable on the dance floor. None of them could avoid noticing his daughter's celebrity status, nor the yards of skirts between them.

As the debs moved onto the floor, a backwash brought hundreds of people into the supper room. There were three sittings: mountains of mixed cakes, oceans of tea and coffee and soft drink, hours of washing up.

The women bustled about bringing out more cakes, refilling sauce dishes, warming sausage rolls, working purposefully and harmoniously.

Out in the foyer Kylie and Scott rushed around, comparing notes with friends and watching the replay on the video screen that Dave the baker had set up. Kylie's followers were there, too, taking a breather. Lorraine was delighted with the way the evening had turned out. Kylie's father was less forthcoming.

When I came to visit two months later, Kylie Eade was still keen to talk about the deb ball. Her dress had made her feel special that night.

'It just made me feel older than I was. It made me feel like I'm . . . different, 'cause no one else had a dress like it, and so it made me stand out a bit. A few people when I got back to school said it was the nicest one there, and I was happy when they said it.'

Kylie thought she would like to wear her deb dress as a wedding dress in four or five years' time, although she would probably get it changed a bit. The Deb had also taught her a few things 'about organizing the dress and the make-up and hair for the bride, and everything personally for her.'

Some women rejected the deb ball in various ways. Lyn Halloran, a senior teacher at Timboon, knew the importance the Deb had for her students, but had reservations about the values it promoted.

'A lot of us are spending time trying to encourage girls to avoid the stereotypes, and yet that deb ball is highlighting and glamorizing everything about that stereotyping. When we talk about equal opportunity things at school, people get really offended that we may be suggesting that girls mustn't get married. They immediately interpret it in that fashion. So you can see, any moves to speak against the deb ball would be met with great resistance and antagonism.'

Others thought that it would be 'more appropriate, more inclusive, more egalitarian and less stereotyped to run a family bush dance including the folk dances from our multicultural heritage'.

But how could a family bush dance give these young women their moment of glory, their few seconds in the limelight, and the acknowledgement of their sexual maturity by their community, by their fathers?

The women presided over the deb ball: they organized it, prepared the girls and their partners, and their daughters starred in their production. Yet, although the men attended their daughters' 'coming out' ceremony reluctantly, and remained largely disengaged, their presence, their authority, was essential. It was like a wedding, when the bride's second dance is with her father, who has just 'given her away'. As at a wedding, the elaborate gown – of virginal white – also allowed the parents to display their wealth (despite the mothers' protestations about trying to make the dresses cheaply). The deb was a bride-in-training, and it was in this role that she received the respect and admiration of her community.

Until the 1970s the debutante ceremony was well-integrated into the young women's social world. This is no longer the case.

For the women of that most-married, youngest-marrying post-World War 2 generation, for whom marriage was inevitable and an end in itself, pride in their daughters' debuts was touched with poignancy. While the ceremony endorsed the choice they made to become brides, it also confronted them with their loss: the loss of their own youth and, inevitably, the loss of their daughters. In relinquishing their daughters to the comparative freedom of adulthood, the mothers faced the more profound loss of their daughters' departure from the community, as almost any job or training would take them away from home. Away from the community and its values, and outside the network of women's work, the intimacy of that relationship might be lost altogether.

The debutante ceremony, while claiming to be a letting go, was also a holding on. It exerted a pressure for the young woman to stay – to become like her mother – at just the moment when she was in theory mature enough to go her own way. The deb rehearsed the role of the bride, learning the appropriate dress, preparations and behaviour. As the debutante balls in this country district have become hugely popular, increasingly elaborate, and more closely resembling weddings, the young women continue to leave. Eighteen months after she did her deb, Kylie left the district and began a college course. Her deb dress sleeps in its plastic bag in the wardrobe at home.

Notes
1. This information came from informants at Golspie, NSW, in 1987, as described in 'The Golspie Hall', *Meanjin*, 4/1988; and from informants at Ecklin South, as part of field work for a study of a dairy farming community, 1989.

Jenny Maher
RURAL WOMEN'S SYNDROME[1]

I have been a rural person all my forty-eight years. I grew up on a grape farm at Nyah West on the Murray River in Victoria. We were farming battlers, but our family was well provided for. My parents worked hard, especially my mother. As a child I can remember my mother sewing, cooking, bottling fruits and washing in an outside copper till the early hours of the morning. With only a few hours sleep she would be up and about working the next day inside and outside the home. She also looked after her sick father as well as other workers on the farm. She was a busy and resourceful woman, and although I could never understand why she had to work such long hours I recognised the injustices of her situation. It wasn't fair that the men went to the pub while my mother had to do their washing, cooking and cleaning up after them. However, unfair as it was, I simply accepted this as a way of life and I also accepted that I would marry and follow my mother's path. My mother's ambition was to be a nurse, but her mother would not allow it because it was 'dirty' work – what a contradiction!

When I was nearly sixteen I entered the nursing profession at a District Hospital thirty-five kilometres away. In those days it was considered that girls be nurses, hairdressers, teachers or secretaries. I continued nursing until I married a wheat and sheep farmer twenty kilometres from my home town. To me it was the end of the earth and I had a difficult time adjusting to the harsh surroundings and poor living conditions. I often cried over my loneliness and longed for other human contact, especially women.

There was no electricity and about once a week an overhead tank was filled with water pumped from a dam. This was achieved by towing an old tractor around to get it started. The dam was filled once a year, channelled from hundreds of kilometres away. So there was limited water which meant little or no garden or trees. This in turn meant that during the summer experiencing months of extreme heat waves was no picnic. With hardly any protection around the house and louvre windows, I had to shovel the dirt out of the house after many violent dust storms.

I had a copper in an outside wash house which I stoked up once a week to do the arduous task of washing. Smoke used to fill the wash house and I can remember hanging my head out the doorway gasping for air with watery eyes and a running nose. I did my ironing with a shellite iron and sometimes with just a heavy cast iron which I used to heat up on the gas stove. I also had a wood stove with a hot water supply through it. Furniture was a limited commodity, so kerosene tins were used in the lounge room where my husband and I sat around the open fire at night and listened to a big old battery operated wireless with the tilly lamp burning. A kerosene fridge was a blessing, as was the party line telephone shared by six farmers. The phone number was 23K and when I wanted to ring out I had to manually ring a long, short and a long code. When the phone was out of order we had to go out along the line to find the problem, and fix it ourselves.

During the first year of our marriage our son was born and the following year electricity was connected to our home. We couldn't afford much but we bought a second-hand washing machine and other essentials. On the birth of my second son I was pleasantly surprised with a new fridge and a TV. I felt life was going to become easier at last! We also erected an electric water pump from the dam so I could have an endless supply of water, which meant I could have a small garden.

By the time my third son was born I had decided to go back to nursing, it felt good, it was 'my' decision. I worked mostly night duty for a short time but my health deteriorated trying to manage on a few hours sleep, usually taken when the children were put to bed at 7.30 p.m.

As the years progressed we worked hard to hold onto the farm. My daughter, born during these years, was put into private child care and I took on seasonal work to help financially. My husband did seasonal work too carting grapes to wineries across Victoria which kept him away nights at a time. I did some more part-time nursing, took in sewing, cake decorating, did Home-Help (for eleven years) and was actively involved in community activities, centred mainly around my children's education.

When my daughter started school I extended the seasonal job to working all year round on properties and I learnt everything about vegetable and fruit growing. I even rented a plot of ground and grew and marketed vegetables myself. It was labour intensive work but there was something about working in that environment, here were harmony and serenity! I met and worked with lots of women, and as we worked together we discussed many issues and formed bonds and friendship that have been everlasting. We shared our experiences helping each other to face the many difficulties confronting rural women. I loved this social contact and was amazed at the number of women working in the fields. A couple of growers I spoke to said they would not employ men because they are unreliable. They said that 'women are much more responsible, reliable and hard working and take pride in their work.' The money I earnt working in the fields was put towards food, clothing and the education of my children.

My relationship with these women sparked a type of sisterhood. I no longer felt isolated. I became more independent in my thinking and doing and went out and bought myself a car. Initially, my husband was not impressed with this, but recognised the need for the step.

At the beginning of 1980 we could see our way clear to renovate our home, at last! The farm had built up reasonably, and we were (ill-)advised by the bank to expand (the same advice was given to many other farmers). However, the rural crisis soon hit with high interest rates coupled with low commodity prices in wheat and sheep throughout Australia. Consequently, this saw us and many other farmers in dire straits and the effects of this caused severe emotional strains on the whole family. We joined a support group for the depressed farming community all facing the same fear of losing everything we all had worked for. We made many friends through this network and shared many tears and laughter but realising how bad it was for other families I could see what lay ahead for us.

I remember one particular meeting attended only by women during the harvest period. The men were too busy to attend. At this meeting I saw and shared the despair, distress and frustrations with these women. It was clearly evident that these women were extremely resourceful and were the strength behind their menfolk and the farm gate. It was a very intimate meeting where we exchanged our experiences and shared our innermost feelings about our position as women: we were not the decision-makers or responsible for our predicament but we all had to bear the consequences. The meeting also showed that the women wore two hats – one for the mixed meetings where the males dominated the discussion, just like the decisions made on the farms. At the women's meetings we were extremely forthright, honest and shared a real sense of sisterhood. As a result of this we decided to continue with women only monthly meetings. This gave us great confidence and strength through a shared awareness of our circumstances and our unequal status as rural women.

I worked even harder during the crisis which still continues. I kept up the seasonal work and took on added jobs such as roustabouting and shearer's cook which took me into NSW 400 kilometres away. I did anything I could make a bob out of!

I could not foresee any financial security in the farm. My sense of self worth had been shattered and I decided I had to do something about this to prove that my mind had not stagnated nor become completely corroded over the years. Facing this dilemma head-on, I decided to do an external university degree in Social Science which I began in 1988 as a result of my contact with the rural women's support group. A big step for someone who hadn't had much time even to pick up a book in twenty-three years. A terrifying thought!

At this point, permanent jobs were hard to get but I kept applying and gained a part-time position as a cook at the local hospital and another part-time job working with the intellectually disabled, which in turn led me to my present full-time job. During the first year of my course we lost our battle to retain the farm. We suffered badly from this experience. Doing exams and moving house is something I cannot put into words. Losing almost everything was just like going through a grieving process. There is still much hurt in losing the historical identity of that farm. I feel that I have gone through a great deal in the course of twenty odd years in building up the home and farm then to accept and forget it – I can't. But I realise that life has to go on and I am now ready to start over again. We are trying to re-establish a small farm next door to the one we lost. Our only source of water has been rainwater, and recently we have been connected to piped water pumped from the Murray River forty kilometres away. It took a woman in parliament, Joan Kirner, to make the overdue decision to pipeline the Mallee. The pipeline (my lifeline) has been one of the highlights of my life. It was so hard without this essential commodity. I can now start a garden and plant lots of trees.

Through studying I have gained more self confidence and my whole life has changed. I still work on the farm and my study is always fraught with interruptions. It is rare that I can come home and relax, there are always farm issues, housework and my full-time work to attend to. Often I feel there's not enough of me to go around!

Through my studies I have had the opportunity to major in Women's Studies. When I first looked at the subject material I thought this was just too far out for me, but when I looked a little closer it was all about me! I always felt that there was something wrong with the way women were treated but could never put my finger on the cause. Now I can name it! I have found a peace with myself knowing what has troubled me all these years and by virtue of this event my life has taken on a whole new dimension in finding strategies to fight rural women's oppression.

Working through all this my priorities in life have changed. I would like to think that I can now stand up and be counted. Although life has been a battle I have become a much stronger person because of my experiences. I dare say we change, I know I have. I now appreciate the harshness and wilderness of the Mallee terrain and I look forward to coming home to the isolation where I can take a walk and enjoy the peace and tranquility of nature around me. This is my treat for the week where I can escape the hustle and bustle of city life. The bird life is magnificent where I live, it's funny how I never noticed it before!

Notes
1. Syndrome = recognisable pattern of behaviour.

Terry Whitebeach
WILL THE REAL TASMANIAN ABORIGINES PLEASE STAND UP?

If I'm asked 'Are you black or white?' I want to say, 'I'm both.' I want to say that Aboriginality is a part of me, the strongest part of my spirituality but I was brought up by white parents in a white society, as a white person, that's been so for generations in our family. So how can I say I'm Aboriginal? I'd be lying.

Trying to find traditional Aboriginality in Tasmania would be the equivalent of white people saying, for us to be really white, or English, we have to be the way we were when our ancestors came from England. So we'd better dress the same, revive all the old folk songs and have the same sexual mores, the same values and economic systems.

For white people that's no longer relevant and I think there's got to be the same sort of change happening with Aborigines, and that means people getting in touch with their Aboriginality as it is NOW.

Searching out your Aboriginality is not necessarily to go mutton birding every year; it is to make that direct link with that Aboriginal ancestor, to find the connection, which for me is a spiritual one.

We none of us really understand our connectedness with this land. We don't understand our Aboriginal connections. We come from a place of not knowing: the ancestors are dead and the earth speaks a language we have forgotten.

The two quotations above, and others, demonstrate clearly some of the difficulties, contradictions and confusion surrounding the notion of Aboriginality in Tasmania today.[1]

The island of Tasmania is separated from the Australian mainland by approximately 500 kilometres of ocean, the floor of which is littered with shipwrecks from the last 200 years of European maritime activity. For these are the notorious 'Roaring Forties' latitudes, which saw the early European explorers blown to the coast of the great south land, or Terra Incognito Australis, as it was once known. The 50 windswept Bass Strait islands are all that remain of the landbridge that once linked Tasmania with the Australian mainland. The Furneaux Islands, off the north-east tip of the Tasmanian coast, Cape Barren and Flinders Islands in particular, are especially significant in Tasmanian Aboriginal history and affairs.

Cut off as they were from their mainland counterparts by the subsidence of the landbridge after the last Ice Age, the Tasmanian Aborigines lived a relatively isolated, but harmonious existence as hunter-gatherers. At the time of first European contact there were approximately 4,000 Aborigines in Tasmania. They lived in small bands, each band inhabiting a clearly defined territory.

Their way of life made little impact on the land, and the absence of imposing structures, man-made wastelands and non-degradable rubbish heaps, was later used as evidence of their primitiveness. The main evidences of their long habitation are the numerous shell middens around the coast-line and river banks, the petroglyphs at Rocky Cape and Mt Cameron West and the paintings in the Ballawinne cave in South West Tasmania, the discovery of these last hinting at a richness of culture and spiritual expression previously unsuspected by European chroniclers of Tasmanian Aboriginal history.

Early contacts with Europeans were largely cordial. The indigenous people were initially courteous and hospitable, although little interested in the trinkets offered them by the visiting scientists and explorers. And as they did not evince a European-type ownership of the land, Captain James Cook, in 1777, felt that they would not oppose British settlement. Plans had been made to turn Van Diemen's Land, as it was known at the time, into a penal colony.

Later scientists did not share the early enthusiasm for the indigenous race: Peron described them as a miserable horde, the most primitive of all races, thus unwittingly providing scientific justification for their later dispossession.

> *In the dark I hear a sound*
> *like Aboriginal clapping sticks.*
> *It is frogs, I think.*
> *This land is pregnant with the presence*
> *of the displaced tribes.*
> (Little Swanport, home of the Oyster Bay tribe)

Within twenty-five years of the settlement at Risdon Cove in 1803, hundreds of Aborigines had been killed and most of their land taken by Europeans. Violent resistance superceded the earlier courteous hospitality. They were initially proclaimed to be under the protection of British law, but their land rights, although upheld in the European courts of the day, were ignored by the Colonial governments in Tasmania. Most settlers wished to be rid of them completely, and several attempts at extermination were made. Very few penalties were inflicted on Europeans who murdered Aborigines, science conveniently providing a balm to conscience by describing the 'primitive' indigenous race as less than human. This was a disgraceful period of Tasmania's history.

The only value they were seen to have was as scientific curiosities. Named the 'most primitive race on earth' their anatomy and physiology were the subject of much study, and the bodies of Aborigines taken to the museums of Europe. (A present-day project of members of the Tasmanian Aboriginal community is to retrieve and bury the remains of their ancestors.)

Finally, Governor Arthur decided on a policy of pacification, protection, and exile from white settlement, measures which were adopted by other Australian states under the segregation policy, and he appointed George Augustus Robinson to capture the remaining Aborigines, and to confine them in protective custody.

With the aid of several Aboriginal helpers, most famous of whom was Truganini, the so-called 'last Tasmanian Aborigine', Robinson went on his famous conciliation mission, where he rounded up the remaining 400 Aboriginal people, and took them in 1835 to a dreary settlement called Wybalenna, on Flinders Island. (Ironically, the name means 'home' or 'resting place'.)

Robinson's stated aim was to Christianize and civilize the natives into a docile and obedient peasantry. In 1838 he left them to their fate, going off to a more lucrative post as protector of Aborigines in Port Philip.

By 1847, only forty-four Aborigines of the original 400 were still alive, and all were in poor health and low spirits. These survivors, amidst hostile opposition from the settlers, were transferred to the unhealthy, low-lying swampland near Oyster Cover, where they succumbed to alcohol and European illnesses. Truganini, the last of this ill-fated group, died in 1876.

What we have dealt with so far is 'fact'. Tasmanian history. And now the difficulty arises, for the history books tell us that the Tasmanian Aboriginal people are no more. N. J. B. Plomley, author of *Weep in Silence*, considered by some the definitive work on the history of the Tasmanian Aborigines, states baldly: 'The Tasmanian Aborigines are an extinct race.' The 5,000 Tasmanian Aborigines alive in Tasmania today naturally take issue with that statement.

As a school child I was taught that Truganini was the last of her race and that she had died nearly a hundred years ago. This view is still widely held. Recently I read a series of essays by students of the Flinders Island District high school. Statements like the following appeared over and over again: 'Wybalenna was the settlement which saw the Tasmanian Aborigine die out as a race of people'; 'Wybalenna stands as a stark reminder of the destruction of an entire race of people'; and again, 'the extermination of the race ended with the death of Truganini on the 8th of May 1876'. Historical fact. The students who wrote these essays probably have Aboriginal classmates and neighbours.

A lot of the records have been destroyed and a lot of them have been written by people who don't want a lot of things known about themselves. Most people in Tasmania, if they've been here for five generations, have got stuff they don't want out.

Tasmania is a place of contradictions and paradoxes, a place where lies and secrets and silences, to appropriate Adrienne Rich's phrase, abound. It seems that it is possible both to hold the belief that there are no Aborigines in Tasmania, and to name individual Aboriginal people, and to express clichéed views about them, that they are good sportspeople, academic failures, or alcoholics. The illogicality of this stance doesn't seem to occur to most people.

It seems the closer you are, geographically, to the unspeakable events of a history, the more strenuously these events are denied, or coloured by an official line, and Tasmania is no exception. For it did try to wipe out its indigenous people: that it failed is a credit to the survival skills of the Aborigines, 5,000 of whom still exist today, to the embarrassment of many of the descendants of those early settlers. And the contentious issue then, as now, is land rights.

It pisses me off that we have to make so many concessions to white people for our survival. But WE HAVE SURVIVED, that's the thing. And no matter how much they have this thing that we haven't got – a culture – we're still getting stuff from the ancestors, or we're still getting stuff just from being around with other Aboriginal people. And that culture is still surviving.

And now we must go back a bit in history, if I am to support my claim that 5,000 Aboriginal people still live in Tasmania. It's true that most of the people rounded up by Robinson died, but that was not the end of the story. It is the way the remainder managed to survive that has generated the controversy that surrounds the notion of Aboriginality in Tasmania today.

Bass Strait was the focus of a vast sealing industry in the late eighteenth and early nineteenth centuries and many Aboriginal women joined, or were kidnapped by, sealers to work around the islands. The women were a tremendous asset to the sealers: powerful swimmers, they were also able to camouflage themselves and creep up amongst the unsuspecting seals basking on the shores.

It is true that many of these women were abused and treated shamefully, but it is a grim irony that those like Truganini who persuaded their fellows to give themselves up to the protection of Robinson and the government all died, but those who threw in their lot with the rough and undisciplined sealers survived. It is mostly their descendants, concentrated initially on Flinders and Cape Barren Islands, who are the Tasmanian Aboriginal community of today.

And that is the heart of the conflict, for these offspring have mixed-race parentage, and it was officially denied for many years, and still is widely believed, that these people are not truly Aboriginal. The fact that most of the languages, culture and way of life of the people, and many of the distinguishing physical characteristics of the race, are lost, makes this point of view more persuasive, as does the fact that not all descendants of these island people identify themselves as Aboriginal.

We weren't known as Aboriginals, early on, when we lived on the island, the word was half-castes. And to me that was the most misbegotten word that anybody could be called. It was not what our parents called us, we were forced to take that name. We knew we were different and we were made to be ashamed we weren't either, just half of black and half of white.

People have said niggers or half-castes but all the time it never changed my feeling. I didn't like what they said, or I'd probably say something to them, but it's never changed my feeling about my Aboriginality. It's always been there. I knew I was something different on Cape Barren. We were called half-castes and I felt the same then as I do now: we're Aboriginal.

Some people chose to remain on Cape Barren Island, where land was granted to the community and where, to this day, the majority of the island's inhabitants are Aboriginal. Others were assimilated into the white community, in line with a deliberate Government policy. The Aboriginality of many families was denied or hidden, so that their children would escape the penalties of being Aboriginal. Names were changed, history falsified. Aborigines have suffered greatly in Tasmania, and on the mainland: it was only in 1967 that they were able to become Australian citizens, with the right to vote. Since then they have begun to organize, assert their rights and argue for landrights and compensation. But the denial of Aboriginal rights, identity and dignity has inflicted deep psychic wounds, witnessed in the confusion and division within the community. People differ in their understanding of, and pride in, being Aboriginal.

The only thing we've got left going for us at the moment is our cultural food. We love to go around the beaches and get limpets and periwinkles and any sort of shellfish. We go out in the bush and get wild cherries and cranberries and tater vine. I was taken mutton birding when I was six months old, on Chappell Island. I go every year and even today it's funny, it's a thing that comes back to the Aboriginal people.

This is where things are changing for the better for us today. Our grandparents and parents never talked much about a lot of things to their children, but we can see the wrong in that now. So hard to track back – and you can't track back. But we now can pass on our type of thing to our children, hoping it will be passed on to our children's children.

396

For those who have escaped the penalties of racism, by having their Aboriginality denied, or hidden from them, the spiritual vacuum they have been placed in is profound. They look inside and see only the wind sighing through an empty landscape. They search their own and their families' faces for clues and find nothing, for they belong to a people who are not there, either historically or psychically, it is said. They speak uncertainly of old memories, half-forgotten, of dead relatives, of conversations overheard and later denied, hints dropped and then retracted. Their families are full of mysteries and secrets.

It has cost so much to suppress the truth. It would cost even more to reveal it. Things have been left unsaid for too long now. The longings have no names. They don't fit. They are muddled with the dreaming of other races.

There were and still are powerful reasons for denying the continued existence of Aboriginal people: the question of blame, of white guilt, and of recompense, in the form of recognition, financial assistance and land grants. And of course, the enormous and overwhelming task of coming to terms with the attempted genocide of the indigenous people of Tasmania. Past and present-day Tasmanians have baulked at this task. They would like the blame to rest firmly in the past, so that they would not have to acknowledge that the same racism, the same vested interest which originally dispossessed the Tasmanian Aborigines still exists today.

But at least Aboriginal people have won the right to define themselves, by their own criteria, and these are not colour, physical characteristics or philosophy, but by identifying as Aboriginal, and by being accepted as Aboriginal by the Tasmanian Aboriginal community. So, in a sense, being Aboriginal is a matter of choice in Tasmania.

I never taught my children they had to be Aboriginals. I thought, they've got to accept it themselves. I think the proudest day of my life was when my daughter came home from school and said, 'Mum, we had to write on Cape Barren Island Aboriginals and I put my hand up and said, "Sir, I can, because I am one and my mother and her people are."' And that to me was the proudest day of my life.

When I identified as Aboriginal Mum didn't like it at first. We had some quite heated arguments, where I just had to lay it on the line.

'Look,' I said, 'I have a right to determine my own future and the right to choose what path I take. If you want to deny that you've slept with a black man for twenty-five years and have seven or eight children to him, and one of them decides to stay with the Aboriginal part of her life, then that's your right.'

She accepts it now. When we were kids things were very different. Aboriginals weren't in vogue then. It was very hard for people and easier just to deny the things that made it harder.

There are a lot of problems inherent in the notion of Aboriginality in Tasmania, particularly as it exists in identification and feeling, rather than degree of Aboriginal 'blood' (the way native American nationality is defined in the USA and Canada), and there are many contentious areas of discussion, such as the degree of involvement in the community defining the legitimacy of one's claim to Aboriginality, and the way the right to grants and funds is decided. Colonialism's legacy is very apparent still.

Gains by the Aboriginal community have been slow but significant. Oyster Cover has been returned to their custody, and other sites of spiritual, economic, historical and social significance are being considered by the state government. Aboriginal Studies units have been developed and are available in some schools and colleges; the first crop of university graduates has entered the professions; and Aboriginal Centres, including legal services, creches and a Women's Centre have been set up in both Hobart and Launceston. Aboriginal Liaison Officers are attached to schools, and camps, where Aboriginal students can get together, are conducted regularly.

We can't keep on the bitterness with our children. How do the next generation of kids see their Aboriginality? Do they see it only as a focus for landrights or do they see it as a part of their dreaming, as part of their spirituality? Where is it going to take them?

Things are still far from ideal: as one woman said, 'There's so much pain with all of us, collectively and individually, that I don't know if we're ever going to work through that.' Divisions in the Aboriginal community are deep, especially between the conservative and radical elements. In radical circles, racism is seen as the main political issue, and women's rights are a secondary consideration. Women suffering domestic violence, for example, are urged not to 'betray' their black brothers by seeking out services in the wider community. Oppression has its roots in the white community, and feminist issues detract from the fight against racism, goes the party line. This has put many Aboriginal women in a difficult position.

It really drags me down that as Koori women we've never met together as a state group. If we ever get together on an issue, for example, we have to have the men involved. But there's women's business we really need to work out. And it's women's spirituality that's really negated as well, because women's spirituality is a lot different from men's. It goes together, but it's different.

For some, the understanding of their Aboriginality lies chiefly in connections with the land or with family ties; for others it is found in political action, winning rights and recognition; for others again it is in succeeding in the white community, whilst retaining a sense of Aboriginality. For some people it is all of these. My particular burden is the retrieval of the language, so that it can be heard and read again today, for language is so revealing of the social and spiritual temper of a culture. And it can be argued that a culture consciously retrieved and recreated is as authentically alive as it was in the past, as would be a music score that has lain unplayed for many years, and then is discovered and taken up again. Its temporary invisibility has not rendered it illegitimate.

It is in the spoken language, in poetry and performance, and in works of visual art created by those whose consciousness is bathed in their Aboriginality, as much as in the family and community ties of Tasmanian Aboriginal people, that not only the physical, but the psychic and spiritual continuity of the Aboriginal people of Tasmania be evidenced and continued.

It's good that as artists, as Aboriginal artists, we're writing our history for now, for future things. And as far as my art goes, I hope it is seen as crossing the boundaries of being something that can be seen as a future thing. It's not just dwelling on the past. I can't change my past and I can't change what happened there. And I know that I feel greatly and emotionally about that, but I also see it as a continuum into future hopes, of feelings that I have. Something like that.

Note
1. The quotations are from interviews with Tasmanian Aboriginal women for a forthcoming book: *We Who Are Not Here.*

Terry Whitebeach
MT STRZELECKI – FLINDERS ISLAND

Mena lageta – I will tell you –
how I climbed
the rock-peaked mountain
the poymalangta

I found a track – rialuggana –
made by the one-toed,
no puggaluggana – blackman's footprints –
on this hill.

Niripa crawled below me,
her white waves curling,
lukagana leapt among the gum trees
blowflies drank my sweat.

Pallanubra-na, the sun was high,
but still I trembled – mienni tyack –
for this poymalangta holds warrawena,
spirits of the dead.

3
RESOURCES

National
Lesbian Network, quarterly newsletter, PO Box 215, Rozelle 2039.

Victoria
Women's Information Referral Exchange (WIRE). 247 Flinders Lane, Melbourne
3000. (03) 654 6844
Out Loud, lesbian magazine. PO Box 535, Eltham 3095. (03) 439 7942
Lesbiana, magazine. PO Box 334, Fitzroy 3065, (03) 417 7388
Tourism Victoria (RACV), 230 Collins Street, Melbourne 3000. (03) 790 3333,
Hotline, (03) 790 2121, (008) 33 7743

New South Wales
Lesbians on the Loose, free magazine available from bookshops, pubs, women's
health centres.
Tourism Commission of NSW, 44 Martin Pl, Sydney 2000. (02) 231 4444
Young Women's Resource Centre, 23 Sheriff, Ashcroft 2168. (02) 607 7536
South Sydney Women's Centre, 231 Abercrombie, Chippendale 2008.
(02) 319 2613
Women's Centre Albury Wodonga, 440B Wilson Street, Albury 2640.
(060) 41 1977

Australian Capital Territory
Women's Information Referral Centre, Ground Floor, North Building,
London Circuit, Canberra 2600. (06) 245 4650/4654
WomanNews, available from Club Veg, 9A Sargood St, O'Connor 2601.
Women's House, 3 Lobelia St, O'Connor 2601. (06) 247 6679

South Australia
Women's Information Switchboard, 122 Kintore Avenue, Adelaide 5000.
(08) 223 1646, (008) 18 8158
Lesbian Times available from Women's Health Centres, Murphy Sisters Bookshop,
Women's Information Switchboard. (08) 267 3633.
Liberation magazine, available from the Women's Studies Resource Centre,
64 Pennington Terrace, North Adelaide 5006. (08) 2677 3633
Tourism South Australia, 18 King William St, Adelaide 5000. (08) 212 1505

Queensland
Women's Infolink, Pavilion Building, Queen Street Mall, Brisbane 4000.
(07) 229 1264/1580, (008) 17 7577
Queensland Tourist and Travel Corporation, 123 Eagle, Brisbane 4000.
(07) 833 5400
Queensland Government Travel Centre, 196 Adelaide St, Brisbane 4000.
(07) 221 6111

Western Australia

Women's Information Referral Exchange (WIRE), Ground Floor, 32 St Georges Terrace, Perth 6000. (09) 222 0444, (008) 19 9174

Western Australian Tourism Commission, Albert Facey House, Forrest Place (cnr Wellington St), Perth 6000. (09) 483 1111

Tasmania

Women's Information Service, 3rd Floor, Executive Buildings, Franklin Square, Hobart 7000. (002) 34 2166, (008) 00 1377

Lilac, lesbian newsletter. PO Box 1664 Launceston, Tasmania 7250. (003) 34 1060 or (002) 73 2627

Tasmanian Travel Centre, 80 Elizabeth St, Hobart 7000. (002) 30 0250

Northern Territory

Women's Information Centre, Helm House, Bath Street, Alice Springs 0870. (089) 51 5886

Women's Information Centre, Shop 5, Casuarina Plz, Casuarina 0810. (089) 22 7166, (008) 01 9132

Women's Embassy, PO Box 1105, Darwin 0801

Lesbian Territory, magazine available from Women's Embassy

Northern Territory Tourist Commission, 67 Stuart Hwy (North), Alice Springs 0870. (089) 51 8555, 33 Smith St Mall, Darwin. (089) 81 7899

Northern Territory Government Tourist Bureau, Shop 2, Ford Plaza Todd Mall, Darwin 0801. (089) 51 5470, 33 Smith St Mall, Darwin 0801. (089) 81 6611

SEXUAL ASSAULT SERVICES

Victoria

Telephone Service Against Sexual Assault, PO Box 4313, Melbourne University, Parkville 3052, (03) 349 2466, (ah) (03) 349 1766, (008) 80 6292 (Metro Barred)

Centre Against Sexual Assault, 270 Cardigan Street, Carlton 3053. (03) 344 2210

Regional services can be contacted on the following numbers: Collingwood (03) 419 6155; Bendigo (054) 41 0222; Heidelberg (03) 450 5770; Warrnambool (055) 61 2821; Footscray 3011, (03) 687 5811; Ballarat (053) 32 1771; Horsham (053) 81 9111; Geelong (052) 22 4802; Shepparton (058) 31 2343; Morwell (051) 34 3922; Mildura (050) 22 3444; Wangaratta (057) 22 2203

New South Wales

Sydney Rape Crisis Centre, PO Box 188, Drummoyne 2047. (02) 819 6565

Regional services can be contacted on the following numbers:

Gosford (043) 25 9111; Newcastle West (049) 69 4022, (ah) (049) 26 6234; East Maitland (049) 33 4422; Taree (065) 52 2799; Nowra (044) 21 3322, (ah) (044) 21 3111; Tamworth (067) 68 3240, (067) 66 1772; Albury, (060) 23 0340, 23 0370, (ah) (060) 23 0310; Wagga Wagga (069) 23 4816, 23 4815, 23 4818; Griffith (069) 62 3900; Forbes (068) 52 1000; Orange (063)

62 1411; Bathurst (063) 33 1311; Condobolin (068) 95 2600; Goulburn (048) 21 5755, (008) 02 4934; Young (063) 82 1522; Bega (064) 92 9196, (ah) (064) 92 9177; Cooma (064) 52 2777; Queanbeyan (062) 99 1432, (062) 97 2266; Dubbo (068) 85 8999, (068) 85 8927; Coffs Harbour (066) 52 2000, (066) 52 2866 (24hr); Lismore (066) 21 8000; Tweed Heads (075) 36 0440, (075) 36 2431; Port Macquarie (065) 83 1066, (065) 83 3944

Australian Capital Territory
Rape Crisis Centre, PO Box 31, Lyneham 2620. 247 2525

South Australia
Adelaide Rape Crisis Centre Inc., PO Box 164, Plympton 5038. (08) 293 8666
Sexual and Domestic Violence Crisis Care Unit, (08) 232 3300, (008) 18 8188

Queensland
Brisbane Rape Crisis Service, 30 Victoria Street, West End 4101. (07) 844 4088
Rape Crisis Support, 7 Miller Street, Parramatta Park, PO Box 142, North Cairns 4870. (070) 31 3590
Sunshine Coast Rape Crisis Service, Parker Street, Maroochydore, PO Box 74, Cottontree 4558. (074) 43 4334, (008) 01 2023; Gold Coast Sexual Assault Centre, (075) 91 1164

Western Australia
Sexual Assault Referral Centre, PO Box 842 Subiaco 6008. (09) 382 3323, (008) 19 9888
Geraldton Sexual Assault Referral Centre, (099) 64 1833; Waratah Women's Support Centre, (097) 91 2833; Kalgoorlie Women's Health Care Centre, (090) 21 8266

Tasmania
Hobart Sexual Assault Service, PO Box 217, North Hobart 7002. (002) 31 1811
Burnie Sexual Assault Referral Service, North West General, Hospital, PO Box 258, Burnie 7320, (004) 31 3033
Northern Sexual Assault Group, Community Based, PO Box 1062, Launceston 7250. (003) 34 2740

Northern Territory
Ruby-Gaea, Darwin Centre Against Rape, PO Box 42082, Casuarina 0811. (089) 45 0155
Sexual Assault Referral Centre, PO Box 40596, Casuarina 0811. (089) 22 7156
Community Health Clinic, PO Box 721, Alice Springs 0871. (089) 51 5888

WOMEN'S HEALTH SERVICES

There are many women's health centres throughout the country. Regional health centres can be located by contacting the ones listed below.

Victoria
Healthsharing Women, 5th Floor, 318 Little Bourke Street, Melbourne 3000.

(03) 663 3544, (008) 13 3321 referral and information service.

New South Wales

Women's Health Advisory Service, 187 Glenmore Road, Paddington, 2021.
(02) 331 5014/1294 – referral and information
Women's Health Information, 122A Norton Street, Leichhardt 2040.
(02) 559 5029, referral and information

Australian Capital Territory

Women's Health Service, Ground floor, ACT Health Building, Corner Moore St
and Alinga St, Canberra 2600. (06) 205 1078

South Australia

Adelaide Women's Community Health Centre, 64 Pennington Terrace,
North Adelaide 5006. (08) 267 5366, (008) 18 2098

Queensland

Women's Health Centre, 165 Gregory Terrace, Spring Hill 4000. (07) 839 9988
Women's Health Information and Referral Service, 47 Cambridge Street,
Rockhampton 4700. (008) 01 7382

Western Australia

Women's Health Centre, 114 South Fremantle 6160. (09) 335 8214
Women's Health Care House, 100 Aberdeen Street, Northbridge 6003.
(09) 227 8122, (008) 998 399

Tasmania

Women's Health Centre, 326 Elizabeth Street, North Hobart 7000.
(002) 31 3212, (008) 001 373
Women's Health Foundation Clinic, 9 Pierce Street, Moonah 7009.
(002) 28 0997

Northern Territory

Bath Street Medical Centre, Bath Street, Alice Springs 0870. (089) 52 2991,
not specifically for women, but female doctors in attendance
Central Clinic, 76 Todd St, Alice Springs 0870. (089) 52 1088, not specifically for
women, but female doctors in attendance
The Health & Relaxation Centre, 1 Griffiths Place, Alice Springs 0870.
(089) 52 4374, women-run massage and alternative medicine

LEGAL RESOURCES

Victoria

Women's Legal Resources Group, 1st Floor, 165 Gertrude Street, Fitzroy 3065.
(03) 416 0294/0272, (008) 13 3302 (Monday and Friday 10am–1pm,
Wednesday 6–9pm)

New South Wales

Women's Legal Resources Centre, PO Box H154, Harris Park 2150.
(02) 637 4597, (008) 80 1501

Lesbian and Gay Legal Rights, PO Box 9, Darlinghurst 2010. (02) 360 6650

South Australia
Women's Centre at St Peters, 64 Nelson Street, Stepney 5069. (08) 362 6571

Queensland
Women's Legal Service, 81 Russell St, West End 4101. (07) 846 2066

Western Australia
Women's Lawyers Association, (09) 221 3391

Northern Territory
Legal Aid Commission, 16 Leichardt Terrace, Alice Springs 0870.
   (089) 52 1088, not specifically for women
Women's Lawyers Association, GPO Box 4369, Darwin 0801. (089) 81 8322

GALLERIES/BOOKSHOPS/LIBRARIES

Victoria
The Women's Gallery, 375 Brunswick St, Fitzroy 3065. (03) 419 0718
Colari Bookshop and Gallery, Pakington Street, West Geelong 3220.
   (052) 21 7970
Shrew Women's Bookshop, 37 Gertrude Street, Fitzroy 3065. (03) 419 5595
Eltham Bookshop, 22 Commercial Place, Eltham 3095. (03) 439 9606
Bellcourt Books, 63 Gray Street, Hamilton 3300. (055)72 1310

New South Wales
The Feminist Bookshop, Shop 9, Orange Grove Plaza, Balmain Road, Lilyfield
   2040. (02) 810 2666
Bent Books, lesbian and gay bookshop, 43 Terania Street, North Lismore 2480.
   (066) 21 8992
Jessie Street Library, GPO 2656, Sydney 2001; located in the NSW Writers
   Centre, Rozelle Hospital grounds, Balmain Road, Rozelle 2039.
The Women's Library, PO Box 271, Newtown 2042.
Playworks, PO Box 1523, Darlinghurst 2010. (02) 212 3736

Australian Capital Territory
A–GOG Women's Gallery, 71 Leichhardt St, Kingston 2604. (06) 295 3180

South Australia
Blue Expressions Gallery, 69 Semaphore Road, Semaphore 5019. (08) 242 0688
Murphy Sisters, 240 The Parade, Norwood5067. (08) 332 7508
Sisters by the Sea Bookshop, 14 Semaphore Road, Semaphore 5019. (08) 341 7088
Reading Matters 17 Gawler Street, Mount Barker 5251. (08) 398 2993
Women's Studies Resource Centre, 64 Pennington Terrace, North Adelaide 5006.
   (08) 267 3633

Queensland
Boulder Lodge Concepts (gallery), 270 Wickham St, Fortitude Valley 4006.
   (07) 852 2093 (not specifically women's)

Metro Arts, 109 Edward St, Brisbane 4000. (07) 21 1527 (not specifically women's)
The Women's Bookshop, 15 Gladstone Road, Highgate 4101, (07) 844 6650
Emma's Bookshop, 82a Vultura Street, West End 4101. (07) 844 4973
Elspeth Douglas, 16 Jumbuck Street, Jindalee 4074. (07) 870 8457

Western Australia
Arcane Bookshop, 212 William Street, Perth 6000. (09) 328 5073
Kimberley Bookshop, 34 Dampier Terrace, Broome 6725. (091) 92 1944
The Lespar Library of Women's Liberation, 29 Allpike Rd, Darlington 6070.
    (09) 299 6594

Northern Territory
Arunta Art Gallery and Bookshop, Todd Street, Alice Springs 0870. (089) 52 1544
Araluen Arts Centre, Larapinta Drive, Alice Springs 0870. (089) 527 581
Arid Lands Environment Centre (bookshop), Shop 3, Gregory Terrace, Alice
    Springs 0870. (089) 52 6782
Tivoli Books & Music, 27 Cavanagh Street, Darwin 0800. (089) 81 8470

RADIO
Programme names may change – check radio guides listed in metropolitan and
local newspapers.

National
ABC Radio National, various frequencies – The Coming Out Show (repeated).
    Community Radio Stations – Women on the Line (see separate listings below).

Victoria
3CR, 855 AM – Women on the Line, (national), Out 'n Out (national
    gay/lesbian), Women's Arena (sport), Taking Control (various interest groups),
    Fair Start (single mothers), Union of Australian Women, World Women's beat
    (international music), Not Another Koori Show, Voice of the Arabic Women,
    Eve's Cabin (folk music), 2nd Opinion (health), Women's World (elderly),
    Lesbian and Gay Show, Women's Home Time (current affairs), In Your Face
    (lesbian/gay youth), Masalda (Spanish women), Dustless Houses (unemployed),
    Sistamatic.

New South Wales
2SER, 107.3 FM – Women on the Line, (national), Out 'n Out (national
    gay/lesbian), Jezabelle's (music), Broadscast News (current affairs), Broads on
    Brecky, Crystal Set, Gay Waves (lesbian/gay), Women's Jukebox.

Australian Capital Territory
2XX, 1008 AM – Women's Revolutions per Minute (music), Women Behind the
    Lines, Fantasy (magazine), Women on the Line (national).

South Australia
5UV 531 AM – No Frills, Women on the Line (national).

Queensland
4ZZZ, 102.1 FM – Queer Radio (lesbian/gay; lesbian only every third week),
Megahers.

Western Australia
6RTR, 92.1 FM – Burning Down the House (twice a week), Women's Music
Program.

RESTAURANTS/CAFÉS/NIGHTCLUBS
Nightclub venues change frequently – pick up the local magazine for up-to-date
listings.

Victoria
The Angel Cafe, 362 Brunswick St, Fitzroy 3065. (03) 417 2271
Women's Oasis, every Friday night at Oasis Oz Hotel, cnr Queensberry &
Dryburgh Streets, North Melbourne 3051.
Feminique, Wednesday nights at Golden Gate hotel, Cnr Coventry & Clarendon
Sts, South Melbourne 3205.
Rochester Castle Hotel, 202 Johnston Street, Fitzroy 3065. Sunday nights,
(03) 416 3133
The Inkspot, 375 Inkerman St, East St Kilda 3182.
Glasshouse Hotel, 51 Gipps St, Collingwood 3066. Lesbian and gay.
Temple, Saturday nights, 2nd Floor, 164–170 Flinders St, Melbourne 3000.
Lesbian and gay
Masai, Thursday–Saturday nights, 2 Arthurton Road, Northcote 3070. Lesbian and
gay.
Three Faces, 143 Commercial Road, South Yarra 3141. (03) 826 0933. Gay and
lesbian nightclub, changes daily, ring for lesbian/mixed nights.

New South Wales
Club 77, 77 William Street, East Sydney 2000. (02) 361 4981 (Fri/Sat).
Curry Connection restaurant, 1st Floor, Agincourt Hotel, Cnr George and Harris
St, Broadway, 2007. (02) 212 7409
The Britannia Hotel, 103 Cleveland St, Chippendale 2008. (02) 310 2308

Australian Capital Territory
Tilley's Café, Wattle Street, Lyneham 2602. (06) 249 1543
The Meridian Club, 34 Mort Street, Canberra 2600. (06) 248 9966

South Australia
Babettes Eatery, 69A Semaphore Road, Semaphore 5031. (08) 341 6606
Café Bohemian, Unit 1/139 Henley Beach Road, Torrensville 5031. (08) 43 3643
Kookaburra Café, Cottage Kitchen, 160 St Vincent's Street, Port Adelaide 5015.
(08) 346 1784. Lesbian and Gay night every second Saturday
Performing Women Friday once a month. Enquiries (08) 267 3633

Queensland
TKs lesbian and gay coffee shop, 44 Spence St, Cairns 4870. (070) 51 8200
Cinema Café, 158 Oxford St, Bulimba 4171. (07) 899 2276
Stray Cats, Shafston Hotel, Lytton Rd, East Brisbane 4169. Alternate Saturdays.
Options, lesbian and gay nightclub, Spring Hill Hotel, Spring Hill 4000.

Northern Territory
Witchetty's Bar and Restaurant, Araluen Arts Centre, Larapinta Drive, Alice
    Springs 0870. (089) 52 7581
Swingers Café, Cnr Bath St & Gregory Terrace, Alice Springs 0870.
    (089) 52 9291
White Gums Tearooms and Fauna Park, Honeymoon Gap, Alice Springs 0870.
    (089) 55 0366
The Saloon, 21 Cavenagh Street, Darwin 0800. Lesbian and gay-friendly.
(None of these are women only.)

TRAVEL SERVICES

Victoria
Victoria Aboriginal Land Council, 2 Watt Street, Thornbury 3071.
    (03) 480 6644, fax (03) 416 9092
Women's country guest house, PO Box 82, Trentham 3458. (053) 686 775
Wandering Women, (03) 489 9474, voluntary group organising tours.
Fitzroy Stables self-contained accommodation, 124 Victoria Street, Fitzroy 3065.
    (03) 415 1507

New South Wales
New South Wales Aboriginal Land Council, 103 Moore Street, Liverpool 2170.
    (02) 601 4766, fax (02) 601 1936
Wildwise, adventure holidays for women, 2nd Floor, Suite 19, 94 Oxford St,
    Darlinghurst 2010. (02) 360 2099, (008) 65 5325
BreakOut, GPO Box 3801, Sydney 2001. Travel for women.
    Also Bush Strolls and Hampers, tours around Sydney for women
    (02) 550 0328, fax: (02) 560 7167.
Friends of Dorothy Travel (gay and lesbian), 2nd Floor, 77 Oxford St,
    Darlinghurst 2010. (02) 360 3616
Stringybark Farm, (063) 79 1182
Woodhill Mountain Lodge, (044) 64 2013
The Sibyls, holiday cottage, (02) 597 2508
Trillium, Blue Mountains retreat, 71 Seventh Avenue, North Katoomba NSW
    2780. (047) 82 6372
Moonraker Farm, RMB 236 Wattamolla Road, Wattamolla 2535.
    (044) 65 1240
Tara Country Retreat (lesbian & gay), RMB 218, Berry, NSW 2535.
    (044) 64 1472

Northern Territory
Central Aboriginal Land Council, 33 Stuart Highway, Alice Springs 0870.
(089) 51 6211, fax (089) 53 4343
Desert Tracks, PO Box 8706, Alice Springs 0871. (089) 50 5411, 52 8984
Desert Rose, Alice Springs, (089) 52 6251, can conduct private tours.
Discovery Ecotours, Alice Springs, (089) 53 0881, must be group booking.
Ipolera Cultural Tours and campground, Alice Springs (089) 56 7466

South Australia
Aboriginal Lands Trust, Tandanya, 253 Grenfell Street, Adelaide 5000.
(08) 232 3732, fax (08) 223 2620
Women of the Wilderness Australia, PO Box 340, Unley 5061.
(085) 56 3586, run regular trips and courses in outdoor skills and sports.

Queensland
South East Queensland Indigenous Regional Council, GPO Box 165, Brisbane
4001. (07) 229 8277, (07) 221 6008
Witchencroft women's guest house, Atherton (near Cairns) PO Box 685,
Queensland 4883. (070) 91 2683 (ah)
BeBee's Tropical Apartments, PO Box 120, Edgehill, Cairns 4870. (008) 80 8390.
Lesbian and gay

Western Australia
Aboriginal Lands Trust, 1st Floor, Havelock Street, West Perth 6005.
(09) 483 1222, fax (09) 321 0990
Leaps and Bounds, adventures for women, contact Ricky Coates, PO Box 205,
Margaret River 6285. (097) 572 947
Bushtucker Tours, with Helen Lee, 2 Willmott Avenue, Margaret River 6285.
(097) 57 2466/2911, fax (097) 57 2550
Backpackers Bush Tour, with Lyn Clarke, 57 Vickery Crescent, Bunbury 6230.
(097) 21 4248

Tasmania
Tasmanian Aboriginal Regional Council, GPO Box 8A, Hobart 7001.
(002) 34 8055, fax (002) 34 8072
Mullaine Cottage women's self-contained accommodation, 21 Seventh Avenue,
Tasmania 7009. (002) 73 2627
Radclyffe Hall women's hostel, 139 Tarleton Street, Tasmania 7310.
(004) 27 9219
Women's Adventure Network, Outdoor activities, contact Laurel 002 23 4157
or Vicki (002) 24 0253

Recommended Reading
There are lots of books we could refer you to in this section. The following is a
select list and it contains books that are most likely to be useful in information on
travelling, reading not covered by pieces in the book, or as a guide to some aspect of

Australian women's culture. For further information visit any of the bookstores listed.

Travel Books
Lonely Planet has an excellent guide to Australia, and state guides are in preparation.
John Chapman and Monica Chapman. 1992. *Bushwalking in Australia 2nd Edition.*
Hawthorn: Lonely Planet.
Explore Australia. 1993. Melbourne: Viking O'Neil, (regularly updated, with good maps. (Road Atlases are also available).
Ron and Viv Moon. 1989. *Cape York: An Adventurer's Guide.* Chelsea: Kakirra Adventure Publications.
Ron and Viv Moon. 1989. *The Kimberley: An Adventurer's Guide.* Chelsea: Kakirra Adventure Publications.
Reg Morrison and Helen Grasswill. 1981. *Australia: A Timeless Grandeur,* Lansdowne Press.

Literature
Anthologies give a good idea of the general cultural drift. The following are just a few of the many anthologies that have focused on women's writing over the last decade or so. Also see books by contributors listed in biographical notes.

Anthologies
Debra Adelaide ed. 1988. *A Bright and Fiery Troop: Australian Women Writers of the Nineteenth Century.* Ringwood: Penguin. Available from Spinifex Press, Melbourne.
Debra Adelaide, 1988. *Australian Women Writers: A Bibliographic Guide.* Sydney: Unwin Hyman Limited.
Margaret Barbalet et al. 1988. *Canberra Tales.* Ringwood: Penguin.
Jillian Bartlett and Cathi Joseph eds. 1991. *Body Lines: A Women's Anthology.* Sydney: Women's Redress Press.
Margaret Bradstock and Louise Wakeling eds. 1987. *Words from the Same Heart.* Sydney: Hale and Iremonger.
Cathie Dunsford and Susan Hawthorne eds. 1990. *The Exploding Frangipani: Lesbian Writing from Australia and New Zealand.* Auckland: New Women's Press.
Flora Eldershaw ed. 1988. *The Peaceful Army.* Ringwood: Penguin. Available from Spinifex Press, Melbourne.
Anna Gibbs and Alison Tilson eds. 1982. *Frictions.* Melbourne: Sybylla.
Sneja Gunew ed. 1988. *Telling Ways: Australian Women's Experimental Writing.* Adelaide: Australian Feminist Studies Publications.
Sneja Gunew and Jan Mahyuddin (eds). 1988. *Beyond the Echo: Multicultural Women's Writing.* St Lucia: University of Queensland Press.
Susan Hawthorne ed. 1985. *Difference: Writings by Women.* Sydney: Waterloo

Press. Available from Spinifex Press, Melbourne.

Susan Hawthorne and Jenny Pausacker eds. 1989. *Moments of Desire: Sex and Sensuality by Australian Feminist Writers*. Ringwood: Penguin.

Drusilla Modjeska ed. 1989. *Inner Cities: Australian Women's Memory of Place*. Ringwood: Penguin.

Jocelynne Scutt ed. 1992. *Breaking Through*. Melbourne: Artemis Publishing.

Jocelynne Scutt ed. 1992. *Writing as a Woman*. Melbourne: Artemis Publishing.

Jocelynne Scutt ed. 1993. *Glorious Age*. Melbourne: Artemis Publishing.

Second Degree Tampering: Writing by Women. 1992. Melbourne: Sybylla Feminist Press, Melbourne

Roberta Snow and Jill Taylor eds. 1993. *Falling for Grace: An Anthology of Australian Lesbian Fiction*. Sydney: Blackwattle Press.

Dale Spender ed. 1991. *Heroines: A Contemporary Anthology of Australian Women Writers*. Ringwood: Penguin.

Dale Spender ed. 1988. *The Penguin Anthology of Australian Women's Writing*. Ringwood: Penguin.

Lynne Spender ed. 1988. *Her Selection: Writings by Nineteenth-Century Australian Women*. Ringwood: Penguin.

Poetry and Plays

Irene Coates, Nancy J. Corbett and Barbara Petrie eds. 1987. *Up From Below: Poems from the 1980s*. Sydney: Women's Redress Press.

Susan Hampton and Kate Llewellyn eds. 1986. *The Penguin Book of Australian Women Poets*. Ringwood: Penguin.

Kate Jennings ed. 1975. *Mother I'm Rooted*. Melbourne: Outback Press.

Kevin Gilbert ed. 1988. *Inside Black Australia: An Anthology of Aboriginal Poetry*. Ringwood: Penguin.

Around the Edge: Women's Plays. 1992. Adelaide: Tantrum Press.

Fiction (bracketed place names after entry indicate main setting)

Jessica Anderson. 1987. *Stories from the Warm Zone and Sydney Stories*. Ringwood: Penguin. (Sydney)

Thea Astley. 1988. *It's Raining in Mango*. Ringwood: Penguin. (North Queensland)

Barbara Baynton, see Sally Krimmer & Alan Lawson. 1980. Barbara Baynton. St Lucia: University of Queensland Press. (Gippsland, Victoria)

Carmel Bird. 1990. *The Bluebird Café*. Melbourne: McPhee Gribble. (Tasmania)

Kaz Cooke. 1992. *The Crocodile Club*. Sydney: Allen and Unwin. (Darwin)

Anna Couani and Peter Lyssiotis. 1989. *The Harbour Breathes*. Sydney: Seacruise. (Sydney)

Beverley Farmer. 1992. *Seal Woman*. St Lucia: UQP. (Victorian South Coast)

Miles Franklin. 1901. *My Brilliant Career*. Sydney: Angus and Robertson. (The High Country, NSW)

Helen Garner. 1978. *Monkey Grip*. Melbourne: McPhee Gribble; *The Children's*

Bach. Melbourne: McPhee Gribble. (Melbourne)

Andrea Goldsmith. 1990. *Gracious Living*. Ringwood: Penguin. (Melbourne)

Kate Grenville. 1988. *Joan's History of Australia*. St Lucia: UQP; 1987. *Lilian's Story*. Sydney: Allen and Unwin. (Sydney)

Barbara Hanrahan. 1982. *Dove*. St Lucia: UQP. (Adelaide)

Susan Hawthorne. 1992. *The Falling Woman*. Spinifex Press, Melbourne. (Central Australia and Riverina, NSW).

Dorothy Hewett. 1985. *Bobbin Up*. London: Virago. (Sydney)

Helen Hodgman. 1989. *Broken Words*. Ringwood: Penguin. (Goondawindi)

Janette Turner Hospital. 1990. *Isobars*. St Lucia: UQP. (Queensland)

Dorothy Johnston. 1988. *Maralinga, My Love*. Melbourne: McPhee Gribble. (Central Australia)

Elizabeth Jolley. *Palomino*. St Lucia: University of Queensland Press; 1987. *The Well*. Penguin. (South West Western Australia)

Eve Langley. 1942. *The Pea Pickers*. Sydney: Angus and Robertson. (Gippsland, Victoria)

Finola Moorhead. 1993. *Remember the Tarantella*. London: The Women's Press. (Melbourne); 1991. *Still Murder*. Ringwood: Penguin. (Sydney)

Christina Stead. 1945. *For Love Alone*. Sydney: Angus and Robertson. (Sydney)

Glen Tomasetti. 1976. *Thoroughly Decent People*. Melbourne: McPhee Gribble. (Melbourne).

Kylie Tennant. 1941. *The Battlers*. Sydney: Angus and Robertson. (Rural NSW)

Aina Vavere. 1990. *The Blue Mountain in Mujani: Stories of the Immigrant Experience*. Ringwood: Penguin. (Adelaide)

Amy Witting. 1989. *I is for Isobel*. Ringwood: Penguin. (Sydney)

Poetry

Caroline Caddy. 1989. *Beach Plastic*. Fremantle: Fremantle Arts Centre Press.

Lee Cataldi. 1990. *The Women Who Live on the Ground*. Ringwood: Penguin.

Terry Whitebeach. 1993. *Bird Dreaming* in *Four New Poets*. Ringwood: Penguin.

Autobiography

Ellie Gaffney. 1989. *Somebody Now*. Canberra: AIATSI Press. (Torres Strait)

Pat Malcolm. 1993. *The First Cuts are Deepest*. Fremantle: Fremantle Arts Centre Press. (WA)

Ruby Langford. 1988. *Don't Take Your Love to Town*. Ringwood: Penguin. (NSW and Qld)

Sally Morgan. 1987. *My Place*. Fremantle: Fremantle Arts Centre Press. (WA)

Glenyse Ward. 1987. *Wandering Girl*. Fremantle: Fremantle Arts Centre Press. (WA)

History

Diane Bell. 1993. *Daughters of the Dreaming*. Sydney: Allen and Unwin. *Generations*. 1988. Ringwood: Penguin.

Miriam Dixon. 1976. *The Real Matilda: Woman and Identity in Australia 1788 to 1975*. Ringwood: Penguin.

Eve Mumewa Fesl. 1993. *Conned*. St Lucia: UQP.

Lucy Frost. 1984. *No Place for a Nervous Lady: Voices from the Australian Bush*. Melbourne: McPhee Gribble.

Patricia Grimshaw, Marilyn Lake, Ann McGrath and Marion Quartly. 1994. *Creating a Nation*. Ringwood: McPhee Gribble/Penguin.

Sue Hardisty. 1991. *Thanks Girls and Goodbye*. Melbourne: Viking O'Neil.

Susan Hawthorne. 1993. *The Spinifex Quiz Book: A Book of Women's Answers*. Melbourne: Spinifex Press.

Beverley Kingston. 1975. *My Wife, My Daughter, and Poor Mary Anne*. Melbourne: Nelson.

Wendy Lowenstein and Moragh Loh. 1982. *The Immigrants*. Ringwood: Penguin.

Jan Mercer (ed). 1980. *The Other Half: Women in Australian Society*. Ringwood: Penguin.

Heather Radi ed. 1988. *200 Australian Women*. Sydney: Women's Redress Press Inc.

Julie Rigg and Julie Copeland eds. 1985. *Coming Out! Women's Voices, Women's Lives*. Melbourne: Nelson.

Marian Sawer. 1990. *Sisters in Suits: Women and Public Policy in Australia*. Sydney: Allen and Unwin.

Jocelynne A. Scutt. 1991. *Women and the Law*. Sydney: The Law Book Company.

Jocelynne A. Scutt. 1994. *The Sexual Gerrymander*. Melbourne: Spinifex Press.

Anne Summers. 1994. *Damned Whores and God's Police: The Colonization of Women in Australia*. Ringwood: Penguin.

Journals, magazines, newsletters, directories

Australian Feminist Studies. Research Centre for Women's Studies, University of Adelaide, GPO Box 498, Adelaide 5001.

Australian Women's Book Review. Victoria University of Technology, PO Box 14428, Melbourne 3000.

Australian Women's Studies Association Newsletter. PO Box 10, Kingswood 2747.

Hecate: An International Journal of Women's Liberation. PO Box 99, University of Queensland, St Lucia 4067.

Journal of Australian Lesbian Feminist Studies. PO Box 364, Glebe 2037.

Lilith: A Feminist History Journal. PO Box 4354, University of Melbourne, Parkville 3052.

Refractory Girl: A Feminist Journal. PO Box 648 Glebe 2037.

WIFT. 1991. *Women Working in Film, Television and Video*. Women in Film and Television Inc, Sydney.

Women's Studies in Australian Universities: A Directory. 1992. Women's Research Centre, University of Western Sydney, Nepean.

CONTRIBUTING AUTHORS AND PHOTOGRAPHERS

ROBYN ADAMS lives in bushland near Melbourne. She is a botanist and soil scientist who lectures in environmental management, and her major research interests are in the areas of arid zone ecology, plant-soil relationships, fire ecology and archaeobotany. She has a long involvement with environmental education, dealing with professional vegetation managers as well as volunteer groups. She has walked extensively in south-eastern Australia, and is a keen photographer of plants and wild places.

ROBYN ARIANRHOD is a mathematician who works at Monash University. She lived for many years in Armidale and Bellingen where she was involved in the establishment of the alternative magazine, *Maggie's Farm*. When she moved back to Melbourne in the early 1980s, she quickly became one of the founding members of Salon-A-Muse, an arts salon for women. She is currently working on a book about women and maths.

FAITH BANDLER was born in Tumbulgum on the North Coast of New South Wales. She was educated at Murwillumbah Public school and the Cleveland night school in Sydney. After serving in the Australian Women's Land Army during the war she studied piano and singing while working in a fashion house. Her father Wacvie Mussingcon was brought from the Pacific Island of Vanuatu by the Australian slave traders in the last century to work on the sugar cane in North Queensland. Her works include *Wacvie* (1977), *Marani in Australia* (1980 with Len Fox), *The Time Was Ripe* (1983 with Len Fox), *Welou, My Brother* (1984) and *Turning the Tide* (1988). She was awarded the Braille Book of the Year in 1977 and the Pandora Award in 1989. Faith Bandler has been an active advocate for Aboriginal rights for over thirty years as a member of the Aboriginal Rights Council for the Advancement of Aboriginal and Torres Strait Islanders and as co-founder for the Aboriginal Australian Fellowship, organisations which successfully worked for the removal of discriminatory legislation and the establishment of Government services directed at Aboriginal and Islander people. She was the NSW director for the 1967 National Referendum campaign to recognise the citizenship of Aboriginal and Islander people. She accepted an Order of Australia in 1984, having declined an MBE in 1974. She is currently working on a new manuscript and has recently been appointed to the Literature and History committee of the NSW Arts Advisory Council. She gave the key-note address at the NSW State Literary Awards in 1993.

DIANE BELL grew up in Melbourne and after graduating as a 'mature student' she lived in central Australia working as an anthropologist and consultant on Aboriginal law and land rights. She has also been involved in making links between Aboriginal women's customary law and the ways in which Australian women's culture is represented. She is the author of numerous books and articles including *Law: The Old and the New* (1980/1984) *Daughters of the Dreaming* (1983/1993), *Generations: Grandmothers, Mothers and Daughters* (1987), and co-editor of *Religion in Aboriginal Australia* (1984), *This is My Story* (1990) and *Gendered Fields* (1993). She lives in Massachusetts, USA.

SUZANNE BELLAMY is an artist, writer and radical feminist, with a diverse background in academic history and Women's Studies, ceramics, printmaking, sculpture and storytelling. She began her creative work in urban Sydney, but in 1983 moved to the country. For ten years she lived in the southern mountain ranges of New South Wales, south of Canberra, the national capital. She set up a studio on an old sheep farm by a creek in the high country of the Monaro, surrounded by eucalypt forest, native animals and granite rock formations. In 1993 she moved to land near Braidwood, still south of Sydney, but closer to the south coast beside the Bandawang National Park. She is building a studio there, in the bush. She can be contacted by writing to her c/- PO Box 142, Braidwood, NSW 2622, and she welcomes enquiries and planned visits, particularly from other artists, builders and gardeners. In time she hopes to build guest studios with labour exchange programmes.

LISA BELLEAR is from the Noonuccal tribe and is a poet, radio personality and post-graduate student at the University of Melbourne. She has been active in the Koori and women's movements in Melbourne for many years. She is currently working on a book with Destiny Deacon entitled, *Dreaming in Urban Areas* (Spinifex, forthcoming).

JANINE BURKE was born in Melbourne in 1952. She is the author of eight books of fiction and art history. In 1975 she organised the pioneering exhibition Australian Women Artists, 1980–1940, the subject of her first book. She is a well-known critic publishing in journals, catalogues and newspapers. She has also curated exhibitions of contemporary art. From 1977 to 1982 she lectured in art history, resigning her job to write fiction full time. *Second Sight* won the 1987 Victorian Premier's Award for fiction. Her other novels are *Speaking, Company of Images, Lullaby* and *A Journey to Bright Water*, a novel for teenagers. She has also written a biography, *Joy Hester* and *Field of Vision, A Decade of Change: Women's Art in the 70s.* She has degrees from Melbourne and La Trobe Universities. Her travels have included the USA and Europe, and she has stayed for long periods in Paris and Tuscany, the latter inspired *Second Sight.* She has decided that St Kilda, where she lives now, is the next best thing to Paris.

CAROLINE CADDY was born in Western Australia but spent her childhood in the USA. Since then she has lived in Western Australia mainly on the south coast. She has published four books of poetry: *Singing at Night, Letters from the North, Beach Plastic* (which won the Premier's Literary Award in 1990) and *Conquistadors* (which won the National Book Council Award in 1991). Recently she has travelled to Antarctica with the Australian Antarctic Division and spent some time in China. She is currently working on books of poetry concerning these areas.

JANE CAFARELLA is a journalist and cartoonist with the Melbourne *Age.* She was on maternity leave and had just moved from the inner city to the Dandenong Ranges, about one hour from Melbourne, when she wrote this story for her weekly column, 'A New Life Journal'. Since then, things have gone from bad to worse. If she forgets to put the seed out early in the morning, the cockies pace up and down the verandah peering in at the kitchen window. If she does not emerge, seed in hand, they chew holes in the verandah posts. Recently, she ran out of seed and could not go out to buy more as both her children were at home sick. In desperation, she grabbed the packet of Nutrigrain (breakfast cereal) and poured half it into the bird tray. The cockies flew down in eager anticipation but . . . well, that's another story.

BARBARA CREED teaches film at La Trobe University. She has spoken and written widely on issues related to film theory and popular culture. She is the author of *The*

417

Monstrous-Feminine: Film, Feminism, Psychoanalysis (Routledge, 1993) and co-editor of *Don't Shoot, Darling: Women's Independent Filmmaking in Australia* (Greenhouse, 1987). Barbara grew up on a farm in rural Victoria in the 40s but now lives in Melbourne – although she leaves for the country/beach at every opportunity. Her favourite pursuits are watching movies, reading and horse-riding.

DESTINY DEACON has been active in the Koori and women's movements since the 1970s. She is a photographer and writer. Her photographs have been exhibited throughout Australia and are held in several major gallery collections. She teaches English Literature at the University of Melbourne. She is currently working on a book with Lisa Bellear, *Dreaming in Urban Areas* (Spinifex, forthcoming).

JEANNIE DEVITT is an anthropologist who has worked extensively in northern Australia with Aboriginal communities. Her principal research interest is the relationship between traditional and contemporary Aboriginal dietary practices. Currently living in Darwin, and working as a consultant she now also undertakes research into traditional systems of land tenure for Aboriginal communities preparing land claims.

SARA DOWSE was born in Chicago, USA, lived in New York and Los Angeles, and migrated to Australia just before she turned twenty. She settled in Sydney, and ten years later moved to Canberra, the Australian capital, where she became the first head of what is now the Office of the Status of Women in the Prime Minister's Department. She resigned this position to become a full-time writer. Her work has appeared in a wide range of publications. She was co-author of the Seven Writers' *Canberra Tales*, and her books include *West Block, Silver City, Schemetime,* and *Sapphires*. She is currently working on a biography of a great aunt who is believed to have died in Stalin's purges.

SUE EDMONDS is a musician and songwriter. Living in Hobart in the 1970s, she was a member of the Ovarian Sisters band. In 1983 she moved to Wollongong, NSW where she began working with Aboriginal mural artists. She is currently travelling Australia with her hubaphone, a percussion instrument made from used car hub caps.

CATHERINE ELLIS is a leading scholar in Central Australian Aboriginal music. She has done extensive work on women's secret ceremonies in South Australia, and later established the Centre for Aboriginal Studies in Music in Adelaide. She has been Professor of Music at the University of New England since 1985, a position that acknowledges her role as a music educator and performer.

VIRGINIA FRASER is a photographer, journalist and film-maker. She is the author of *A Book of Australian Women* (Melbourne: Outback Press, 1974), one of the first feminist books of photographs and text published in Australia.

SABINE GLEDITSCH was born in Germany in 1955 and came to Australia in 1987. Despite earlier doubts over the possibility of using a second language in a professional capacity, she has for the last four years worked as a news journalist, writing news copy and reporting for Radio 3EA, the Melbourne-based radio station of the Special Broadcasting Service (SBS). Sabine defines herself as a lesbian feminist first, and a privileged migrant second – privileged because she spoke English on arrival, is well-educated and comes from an industrialised Western culture with no dependants in her care and a career instead, which gives her more choice than other migrant women have. Journalism satisfies her curiosity about life, and in her spare time she is active in Melbourne's lesbian community, works towards personal growth, reads a lot, likes photography, and enjoys beach walks and camping in the bush and the desert.

HEATHER GRACE was born in Melbourne in 1951. Since 1983 she has lived in the Kimberley in Western Australia. Her work has been published in *Angry Women: Anthology of Australian Women's Writing*. Her novel, *Heart of Light* was published by Fremantle Arts Centre Press in 1992.

SNEJA GUNEW has worked for many years to highlight the contribution of migrant writers. She has contributed many articles to journals and books internationally. She is co-editor of two volumes of fiction, *Beyond the Echo: Multicultural Women's Writing* and *Telling Ways: Australian Women's Experimental Writing*, and she is the editor of two volumes of feminist theory, *Feminist Knowledge: Critique and Construct*, and *A Reader in Feminist Knowledge*. She teaches at the University of Victoria, in British Colombia, Canada.

JANINE HAINES was born in South Australia in 1945 and is married with two adult daughters. She is an Arts/Science graduate of the University of Adelaide in South Australia and taught senior school mathematics and English between 1967 and 1977. In 1977 she was appointed to the Australian Senate and re-elected in the 1980, 1983 and 1987 Federal elections. She became Deputy Leader of the Australian Democrats in 1985 and, in 1986, became the first woman to lead a political party in Australia when she was elected Federal Parliamentary Leader of the Australian Democrats. Her main concern as a member of parliament was to use the legislative process to improve the legal, social and economic position of women in Australia. Following her defeat in the 1990 Federal election and her subsequent retirement from politics, she wrote *Suffrage to Sufferance: 100 Years of Women in Politics* published by Allen & Unwin in 1992.

GILLIAN HANSCOMBE (b. 1945, Melbourne) and SUNITI NAMJOSHI (b. 1941 Bombay) live together in a small village in Devon, surrounded by thatched cottages, green pastures, dairy herds, flocks of sheep, and other set pieces of English rural life. Separately they have published books of poetry, fiction, satire, and literary criticism, as well as poems, articles and other work in various anthologies, collections and periodicals. Jointly they have written in a variety of modes in both poetic and prose forms. Suniti is well known for her *Feminist Fables*, reissued in 1993 by Spinifex Press, who also published her latest extended fable, *St Suniti and the Dragon*. Gillian's most recent book, *Sybil The Glide of Her Tongue*, was published by Spinifex in 1992. Their joint work began with *Flesh and Paper* (1986), a sequence of poems written while Gillian was living in London and Suniti in Toronto, where she taught at the University of Toronto for seventeen years. Their most recent extended joint work is a theatre piece called *Kaliyug: Circles of Paradise*, a satire for a singer, two principals, and a chorus. As lesbian feminist writers they have given a large number of joint readings in Britain, North America and Australia, but between travels, do their best to write full-time.

PONCH HAWKES is a Melbourne-based freelance photographer who has exhibited in solo and group shows. Her photographs are published widely in books, newspapers and magazines. Publications include, *Generations: Grandmothers, Mothers and Daughters*, by Diane Bell and photographs by Ponch Hawkes, a book about the way culture and values are passed down from one generation of women to another, and *Best Mates*, a study of male friendship. Currently she works happily as an artist and freelance photographer and is completing her latest book about the AIDS Memorial Quilt.

SUSAN HAWTHORNE grew up on a farm in the Riverina in southern NSW. She loves travelling and although she has travelled extensively throughout Australia since she was seventeen, there are still many places she would like to visit. She has worked as a teacher, youth worker, festival organiser and publisher. She is the author of a collection of poems, *The Language in My Tongue*, (published in the volume *Four New Poets*), a novel, *The Falling Woman* and *The Spinifex Quiz Book*, translated into German, it will appear in 1994. She is the editor or co-editor of four anthologies of women's writing including *Difference*, *Moments of Desire*, *The Exploding Frangipani* and *Angels of Power*. She has been active in the women's movement for more than twenty years.

DIANA JAMES currently runs Desert Tracks tours with Nganyinytja, an elder of the Pitjantjatjara people of Central Australia. Diana is an anthropologist and teacher who has worked with Nganyinytja since 1980, when they worked together gaining political recognition of Pitjantjatjara women as land owners and custodians in the Land Rights struggle. Diana was born in 1954 in Sydney. In 1975 she left to work as an art and craft advisor at Fregon with Pitjantjatjara women. Since then her life has been spent with these people, learning their language and way of life. She has worked as a bilingual teacher, a community advisor and now as a cross-cultural guide.

SANDY JEFFS is a poet whose book, *Poems from the Madhouse* was published by Spinifex Press in 1993. Her poetry has also appeared in anthologies, such as *Difference* and *The Exploding Frangipani*, and in literary magazines. Born in Ballarat, Victoria she now lives on the fringes of Melbourne.

EVA JOHNSON has worked in Aboriginal theatre for many years. She is the author of six plays including *Tjindarella, Murras, Miminis Voices, What do They Call Me, Two Bob in the Quid, Heartbeat of the Earth*. Her poetry and plays have also been published in anthologies including *Inside Black Australia, Difference, The Exploding Frangipani* and *Heroines*.

KAYE JOHNSTON is a lesbian feminist, teacher, organic farmer and permaculturist. Her work is teaching women, growing plants, creating healthy food and landscapes. Kaye and her partner Andrea Lofthouse established Moonraker Farm in Kangaroo Valley, a very beautiful area of the South Coast of New South Wales. Born in 1946 in Sydney, she grew up in the inner city and western suburbs, and moved to the country in 1984. Her interests include writing fiction and non-fiction, writing and performing comedy items. She is learning to play the trumpet and is in a jazz band and the town band, Berry Silver Band.

ELIZABETH JOLLEY was born in 1923 of Austrian British parents and grew up in the Midlands of England. Trained as a nurse, since migrating to Australia in 1959 she has worked at a variety of jobs. She wrote for twenty years before publishing her first collection of short stories *Five Acre Virgin* in 1976. Her first novel *Palomino* was published in 1980. She is a widely acclaimed novelist throughout the English speaking world whose many prizewinning books include *Milk and Honey, The Well, Miss Peabody's Inheritance, Foxybaby, Mr Scobie's Riddle, My Father's Moon* and *Cabin Fever.* For her service to Australian literature, Elizabeth has been awarded the Order of Australia (1988) and the Advance Australia Award (1989). Her novels have been translated into French, Spanish and German. In 1989 the West Australian University of Technology awarded Elizabeth an honourary doctorate. She currently lectures at Curtin University, Perth, Western Australia and cultivates a small orchard forty miles from Perth. Her most recent book, *The George's Wife*, won the *Age* Book of the Year Award in 1993.

ROSEMARY JONES was born in Adelaide, South Australia in 1954. She is the author of numerous short stories which have appeared in magazines and anthologies. She was one of the founding editors of a literary magazine, *Ash Magazine* in 1979 which she continued to edit until its termination in 1984. A former resident of Coober Pedy (in the far north of the state) she now lives and teaches in Whyalla, South Australia, a small city poised between the sea and the desert.

LAURENE KELLY worked for five years running the Mole Creek Wildlife Park in northern Tasmania. She is currently living on women's land, on the East Coast of Tasmania. She has previously lived on women's land in NSW and in Wales. She has also worked extensively in women's services and considers herself a gut women's liberationist. Writing is an ambition she has had since childhood and she aims to have more published works before the turn of the century. She is a Sagittarian and remains ever optimistic for a better world for women and children. She lives with her lover, her 10-year-old dog and two other women, hundreds of wallabies and other nocturnal species.

RENATE KLEIN was born in Switzerland and has lived and worked in many different places including East Africa, Tunisia, Paraguay, USA, Britain and Australia. Well known for her work in Women's Studies and women's health, she is the author and (co-)editor of numerous books including, *Theories of Women's Studies, Test Tube Women, Infertility, Radical Voices, The Exploitation of a Desire, Angels of Power* and *RU 486: Misconceptions, Myths and Morals.* She is a Senior Lecturer in Women's Studies and Deputy Director of the Australian Women's Research Centre at Deakin University. She is working on an international anthology on radical feminism with Diane Bell, and researching the unethics of Hormone Replacement Therapy with Lynette Dumble.

RUBY LANGFORD GINIBI was born on Boxbridge Aboriginal mission, NSW, in 1934 and grew up in Bonalbo, near Casino in northern NSW. In 1988 Ruby's autobiography, *Don't Take Your Love to Town* was published to wide acclaim. Her second book, *Real Deadly* was published in 1992. Her third book, *My Bundjalung People,* published in 1994, tells of her return to the mission where she was born after a 48 year absence, to find her roots and reconnect with her extended family. She lives in Sydney where she is currently working on her fourth book which explores the incarceration of Aboriginal people in Australian jails through the story of her son Nobby's imprisonment. Aboriginal people are the most incarcerated in Australian jails. She is also working on a book of Koori humour to be entitled *Only Gammon* (meaning, 'not real').

TANIA LIENERT was born in Woomera in South Australia in 1966 and lived there until she was fifteen. After finishing secondary school in Adelaide she worked as a journalist for the *Adelaide Advertiser*, a community arts officer on rural Eyre Peninsula in South Australia and a theatre company administrator in the South East of South Australia. In 1991 she moved to Victoria and completed a Post-graduate Degree in Women's Studies at Deakin University, Geelong. She is of German, Scandinavian, Irish and Scottish descent, her ancestors having emigrated to South Australia in the 1800s. Her interests include the history of female friendship and lesbianism, feminist theology and spirituality, the women's peace and environmental movements, community radio, world music festivals, bushwalking and gardening. Her ambition is to live in a forest in a warm climate near a river and set up a women's university/learning centre by the sea.

KATE LLEWELLYN was born in Tumby Bay, South Australia and moved to the Blue Mountains, New South Wales in 1985. Kate has published six books of poetry, among them *Luxury, Honey, Figs* and *Selected Poems*. She co-edited *The Penguin Book of Australian Women Poets*. Her first book of prose, *The Waterlily*, was a runaway best-seller and has been reprinted five times so far. *Dear You* and *The Mountain* completed the trilogy of which *The Waterlily* was the first part. *Angels and Dark Madonnas* is a book of travel in Italy and India. Her new book, *Lilies, Feathers and Frangipani*, continues her travel writing.

UYEN LOEWALD was born in Vietnam and fought against the Diem Government supported by the Americans and subsequently was imprisoned for six months. She studied mathematics and literature in Vietnam, the US and Australia and has lived in the US, Germany, France and is now settling in Australia. The author of *Child in Vietnam* (1987), she regularly contributes to *Short Story International*, NY and is currently working as the Co-ordinator of the Migrant Resource Centre of Canberra and Queanbeyan Inc. She is also researching on cultures and their impact on learning and training.

SALLY MACARTHUR was born in 1950 in the NSW country town of Bombala. As a child she studied piano and later, composition. In 1968 she won the school composition prize and performed one of her works at the International Society for Contemporary Music's New Bloom Concert in Sydney in 1969. On graduating from the Sydney Conservatorium in 1972, she became Director of Music at Walford Church of England Girl's Grammar School in Adelaide while simultaneously furthering her musical studies at the University of Adelaide where she graduated in 1976. Since returning to Sydney in 1977, Sally has been lecturing in the Division of Musicology at the Sydney Conservatorium and, during 1993, she has also been teaching in the Music and Women's Studies Departments at the University of Sydney. She is currently undertaking postgraduate research, applying feminist theory and semiotics to the analysis of music by Australian women composers. Sally has published extensively in local and overseas journals and books. She is currently editing *New Music Australia* (Sounds Australian, 1993), a special issue of *Sounds Australian* on feminism and music (Summer, 1993), and she is contributing a chapter to an Australian feminist reader (Barbara Caine, Elizabeth Grosz and Rosemary Pringle, eds.) which will be published by Allen & Unwin in 1994.

BETTY MCLELLAN is a radical feminist psychotherapist practising in Townsville, North Queensland. Since returning from study in the United States in 1977 she has been active in Australian feminist politics and is a frequent speaker at political demonstrations and conferences throughout the country. She is a consultant to the Aboriginal and Torres Strait Islander Mental Health program recently set up in Townsville. Betty is responsible for establishing the annual Winter Institute for Women held in Townsville. She is the author of *Overcoming Anxiety: A Positive Approach to Dealing with Severe Anxiety in Your Life* (Allen & Unwin, 1992) and of *Beyond Psychoppression: A Feminist Alternative to Therapy* (Spinifex, 1994).

RUTH MADDISON was born in Melbourne, Australia in 1945. When young she married, had three children and divorced in quick succession. She spent several years being a kitchen-hand, waitress and driver. In 1976 she picked up a camera and became a photographer. Self taught, she works as a freelance photographer, artist and occasional lecturer. She has had nine solo exhibitions since 1979, and her work has been seen in group shows every year since 1980, including important survey shows mounted by the National Gallery of Victoria and the Australian National Gallery. She has been published in many books, magazines and newspapers and is represented in many major collections, including the National Gallery of Victoria, the Australian National Gallery and the Jewish Museum of Australia.

JENNY MAHER was born in 1945 and grew up on a grape farm at Nyah West on the Murray River in Victoria. She entered the nursing profession when she was almost sixteen and left when she married a wheat and sheep farmer in 1964. She has four grown children, three sons and one daughter. She sees herself as a typical rural women who has had to sustain a variety of jobs to survive in rural Australia, but is happy to declare her independence, an achievement in male-dominated Australia. She is interested in the lives and plight of rural women, especially the backlashes and consequences suffered by them under patriarchy. She is particularly interested in the present rural crisis and the effects of this on rural women and their families. In 1993 she completed her degree in Social Science at Deakin University, majoring in Women's Studies and is now a full-time Training Officer for the disabled.

JUDITH MARTYN-ELLIS is the youngest daughter of Catherine Ellis, introduced to traditional performance before her birth and named by the Pitjantjatjara people after a song that was being researched at the time of her birth. She is currently completing a Combined B. Mus/B.A. at the University of New England, at Armidale, New South Wales.

FINOLA MOORHEAD was born in Victoria. She graduated from the University of Tasmania in 1968 and has been a full-time writer since 1973. She wrote several plays in the 1970s and was a member of the Women's Theatre Group in Melbourne. She is the author of the prize-winning novel, *Still Murder*, as well as *Remember the Tarantella*, *A Handwritten Modern Classic* and a collection of short works, *Quilt*. Her work has been published widely in magazines and anthologies. In 1986 she wrote 'Miss Marple Goes to Ayers Rock', as part of a play, *Lindy and Dingo*. She lives in northern New South Wales.

MERRILEE MOSS is a playwright. Her first full-length play, *If Looks Could Kill*, was a sell-out success at La Mama Theatre in 1988 and had a return season in St Kilda 1989. Her second play, *Over the Hill*, had seasons in Canberra and Melbourne in

1990/91 before touring community venues in NSW, Victoria and Tasmania. *Over the Hill* will tour Western Australia in 1994, has been translated into Mandarin and was recently made into a video by the Family Planning Association. A third play, *About Face*, was commissioned by the ACT Arts Council and had a successful season at the Ralph Wilson Theatre, Canberra in 1991. *And Empty Suitcases*, Moss's fourth play – about women, travel and adventure – was produced in Canberra in 1993. Merrilee Moss has also written nine novels for adolescents under two different names. Five of those novels were included in the Dolly Fiction series – *Stroke of Luck*, *Hungry for Love*, *Behind the Scenes*, *Best Friends* and *Forget Me Not*. These 'romance' books focus on issues important to girls – success, sport, anorexia, non-traditional occupations and body image. Her four titles in the romance-adventure series *Hot Pursuit* (devised and written in collaboration with fellow author Jaye Francis and published by Penguin) are: *Franca*, *Louise*, *Kristi* and *Semra*.

SUNITI NAMJOSHI was born in India and has lived in Canada and Britain. A poet, fabulist and novelist she is the author of *Feminist Fables*, *Conversations with Cow*, *The Blue Donkey Fables*, *The Mothers of Maya Diip*, *Because of India* and most recently, *St Suniti and the Dragon*.

OODGEROO NOONUCCAL is one of Australia's best known poets. Her collection *My People* has become a classic of Australian literature. Born of the Noonuccal people of Stradbroke Island, Queensland, Oodgeroo was a committed activist for Aboriginal rights. She is also the author of *We Are Going* (1964), *The Dawn is at Hand* (1966), *Stradbroke Dreamtime* (1972), *Father Sky and Mother Earth* (1981) and *Quandamooka: The Art of Kath Walker* represents her visual art. She has worked as an actor in the film, *The Fringe Dwellers* and was joint scriptwriter and producer with her son for the TV programme, *The Rainbow Serpent*. Oodgeroo Noonuccal died in 1993.

HELEN O'SHEA was born in 1951 and grew up on the outskirts of Melbourne. Her degree in literature from the Australian National University, Canberra, took her to Ireland where, for two years, she wrote a masters thesis on Irish poetry while learning folklore collecting and fiddle playing. After ten years at Australian universities working in teaching, administration, publications and community relations, she turned to free-lance work as a folklorist, historian and author. She is currently completing an ethno-graphic study of rural community life, sponsored by the National Library of Australia, the Australian Folk Trust, the Victorian Ministry for the Arts and the Literature Board, while teaching Australian Studies at the University of Melbourne and playing Irish music.

PAULINE REILLY is an ancient grandmother, born 5 December 1918, who lives by the sea, loves people, surfing, reading, theatre, music, walking in the bush, jigsaw puzzles, enjoys a long-sustained marriage (retired husband happy with role-reversal), loathes housework, shopping and cooking. She is the author of more than twenty books, co-author of *The Atlas of Australian Birds* and has been involved with birds for forty years in bird-banding research and writing papers, especially about penguins. Her latest project is *Penguins of the World* for Oxford University Press, due July, 1994. She spent three months, aged 60, on study in Antarctica. She is a compulsive writer but to date most of her fiction is not YET appreciated by publishers.

ALISON RICHARDS is a theatre director, performer and theorist. She attended early Circus Oz workshops, but gracefully retired when she found out how many one-armed chin-ups it took to train for the trapeze. She is now Lecturer in Theatre at Deakin University, Geelong.

MERREN RICKETSON was born in Melbourne, Australia in 1954. Apart from lengthy sojourns in Europe, India and interstate she has lived in Melbourne all her life. She has been involved with women's arts practice and education for over 10 years and has organised many exhibitions of women's work. She is currently the Co-Director of Artmoves, an organisation which works to promote women artists through exhibitions and publishing. Merren is also the Co-ordinator of the Women's Art Register, an extensive archive of images and information on Australian women artists located at the Carringbush Library.

PORTIA ROBINSON is the Associate Professor of History at Macquarie University. Publications include: *The Women of Botany Bay*, a reinterpretation of the role of women, Macquarie Library (1988) and Penguin (1993); *The Hatch and Brood of Time*, OUP (1985). Current European-based research includes: criminal women in society; migrant women to Australia; the Irish and an Australian identity. She became a member of the Order of Australia in 1993 for her works on colonial history. (She has 1 husband, 4 children, 8 grandchildren and a cat. Hobbies: cooking, gardening and surfing.)

ROSA SAFRANSKY was born in Paris in 1948 and migrated to Australia with her family in 1949. Her background is Polish Jewish. She considers herself a cultural mish-mash which makes her life very interesting. She studied textile design in New York and her daughter was born in the Bronx. Rosa has been writing for a number of years and has won prizes in the *Age* Short Story Competition, The ABC Bicentennial Short Story Award, and the *Canberra Times* National Short Story Award. In 1988 she was awarded a fellowship by the Literature Board of The Australia Council. In 1991, she was Writer in Residence at Deakin University and she has also taught creative writing for a number of years. Her work has been anthologised in collections in Australia and overseas and her first collection *Can A Morris Minor Break the Speed of Sound?* will be published by Pan Macmillan in 1994.

JOCELYNNE A. SCUTT is Australia's best known feminist lawyer. A frequent speaker at rallies, book launches, seminars and conferences, Jocelynne Scutt is widely admired for her efforts in raising issues around violence. She is the author and editor of many books including *Even in the Best of Homes*, *The Baby Machine*, *Growing Up Feminist*, *Different Lives* and *Women and the Law*. In 1992 she co-founded Artemis Publishing which has published anthologies of Australian women's autobiographical writings, the 'Women's Voices, Women's Lives' series. Her most recent book is *The Sexual Gerry-mander* (Spinifex 1994).

DIANNE SIMMONS lives in bushland near Melbourne. She is a botanist who lectures in environmental management, and her research interests include fire ecology, weed ecology, habitat fragmentation and biodiversity, archaeobotany and the reconstruction of prehistoric environments. She is committed to the conservation of wilderness areas and native vegetation in Australia, and she has walked extensively in remote parts of southeastern Australia, particularly in Tasmania, for over twenty years.

DALE SPENDER is an Australian who has walked down the main street of every major city on the continent. She has also lived in England for many years and has a 'second home' in the United States. Portable computers have made an enormous difference to her life and she is now able to write no matter where she is. Her current research is on women and the electronic era and *Nattering the Nets: Women, Power and Multimedia* will be published by Spinifex in 1994. She is also working on *Brains and Beauty* (Transworld) and *Weddings and Wives* will be available from Penguin in 1994.

DIANA STARSKI lives with her canine companion in a leafy suburb of Melbourne. She is a teacher, writer, artist and astrologer. Diana has had a longstanding interest in women's history and ancient religions. She is currently working on a series of icons which depict facets of lesbian culture, both ancient and modern.

JAN TEAGLE KAPETAS was born in 1947 and is a fourth generation Australian. She is an artist, festival co-ordinator, teacher, writer, feminist and mother of two children. Her short stories and poetry have won awards, (including the Arafura Short Story Award in 1990, 1991 and 1992) and she has had two plays produced in 1991 and 1992, (*Staying True* and *From Another Place*). Her work has been published in magazines, art catalogues, and anthologies and deals with issues of migration, place, and culture in women's lives. She has lived in South Australia, Greece and the Northern Territory. Most recently she was Writer in Residence in Angurugu, Groote Eylandt and is now, after five months of travelling around Australia, delighted to be living in Fremantle, Western Australia completing a novel with the assistance of a grant from the Literature Board of the Australia Council.

BARBARA TIERNAN was born in Melbourne in 1947 and has been a professional arts administrator since 1978. Her work has taken her all over Australia, managing major theatre companies, visual art galleries and performing arts tours. She is active in the development of performing arts touring circuits in regional and remote areas of Australia as well as devising improved access for geographically disadvantaged people to the best of Australia's theatre events. Barbara was the Director of Araluen Arts Centre, Alice Springs from 1987 to 1990. She is currently the Director of a theatre venue in Sydney.

TERRY WHITEBEACH was born on the east coast of Tasmania, the second of a family of six girls. She spent much of her early life roaming the middens and beaches of South East Tasmania, unaware that her companions, whom she names 'the silent ones' were the spirits of her Aboriginal ancestors. Educated at the University of Tasmania, where she studied Mediaeval Literature and Philosophy, she interrupted her studies to produce four children. About twenty years later she began to write again, seriously. Her work has been published in anthologies and journals in Australia, New Zealand and America, and performed in many venues in Australia and the USA. Her first collection of poetry *Bird Dream* was published by Penguin in *Four New Poets*. It has been short-listed for the Western Australian Premier's prize. She works as a community artist, and is presently studying part-time for an MA in literary criticism and performance. She now lives in Western Australia and is collaborating with Darwin Aboriginal performer June Mills, to produce a show that addresses (both seriously and humourously) some of the issues facing women, in particular, Aboriginal and mixed-race women.

426

MAVIS YEN was born in Perth, Western Australia in 1916 of an Australian mother and a Chinese father. She was educated in Australia, Shanghai, Hong Kong and the Pearl River delta. She was in Hong Kong when it was surrendered to the Japanese in 1941 but managed to reach Free China where she spent two years doing war work in Chungking. Returning to Australia in 1944, her wartime experiences led her back to China again. A job in the Chinese Industrial Co-operatives movement in Shanghai in 1949 enabled her to move to Peking, the capital of the new people's republic. She stayed on to teach English and correct English scripts. But the cultural revolution taught her more about China and the Chinese people than any other period. Today she lives in Canberra but finds herself suspended between two cultures. Her current interest is the history of the early Chinese in Australia.

ACKNOWLEDGEMENTS (FOR REPRINTED MATERIAL)

For permission to reprint the works in this anthology, acknowledgement is made to the following:

Faith Bandler. Extract from *Wacvie*, published by Rigby, Adelaide, 1977. Permission from the author.

Diane Bell. Extract from 'Sheroes of Mine'. Published in *Heroines: A Contemporary Anthology of Australian Women's Writing*. 1991. Edited by Dale Spender, Penguin, Ringwood. Permission from the author and the publisher.

Lisa Bellear. 'Chops & Things'. Previously published in *Hecate*. Permission from the author.

Jane Cafarella. Published in the *Age*, 22 September 1993. Tempo p. 18. Permission from the author.

Destiny Deacon. This speech was given at The Australian Women's Movement: 1970–1990 Conference held at The University of Melbourne, 1991. Published with permission from the author.

Ruby Langford Ginibi: An extract from Chapter 7 of Ruby Langford Ginibi's autobiography, *Don't Take Your Love to Town*. 1988. Ringwood: Penguin. In it she describes life in rural Australia in the 1950s. Permission from the publisher and author.

Virginia Fraser. First published in *The National Times*, 1980. Permission from the author.

Sneja Gunew. Extract from 'Who's on Whose Margins: Migrant Women Writers'. First published in *Meanjin*, 1985.

Janine Haines. Extract from *Suffrage to Sufferance: 100 Years of Women in Politics*. 1992. Sydney: Allen and Unwin. Permission from the publisher.

Susan Hawthorne. 'The Great South Land' published in *Kunapipi* Vol. XI, No.2, 1989. Permission from the author. Extract from 'History of the Contemporary Women's Movement'. Published in *Journal of Australian Lesbian Feminist Studies*, No. 3, 1992. Permission from the author. Extract from 'Innovative Feminist Fiction'. First published in *Top Shelf, Australian Book Review*, September 1991. Permission from the author.

Eva Johnson. Extract from 'Alison'. First published in *The Exploding Frangipani*, edited by Cathie Dunsford and Susan Hawthorne. New Women's Press, Auckland, 1990. Permission from the author.

Kaye Johnston. Extract from 'The Revolutionary Nature of Lesbian Organic Gardening'. First published in *Journal of Australian Lesbian Feminist Studies*. No. 3, 1992. Permission from the author.

Elizabeth Jolley. 'A Sort of Gift: Images of Perth'. First published in *Inner Cities: Australian Women's Memory of Place*, edited by Drusilla Modjeska, Penguin Books, 1989. Also published in *Central Mischief*, Viking Penguin, 1992. Permission from Australian Literary Management.

Kate Llewellyn. Extract from *The Mountain*, published by Hudson, Hawthorn 1990. Permission from the publisher.

Finola Moorhead. Extract from 'Miss Marple Goes to Ayers Rock'. Published in *Heroines: A Contemporary Anthology of Australian Women's Writing*, edited by Dale Spender, Penguin, Melbourne, 1991. Permission from the author and the publisher.

Suniti Namjoshi. 'Australian Notebook'. First published in *St Suniti and the Dragon*, Spinifex Press, Melbourne, 1993. Permission from the author.

Oodgeroo of the tribe Noonuccal Custodian of the land Minjerribah: 'Oh Trugganer' from *My People*, Jacaranda Wiley Ltd 1990, Qld to Jacaranda Wiley.

Oodgeroo of the tribe Noonuccal Custodian of the land Minjerribah: 'Summer' from *My People*, Jacaranda Wiley Ltd 1990. Permission to reproduce this piece is from Collins/Angus and Robertson Publishers, Sydney.

Helen O'Shea. A slightly different version of this paper appeared in the *Women's Knowledge* issue (Vol. 51, No. 1, Autumn 1992) of the cultural quarterly *Meanjin*, published by the Australian Centre, University of Melbourne. Permission from the author.

Alison Richards: A version of this article was first published in the Women's Knowledge issue (Vol. 51, No. 1, Autumn 1992) of the cultural quarterly *Meanjin*, published by the Australian Centre, University of Melbourne. Permission from the author.

Rosa Safransky. 'Blume, the Borgia of Chapel Street'. Published in *Can a Morris Minor Break the Speed of Sound?* Pan-Macmillan, Melbourne, 1994. Permission from the author.

Jocelynne A. Scutt. 'The Incredible Woman' originally published as 'The Rape of Equality' in *Weekend Australian*, 28–29 September 1991, p. 31.

Dale Spender. Extract from 'Introduction' published in *The Penguin Anthology of Australian Women's Writing*, edited by Dale Spender, Penguin Books, Ringwood, 1988. Permission from the publisher and the author.

Every effort has been made to trace copyright holders, but in a few cases this has proved impossible. The publishers would be interested to hear from any copyright holders not acknowledged here or acknowledged incorrectly.

PHOTO CREDITS

430

ACKNOWLEDGEMENTS

When a book has been in the making a long time, it is difficult to adequately thank everybody involved. Our heartfelt thanks go to Hilke Schlaeger and Gerlinde Kowitzke of the German publishing company, Frauenoffensive for initially asking us to edit *Australia for Women* as part of their Travel Series. Enormous gratitude goes to Ursula Grawe – translator extraordinaire – who not only translated for the German edition of this book but who also provided editorial feedback for the English language edition. For their patience and their enthusiasm we thank all our contributors who have made *Australia for Women* come alive. Many thanks also to the photographers, in particular to Ponch Hawkes and Ruth Maddison. Rose Mildenhall has been busy touring the country and sending us bits of information which have been incorporated into the Section Introductions and the Resource List. Jane Farago pulled together the Resource List from a wide range of sources. And without the typesetting and editorial assistance of Michelle Proctor, the work on this book would have been much more arduous. Finally, we'd like to thank Lin Tobias for the cover design, Claire Warren for design and typesetting, and Morgan Blackthorne for her production expertise and not losing her cool at the excessive length of this book.

The process of putting *Australia for Women* together has been most rewarding not least because of the inspiring diversity of Australia's women. Much still remains unknown and unrecorded about women's contribution to Australian travel and culture – so this book is only a beginning. We would be delighted to hear from readers with updates for the Resource List.

Melbourne, January 1994
Susan Hawthorne and Renate Klein